Governing America

Governing America

* History
* Culture
* Institutions
* Organisation
* Policy

TIM HAMES
and NICOL RAE

Manchester University Press

Manchester and New York

distributed exclusively in the USA and Canada by St. Martin's Press

Published by Manchester University Press
Oxford Road, Manchester M13 9NR, UK
and Room 400, 175 Fifth Avenue, New York, NY 10010, USA

Distributed exclusively in the USA and Canada
by St. Martin's Press, Inc., 175 Fifth Avenue, New York, NY 10010, USA

British Library Cataloguing-in-Publication Data
A catalogue record for this book is available from the British Library

Library of Congress Cataloging-in-Publication Data
Hames, Tim.
   Governing America: history, culture, institutions, organisation, policy/
Tim Hames and Nicol Rae.
         p.   cm.
   Includes bibliographical references and index
   ISBN 0-7190-4077-9. — ISBN 0-7190-4078-7 (pbk.: alk. paper)
   1. United States—Politics and government.   I. Rae, Nicol C.
II. Title.
JK421.H28   1996   95-39217

ISBN   0 7190 4077 9   hardback
          0 7190 4078 7   paperback

First published 1996

00 99 98 97 96   10 9 8 7 6 5 4 3 2 1

Typeset by Carnegie Publishing Ltd, Preston
Printed in Great Britain by Bell & Bain Ltd, Glasgow

Contents

Illustrations

Tables

Preface

Any book such as this spawns a great deal of thanks and acknowledgements. Tim Hames is indebted to the Warden and Fellows of Nuffield College where he was situated while most of this book was written. He would also like to thank the Andrew Mellon Fund for its support on numerous occasions. He would further like to thank all his colleagues the University of Oxford who teach American politics for their help and many conversations that have helped in his intellectual evolution. In particular Professor Byron Shafer, Nigel Bowles, and Gillian Peele deserve mention. Beyond Oxford, Professor Richard Hodder-Williams and Professor Nelson Polsby have also been the source of much stimulation. He would also like to thank his long-suffering wife Julia and stepchildren Edward and Tom.

Nicol Rae has enjoyed the backing of the faculty at Florida International University, Miami, Florida. He would like to show his gratitude to his secretary, Dorinda Mosby, and teaching assistant Carlos Maceo. Thanks also go to his colleagues Mary Volcansek, Joel Gottlieb, and John Stack for their support, and John Loza, Dario Moreno, Chris Warren, Francois Illas, and Kevin Hill for interesting discussions and observations on US politics. Finally, his mother Lily Rae deserves thanks for her constant support and encouragement.

Both authors would like to thank the team at Manchester University Press led by Richard Purslow for all their efforts at turning out this volume in its current condition.

None of these good people are, alas, responsible for any errors, omissions, or arguments generated by this book.

<table>
<tr><td>Tim Hames</td><td>Nicol Rae</td></tr>
<tr><td>Oxford</td><td>Miami</td></tr>
<tr><td>England</td><td>Florida, USA</td></tr>
</table>

Dedicated to Julia Hames, Michael Hart, and Lily Rae.

Introduction

The United States of America is both a fascinating and frustrating nation for students of politics and interested observers. In many senses its political process operates within a unique set of conditions and constraints. It is a liberal democracy with a large (nearly 260 million) and extraordinarily diverse population set in a physically huge (over 3,600,000 square miles) setting. It has been governed from its outset by the principles of federalism (significant exercise of power by the states) and a system of separated political bodies with overlapping jurisdictions and checks and balances. It deploys the single plurality or first-past-the-post electoral system for its inter-party contests and uses the direct primary for intra-party candidate selection. No other country matches this bundle of elements.

Because of this, governing the United States has never been easy and has always been complex. It will be the objective of this book to make some sort of sense out of a political system whose day-to-day practice frequently appears to defy rational analysis. In fact, once the ground rules and cultural influences that shape American politics and society are understood, then much of the sound and fury that dominates the modern process of government becomes much more comprehensible.

To try and give as complete a picture of American politics as possible this book is organised into four parts. The first offers an overview of American political history, focusing on those incidents that the modern observer of politics really needs to know. This part will also attempt to outline what sort of country the United States is, how a distinctive political culture has developed, and why understanding that culture is vital to anyone attempting to understand contemporary political outcomes.

The second part will examine the major political institutions through which government of some form or other emerges. The Presidency, Congress, Supreme Court, and the States and local government will all be discussed in detail.

The third part will survey those elements of political organisation that are not part of the formal structure of government (indeed, none of them are explicitly mentioned in the American Constitution) but which are absolutely vital to the actual practice of public policy. Hence the roles of the federal bureaucracy, political parties, interest groups, and the mass media will be outlined.

The final part will attempt to bring all the preceding elements together: history; culture; institutions; organisation; and demonstrate their impact on those parts of American government most familiar to outside observers –

elections for public office, the conduct of economic policy and the nature of American foreign policy. From there a few concluding thoughts about the overall pattern of American politics in the 1990s and probable directions for the next century will be offered.

Although both of the authors have been involved in, and take responsibility for, all the chapters, inevitably different issues have seen either author dominate.[1] It should perhaps be said that Nicol Rae was primarily the author of the first section, Tim Hames took charge of the final part, and the chapters concerning political institutions and organisation were split evenly between the two.

A number of important themes should run across this book and help shape the bigger picture about how we think about modern American political life. They are worth emphasising right at the beginning so that they may be more transparently seen as they reappear at periods throughout the text. Those themes include:

o That an appreciation of American political history and the highly distinctive political culture of the United States is critical to an understanding of current events.

o That while governing the United States has never been a simple procedure, the operation of politics has become much more complicated over the last quarter-century, for reasons that will be regularly illustrated. In particular, being or trying to be any sort of leader (President, Congressional Leader, Supreme Court Chief Justice, State Governor, State Legislator) has become much harder, some would say almost impossible. As Charles O. Jones has noted in his recent discussion of the perils of the American presidency,[2] the United States has a separated system of government and it appears to be becoming more separated.

o That whilst the conditions for conflict between political institutions have always existed and often been practised in the American political system, the degree of conflict between the various arms of the federal government seems to have grown over the past two decades. One by-product of this basic disagreement over national priorities at the national level – the American budget deficit – has assisted a process in which states and local governments, largely perceived as withering on the vine twenty years ago, have become much more significant actors in recent times. Although, as will be shown, this rise in responsibility can be a distinctly double-edged sword for many of the individual politicians concerned.

o That the number of different bodies attempting to influence, and be involved in, American government has also risen sharply, a process that brings both more democracy and greater problems of control and co-ordination into the system. Within Congress political authority is now much more diffusely spread. The weakness of political parties in terms of controlling who are its standard-bearers means that it is far easier for previously inexperienced individuals to stand for very senior public office. The most extraordinary example of this is the candidature for President in 1992 of H. Ross Perot, a Texan billionaire with no political pedigree whatsoever, who none the less mobilised a national campaign which in five weeks saw him win 19 per cent of the popular vote – the second highest for an independent candidate this century.

There are many other examples of what economists would call falling barriers to entry affecting the modern process. As will be signalled here, both the numbers and range of interest groups attempting to sway public (especially congressional) opinion have snowballed. Whether this is – on balance – a good thing is a matter for heated debate. Similarly, there has been a revolution in the way that political action is reflected to the outside world. As the chapter on the media will demonstrate, there are more and varied means of media coverage which have had a powerful knock-on effect on the way politics is conducted, especially the nature of modern American election campaigns.

o Despite all these new means of influencing the process – possibly because of the further complexities they provide – American citizens do not appear particularly happy either about those they elect or the political system more generally. The past two decades have seen a collapse in public faith in the basic capacity of governments to manage public affairs competently and honestly. Successive political candidates (including some consummate political insiders) have found it profitable to campaign 'against Washington'. Ross Perot's mercurial candidacy in 1992 was but one part of a pattern of political dissatisfaction being expressed by ordinary voters. Although it speaks volumes about American political culture that, in times of great voter unrest, the man seized upon as saviour by twenty million voters is not a socialist revolutionary but a populist billionaire. It was also seen in more conventional form by the extraordinary Republican triumph in the congressional elections of 1994.

One simple example of this discontent: in the period 1913–1975 every incumbent President who sought re-election bar one (the hapless Herbert Hoover, overwhelmed by the Great Depression in 1932) won. Since 1975 three incumbents (Gerald Ford, Jimmy Carter, and George Bush) have been beaten. Indeed, since Dwight Eisenhower's retirement in 1960 only one man (Ronald Reagan) has successfully won re-election and served out two full terms as Eisenhower did.

o Allied to all this has been a very substantial change in the national and international environment in which United States politics exists. Thirty years ago the United States clearly constituted the globe's largest economy, with nearly one-third of all the planet's economic output coming from it. This dominance was in part artificial because of the devastating impact that the Second World War had on the economies of other countries. That figure has fallen to under one-quarter, about the same standing as 1938. Whilst neither author would like to wade into the waters of those who claim an inevitable American economic decline with parallels to Imperial Rome or Bourbon France[3] some relative change has to be noted. In recent years economic – and hence wider domestic – policy has been dominated by the voluminous American budget deficit which has paralysed the federal government and seen the United States shift from being the world's largest creditor to the world's largest debtor. In terms of the international economy matters have been similarly influenced by record American trade deficits. The meaning of all this is disentangled in Chapter 13.

Finally, there is the international position. The end of the superpower struggle has left the United States as the planet's sole military, economic, political and cultural superpower. Yet it seems a curiously insecure one. In the absence of the grand conflict with the Soviet Union, the United States needs to reassess what its national interests and goals are, and what sort of international system would be complimentary to those objectives. As the experience of the Clinton Administration has demonstrated, and as Chapter 14 discusses, this transition has proved far from comfortable.

These themes and many sub-themes will be woven through the fourteen chapters presented here, and the conclusion that attempts to look beyond them. They can be further fleshed out via the bibliography presented at the end of this volume. We hope that by its finale this book will have helped the reader to understand the complicated kaleidoscope that constitutes the contemporary American political system. Hopefully, the reader will feel, as the authors do, that the fascinations of the United States far outweigh the frustrations.

Notes

1 Like Howard Rourke in Ayn Rand's *The Fountainhead* (New York, Cassell & Co., 1947), the authors believe there can no more be a collective mind than a collective stomach.
2 Charles O. Jones, *The Presidency in a Separated System* (Washington, DC, Brookings Institution, 1994).
3 Paul Kennedy, *The Rise and Fall of Great Powers* (New York, Vintage, 1987).

Part One

Political history and culture

1

Political history – an overview

History is more or less bunk. *Henry Ford*

The youth of America is their oldest tradition. It has been going on now for three hundred years. *Oscar Wilde*

Without some grasp of the history of a nation, its politics and government will make little sense to the outsider. The political habits and institutions of the present have been forged in the events and struggles of the nation's past, and their contemporary shape is the outcome of an unending series of adaptations to changing historical circumstances.

Yet Americans are not a very history-conscious people. Unlike Europeans – who often appear preoccupied with history to the point of obsession – most Americans, like Henry Ford, view the history of their country as irrelevant and uninteresting. American culture has traditionally encouraged Americans to look forward, not back, and to see the past as something to be overcome rather than emulated. The overall American outlook on their history, then, is 'progressive' in the sense that history is understood as a progression towards a higher state of civilisation, both ethically and technologically. Change and reform are thus to be welcomed rather than feared, and the American is encouraged to look towards the opportunities of the future rather than to dwell on nostalgia for the past.

The dominance of the progressive outlook in American culture is certainly connected to the perpetual 'youthfulness' of Americans alluded to by Oscar Wilde. Since colonial times, the 'youthfulness', dynamism, innocence, and naivety of Americans in comparison to the traditions, indolence, decadence, and cynicism of the Old World have been emphasised by writers and commentators on both sides of the Atlantic. The reality is considerably more complex, however. As a nation–state the United States is older by a century than Germany or Italy, to say nothing of most of the contemporary nation–states of Africa and Asia. The US is also governed under a constitution that is older than that of all but a handful of present-day nations.

As a nation America is thus no longer so young in relative terms. What Wilde and others have really meant when they have alluded to American youthfulness, however, has been America not as a nation–state but as a culture: and here they are on much firmer ground. American society and culture are distinctive in important ways that are linked to the emigration of peoples from the Old World in search of 'new' opportunities and a 'new' and different kind of society to that they had left behind in Europe. This deliberate repudiation of the Old World and the urge to start over again helps to explain America's necessary conception of itself as an eternally young and vigorous country, continually setting a new example to mankind, and refusing to be bound by the fetters of tradition.

Of course, while the progressive strain has been dominant in American history, it has not been unchallenged. The US Constitution, authored by the patrician political class of the 1780s, with its federal structure and separated political institutions, has proved to be the most significant political constraint on the progressive impulse by ensuring that any reform must command a truly remarkable degree of public consensus before it can be effected. Moreover, white Southerners (inhabitants of the only section of the US to have suffered defeat and occupation) and blacks (with their unique experience of involuntary deportation and slavery) have also traditionally stood somewhat outside the dominant progressive culture in different ways. Finally, the unusual degree of pessimism among academic and cultural elites over the state of the US since the Vietnam/Watergate era, and the nostalgia for the social *mores* of the Eisenhower era, evinced by some contemporary American conservatives, might also signify a final loss of American innocence and the emergence of a new American 'maturity' in the wake of the traumas of the 1960–80 period (although they could equally well be manifestations of the pessimistic world view of a declining social and political class).

Some of these social and cultural issues will be explored at greater length in Chapters 2 and 3. The remainder of this chapter provides a brief, but necessary, summary of the most significant American political developments from the early settlements to the end of the Cold War.

Colonial America: 1607–1776

The nature of the settlement and colonization of the North American colonies by the British differed significantly from the Spanish Empire in Central and South America. Settlers in British North America were by and large not *conquistadors* set on making a rapid fortune by exploiting the natural resources of the New World, but people who were seeking new opportunities and a different kind of society to that of seventeenth-century England. The Pilgrim Fathers and the other groups of religious dissidents who established colonies in British North America (such as the Quakers in Pennsylvania, and the Catholics in Maryland), had been oppressed by the Anglican English establishment, and set out explicitly to form colonies that would be governed according to their religious precepts. As we shall see, these dissidents – and particularly the Massachusetts Puritans – have continued to exercise a profound influence over American political culture.

Not all the colonists were religious dissidents, however. In the southern states settlers were attracted by the prospects of making money on cash crops like tobacco and sugar, using cheap slave labour imported from West Africa.

Southern settlers were more likely to be members of the rural Anglican gentry (though not generally from the higher nobility) and their indentured servants. During the eighteenth century there was a further influx of poor Irish Protestant settlers from Ulster (still referred to today as the 'Scotch–Irish') into the then 'frontier' region of the Appalachian mountain chain. Colonial America was thus a diverse society, and historian David Hackett Fisher has interestingly pointed out how the social and cultural differences between the northern and southern states have their origins in the different social and geographic backgrounds of the original settlers from the British Isles.[1]

Another contrasting factor between British and Spanish America was the role and treatment of the native population. Whereas in much of Hispanic America native populations had been concentrated and had reached a fairly advanced level of social development, the North American Indians were scattered, nomadic, and less technologically advanced. This had two important consequences. First, after the initial settlement period, the native populations constituted no serious threat and were either wiped out or retreated into the interior. Second, whereas British settlers generally came to North America in families, the *conquistadors* tended to leave the women behind during the period of conquest. One outcome of this was the advent of massive interbreeding and intermarriage between the Spanish and the natives, which did not take place in the North American colonies. The Spanish obsession with the conversion of the natives to Christianity through the Catholic missions, was also not emulated by the overwhelmingly Protestant British colonists.

By the mid-eighteenth century the British North American colonies were developing in an increasingly diverse direction from the homeland. The middling economic status of the religious dissidents who largely settled New England and the Middle-Atlantic states led to the development of a society that was remarkably unstratified socially in contrast to the class divisions of eighteenth-century England. The northern colonies were also becoming increasingly prosperous, with the development of trade and manufacturing in the major urban centres and ports of Boston, New York, and Philadelphia. Finally, the diversity of religions among the settlers and the continual fragmentation of denominations, meant that the colonies displayed a quite extraordinary degree of religious pluralism and tolerance by comparison with contemporary Britain.

In addition to an increasingly autonomous economy and society, the colonists also had a high degree of political autonomy. Almost all the colonies had vigorous colonial assemblies which had severely curbed the powers of the British colonial governors. The colonists' political views were also predominantly 'Whig' (that is, they regarded individual liberties and government by popular consent as the supreme political values), while the social class that might have sustained a more pro-governmental and aristocratic 'Tory' outlook were conspicuous by their absence in North America, though it was still very powerful back in the homeland.[2] When the French threat was ended for good after the Seven Years War (1756–63) and the British acquisition of Canada, and with Spain clearly in decline, the relationship between London and the North American colonies inevitably become increasingly problematic.

Rebellion, Independence, and the 1789 Constitution

Unsurprisingly, it was an issue that particularly aroused the colonists' Whig political sensibilities that acted as the catalyst for the American Revolution. The idea that individuals should not be taxed by their government unless they were represented in that government was an absolutely fundamental tenet in the Whig political canon, dating from the period when Charles I had attempted to impose taxes without parliamentary approval and had plunged England into civil war and the temporary abolition of the monarchy. When King George III's government, in which the colonists had no representation, sought to impose duties on North America after the end of the Seven Years War, it precipitated an escalating war of words with the colonists that culminated in the outbreak of armed hostilities in 1775 and the Declaration of Independence a year later.

Given the gradual drifting apart of Great Britain and her thirteen North American colonies, the relationship was bound to collapse eventually. The colonies could not be governed from London in defiance of their wishes, and London could not effectively suppress a rebellion at such a distance in the face of a hostile population, as the course of the revolutionary war demonstrated. Indeed it is surprising that the colonists delayed their Declaration of Independence as long as they did. The struggle for independence united both North and South and produced an extraordinary generation of revolutionary-leaders – Thomas Jefferson, James Madison, Alexander Hamilton, Benjamin Franklin, and John Adams – and an authentic national leader and hero in the Virginia farmer and general, George Washington.

The 1776 Declaration of Independence, written by another Virginia gentleman, Thomas Jefferson, was the clearest possible statement of radical, revolutionary Whiggery with its ringing statements 'that all men were created equal' and were also 'endowed with inalienable rights to life, liberty and the pursuit of happiness'. But in the American context of 1776, this statement was not really very revolutionary and merely confirmed the Whig beliefs held by most Americans. In terms of its immediate effects on the structure of American society, the American 'Revolution' was barely a revolution at all.

Nevertheless, by successfully throwing off the British yoke, and doing so in terms of natural rights and the equality of man, the Americans set a very powerful example indeed to oppressed classes in other nations, and helped undermine the authority of the European *anciens régimes*. Absolutism would never be quite so easily accomplished anywhere again after the American Revolution. Domestically, while the short-term impact of the revolution was slight in terms of altering the basis of American society, its long-term impact, as Gordon Wood has demonstrated, was to assist the transformation of a Whig

George Washington.

George Washingon (1732–99) was the first President of the United States (1789–97) and its first great national hero. Like other founders of great nations, the figure of Washington became shrouded in myth (for example, the story that he never told a lie), but he nevertheless remains among the greatest of American Presidents. A Virginia gentleman-farmer and state legislator, Washington was already a legendary figure prior to assuming the presidency as he had successfully commanded the revolutionary forces throughout the War of Independence from 1775 to 1783. Washington had also presided over the 1787 constitutional convention in Philadelphia. He was thus the logical and inevitable choice to occupy the new office of President, and during his two terms in office the political and economic system of the infant Republic became firmly established. As President, Washington adopted a general conservative course, being wary of revolutionary France and sympathetic to the pro-business economic policies of his Treasury Secretary Alexander Hamilton. True to the classical Republican model of Cincinnatus, the Roman leader who retired to his farm after serving his country, Washington returned to his Mount Vernon plantation after leaving office.

society still dominated economically, socially and politically by a relatively small elite of planters and merchants into a democratic society dominated by an expanding and energetic middle class. It is unlikely that this would have happened quite so rapidly and peacefully without the 1776 Declaration and the democratising and egalitarian forces that it unleashed.[3]

America's first constitution was the 1776 'Articles of Confederation', under which the US was governed for thirteen years. The limited nature of the US government created by the Articles, based on a 'Continental Congress' of delegations from the new states and no executive, demonstrates the uncertainty of the framers as to quite what kind of nation they were creating. The original consensus was for a loose confederation, with the national government providing only very basic military and diplomatic functions and sovereignty lying with the individual states.

Once the national unity that sustained the war against the British subsided after peace was made in 1783, the limitations of the Articles were rapidly revealed. With the hungry predators Britain, France, and Spain still lingering around the western hemisphere, it seemed unwise to leave the central government of the infant Republic in such a weakened condition. Domestic elites were also frightened by outbreaks of armed resistance to government authority by angry farmers in western Massachusetts and western Pennsylvania. Finally, the national government found it hard to raise enough money to pay its debts. These threats were sufficient to scare the Republic's national political elite into calling a constitutional convention in Philadelphia in 1787 to provide for a stronger federal government.

The Constitution (which will be considered more closely in Chapter 3) was by no means a radical document. Indeed the conservative Whig gentlemen who wrote it intended it as a check on the radical, democratising forces within American society. The Federal government was strengthened with a directly elected House, and an indirectly elected executive. It was given tax-raising powers, and enhanced authority to deal with foreign threats and domestic subversion. However the House was to be restricted by a Senate elected by the state legislatures, and a federal judiciary was created with implicit veto powers over certain federal government actions. Finally, most government activity was still left to the states.

The 1787 Constitution thus was anything but a democratic document, and the wary framers must have been reassured when George Washington agreed to accept the office of President when the Constitution came into operation in 1789. As we shall see, the consensus among its authors on the future course of the new nation would not last for very long.

Democratisation and expansion: 1789–1850

The consensus among the founding elite that authored the Constitution broke down during Washington's presidency principally over two issues: foreign policy, and the power of the national government *vis-à-vis* the states. Treasury

Secretary Alexander Hamilton and Washington's Vice-President and successor John Adams were the leading 'Federalists', believing that the US's natural ally in foreign policy and main trading partner should be Great Britain as opposed to revolutionary France, and that the federal government should engage in an extensive series of measures to encourage the growth of American manufacturing and trade. Thomas Jefferson ultimately resigned as Washington's Secretary of State in protest at Hamilton's policies, being more sympathetic towards the French and suspicious of a powerful federal government. Jefferson and James Madison formed the 'Democratic–Republican' party, and ultimately ousted the Federalists from the presidency in 1800.

As President, Jefferson actually pursued a conciliatory approach towards the defeated Federalists and did not radically depart from the policies of his predecessors. After the death of Alexander Hamilton in a duel with Vice-President Aaron Burr, the Federalist party faded away as an effective national competitor for the Jeffersonian Democrats, and Jefferson's administration ushered in the so-called 'Era of Good Feelings' – a period of single-party rule and national consensus in policy that persisted through the Madison and Monroe administrations until the outbreak of the Jacksonian revolution in the 1820s. Beneath this apparent consensus, however, significant developments were in train regarding America's constitutional and political development.

The breakdown of consensus among the founding generation and the party conflict of the 1790s fatally undermined the conservative intentions of the framers of the 1789 Constitution regarding the selection of the President. Instead of being chosen in an electoral college of local notables selected by state legislatures, the pressures of party competition opened up the elections to the electoral college to popular influence. By the mid-1820s virtually all the states were choosing their presidential electors in direct popular elections, a development that was to be ruthlessly exploited by the Jacksonian Democrats after the clear popular favourite General Andrew Jackson was denied the presidency in 1824. Also by the mid-1820s most property restrictions on the franchise had been removed under popular pressure, meaning that America had more or less complete adult, white, male suffrage and a mass electorate.

The conservative devices of the framers thus proved to be too weak to restrain the democratic, egalitarian forces unleashed by the American revolution. The most obvious manifestation of this was the outbreak of the Jacksonian revolution during the 1820s. Robbed of the presidency in 1824, the war hero General Andrew Jackson formed the Democratic party as a vehicle for his ideas and his presidential ambitions. The Jacksonian movement represented the 'out' groups of 1820s America – the frontiersmen, small farmers, artisans, and labouring classes – against the merchant and planter elites of the eastern seaboard who dominated the national government. In the election of 1828 the Jacksonian national organisation mobilised the General's supporters behind slates of presidential electors committed to Jackson, who thus won an overwhelming victory.[4]

In office Jackson continued his polarising, radical approach towards his political opponents. The commitment to states' rights, as opposed to an over-weening federal government controlled by a narrow economic elite, was the fundamental principle of Jacksonian Democracy, and in office the President raised the stakes even further by dismantling the hated National Bank of the US in the face of fierce opposition. Energised by the Bank conflict, Jackson's opponents realised the need to organise on a national level against him, and the Whig party was born. So effectively did the Whigs duplicate the populist style of the Jacksonian Democrats, that this coalition of north-eastern and southern patricians was able to win the presidency from the Democrats in 1840 with another military hero, General William Henry Harrison.

The divisions between the parties were similar to those that had divided the Federalists and Jeffersonians. The Whigs stood for an energetic national government led from the Congress to promote economic growth and development through national improvements and pro-business policies. The Democrats, by contrast, sought a strong presidency to curb the ambitions of a Congress dominated by commercial interests and to restore power to the states. Ironically, both the elected Whig presidents – William Henry Harrison and Zachary Taylor – died within a years of taking office, and party was mainly led from Congress by House Speaker (and later Senator) Henry Clay of Kentucky for most of its existence.

In foreign affairs the first half-century of America's existence saw the continual expansion of American territory and influence over the western hemisphere. Jefferson's Louisiana Purchase in 1804 brought the entire Mississippi River valley into the US and removed France as a serious power. In 1819 Florida was acquired from Spain, and Texas (an independent republic from 1836 to 1845) and the Rocky Mountain and Pacific coast states had been acquired from Mexico by 1850. The US also saw off a final invasion by the British in the war of 1812. The clearest manifestation of America's intentions in foreign policy during this period was President Monroe's 1823 warning to the European powers not to interfere in the western hemisphere, popularly referred to as the 'Monroe Doctrine'. From being a small, isolated confederation of thirteen Atlantic seaboard states, the US had expanded into a dominant continental power by 1850.

Slavery, civil war and reconstruction: 1850–1876

Ever since the founding of the Republic the slave issue had troubled many Americans. Keeping millions of blacks in involuntary servitude in the southern states was clearly at odds with the egalitarian sentiments of the Declaration of Independence ('All men are created equal'), but the Declaration's author and many of the Founding Fathers were slave-holders. As the US territory expanded and more and more states were admitted to the Union the slave issue became increasingly vexing. The northern states, which prohibited slavery, were prepared to tolerate it in the southern states where it sustained the plantation economy. What they could not countenance, as they aggressively pursued industrialisation, was the expansion of slavery into the new western territories, which might eventually give pro-slavery forces complete dominance over the federal government.

The matter was temporarily resolved by the Missouri compromise of 1820, which proclaimed that slavery would be excluded from the Louisiana Purchase territory north of latitude 36° 30'. However, tensions over the admission of new territories continued and were augmented by the growth of a militant abolitionist movement in the northern states, and an increasingly hysterical defence of slavery in the South. The issue also challenged the very authority and legitimacy of the federal government. John C. Calhoun, the leading political theorist of the slave-holders, held that the federal Congress had no authority to prohibit slavery under the Constitution, or indeed to pass any measure affecting the 'peculiar institution' to which the South objected.[5] The Missouri Compromise broke down after the 1854 Kansas–Nebraska Act, which established popular sovereignty as the basis for whether the state should be slave or free. This only served to precipitate violence in the western states between slaveholders and settlers from the free states. Finally, the Supreme Court declared the Missouri Compromise unconstitutional in its infamous 1857 decision, *Dred Scott* v. *Sanford*. Divisions over slavery destroyed the Whig party and also divided the Democrats. As a result a new party committed to curbing the extension of slavery – the Republicans – rose to dominance in the northern states. With the election of the Republican Abraham Lincoln to the White House in 1860, the secession of the southern states became inevitable.

The South's attempted secession was the greatest challenge that America had yet faced, and task of upholding the authority of the Constitution fell upon the shoulders of Lincoln and the Republicans. Many in the North were ambivalent to say the least about fighting the southerners over this issue, and the South's early military successes several times came close to forcing the Union government to come to terms. Despite domestic and foreign pressure to accept secession, however, Lincoln remained determined to save the Union, and once he had issued the Emancipation Proclamation on 1 January 1863, there could be no turning back. Eventually the tide turned after Robert E. Lee's defeat at Gettysburg in July 1863, and the assumption of command of the northern armies by generals Grant and Sherman.[6]

Lincoln had intended to pursue a fairly limited reconstruction policy towards the South, but after his assassination the presidency fell upon his southern (and Democratic) Vice-President Andrew Johnson, who lacked the authority to carry through such a policy. The most destructive conflict of the nineteenth century had created a reservoir of bitterness on all sides, a bitterness that was exacerbated by the occupation of the southern states by Union armies and the imposition of Republican Reconstruction regimes. Eventually the Republicans lost their enthusiasm for Radical Reconstruction and black rights in the South, and as a result of a sordid electoral deal to keep the Presidency in 1876, the

Abraham Lincoln.

The second towering figure in American history, Abraham Lincoln (1809–65), served as America's sixteenth President during the Civil War (1861–65). Lincoln's successful defence of the Union confirmed the sovereignty of the federal government, and his 1864 Gettysburg Address reformulated the American creed for a more democratic society. His assassination at the end of the war guaranteed Lincoln's status as America's greatest martyr. A lawyer who had served one term in the US House as a Whig from Illinois, Lincoln was appalled by the 1854 Kansas–Nebraska Act which threatened the spread of slavery to the western territories. After joining the Republican party, he gained national prominence in a series of public debates on slavery with Democratic Senator Stephen A. Douglas in 1858. Two years later the Republicans nominated Lincoln for President, but his election immediately resulted in the secession of eleven southern slave-holding states. During the war Lincoln remained determined to save the Union at all costs in the face of reluctant generals and calls for compromise with the South from some quarters. Although he had never been an abolitionist, Lincoln's Emancipation Proclamation signalled the end of slavery in the US.

Union armies were finally withdrawn. Restored to white rule, southern state governments soon proceeded to reverse all the gains that blacks had made as a result of Reconstruction policies, and reimposed an oppressive regime of disfranchisement and segregation of the black population.[7]

The Civil War was still a pivotal event in US history however. The defeat of slavery not only ended the secession question for good and finally established that the US was a federal state and not a confederation, but was also a victory for the democratic, egalitarian principles set out in the Declaration of Independence and rearticulated in Lincoln's 1863 Gettysburg Address. This was confirmed by the passage of three post-war amendments to the Constitution: the Thirteenth, which prohibited slavery; the Fourteenth, which guaranteed 'due process of law', and 'equal protection of the laws' to all citizens of the US (and which would ultimately greatly expand the scope and authority of the federal government); and the Fifteenth, which guaranteed the right to vote. The defeat of the old South thus ensured the irrevocability of the Union, and marked another triumph for the principles of the Declaration of Independence.

The Gilded Age and the Progressives: 1876–1917

With the slavery and secession questions definitively settled, the last quarter of the nineteenth century saw America surge forward as a major economic and military power. Industrialisation proceeded at a rapid pace, thanks to the high external tariffs and other pro-business policies promoted by the mainly Republican presidents and Congresses of the period. Such rapid industrial development also encouraged the making of vast fortunes by major manufacturers and speculators: Rockefeller, Carnegie, Mellon, Vanderbilt, and J. P. Morgan became household names and role-models for young Americans to emulate as they exemplified the myth of the self-made American. At the same time their wealth and the means of acquiring it were bitterly attacked by many members of the old patrician class and in the popular press, where they were referred to as 'robber barons', and the entire period was ironically described as the 'Gilded Age'.

Such rapid industrialisation naturally brought a plethora of social problems in its wake. The population became more urbanised as the masses crowded into the new industrial centres and this brought overcrowding, poverty, disease and crime. Massive numbers of immigrants from northern, eastern and southern Europe – Jews, Italians, Poles and other Slavic groups, Scandinavians, Greeks – joined the Catholic Irish and the Germans who had already arrived in large numbers prior to the Civil War. The immigrants were not only a constant source of cheap labour, but also transformed the nature of American politics and society. Party machines based largely on immigrant votes (but also closely tied to local business interests) and led by the legendary party bosses controlled most of America's major cities at the end of the century.

The pervasive corruption of the Gilded Age eventually created a backlash from those groups that felt themselves to be excluded from a system built around big business and party bosses. Rural America, which had been rapidly settled by homesteaders after the granting of free land in the 1862 Homestead Act, had endured a series of debilitating depressions due to over-production. Damaged by external tariffs erected by the federal government to benefit industry (but which provoked retaliation in the prairie farmers' export markets), and heavily dependent on eastern-controlled banks, merchants, and railroads, the rage of agrarian America spilled over in the Populist revolt of the 1890s.[8] In 1892 the Populist party mounted a serious challenge for the presidency, and in 1896 an anti-industrial coalition took over the Democratic party under the leadership of William Jennings Bryan. Eastern industrial workers, however, were alienated by an agrarian radicalism that potentially threatened their livelihoods, and they rallied behind the pro-business Republicans.

After the 1896 election, the Republicans solidified their grip on the national government, and the Democrats dominated only the racist, impoverished, and economically backward southern states. With single-party domination now being the rule in most major states and cities, the excesses of the dominant party's machines (who now effectively chose the office-holders) seemed all the greater. In reaction to big business and the bosses another protest movement erupted against the materialistic, *laissez-faire* values of the Gilded Age – Progressivism.

Progressivism succeeded where Populism failed because instead of looking backwards towards an idyllic rural past, its precepts were more relevant to the growing sectors of American society at the turn of the century – most importantly, the new, professional middle class. These corporate managers, lawyers, and teachers had been trained to think of problems in terms of rational or technical solutions, and therefore preferred a government based on rationalism and expertise rather than on personal ties and ethnic affiliations.[9]

Under the leadership of Presidents Theodore Roosevelt (a member of the old north-eastern patrician elite that despised the materialistic values of the *nouveaux riches* of the Gilded Age) and the Princeton academic Woodrow Wilson, the Progressives succeeded in passing national legislation to curb the power of major agglomerations of capital – the so-called 'trusts' – and promote greater competition. At the state and local level Progressives succeeded in many states – especially in the Upper Midwest and the Pacific Coast – in establishing legislation to improve workers' hours and conditions, and public health. They also pioneered the introduction of the primary election as a means of taking the choices of candidates and office-holders out of the hands of the local party machines. At all levels of government, the Progressives introduced a merit civil service based on expertise as opposed to the patronage and nepotism that had prevailed since the Jackson era. All of these changes were dictated by the emergence of America as a modern industrial society, and would have a lasting impact over the American political process, as we shall see in subsequent chapters.

America's rapid industrial growth was paralleled by its growing importance as a world power. The arrival of the US on the world scene was heralded by the defeat of Spain in the 1898 Spanish–American war which established America as the dominant power in the Caribbean and the Pacific Ocean. Theodore Roosevelt was an unabashed imperialist and revelled in America's new great power status. Woodrow Wilson was more ambivalent, but once he had committed US forces to the First World War in 1917, he became the dominant figure among the allied leaders, and his 'fourteen points' based on the American principles of anti-imperialism and 'self-determination' were intended to be the guiding principles of a new post-war international order, of which the US would be the ultimate guarantor.

Normalcy and the New Deal: 1917–1945

The 1920s witnessed a backlash against the Progressive impulse both at home and abroad, and a longing for the return to what President Warren Harding described as 'normalcy'. Business regained the ascendancy it had held during the Gilded Age, and the three Republican presidents – Harding, Coolidge, and Hoover – elected during the decade pursued a *laissez-faire* approach to the economy. As the economy boomed during the 1920s and the Democratic party remained hopelessly divided between its northern ethnic machines and the reactionary white South, the 'old guard' Republicans reasserted their grip on the national government.[10]

Yet the long-term social changes that had produced Progressivism were not arrested during the 1920s, and even Harding & Co. were unable to reverse the Progressives' expansion of the scope of federal government activity. Progressivism had exhausted itself by 1920, but when the opportunity arose for a further period of government activism it would reappear in a slightly different form. With Progressivism in abeyance, continuing unease over the untrammelled power of northern capital and the emerging consumer society manifested itself in support for reactionary movements like the Ku Klux Klan in both North and South. Even more remarkably, anti-alcohol forces succeeded in placing an amendment prohibiting the sale and distribution of alcohol in the Constitution in 1919. Mass immigration was finally arrested by the blatantly racist 1924 Immigration Act, which effectively ended eastern and southern European immigration.

None of these developments changed the overall direction of American society. The Klan petered out in the depression years as its white, Protestant, small-town constituency became preoccupied with economic matters. Prohibition proved to be an abysmal failure that only succeeded in promoting the rise of organised crime, and was finally reversed by another constitutional amendment in 1933. The Immigration Act (passed under pressure from white, Protestant nativists and labour unions who feared imported cheap labour) did largely close the door on immigration, but the large numbers already admitted were only beginning to exercise their social and political power.

Photograph 1.3. Franklin Roosevelt.

The greatest of twentieth-century Presidents and usually ranked with Washington and
Lincoln by historians, Franklin Delano Roosevelt (1882–1945) served as the thirty-
second President of the US during the Great Depression and the Second World War
(1933–45): a period that saw America's rise to world power. At home, Roosevelt's
New Deal dramatically expanded the scope of federal government activity, and helped
to save American capitalism from its greatest crisis. Roosevelt's use of radio in his
'fireside chats' also made him the first President with whom millions of Americans felt
they had personal contact. Abroad, Roosevelt mobilised America to lead the global
resistance to Hitler after 1940, and his liberal internationalist principles helped set out
the framework for the post-war world. Like Lincoln, he died in his hour of triumph,
just prior to the conclusion of the war.

In foreign policy the general disillusion with the Versailles peace settlement
and the apparent failure of American ideals to prevail led to the rejection of
the Treaty and the League of Nations Covenant by the Republican-controlled
Congress in 1920. After Woodrow Wilson's departure from the presidency,
the Republicans attempted to revert to the 'isolationist' foreign policy of the
pre-Progressive period. Again, however, this reversion was more apparent
than real. The US was more committed overseas – particularly in the economic sphere – than ever before, and found it increasingly hard to disentangle
itself from foreign conflicts that affected its crucial European and East Asian
markets.

Normalcy during the 1920s was little more than a holding operation by traditional elites against the deeply-rooted, long-term, modernising forces in American society and politics, and it collapsed completely in the face of the 1929 crash and the onset of the Great Depression. Franklin Roosevelt did not campaign as a radical economic interventionist in the 1932 election, but once in office, government intervention to deal with the collapse of the banking system and the widespread human suffering of the 1930s was the only available option, as Republican austerity under Herbert Hoover had failed to end the economic downturn. Roosevelt's 'New Deal' was a haphazard, quick-fix operation that only alleviated but did not end the Great Depression. It nevertheless established the federal government's responsibility over the whole range of economic and domestic policy: most particularly in the areas of welfare and government management of the economy. It also ended the post-Civil War Republican ascendancy and established the Democratic party in control of the federal government for a generation.[11]

Abroad, the US tried desperately to evade military intervention in European and East Asian affairs during the 1930s, but ever-growing foreign commitments and the evident threat posed by Hitler and the Japanese militarists to American interests made it inevitable that they would eventually be dragged into the conflict. After the defeat of Nazism and the use of the atom bomb in 1945, America stood alone as the world's major power, with its economic strength intact and the potential to obliterate much of the globe. This time it was impossible for the US to refuse the burden of leadership over a shattered world.

Superpower: 1945–74

The period after the Second World War saw American power and prosperity at unprecedented levels. Abroad, of course, US supremacy was challenged militarily by the Soviet Union, which had achieved a potentially hegemonic position through its occupation of most of Eastern and Central Europe after the war. To thwart Soviet ambitions, the Truman Administration (1945–53) gave Marshall Aid to the West European nations, so that their shattered economies (and valuable US markets) could be rebuilt. In the Bretton Woods Agreements, the world's economic and monetary order was re-established by the US by making the dollar the major international reserve currency, and the creation of the International Monetary Fund, the World Bank, and the General Agreement on Tariffs and Trade. In the security sphere the Americans signed the NATO Treaty in 1949, which committed them to come to the aid of Western Europe should the latter come under direct Soviet attack.[12]

Fearful of Soviet ambitions, the US committed itself to contain the spread of Communism on a global scale. After Communist North Korea invaded the South in 1950, America fought the Korean War against North Korea and China, at the cost of 50,000 American lives. At home, the Communist takeover in China, the USSR's development of nuclear weaponry, and the frustrating stalemate in Korea encouraged the growth of a vehement hysteria over the dangers of domestic Communist subversion, which became known as McCarthyism after the most prominent of the witch-hunters, Senator Joseph McCarthy. By the time that the scare petered out after McCarthy's downfall in 1955, it had ruined the careers of many leading American politicians, diplomats, government servants and artists.[13]

In 1952, the Republicans recaptured the White House after twenty years with the Second-World-War hero General Dwight Eisenhower at the head of their ticket, but the Roosevelt–Truman policies of containment abroad and interventionism at home were maintained. As the long post-war boom continued, the 1950s were a period of seemingly never-ending prosperity for the US. Perhaps the most significant development of the decade as far as the future of American politics and culture was concerned was the advent of television. In the election of 1960, television was to have a major impact in the victory of Democrat John F. Kennedy over Eisenhower's Vice-President Richard Nixon.[14] Kennedy's election ushered in the turbulent 1960s, which blew apart the New Deal political system and the complacent prosperity of the Eisenhower era. His assassination in November 1963 was almost symptomatic of the violence and turmoil of the new decade.

The first major social explosion was on civil rights. From the mid-1950s onwards, southern blacks led by the Revd Martin Luther King, Jr had begun an accelerating series of protests against southern racial segregation and disfranchisement. King's cause was strengthened by the Supreme Court's 1954 *Brown* v. *Board of Education* decision that had decisively declared segregation to be unconstitutional, but that had also been largely ignored by the southern state governments. In the early 1960s, as black protests gathered force, southern whites began to resist with violence, and the Kennedy Administration was compelled to intervene to uphold the law of the land. Finally, after Kennedy's death, Congress passed the Civil Rights Act of 1964, which finally guaranteed southern blacks their rights almost a century after the end of the Civil War, and the Voting Rights Act of the following year ended disfranchisement.[15]

Even more traumatic than the long-struggle for black civil rights was the Vietnam War. As in Korea, the US had committed itself to defend the regime of South Vietnam against the local Vietcong guerrillas and Communist North Vietnam. To prevent the collapse of the corrupt South Vietnamese regime, President Lyndon Johnson sent large numbers of US ground forces to Vietnam in the summer of 1965. By 1968 the US had over half a million troops engaged there and had also conducted a sustained aerial bombardment of North Vietnam, but was no nearer victory.[16] At home the war was particularly unpopular on college campuses and a large anti-war movement broke out first in California and then nationally. The anti-war movement succeeded in effectively forcing President Johnson out of the race for re-election in 1968, but Johnson's withdrawal was merely the prelude to an extremely turbulent year, that witnessed the assassinations of both Martin Luther King and Robert Kennedy, and outbreaks of street violence between anti-war protesters and the police during the Democratic National Convention in Chicago. The anti-war movement also provoked a backlash 'law-and-order' presidential candidacy from the Alabama segregationist George Wallace that won 14 per cent of the national vote in November.

The eventual winner of the 1968 election was the Republican Richard Nixon, who had promised to end the war, but found this to be easier said than done once he took office. Indeed Vietnam had been the catalyst for a broad revolt by the post-Second World War 'baby-boom' generation against the conservative *mores* of their elders. This revolt included the sexual revolution and the rise of feminism (and later, the gay rights movement), together with the widespread use of drugs. Among many urban blacks in the North, the non-violent protests of Dr King had been transformed into the violent rhetoric of 'black power' after the virulent race riots of 1965–68. In the face of these changes Nixon claimed to speak for the 'Silent Majority' who disapproved of the so-called 'counter-culture'. As a result the US was bitterly divided on Vietnam and a whole range of social issues in the early 1970s.

The social temperature declined somewhat when Nixon finally succeeded in extricating the US from Vietnam in 1973, but no sooner had this been accomplished than it was revealed that his aides had been involved in an inept burglary of the Democrats' election headquarters during the 1972 campaign. As the 'Watergate' scandal unfolded it became increasingly apparent that Nixon had been involved in an elaborate cover-up, and in the summer of 1974 he was eventually forced to resign the presidency in the face of impeachment and likely conviction by the Senate. Thus the most turbulent period in US history since the Civil War ended with the first-ever resignation of an incumbent President.[17]

Post-imperial decline?

Vietnam and Watergate were not the only traumas that afflicted America during the 1970s. President Johnson's expansion of the welfare state and the costs of Vietnam led to the onset of inflation and a corresponding squeeze on American incomes. The situation was exacerbated by the 1973 oil price-rises, followed by another oil shock in the later 1970s. Now inflation was accompanied by rising unemployment, zero-growth, and a growing federal budget deficit. In addition to these domestic travails, President Jimmy Carter in the late 1970s also had to deal with the fall of US allies in Iran and Central America, and a new Soviet adventurism in Afghanistan, coupled with a growing resistance to nuclear deployments in Europe. At the tail-end of Carter's presidency American confidence appeared to have sunk to unprecedented depths.

Republican Ronald Reagan succeeded in restoring much of that confidence during the 1980s. This decade was characterised by low inflation, lower unemployment, and an economic boom encouraged by Reagan's heavy cuts in income taxes. Reagan and his Vice-President and successor George Bush could also take some credit for the collapse of Soviet power towards the end of the decade. America had finally won the Cold War and defeated Communism as a significant international force. Once again the US stood alone as the world's only economic and military superpower in the early 1990s.

Yet the US's relative economic position was much weaker than it had been in 1945. Much of this was due to the fact that the shattered post-Second-World-War economies of Western Europe and Japan had assumed their natural strength, but historians and commentators could also make a strong case that America's economic position had begun to show significant signs of absolute decline. The Bretton-Woods economic system and the dominance of the dollar had broken down in the early 1970s. Reagan's economic policies had raised the federal budget deficit to unprecedented levels and turned the US from the world's largest creditor into the largest debtor nation. Moreover, US manufacturing showed clear signs of weakness against sustained competition from Japanese imports in major industries such as cars and consumer electronics. The sustained growth in real family incomes that had characterised the post-war era had come to a halt in the early 1970s, and the great American middle class began to suffer a decline in real living standards. Falling educational standards, decaying infrastructure, ever-rising crime and violence, and continuing divisions on racial, sexual and cultural issues also gave rise to widespread concern. This pervasive sense of malaise led to the defeat of Reagan's Republican successor George Bush in the 1992 presidential election by Democrat Bill Clinton, and to the extraordinary phenomenon of Texas billionaire H. Ross Perot, who won 19 per cent of the popular vote on a populist national-revival ticket.[18]

Did the loss of American self-confidence in the early 1990s portend that the US was condemned to the eternal loss of its youth, innocence and vitality, and the slow, but inexorable decline that had characterised Great Britain during the twentieth century? The question revolved around what exactly one meant by decline. In relative terms an American retreat from the supremacy of the post-war era was inevitable, and to a large extent, welcome. The end of the Cold War no longer necessitated such a heavy defence burden for the US and allowed for a greater concentration on domestic problems. Rather than a retreat from the world being seen as a sign of weakness, it could potentially contribute to greater US strength over the longer term as scare resources are diverted from defence to deal with economic problems at home. There was also little sign that the American progressive, idealistic, forward-looking spirit had been quelled. Indeed success in the Cold War confirmed the validity of the liberal–democratic ideas on which the US was based.

So despite serious concerns over its relative international position, the US still had the opportunity to prolong its youth a little longer, and act with typical historical irreverence in a post-Cold-War world where it appeared likely to be the leading power for some time to come.

Notes

1 On the differing cultures of the early American colonists see Hackett Fisher, *Albion's Seed*.
2 On the political outlook of colonial American society see Wood, *The Radicalism of the American Revolution*, and Boorstein, *The Americans*.
3 See Wood.
4 On the Jacksonian movement see Arthur M. Schlesinger, Jr, *The Age of Jackson* (London: Eyre & Spottiswoode, 1946).
5 On Calhoun see Hofstadter, *The American Political Tradition and the Men Who Made It*, pp. 86–117.
6 On the conduct of the Civil War see McPherson, *Battle Cry of Freedom*.
7 On the post-Civil War South see Woodward, *The Strange Career of Jim Crow*.
8 On Populism see Lawrence Goodwyn, *The Populist Moment: A Short History of the Agrarian Revolt in America* (Oxford: Oxford University Press, 1978).
9 On Progressivism see Richard A. Hofstadter, *The Age of Reform: From Bryan to FDR* (New York: Knopf, 1955).
10 On the 1920s see John D. Hicks, *Republican Ascendancy: 1921–1933* (New York: Harper & Row, 1960).
11 See William E. Leuchtenberg, *Franklin D. Roosevelt and the New Deal* (New York: Harper & Row, 1963).
12 On the origins of the Cold War see Ambrose, *The Rise to Globalism*.
13 On McCarthyism see David Caute, *The Great Fear* (London: Secker & Warburg, 1978).
14 See Theodore H. White, *The Making of the President: 1960* (London: Jonathan Cape, 1962).
15 On the civil rights movement see David Garrow, *Bearing the Cross: Martin Luther King, Jr., and the Southern Christian Leadership Conference* (New York: Random House, 1986).
16 On Vietnam see David Halberstam, *The Best and the Brightest* (New York: Penguin, 1972), and Stanley Karnow, *Vietnam: A History* (New York: Viking, 1983).
17 On Watergate see Stephen E. Ambrose, *Nixon: Ruin and Recovery: 1973–1990* (New York: Simon and Schuster, 1991).
18 For the best statement of the 'declinist' point of view see Paul Kennedy, *The Rise and Fall of the Great powers: Economic Change and Military Conflict From 1500 to 2000* (New York: Random House, 1987).

2

Economy and society

The business of America is business. *President Calvin Coolidge*

America is God's Crucible, the great Melting-Pot, where all the races of Europe are melting and re-forming. *Israel Zangwill*

Just as it is impossible to grasp fully the essential features of the American political system without reference to American history, so some knowledge of the contemporary American economy and society is necessary to understand recent developments in American politics. This chapter offers a brief discussion of the US economy and some reflections on the state of ethnicity, religion, crime, law enforcement, the arts, and education in modern America. (The news media is so important in the modern American political process that it merits a chapter to itself as an intermediary institution in Part 3.)

As we shall see, the economy and society are not discrete variables but interact with each other in many important ways. Each however has been guided by an important myth.

In the economic sphere, Calvin Coolidge's view that America is essentially about business, and that the interests of business should be paramount in guiding national economic policy, has generally prevailed despite some important exceptions (such as the Progressive era and the New Deal). America is much more deeply committed to free-market capitalism as a guarantor of prosperity, than to the merits of state intervention in economic affairs. Nevertheless the myth articulated by President Coolidge is misleading since American government, from the time of Alexander Hamilton's mercantilistic policies in the 1790s to the military–industrial complex of the Cold War period, has always been intimately involved in the overall direction of the economy.

America's vibrant and fast-moving society has similarly been perceived (until very recently) through the myth of the melting-pot. Peoples from multifarious ethnic origins (and no longer exclusively Zangwill's European races) theoretically have merged their identities into a common American nationality based on the political creed discussed in the following chapter. The elements in the pot have melted much less than the myth assumes, however, and indeed the persistence and tenacity of ethnic identities remains one of the more remarkable features of American society. Moreover, since the 1960s the melting-pot metaphor has been generally rejected in favour of others such as the 'mosaic' or the 'salad' in which the elements retain separate identities while forming a common whole. Whether these new metaphors will achieve the

26

same degree of widespread popular acceptance and durability as the melting-pot remains to be seen.

Demography and geography

The United States, with over 250 million inhabitants, is the world's third largest country in population, and at 3.619 million square miles, the fifth largest in area.

The country is large enough to encompass almost every aspect of geographic diversity, from the semi-tropical marshes of southern Florida to the Arctic wastes of Alaska. America also contains almost every variety of climatic diversity and is prone to virtually all types of natural disasters including hurricanes, volcanoes, and earthquakes. The Mississippi–Missouri constitutes the nation's major inland waterway and the opening of the St Lawrence seaway in the 1950s also gave the states around the Great Lakes a direct outlet to the seas. Most of the population is urbanised to some extent (only 2 per cent lived on farms in 1995) and is clustered in metropolitan areas around the coasts and the Great Lakes.[1]

Table 2.1. *The ten largest metropolitan areas in the US*

Rank MSA*		State(s)	Population in 1990 (millions)	% change 1980–90
1	New York–N. New Jersey–Long Island	NY–NJ–CT	18.1	3
2	Los Angeles–Anaheim–Riverside	CA	14.5	26
3	Chicago–Gary–Lake County	IL–IN–WI	8.1	2
4	San Francisco–Oakland–San Jose	CA	6.3	17
5	Philadelphia–Wilmington–Trenton	PA–NJ–DE–MD	5.9	4
6	Detroit–Ann Arbor	MI	4.7	–2
7	Boston–Lawrence–Salem	MA–NH	4.2	5
8	Washington DC	DC–MD–VA	3.9	21
9	Dallas–Fort Worth	TX	3.9	33
10	Houston–Galveston–Brazoria	TX	3.7	20

Note * MSA = Metropolitan Statistical Area. These areas are defined for statistical use by the Office of Management and Budget and the Census Bureau. In addition to the county containing the main city, the MSA includes surrounding counties having strong economic and social ties to the central county.

Source 1990 census date from *The World Almanac and Book of Facts, 1993* (New York: Pharo Books, 1992).

The US is divided into fifty states, each with its own legislature and state capital: the largest state is California with 28 million inhabitants, and the smallest Wyoming with 479,000. However it makes more sense to think of the US in terms of regions than states for economic and social purposes these days. Most Americans divide the country into four regions – Northeast, South, Midwest, and West – although these may be too crude to represent the degree of regional diversity within the country, they still have a cultural significance. The Northeast, the oldest area of settlement, remains the centre of economic, political and cultural life in the US. The South, also settled early but according to a different pattern and with its regional identity reinforced by the Civil War, remains the most distinctive region in terms of culture. Despite rapid economic growth in some sections of the South, it is also still the poorest region of the country. The Midwest is characterised by traditional heavy industries, particularly in the states around the Great Lakes, and agriculture on the Great Plains. The West, settled later than the rest of the country, is still characterised by the individualism of the frontier, and particularly in California, by its susceptibility to the new and unusual.

Table 2.2. *The megastates*

Rank	State	Population in 1990 (millions)	% change 1980–90
1	California	29.7	26
2	New York	18.0	3
3	Texas*	17.0	19
4	Florida	12.9	33
5	Pennsylvania	11.9	0
6	Illinois	11.4	0
7	Ohio	10.8	1
8	Michigan	9.2	0
9	New Jersey	7.7	5
10	North Carolina	6.6	13
11	Georgia	6.4	19
12	Virginia	6.2	16

Note * By some estimates Texas had overtaken New York to become the second largest state by the end of 1994.

Source 1990 census date from *The World Almanac and Book of Facts, 1993* (New York: Pharo Books, 1992).

Perhaps the most significant geographic cleavage within the contemporary US is the one between the 'Frostbelt' and the 'Sunbelt'. These concepts, originated by political commentator Kevin Phillips in 1969, refer to the shift in population and economic and political power from the traditional industrial and financial centres of the Northeast–Upper Midwest region to the states of the South and Southwest – principally Florida, Southern California, Texas and

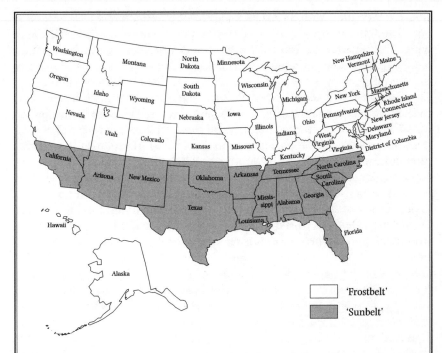

Kevin Phillips coined the expression 'Sunbelt', but even he was not very specific
about its geographical boundaries. It is clear that the 'Sunbelt' includes Florida,
Texas, Arizona, and southern California, all of which have the classic Sunbelt
features: high economic and population growth, a heavy concentration of defence
industries, high immigration from inside and outside the US, a large proportion
of retirees, conservative values, and presidential Republicanism. All the other
states below the line on the map have areas that share many of these features,
such as Atlanta (Georgia), Charlotte and Raleigh-Durham (North Carolina), and
Albuquerque (New Mexico), although there remain pockets of poverty – particularly in the rural South – that the Sunbelt business boom has passed by.

Arizona.[2] This shift has had considerable political implications, as might be
expected, though it is unclear if it will continue during the 1990s, as many
of the Sunbelt's key industries – such as aerospace – have been linked to the
Cold War and the so-called 'Military–Industrial' complex.

The US economy

America still has the world's largest economy, even if it no longer holds quite
the dominant position that it did during the 1950s. In line with other western
nations, the general trend in the US has been away from labour-intensive
traditional 'heavy' industries – coal, steel, cars, shipbuilding – and towards
light manufacturing, pharmaceutical, services, and high-technology electronics.

Since 1945 this has been accompanied by a continuing shift of economic and financial power towards the Sunbelt at the expense of the Frostbelt states. Before the Second World War New York and the northeastern metropolitan area dominated the US economy, reducing much of the South and West to semi-colonial status. Oil wealth in Texas, lower labour costs in the anti-Union southern and western states, the invention of the air-conditioner (which made the Sunbelt habitable during the torrid summer months), and the development of military–aerospace industries, all encouraged the creation of rival centres of manufacturing and financial power in Los Angeles, Houston, Dallas, Miami, Charlotte and Atlanta.[3] Also, while New York has always tended to look across the Atlantic towards Europe, many of the newer financial centres are more oriented towards the Pacific, East Asia, Latin America, or the Caribbean.

One aspect of the US economy that differs substantially from that of the European nations and Japan is the small size of the public sector. The American worship of free enterprise and endemic suspicion of government precluded the creation of a large complex of state industries, and the dirigiste economic approach of the national economic planners in post-1945 Europe. That is not to say that government is not involved in the economy, or that markets are left completely unregulated. Since the Progressive era a large corpus of legislation and federal government-appointed regulatory commissions have regulated key industries – such as railways, the media, the airlines, the stock exchanges, the banks – to preserve competition and safeguard the public interest. One of these regulatory commissions – the Federal Reserve Board or 'The Fed' – acts as America's central bank and regulator of interest rates, and thus has an extremely powerful influence over the rest of the economy.

In comparison with the European democracies, the US has a much smaller percentage of its labour force enrolled in trade unions. Unionisation peaked at about 30 per cent during the New Deal era, and has since been in constant decline to about 15 per cent today, with the only growth sectors for unions being in the public sector. Aside from the traditional American dislike of large political organisations, the weakness of unions can be accounted for by the constant availability of cheap immigrant labour, and the strict 'right-to-work' laws of many states in the South and West, that make labour organisation extremely difficult. In the rapidly growing service sector labour's presence is very weak indeed, and the greater flexibility of the labour market and the availability of low-wage service jobs has largely accounted for the US sustaining consistently lower unemployment rates than the European Union nations during the 1980s.

The most serious challenge facing the US economy in recent years has been the huge trade deficit with Japan that also contributes to America's record budget deficits. Already Japanese products have come to dominate in sectors such as consumer electronics, and have had a devastating effect on America's 'Big Three' automobile manufacturers. During the 1980s the US also experienced an unprecedented degree of foreign investment from the Japanese and others. (This aspect of the increasingly global nature of the US economy created some popular unease as several American landmarks such as the Rockefeller Center in New York, Pebble Beach golf course, Burger King Corp. and the Brooks Brothers clothing chain, fell into the hands of Japanese and European owners.)

Another economic challenge for the US in the 1990s stems from the end of the Cold War era. The containment of Communism involved heavy procurement of military *materiel* from private industry – planes, guns, rockets, scientific research – and led to the creation of what President Eisenhower described as the 'Military–Industrial' complex – a large sector of industry producing primarily for the Pentagon. With the likely reduction of American defence commitments in the 1990s, how will this large sector of the US economy and the states where it is particularly concentrated – California, Texas, Georgia, Florida – cope with the shortage of orders?

How successfully these two challenges are met will determine whether America remains the world's leading economy during the 1990s.

Wages, living standards, wealth and power

America regards itself as a 'middle-class society' and people who would be regarded as working-class or upper-class in comparable liberal democracies persistently refer to themselves as 'middle-class' in the United States. The reality is otherwise of course. America has far greater extremes of wealth and poverty than most other advanced industrial nations. Yet these figures are distorted by the existence of a concentrated, jobless underclass and a relatively small elite of extremely wealthy individuals. Overall US per capita income and living standards are among the highest – if not the highest – of the western industrialised nations.

Poverty in the US is heavily concentrated in the inner cities, the rural South, and the Appalachian Mountains, and among ethnic groups, such as blacks, Hispanics, and lower-status southern whites who inhabit these regions. Extremes of wealth and poverty tend to coexist within certain urban areas – New York, Chicago, and Los Angeles being prime examples – as the middle class has largely fled the inner cities for suburbia. Politically, the poor are one of the weakest groups in modern America, since many of them do not vote, and politicians therefore are not obliged to pay much attention to them. In the US political activity tends to increase with income levels, so that the professional upper-middle classes and the very wealthy tend to have a disproportionate influence over political decisions.

The position of the great American middle class is the most interesting. In the US the term 'middle-class' is used to cover skilled blue-collar workers, the self-employed, small businessmen, and the lower clerical and technical grades. This segment of American society experienced unprecedented rises in living standards and aspirations in the period between the Second World War and the oil-price shocks of the 1970s. Since that period they have been squeezed

Table 2.3. *The relative global economic position of the US*

Rank	Country	GDP ($bn)	Per capita GDP ($)	PPP * (US=100)	average annual % increase GDP 1980–91
1	US	5,686	22,560	100	3.1
2	Japan	3,337	27,919	82	4.3
3	Germany	1,692	21,248	85	2.3
4	France	1,168	20,603	81	2.3
5	Italy	1,072	18,576	74	2.4
6	UK	964	16,748	74	2.8
7	Canada	569	21,254	90	3.1
8	Spain	487	12,461	55	3.2
9	Russia	480	3,220	37	2.0
10	Brazil	447	2,921	22	2.5

Note * PPP = Purchasing Power Parity. Unlike per capita GDP, this statistic accounts for cost-of-living differences by replacing normal currency exchange rates with rates designed to equalise the prices of a standard 'basket' of goods and services, and these are used to obtain PPP estimates of per-capita GDP. Results are normally expressed on a scale of 1–100 with the US, which has the highest standard of living, at 100.

Source The Economist: Pocket World in Figures, 2nd edn (London: Economist Books, 1993).

economically, initially by inflation (which led to the middle-class tax revolt in the late 1970s and early 1980s) and latterly by a dramatic slowing in the rate of economic growth. To maintain living standards, it is now normal for both parents to have jobs outside the home in middle-class families, and middle-class Americans can no longer assume (as they have done for most of this century) that their children will be better-off economically than themselves. The insecurity of this section of society has been further exacerbated by rising crime in urban areas, falling standards in education, and rising immigration.

This explains why the white middle class has been the most volatile segment of the electorate over the past decade or so. In 1980 their votes helped to put Ronald Reagan in the White House and inaugurated the Reagan revolution. When their economic position became precarious again in the early 1990s, middle-class voters formed the backbone of the Ross Perot movement, or voted for Democrat Bill Clinton. Securing these voters is the key to political success in America during the 1990s.

Race and ethnicity

America is a racially diverse and multi-ethnic society. For most of this century public doctrine regarding race and ethnicity in the US has emphasised integration and the need for assimilation. Adherence to the American political creed was supposed to take precedence over racial or ethnic loyalties. Even at the height of the melting-pot era, however, ethnicity had a profound influence over American society and politics. Ethnic ties were the lifeblood of the great urban political machines and also influenced American foreign policy (consider the impact of German and Irish Americans on US foreign policy between the wars). Black Americans were deliberately denied participation in the 'melting-pot', and thus had no opportunity to assimilate. In the 1960s the melting-pot became unfashionable, as following the example of 'black is beautiful' and 'black power', all Americans began to re-emphasise ethnicity and ethnic origins.[4]

Yet assimilation should not be underestimated. Among the white ethnic groups in the United States the marked tensions which existed a half-century ago have eased considerably, and integration and intermarriage have become common. The problem in modern America is not so much one of ethnicity as of race and language.

Black Americans have made significant progress since the Civil Rights Act of 1964. A large black middle class has emerged, and with help of anti-discrimination statutes and 'affirmative action' (positive discrimination) programmes blacks have penetrated institutions and sections of American life that were previously closed to them. Yet America's direst rates of single-parenthood, poverty, deprivation, and crime are still to be found in inner-city poor, black neighbourhoods, and most black Americans still feel that this is largely the result of a continuing pervasive racism in American society.

Table 2.4. *Racial/Hispanic origin breakdown of the US population, 1990*

Race	% of US population 1990	% change 1980–90
White	80.0	6
Black	12.0	13
Asian/Pacific islander	3.0	108
Native American	1.0	38
Other	4.0	45
Hispanic origin *	9.0	53
Mexican	5.0	54
Puerto Rican	1.0	35
Cuban	0.4	30
Other Hispanic	2.0	67
Non-Hispanic	91.0	7

Note * Hispanics may be of any race.

Source 1990 census date from *The World Almanac and Book of Facts, 1993* (New York: Pharos Books, 1992).

Black political leaders are divided on how best to deal with the problem of the inner-city ghettos. The black political establishment within the Democratic party continues to emphasise the need for integration of blacks into the mainstream of American life through traditional remedies like affirmative action and school busing. Others, such as the black Muslims, convinced of the inevitability of white racism, have tended to stress the need for blacks to develop their own institutions, schools and businesses so as to regain self-respect and rebuild devastated inner-city communities.

Traditionally blacks and Hispanics (except for Cuban Americans) have been political allies in support of measures like affirmative action in hiring to assist minorities. However it is doubtful if this alliance can survive the continued influx of Hispanic (mainly Mexican) immigrants into the US. Before too long Hispanics will overtake blacks to become the largest 'minority' group in the US, and in urban areas such as Greater Los Angeles, Dallas and Houston they have already achieved this, although because of low registration rates the demographic changes have not yet been reflected politically. By the middle of the next century it is estimated that in California and Texas (the two largest states in terms of population) over half the population will be of Hispanic origin. While blacks and Hispanics have much politically in common, this would not be the case if the Hispanic population should make more economic progress than blacks.[5] On many issues beyond those concerned with discrimination, Hispanic voters are also more politically conservative than blacks. Finally, both black and white voters are wary of demands for bi-lingual education and equality of Spanish with English on signs and in government documents. Fear of the 'Hispanicisation' of America and Mexican irredentism have given rise to movements to declare English the official language of the US, and to restrict immigration.

In modern public discourse the melting-pot has thus been rejected in favour of other metaphors such as the 'salad' or the 'mosaic' that allow racial and ethnic groups to hold on to their unique characteristics while forming part of a greater whole. Another aspect of the contemporary approach to racial/ethnic relations is the emphasis on 'multiculturalism' and on the promotion of minority cultures in education and culture and the arts more generally. Whether this will be any more successful in achieving ethnic/racial harmony in the US remains to be seen.

Gender and sexuality

No society has taken the 'sexual revolution' more seriously than the United States, and in no other advanced industrial society has the reaction to it been more severe. This is partly a reflection of the diversity of US society but is also related to the contradictory impulses within American political culture with regard to these matters. Americans value individual rights but the democratic culture – as De Tocqueville noted – also encourages conformity, and in a society that has been characterised by constant change the nuclear family has been one of the few social anchors.

America has provided much of the ideology and the leadership of the contemporary women's movement. The writings of Betty Friedan and Gloria Steinem inspired a generation of American women to shake off the shackles of mother and housewife and pursue professional careers on a equal basis with men. The advent of the contraceptive pill and the legalisation of abortion also assisted this process. Despite the failure of the Equal Rights Amendment (ERA) to the Constitution, by the early 1990s women had achieved startling advances in most areas of American society, but most notably in business and the professions. Moreover, the feminist organisations – the National Organization of Women (NOW) and the National Women's Political Caucus (NWPC) – are taken extremely seriously as major political lobbies – particularly within the Democratic party coalition. In the 1992 elections women's votes were instrumental in sending an unprecedented number of women to the US Senate.

Yet American feminism has also had its setbacks. The ERA failed in large part because of feminism's limited popular appeal beyond the well-educated professional and managerial classes. To the vast majority of middle- and working-class American women who must work outside the home but still manage families – often as single parents – or who live in poverty-stricken urban neighbourhoods, the preoccupation of the feminist leadership with issues like sexist language in the workplace might seem much less relevant than finding the next meal for their family.

Another matter that has served as something of a double-edged sword for American feminists has been the issue of abortion. Access to safe medical abortion has been seen by women's organisations as fundamental to women's right to control their fertility, and thus also their careers. Defence of the US Supreme Court's 1973 *Roe* v. *Wade* decision that permitted abortion in the first six months of pregnancy has been a rallying-point, and a major organising and fund-raising asset, for the major women's organisations. On the other hand the issue has also served as a rallying cry for those forces in American society that never felt entirely comfortable with the feminist agenda – most particularly the Roman Catholic Church and the various fundamentalist and evangelical Protestant churches. The need to defend *Roe* at all costs (and few issues are more important to the career-oriented professional constituency that forms the core of the women's movement) has perhaps prevented the feminist organisations from giving sufficient attention to the economic concerns of many millions of American women.

The civil rights movement and the women's movement have also served as models for the gay rights movement that also had its origins in the social and cultural upheaval of the 1960s. While the women's movement has become a national political force, the gay rights movement has been most visible in the major urban centres – such as New York City, San Francisco, and Los Angeles – where gay men and lesbians are concentrated. In these areas political organisation of gays has turned them into an important voting bloc. It is also in those areas that gay rights advocates have been most successful in passing state and local ordinances protecting gays against discrimination in jobs and housing. Widespread suffering and death from AIDS in the gay community have also brought gay-related issues to public attention and served as a rallying-point for gay men in their political activity. As is true for the women's movement there are no other societies where gay men and lesbians are so well organised and influential politically.

As with the women's movement however, the price that has been paid for successful profile and visibility is the counter-organisation of those forces in American society that feel threatened by the gay rights agenda – traditional families and many religious groups. This explains the widespread political controversy over President Clinton's attempt to allow gay men and lesbians to serve openly in the military, and the various recent state and local initiatives to repeal or override gay rights laws and ordinances.

The long-term trend in the US, however, appears to favour the continued expansion of women's rights and gay rights despite the vocal and well-organised nature of the opposition. Opponents of such measures face the problem that their opposition goes against the grain of America's liberal political culture which emphasises equal treatment and equal rights for all. The likely continued advance of women's and gay rights in America is indicated by polls showing that among the youngest voters, these issues are not only heavily favoured, but are regarded as increasingly important.

Religion

America has traditionally prided itself on its religious pluralism. A plurality of religions could thrive there because the notion of the separation of Church and State is deeply embedded in the First Amendment to the Constitution, and the political culture. Yet ironically, despite the secular tradition in public life, Americans are far more committed to individual religions than their counterparts in other western industrialised liberal democracies. On every indicator – belief in God, belief in an afterlife, belief in the Devil, prayer, and churchgoing – Americans rates of commitment are far higher. It may well be that the pressures towards conformity and uniformity in America's middle-class, democratic society explain the greater need for religious commitment as a source of identity for Americans.[6]

Like American society, America's patterns of religious affiliation are in constant flux. It costs little to form one's own denomination or Church in the US, and American religions have been constantly splintering since the Great Awakenings and revivals of the early nineteenth century. In recent times the most interesting development in American Christianity has been declining membership of the 'main-line' Protestant denominations, and the rise in affiliation with the fundamentalist, evangelical and pentecostalist churches. In the 1980s growth in membership of the conservative Churches also was

Table 2.5. *Major religious denominations in the US*

Religion/Denomination	Membership* (millions)
Jewish	6.0
Muslims	8.0
Christian	
Roman Catholic	58.6
Eastern Orthodox	4.0
Protestant	86.7
Major Protestant denominations	
Southern Baptist Convention	15.0
Other Baptists churches	16.0
United Methodist	8.9
Lutheran	7.8
Mormon	4.3
Presbyterian	3.8
Pentecostal	3.8
Episcopal	2.4
Jehovah's Witnesses	0.9
Seventh Day Adventists	0.7

Note * Data supplied by the churches themselves.

Source The World Handbook (1992).

associated with the rise of the television ministries of Oral Roberts, Pat Robertson, Jim Bakker, and Jimmy Swaggert. After tawdry sex scandals had disgraced Bakker and Swaggert, 'tele-evangelism' lost much of its momentum in terms of fund-raising and adherents. It did, nevertheless, mobilise thousands of previously apathetic fundamentalist and evangelical voters in opposition to abortion, gay rights, and Supreme Court decisions prohibiting organised prayer in public schools.

Roman Catholicism has maintained its position in terms of members in the US and seems likely to gain further due to the influx of largely Catholic, Hispanic immigrants. Of course American Catholics have faced the same dilemmas as Catholics in other western democracies, being torn between an increasingly liberal attitude on issues of sexual behaviour and lifestyles, and a generally conservative Church hierarchy. In the US, leading Catholic churchmen such as Cardinal O'Connor, Archbishop of New York, have spoken out frequently against abortion and sexual permissiveness, while those more critical of the Vatican's unbending conservatism in those areas have usually been frozen out of the Church hierarchy. Given their generally poor rural backgrounds, the long-term effect of the new Hispanic immigrants on the Catholic Church is likely to reinforce the conservative position.

Given the overwhelming numerical predominance of the Christian denominations, other faiths often have to struggle for recognition. American Judaism has suffered from intermarriage and from divisions between the orthodox, conservative, and reform denominations, reinforcing its already defensive stance *vis-à-vis* the Christian majority. American Muslims, once largely confined to the fringes of the black community, are likely to become more visible with the growth in immigration from the Indian subcontinent and the Middle-East. Given the wide gulf between American society and the mores of Islam and American opposition to Islamic fundamentalism abroad, the integration of American Muslims into society may well become increasingly difficult.

America's liberal, secular, political culture remains in fundamental conflict with the absolute and universal aspirations of most religions, but the religious pluralism that has characterised American society since colonial times has required that religious toleration be observed for the preservation of the public peace. Religious toleration is one of America's noblest political traditions, and one that would not have survived without the secularisation of the public sphere which the framers intended. At the cost of tolerating the more eccentric religious fringe and occasionally offending the sensibilities of the large Christian majority, America has by and large been spared the kind of religious strife, or battles between the State and organised religion, that has poisoned political life in other portions of the globe.

The shame of the cities?

During the Progressive era at the turn of the century, Lincoln Steffens pioneered the muck-raking style of journalism with his book *The Shame of the Cities*, an indictment of the squalor and corruption that pervaded American urban life at that time. Today America's cities remain a national problem. The old, and not so old, inner cities have become a byword for poverty, drugs, violence, crime and racial enmity. Most Americans, living in suburbs, prefer to push the dire problems of the cities out of their consciousness until the outbreak of really vicious lawlessness on a mass scale – such as the Miami riot of 1989, and the Los Angeles riots of 1992 – reminds them of the ongoing urban crisis in the US.

The problems of the inner cities can largely be attributed to two factors: racial segregation and economic change. Cities that relied heavily on traditional heavy industries – the so-called rustbelt – have been hard hit by the reduction in blue-collar jobs as the service sector of the economy (which pays much less well) has grown. Traditionally, new ethnic groups arriving in American cities occupied the poorest inner-city areas and the worst jobs, but gradually worked themselves out of there to be replaced by new arrivals. The tragedy of America's inner cities is that this did not occur with the last major migration to the old inner cities – that of southern blacks. Racial prejudice made it harder for blacks to break out of their inner city ghettos, and soon after their arrival the old low-paid, unskilled jobs or city jobs began to disappear as a result of the end of machine-based patronage, and the flight of businesses from the inner cities to the suburbs.

As the inner cities became more black, urban police forces remained largely white, and this explosive mixture finally ignited in the urban race riots of the mid-1960s. The riots merely dramatically accelerated a process that was already under-way: the white middle class and much of the working class no longer wanted to live in proximity to racial violence and fled to the burgeoning suburbs in millions, leaving the inner cities blacker and poorer than ever. In one sense this benefited blacks, as black politicians were now able to win mayoral elections regularly and thus control city government in almost all of America's major cities. But ultimately, educated black professionals were also eager to escape the hopelessness of the ghetto, and they too moved into the suburbs. As the black professional and business communities joined the exodus, the situation for those left behind grew worse than ever. Many of America's inner cities have literally become 'no-go' areas: breeding-grounds of poverty, drug abuse and brutality, with danger lurking on every street corner, and federal welfare payments the only source of income.

There are, of course, exceptions to the nightmare. Financial and cultural centres like New York, Chicago and San Francisco have retained wealthy, upper middle-class residents, who are still attracted by what a vibrant inner city has to offer culturally. Indeed as younger, upper middle-class professionals have begun to move back to the cities, gentrification has proceeded apace in several American city centres. Gentrification has not solved the problem however, but merely moved it to another part of town. In the absence of a large middle-class tax base, inner cities can no longer provide essential services without going into heavy debt and even default (as happened to New York City during the 1970s). Shortage of funds also has created major infrastructural problems for American cities – such as poor public transport – which makes it harder to persuade businesses to invest there.

Even the cities of the Sunbelt states, built largely around the motor car (and which are really more collections of suburbs than traditional cities with an urban core), have been suffering from the same problems. Indeed, in some senses the situation is even worse, because in these sprawling politically fragmented and more spatially distant cities the sense of commonality between the various scattered communities is even weaker. The Sunbelt cities, having been built around the automobile, also have to deal with the problems of poor (or often non-existent) public mass transit, congested roads, and environmental pollution.[7]

It is debatable whether the will to address the problems of the inner cities seriously exists in the US today. Most Americans now appear to accept the situation and have decided to live with it by simply avoiding the worst neighbourhoods, and this is easy to do for there is nothing in those neighbourhoods that would lead any non-resident to visit them, except for criminal purposes. Moreover, the nature of modern manufacturing and service industries has led to the growth of what Joel Garreau has called 'edge cities' on the periphery of traditional urban areas.[8] It thus appears likely that, despite the limited movement back to some inner cities by adventurous young professionals and 'outlaw' groups such as gays, the motivation to move further and further out in pursuit of the suburban idyll will persist.

Law and order

America is a violent society by comparison with most other western industrialised nations. The conditions in inner cities described above are part of the explanation for this, but American violence is not confined to the urban ghettos. A large part of the explanation for the high rates of violent crime in the United States, even by comparison with its neighbour Canada, is the easy availability of firearms in most of the country.

The 'right to bear arms' set out in the Second Amendment of the Constitution and repeated like a mantra by the opponents of gun control is almost unique to the United States. The framers saw this right as fundamental to a citizen's right of self-protection against tyrannical or arbitrary government. Moreover, for those Americans living on the constantly expanding 'frontier' the possession of firearms was an essential precaution. In modern America, however, it seems that the problem of easy access to guns has got out of hand. It is not very hard for say, a drug-addicted youth to obtain a small handgun – the infamous 'Saturday Night Specials' – in most states. Fear of violent crime encourages non-violent citizens to purchase firearms as a precaution, and the anxieties of those citizens are played upon by the National Rifle Association (NRA), the leading anti-gun control lobby.

Given the existence of the Second Amendment, truly effective gun control is likely to be all but impossible to achieve in the contemporary US. Several more tentative measures concerning 'assault weapons' and certain other particularly vicious types of firearms have been passed in various states, together with waiting periods and· background checks for gun purchases. In 1993 Congress finally passed the 'Brady' Bill (named after President Reagan's Press Secretary James Brady, who was badly wounded in the 1981 assassination attempt on the President and left severely physically and mentally disabled) mandating a forty-eight-hour waiting period nationwide for persons purchasing a handgun. Despite these reversals the anti-gun control forces, with their large base of support among Americans who like to keep firearms for hunting, is generally better organised and motivated than their opponents, thus making really effective action on the issue very hard to achieve.

The easy availability of firearms of course makes the job of America's police forces and the criminal justice system all the harder. In the urban areas – where violent crime is high, police manpower is constrained by budgets, and the courts and prisons are clogged with cases and criminals – the system of law enforcement occasionally appears to have broken down completely.[9] Again the problem is shortage of revenue, due to the flight of the tax base and escalating crime rates. Poor relations between mainly white police forces and the minority communities in the inner cities have also contributed to numerous incidents of police brutality and massive rioting in response. The tendency of middle-class, suburban, white residents to side unquestioningly with the police in such circumstances creates another degree of racial polarisation within America's troubled urban conurbations. Without effective gun control or a major injection of resources into the system, public order is likely to be even more of a problem in the US during the 1990s.

The great outdoors

The vastness of the United States includes an astonishing variety of topography, flora and fauna. Concern that much of this pristine environment might disappear during the rapid development of the late nineteenth century led to the founding of the conservation movement by John Muir and others during the Progressive era. With support from President Theodore Roosevelt and his Interior Secretary Gifford Pinchot, large areas of land – particularly in the western states – were taken over by the federal government and set aside as national parks or national forest, for the use and benefit of the public.

Despite these measures, up until the 1960s the odds were still stacked in favour of development interests in the battles over public lands. Many states wanted to become more prosperous through extraction of their natural resources, and politicians who controlled the rights to public lands could easily be persuaded or even bought (as in the notorious 'Teapot Dome' affair during the 1920s) by powerful development interests, especially when those interests promised jobs.[10] The 'back to nature' ethic of the 1960s counter-culture, however, also helped to reinvigorate the American environmental movement. Rachel Carson's *The Silent Spring*, which pointed out in dramatic form the effects of pesticides and herbicides on the environment, was one of the major catalysts for the revival.[11] Widespread concern over the effects of pollution, urban traffic congestion, the extinction of various species, and the threat to unique ecosystems also contributed. In response environmental regulation was strengthened, and under the Nixon Administration an Environmental Protection Agency (EPA) was established to enforce them.

The principal environmental organisations – the Sierra Club, the Wilderness Society, the League of Conservation Voters, and the American Wildlife Federation – quickly became major players in state and federal politics, with a large politically active constituency of educated, upper middle-class voters. Nevertheless those business interests that had been the targets of the increased environmental regulation of the period fought back, by spending more on political campaigns, and by arguing that environmental scrutiny might put the jobs of middle- and working-class Americans at stake. In the West the environmental movement produced a backlash from developers and a general public committed to greater development of public lands in the so-called 'Sagebrush Rebellion' of the late 1970s.

Colorado had been the centre of the Sagebrush revolt and two prominent leaders of that revolt, James Watt and Anne Gorsuch Burford, came to

Washington as Interior Secretary and EPA Director respectively with President Ronald Reagan in 1981. Watt and Gorsuch deliberately set out to undo much of the environmental regulation and legislation of the preceding two decades, but their stridency merely provoked the opposition into more vigorous protest. Eventually, after both were forced out of office (due to tactless statements and failure to perform their duties) and replaced by more moderate figures, the temperature on environmental issues settled down for a while.

During the administration of President Bush however, environmental issues again came to the fore in the Pacific Northwest. This time the issue concerned the habitat, in old-growth forest, of the northern spotted owl which had been declared an endangered species by the federal government. This declaration and various federal court orders to implement it essentially put a stop to the lumber industry in the Pacific Northwest. The dispute dragged on into the Clinton Administration, where the President himself tried to negotiate a compromise in the spring of 1993. Clinton's Interior Secretary – the former Arizona governor Bruce Babbitt – seemed likely to pursue a more aggressive anti-development approach than his Republican predecessors, but the prolonged struggle over the great American outdoors between environmentalists and development interests showed no sign of abating.

The crisis in education

Access to free public education has been fundamental to the American ethic, since education theoretically provides the equal opportunity for every American child to succeed. Thus the American states have generally devoted large resources to education at all levels since the early nineteenth century. American children start kindergarten at around the age of four and enter the first grade around the age of seven. From elementary school they proceed to middle school, junior high school, and high school. In contrast to European systems, where basic decisions about life chances and careers are made at a relatively early age, and it is difficult once one has 'dropped out' of the education system to get back in again, Americans believe that options should be maximised for as long as possible. Under the influence of the philosopher John Dewey at the turn of the century, American education has also been less concerned with performance in national tests, but with the development of the individual child. More recently, this type of thinking has been reinforced by the 'self-esteem' movement, which stresses the need for teachers not to be too critical of pupils' performance.

The result is a more open system in many respects, but one in which American schoolchildren are generally behind their counterparts in other western industrialised nations by a year or so in most subjects. Often American students will be dealing with material in their first or second years at university that would certainly have been covered in secondary school in Britain, France, Japan, or Germany. Yet by contrast with those countries, far more American schoolchildren go on to university or higher education, a path that is barred to students in most other countries at an earlier age, and this has to be taken into account in assessing the overall quality of an education system that is too easily dismissed as inadequate by Europeans and critical Americans.

This is not to deny the considerable problems in contemporary American education. In many parts of the country the public schools have suffered from the flight of white students to the suburbs or the private sector, leaving an underclass of minority students stranded in economically deprived and badly underfunded school districts. School busing, which was intended to deal with this problem, has often actually exacerbated the situation by destroying the link between schools and local communities. Problems of drugs, violence, and 'grade inflation' (the dramatic rise in the overall grade level of students over the past two decades) due to parental and political pressure, create further problems for the harassed public-school teacher, now also being criticised by state and federal governments for producing a work-force inadequately educated by comparison with America's major industrial competitors. In the early 1990s state court decisions began mandating states to ensure that all school districts were equally funded. If these are implemented then some redress is likely to take place in favour of the minority districts. However, the problems of educational disparity are more deeply rooted in family and income and are likely to remain formidable.

In the major universities and colleges the quality of education remains high for those who can obtain access. Harvard, Yale, Chicago, Stanford, Berkeley, and Columbia are among the very finest universities on the globe, in terms of the research and the quality of postgraduate education that they provide. At the undergraduate level these are supplemented by many other excellent private and public institutions and liberal arts colleges (a specifically American concept designed around a broad undergraduate curriculum on classical lines). At the state and local level students can gain admission to community college and state universities in their home states with relatively minimal tuition fees. Taken as a whole the American higher education system remains conspicuous by the degree of access that it provides by comparison with other countries.

The major issue in higher education in recent years has been increasing access for women and minorities. In response to the 1960s revolt, American universities at all levels have pursued 'affirmative action' policies to recruit women and minority students that have not been well received by applicants from outside those categories who feel themselves to be disadvantaged in the applications process. Race and gender have also dominated debates over the curriculum, which feminists and minority advocates see as being dominated by the writings of 'dead, white European males' rather than issues relevant to them. Their opponents strike back in defence of the traditional liberal arts curriculum by accusing the advocates of 'multiculturalism' of 'political correctness' and the trivialisation of higher education. Some have gone further and accused multiculturalists of seeking to suppress debate and freedom of speech on grounds of racism and sexism, and there have been countless incidents in recent years where campus attempts to discipline students and faculty for 'racist' or 'sexist' behaviour have become national *causes célèbres*.[12]

If this debate (which is also reflected in curriculum disputes at the secondary level) continues to poison American education then it will detract from the essential problem of the system – training an American work-force that can compete with Europe and Japan. Meeting this challenge is another important test faced by the State and national political leaders during the 1990s.

Culture and the arts: still a contradiction in terms?

The arrogant view on the part of Europeans of American culture as a contradiction in terms still persists, but is badly in need of revision. American cultural vitality is now probably greater than it has ever been, and certainly there appears to be more innovation and energy in arts and culture in the contemporary US than in most of Europe.

Of course, given that America is a democratic, middle-class society, America's greatest cultural contribution to the twentieth century has been the advent of mass culture as opposed to European elite culture. Much to the chagrin of cultural chauvinists in the Old World, the US has proved itself the master of mass entertainment, and no other society in this century has come close to emulating it. World culture is dominated by American popular music, American cinema, and American television, simply because America does these things better.

Even at the elite end of culture, the US now boasts some of the world's finest symphony orchestras, opera companies, and art museums. New York remains at the centre of US elite culture. For visual arts, theatre, music, and latterly even fashion and cuisine, there are few cities on the globe that can compare with the 'Big Apple' in vitality and abundance. It is true that Broadway theatre seems to have lost its capacity for innovation by comparison with London's West End in recent years. Due to the high cost of productions (inflated by the city's powerful unions) producers are only willing to bet on sure-fire successes, which seems to entail a succession of Andrew Lloyd Webber musicals and revivals catering to tourists. On the other hand, fringe theatre on 'off-Broadway' and 'off-off Broadway' is more vital than ever.

American popular culture is based in Los Angeles: home of Hollywood, and most of the television and popular music industries. Reflecting the nature of its mass audience, Hollywood seems to have lost its capacity to innovate and experiment, and the most interesting work in recent US cinema has come from long-time rebels such as Robert Altman, younger directors outside the Hollywood mainstream such as Gus Van Sant, Stephen Soderbergh, David Lynch and Quentin Tarantino, or foreigners such as Stephen Frears. Despite the conservatism of the major studios, American films continue to do remarkably well in international competitions, and no other country was producing more innovative or exciting cinema in the early 1990s.

In popular music the same tendencies towards conservatism are apparent, with the 'Top 40' being dominated by mainstream, middle-of-the-road artists like Michael Bolton or Whitney Houston. Yet again, new forms keep breaking through in spite of this. The 1980s and 1990s saw the emergence of rap music and world music, and new musical forms seem more likely to come to the fore in the US these days. Interestingly, US popular music seems to be becoming more specialised as the FM radio stations cater more to specialised audiences for rock, jazz, classical, MOR, rap and soul and latino music. Again, a notable aspect of the extraordinary diversity in modern American society.

Despite the extraordinary vitality of the arts in the contemporary US however, it cannot be denied that most of the country remains culturally extremely conservative. The clash between small-town and suburban America and the cosmopolitan culture of the artistic elite has been illustrated in recent times by the battles over the National Endowment for the Arts (NEA) awards given to controversial artists such as the late photographer Robert Mapplethorpe. Politicians in Congress led by Senator Jesse Helms of North Carolina have attempted to abolish the NEA altogether or to exert greater control over its awards procedures. During President Bush's administration there was a state of open warfare between congressional Conservatives and the artistic community with the hapless NEA torn between them. Robert Hughes's excellent *The Culture of Complaint* gives the best and most even-handed account of the 'culture wars' that have afflicted the American arts community in the 1990s.[13]

Perhaps the failure of cultural issues to work for the Republicans during the 1992 elections may presage a reduction in the temperature of this debate for the remainder of the decade. Nevertheless the contradiction between the West's most innovative and energetic artistic community and the cultural conservatism of the 'middle-American' television and Hollywood audience remains endemic to American society.

Summary: a society in flux

The essential characteristic of American society is motion. Within certain clearly-set parameters, America is deliberately intended to be a society in flux. Americans are not expected to remain in accepted social positions and roles but to seek perpetual change in their situation, and to transform their lives. Of course living in such a state of flux can be very disconcerting. Today's certainties may become the uncertainties of tomorrow. Americans are perpetually loose and unmoored. In such a situation, fears of a sudden fall in status are much more imminent than in more traditional societies, and this gives rise to movements of fear or resistance such as the advent of the religious right over the past decade or so as a major political force – what historian Richard Hofstadter called the 'Paranoid Style' in American politics and society, that also characterised movements such as the anti-Roman Catholic 'Know-Nothings' in the 1850s, the Populists in the 1890s, and the McCarthyites in the 1950s.[14]

Yet in the end these movements always fail in their objectives. While the religious right may have slowed the pace of change in areas like the acceptance of homosexuality, they have not succeeded, despite the support of the Reagan and Bush Administrations in reversing the right to abortion, in reinstating school prayer, or in ending state support for controversial art. The defensive agenda of resistance runs too much against the grain of America's liberal/progressive political culture: its gets too much in the way of 'business', the perpetual motion of American society.

Notes

1 See *The World Almanac and Book of Facts, 1990* (New York: Pharos Books, 1990), pp. 550–63.
2 See Kevin P. Phillips, *The Emerging Republican Majority* (New York: Anchor Books, 1970).
3 See Sale, Power Shift.
4 See Glazer and Moynihan, *Beyond the Melting Pot.*
5 In Miami, where this has already happened due to the rapid economic and political advance of the Cuban–American community, relations between the two 'minority' communities have been extremely bad. See Alejandro Portes and Alex Stepick, *City on the Edge: The Transformation of Miami* (Berkeley: University of California Press, 1993).
6 See Reichley, *Religion in America Public Life.*
7 In Los Angeles, which deliberately dismantled its excellent public transport system under pressure from the automobile manufacturers in the late 1950s, these problems became so severe that the city began to construct a whole new rail system from scratch in the early 1990s.
8 Joel Garreau, *Edge Cities* (New York: Doubleday, 1992).
9 The availability of the death penalty in many states has also contributed to the ineffectiveness of the court system, despite its widespread popularity. Death-penalty cases have clogged-up the courts even further as defendants pursue the whole series of appeals available to them.
10 'Teapot Dome' was an oil-well on federal land in the state of Wyoming. In 1929 Albert Fall, Secretary of the Interior during the Harding Administration (1921–23), was tried and convicted of having accepted a bribe during the process of leasing the land to private developers.
11 Rachel Carson, *The Silent Spring* (London: Hamish Hamilton, 1963).
12 Roger Kimball: *Tenured Radicals: How Politics Has Corrupted Our Higher Education* (New York: Harper & Row, 1990).
13 Hughes, *Culture of Complaint.*
14 Richard A. Hofstadter, *The Paranoid Style in American Politics* (Chicago: Phoenix Press, 1979).

3

Political culture and the Constitution

In the opening chapter we presented a largely 'progressive' interpretation of American history and some other aspects of American political culture. 'Political culture' is a term used by political scientists to refer to particular sets of beliefs and behaviour associated with politics in different societies. In fact political culture is merely a culture in its political aspect. It should, however, be distinguished from another term, 'ideology', since the latter implies an intellectually coherent and comprehensive world-view such as socialism, nationalism, or liberalism. To say that Americans like their politicians to be 'regular guys', whether they be of the Left or the Right, is to make a statement about political culture, not about ideology.

American political culture is also tied up with the question of 'American exceptionalism': the view that American society and culture are exceptional by comparison with other advanced industrial democracies. Of course this is a truism in the sense that all societies and cultures are different, but adherents of this view hold that there are several features peculiar to American politics and society that particularly distinguish the US from other western democracies. As we have seen from the first two chapters, there is powerful evidence for American exceptionalism from the study of American history and society. In this chapter we shall concentrate on American exceptionalism in its political aspect and discuss the ingredients that make-up American political culture. We then move on to discuss the particular set of political ideas that influenced the framers of the 1787 Constitution, and conclude by examining the most important provisions of the US Constitution itself.

Some who adhere to the 'liberal' interpretation of American history and politics argue that American Exceptionalism is a consequence of a society based on the ideology of Lockean liberal individualism, in contrast to 'Old World' societies based on hierarchy and nationality.[1] Adherents of this view do indeed provide convincing evidence for the continuing (and generally predominant) influence of liberal individualism on American life. We nevertheless find ideology too rigid and imprecise a term to encapsulate accurately the variegated and occasionally contradictory series of themes present in America's political culture. In short, we find more complexity in American political culture than those who take the 'ideological' approach.

The elements of American political culture

What, then, do we take to be the essential elements of American political culture?

Liberalism, defined as the belief in inalienable natural rights and in the

47

importance of the individual and a tendency to view politics in individualistic terms, has undoubtedly been a powerful element ever since the Founding Fathers saw in Locke's writings an intellectual *rationale* for their revolt against George III.

Democracy, belief in government by the people according to the majority will, is often lumped together with liberalism. However the two are distinct and occasionally contradictory concepts. While the framers were undoubtedly largely Lockean liberals, they saw majoritarian democracy – the rule of popular majorities – as a menace. Liberalism and democracy have been persistent influences over the course of American history and politics, but the two are always in dynamic tension with each other, rather than components of a single 'American' ideology.

Both liberalism and democracy have their roots in an older classical *Republican* tradition that has also affected American political culture. This civic humanist tradition, derived from the writings of Cicero and the history of the Roman Republic and revived by Machiavelli and others during the Renaissance, is based on the concept of the *res publica*: the self-governing republic ruled by a virtuous citizenry. The speeches and writings of the framers are suffused with Republican imagery and symbols (statues of George Washington clad in a Roman toga, for example). To this day the American preoccupation with political virtue, periodic popular outbursts against 'corruption', and the reverence for national symbols such as the flag and the Pledge of Allegiance, are redolent of the Republican tradition.[2]

Egalitarianism, the belief in equal rights and equal participation by citizens in politics, is another powerful element in American political culture. Americans are as obsessed by egalitarianism as Old World societies are with hierarchy, and this conflict often provokes some of the most interesting cultural clashes between Americans and Europeans. American egalitarianism, while powerful, is nevertheless limited. As we have seen in Chapter 2, Americans are passionate in their belief in equality of opportunity, but equally passionate in their revulsion at the concept of equality of result.

Dislike and distrust of government in general has also been an abiding element in American political culture. While this element has antecedents in Lockean liberalism, the particular virulence in the American dislike of government can be attributed to the circumstances of the founding and the continuing power of the imagery of George III and British despotism in the American psyche. This has been reinforced by the frontier/western myth rooted in the availability of free land and the desire to escape authority, and also by a persisting classical Republican fear of tyrannical rule.

Pluralism and religious, ethnic, and political toleration have perforce been increasingly important elements in American political culture as the country has become more ethnically and religiously diverse. Religious pluralism, including the separation of Church and State, has been an important element in American culture since the founding. After immigration this pluralism has gradually expanded into the ethnic sphere although, until fairly recently (as we saw in Chapter 2), it has had to contend with the equally powerful image of the 'melting-pot'. Pluralism and toleration of diversity as a view of political life have, however, become quite deeply embedded in American political culture, although they have had to contend with other powerful elements such as Republicanism and Democracy and, in practice, have now expanded beyond religion, race and ethnicity, to embrace life-style groups as well.

Populism, an attraction to politicians who speak in the language of the common man, has been a recurrent feature of American politics since the time of Andrew Jackson and the final consolidation of American Democracy in the 1830s. Ross Perot, David Duke, Jesse Jackson, and Jerry Brown are merely the most recent manifestations of the phenomenon. An outgrowth of America's deep-rooted democratic and egalitarian impulses, populism has sought to mobilise periodic surges of opinion against some perceived internal enemy: 'the Bank', 'the speculators', 'the Eastern Establishment', 'the special interests', 'the Communists'. Populism is the Democratic impulse taken to its ultimate extreme, and as De Tocqueville warned during its first manifestations in the 1830s, is likely to be a perpetual feature of a democratic society. More recently historian Richard Hofstadter described the recurrent outbursts of populist fervour in US history as being linked by a 'paranoid style' endemic to America's middle-class society, with its 'anxiety' over status.[3] Populism's influence is however, generally tempered by other impulses in American political culture such as liberalism or pluralism, with more than a little assistance from the institutional framework erected in the US Constitution.

Messianism, the belief in America's exceptional world role or mission, as expressed in phrases such as the early New England colonist John Winthrop's 'City on a Hill', or 'Last, Best, Hope of Mankind', is rooted in Puritan theology and has been a persistent feature of American political culture ever since. Messianism is perhaps most clearly evident in the American mass reaction to foreign affairs, which has alternated between a universalistic impulse to redeem the world, and an isolationist rejection of the world external to America as irredeemably corrupt.

These, then, are the essential elements of American political culture. There are obvious tensions between some of the various elements, and we are not convinced that they add up to a coherent ideology that one might call 'Americanism'. At different points in US history some elements of the culture have been more dominant than others, nevertheless all of these themes are present in the US Constitution and recur time and again in US history.

The absence of socialism

The preceding review of the central themes in American political culture also explains the feature that most distinguishes the US from comparable advanced western liberal democracies: the absence of a major socialist or social democratic party. After reaching a peak with 6 per cent of the national presidential popular vote in 1912, American socialism virtually disappeared from the political map, and Communism was never a significant political presence outside the fringes of the labour movement, the Arts, and the Academy. In short, socialism as an ideology has never had the kind of mass appeal in American society that it gained among the working classes of Europe.

In Europe socialism became a major political movement in the late nineteenth century due to an explosive combination of social and political factors. Rapid industrialisation created a vast urban proletariat virtually overnight in nations such as Britain, France, and Germany. In these nations the working class was initially completely shut out from political power – in Britain all workers could not even vote until 1918 – and socialism thus took root as a means of mobilising the masses to demand basic political rights and freedoms. The Marxist ideology adopted by most European socialist parties in the late nineteenth century not only justified the claims of the working class to a share in political power, but also promised that their coming to power was a scientific inevitability. The class-ridden societies of late nineteenth-century Europe, moreover, retained social and political structures rooted in feudalism or royal absolutism that prolonged class divisions and class-consciousness into the modern era, and thereby sustained a durable popular base for socialist ideology (albeit in a modified social democratic form after the Second World War).

In the United States virtually all adult white males were enfranchised and included in the political system during the Jacksonian era of the 1830s. Thus when the full force of industrialisation had its impact on American society after the Civil War, most American workers did not experience the explosive combination of economic, social and political deprivation that nurtured such a high degree of class-consciousness in the Old World. American working-class consciousness was also mitigated by the recurrent waves of immigration and the ethno-religious and racial divisions that immigration engendered within the American proletariat. The existence of the western frontier as a safety valve for discontented workers was another factor that alleviated working-class discontent. Instead of feeling oppressed by a rigid and closed social and political hierarchy, as in Europe, the American worker believed in the 'American Dream': that by effort and enterprise he could enhance his economic and social status.

The fundamental reason for the failure of socialism in the United States, however, was that its egalitarian ideology and the mass organisation, discipline, and concentration of governmental power necessary to achieve its ends were fundamentally incompatible with several of the essential precepts of American political culture set out in the preceding section. The Lockean legacy – individualism, the primacy of individual rights, and the concomitant suspicion of concentrated governmental power – were barriers too formidable for socialist thinking to overcome. As we shall see below, colonial America's relatively homogeneous, egalitarian society of farmers, merchants and artisans conspicuously lacked the rigid class divisions between Crown, nobility, and the common people that still characterised eighteenth-century Europe. In Louis Hartz's formulation: America has never had socialism, because it never had the feudal legacy that gave birth to socialism in the Old World.[4]

Two cultures: Puritans and cavaliers

In order to find the origins of American political culture it is thus necessary for us to consider what kinds of people from the Old World settled in the American colonies, and what was unique about the society that they formed.

The Puritan colonists in New England were Calvinist Protestants who had left England due to religious persecution and the desire to build a 'godly commonwealth' in the New World. These were not generally poor people however, but farmers, skilled artisans and merchants – members of the emergent English middle-class of the mid-seventeenth century. In religion they were, of course, devout Calvinists, and Calvinism's emphasis on 'original sin' (and therefore the equality of 'fallen' men), 'predestination' (the notion of an 'elect' which had been 'saved'), and the individual's direct relationship with God inevitably influenced their political beliefs. The non-hierarchical organisational structure of the Calvinist churches, with the clergy being elected by congregations, also contrasted dramatically with the elaborate clerical hierarchies of Roman Catholicism or Anglicanism. This translated into the secular political realm where the Puritans placed authority on 'Covenants' sanctioned by God to form the 'worldly commonwealth' rather than monarchical or aristocratic authority.

By and large the New England colonists came from the same social and theological background as those who supported the English parliamentarians led by Oliver Cromwell against the royal power and divine right. While they prevailed in the English Civil Wars (1642–51) and subsequently executed King Charles I, the English Puritans eventually had to compromise with the aristocracy and countenance the return of a chastened monarchy.

In New England, by contrast, they had the field to themselves and founded a society based on their political precepts. The old Puritan political culture still influences American political behaviour in many ways. American messianism, individualism, egalitarianism, and democratic decision-making are all surviving aspects of Puritanism. Some of the less pleasant aspects of that culture have also persisted. Nathaniel Hawthorne's nineteenth-century novels, *The Scarlet Letter* and *The House of Seven Gables*, are damning indictments of the New England culture's susceptibility to narrow-mindedness, self-righteousness, and intolerance of dissenting views or behaviour. Playwright Arthur Miller also drew the explicit analogy between the Salem witch trials in late seventeenth-century Massachusetts and the McCarthyite hysteria over domestic Communist subversion in the 1950s, in his play *The Crucible*. The 'paranoid style' evidently has theological as well as psychological foundations.[5]

In describing the settlers of the southern colonies as 'adventurers' or 'profiteers', we do not intend these terms to be derogatory, but merely the best description of the other breed of settler who was attracted by the American colonies in the seventeenth century. These settlers were not there because they were fleeing from persecution back home, but because they wanted to advance themselves economically in a new land of opportunity. In contrast to the lower middle-class Puritans, the southern colonists generally came from the English nobility or the lesser gentry, and regarded themselves as gentlemen. Rather than being dissenters, they tended to belong to the established Anglican Church, and of course, in the civil strife of the mid-seventeenth century they were 'cavaliers' who sided with the King rather than Cromwell's parliamentarians.

As mentioned in Chapter 1, they settled in places like Virginia and the Carolinas, attracted by profits in tobacco, sugar, and later, cotton. From quite early on slaves were imported from Africa as cheap labour to work on the plantations. The society of gentleman farmers which they established and to which the most distinguished of the founding generation belonged – Jefferson, Madison, Washington, and Monroe – was one based on a rural economy and status rather than urban commerce and entrepreneurial initiative. They gave the American South its distinctive character and culture.[6]

The South's legacy to American political culture has been its preoccupation with individual freedom and the distrust of governmental authority. Southern culture's impulses in this direction were only enhanced by the arrival of the Scots–Irish migrants in the backcountry and mountain areas in the mid-to-late eighteenth century, for they adhered even more strongly to these values than the gentry of the coastal plain, and carried them to the southwestern states to which they began to migrate later in the nineteenth century.[7]

By the mid-eighteenth century the American colonists, both North and South, had established a society that was becoming increasingly economically and culturally independent of the 'Mother Country'. Despite the pretensions of the southerners, America, unlike England, had no aristocracy and no clear political hierarchy based on birth. In socioeconomic terms, it was a much more homogeneous society of farmers, merchants, and artisans in which there were no deep socioeconomic cleavages and no clear class divisions.

It also had established a tradition of religious toleration from quite early on, despite the severity of the New England Puritans, for the latter were not religiously homogeneous but divided into a whole series of sects such as Presbyterians, Congregationalists, Baptists, Quakers, and Antinomians. There were large numbers of Anglicans in North and South and Maryland had been founded as a haven for Roman Catholics. Other persecuted groups such as the German Mennonites had also found a haven in the expanses of colonial America. Thus religious pluralism was a given in the US from fairly early on and despite the establishment of churches in some states, separation of Church and State was inevitable over the long run.[8]

America in the mid-eighteenth century then was a homogeneous, (relatively) egalitarian, non-feudal, non-aristocratic, non-hierarchical society (or series of societies) with widespread religious toleration, all of which differentiated it from British society at the time. It was also economically self-sufficient and largely self-governing through the various colonial assemblies. The separation with Great Britain was inevitable once it became clear that the two societies were developing in opposite directions.

Intellectual influences on the Founding Fathers

It was against this political/cultural background that the American Revolution came about. The revolutionary slogan 'No taxation without representation' captures the essence of American political culture at the time of the Revolution. The idea that a government in London in which they were not directly represented could levy taxes on them was highly offensive to the egalitarian and democratic-minded American colonists. In their political debates and in their rhetoric against the British the American revolutionaries looked to various political traditions to justify their cause. If we examine the 1776 Declaration of Independence, written by Thomas Jefferson, we can see evidence of all of these traditions. And when it came to drawing up a federal constitution in 1787 the Founding Fathers were largely informed by the same sets of influences, namely the contractarian theory of John Locke; Montesquieu's theory of the separation of powers; the English Whig tradition; the Scottish Enlightenment and its 'mechanical' view of politics; and finally, the classical Republican, 'civic humanist' tradition.

Lockean liberalism's pervasive influence on American political thinking has already been mentioned. Locke's view that political authority was based ultimately on contracts arrived at by individuals in a state of nature, who willingly surrender their natural rights in exchange for the protection of government, perfectly fitted the world-view of the American colonists. Moreover, Locke's belief that government could only be based on the consent of the governed and that it must be reconstituted should that consent ever be withdrawn, provided powerful ideological ammunition for the rebel colonists of 1776. While we do not go so far as Louis Hartz in attributing all the features of American political culture and the Constitution to Lockean liberalism, it has, nevertheless, been a powerful and persistent influence.

The writings of the aristocratic French philosopher Montesquieu, also had a massive influence on western political thought during the eighteenth century. The key element that the framers took from Montesquieu was, in fact, his misinterpretation of the British Constitution of the mid-eighteenth century. Montesquieu admired the constitutional monarchy of Britain by contrast with the absolutism of the French *ancien régime*, and believed that the essence of the British political system was its 'separation of powers' between the legislative, executive, and judicial branches of government. In fact the judicial branch in the UK was not truly a branch of government at all, because of the lack of a written constitution and the absence of judicial review over parliamentary acts. Moreover, in eighteenth-century Britain 'the Crown in

Parliament', or the executive and legislative branches together, was sovereign: a sharing rather than a clear separation of powers. Finally, at the very time the US Revolution was taking place the royal authority was eroding so rapidly that by 1800, the executive power had also devolved upon parliament, leaving the monarch with a purely formal role.

The English Whig tradition had a profound impact on the political philosophy of the framers because it pervaded the whole of colonial American beliefs about politics. That tradition was rooted in the thinking of the anti-royalist forces in the English Civil War and the 1688 political settlement. Its fundamental precepts were that the royal power should be limited, parliamentary authority should be paramount, and if a government violated the natural rights of its citizenry it should be changed, by force if necessary. Given the social composition of colonial America with its essentially bourgeois society there was no effective challenge to the Whig view of politics, in contrast to English Whiggery, which was challenged by court-centred Toryism. Indeed in England the Whigs were largely excluded from political power in the mid-eighteenth century, and Whig leaders could do little more than inveigh against the iniquities and corruption of the system from outside. When the Americans turned against George III, there was therefore a substantial body of anti-monarchical Whig doctrine and rhetoric to turn to for support.[9]

Whereas Whig ideas were present throughout American society the thinking of the contemporary Scottish Enlightenment philosophers was known only to the most highly-educated elites. But at that level their impact was profound. Jefferson, Madison and Hamilton were all familiar with the works of David Hume, Adam Smith and Frances Hutcheson. The Scottish thinkers were pioneers in the scientific study of society, but unlike their French counterparts (particularly Rousseau) they had an essentially pessimistic view of human nature: society did not corrupt men, they were inherently corrupt. In Hume's phrase, human 'reason is the slave of the passions'. To restrain men while still avoiding tyrannical rule, government required institutions 'checking and balancing' each other in a mechanical fashion. This view of government as an intricate machine had a profound influence on the thinking of the authors of the Constitution, as we shall see in the next chapter.[10]

Of course the framers were imbued in their education with the history of the ancient Athenian and Roman Republics, and classical Republicanism, as reformulated by authors such as John Milton and James Harrington in the seventeenth century, had informed the English Whig tradition. The concern with corruption in government and the notion of tyranny as a consequence of corruption was standard classical Republican doctrine. The framers' adoption of classical pseudonyms demonstrates their reverence for classical antecedents, yet they were also aware that most attempts at genuine Republican government had culminated in failure, and they sought to learn how to construct a stable Republican government from the more successful models – classical Rome and renaissance Venice.

The framers of the US Constitution drew on all of these influences. As far as the central institutions of government were concerned however, the Americans had one obvious model to hand – the post-1688 British political system – the underlying principles of which they believed remained basically sound, although those principles had been corrupted by George III and his ministers. America's founding generation, like Montesquieu, believed that the British system worked according to a balancing and separation of powers between executive (King), legislative (Lords and Commons) and judicial (courts) authorities. As we have seen, they were both wrong about the courts, and parliament was gradually acquiring most of the executive and legislative power during the eighteenth century. Nevertheless, at the time of the American Revolution there was more of a genuine separation and struggle between the executive and legislative powers than would be the case a century later. For the generation of the framers it appeared that the British system was the obvious model for a stable political system that protected human freedom.

The failure of the loose and decentralised Continental Congress system of government (which operated from 1776 to 1787) to provide internal political stability, economic prosperity, and adequate protection against predatory European powers led to the calling of the 1787 constitutional convention. Under the 1776 Articles of Confederation there was no genuine executive, and any major decision required the agreement of nine of the thirteen original states. By the mid-1780s this system had proved itself to be totally inadequate to deal with the problems of the infant Republic. Shays's Rebellion – an uprising of indebted farmers against the enforcement of tax and debt collection in western Massachusetts in 1786–87 – in particular terrorised the American political elite, and they were determined to erect a more effective national government that would quickly deal with such disturbances in future and protect the infant Republic externally. This was the essential objective of the constitutional convention called in Philadelphia in the summer of 1787.[11]

The Federalist Papers

Perhaps the most extraordinary feature of the US Constitution is its durability. No other written constitution in the modern world has survived for so long. As the fictional country singer Havon Hamilton puts it in Robert Altman's classic 1975 film *Nashville*, 'We must be doing something right to last two hundred years.'

The US Constitution is also unique in that there is an explicit theory of human nature and government underlying its provisions. This theory is clearly set out in the *Federalist Papers*, written by the principal framers of the Constitution Alexander Hamilton and James Madison (with a little help from John Jay), to persuade the states of its merits and thereby assist the process of ratification. The authors of the *Federalist* succeeded in this objective, although they had to concede the addition of the first ten amendments to the Constitution – commonly referred to as the *Bill of Rights* – which were derived from rather different theoretical premises. In the US Constitution we thus see the revised republicanism of the authors of the seven articles of 1787, combined with the Lockean liberal concern with inalienable natural rights expressed in the Bill of Rights.

America's first great political document, Jefferson's Declaration of Independence, was written from an almost purely Lockean political perspective:

> We hold these truths to be self-evident: That all men are created equal; that they are endowed by their creator with certain inalienable rights; that, to secure these rights, governments are instituted among men, deriving their just powers from the consent of the governed; that whenever any form of government becomes destructive of these ends, it is the right of the people to alter or to abolish it, and to institute new government, laying its foundation on such principles, and organising its powers in such form as to them shall seem most likely to effect their safety and happiness.

This key passage of the Declaration is pure Locke. Men have natural rights, the protection of which is the basis for governments, which in turn derive their authority from the consent of the governed. When government violates the social contract and starts to encroach on natural rights, revolution is justified. George III broke his contract with the American colonists (just as James II had done in Britain in 1688), and thus provided the intellectual justification for the American Revolution.

The perspective of Hamilton and Madison in the *Federalist* is somewhat different, however. They do not have a great deal to say about rights, either because they accepted them as givens or did not regard the protection of rights as their paramount concern in framing the Constitution. Hamilton and Madison were more concerned with establishing a national government that would be stable, durable, and effective: a government that could keep the internal peace and defend the infant Republic against its enemies without collapsing into chaos, or resort to dictatorship and tyranny.

Like all eighteenth-century gentlemen of their station, the authors of the *Federalist* had a thorough classical and historical education, and a deep knowledge of the previous attempts to found lasting, self-governing political communities. In all of human history what they called 'Republican Government' – a polity governed by its citizens – had been the exception rather than the rule. Even the celebrated 'democracies' of classical Greece (principally Athens) had generally been of short duration and inherently unstable.

Perhaps the reason that the Roman Republic lasted so long was that it had the 'mixed' political constitution preferred by Aristotle, with checks and balances and separate representation for the different components of Roman society. The plebs had their tribunes, the patricians had the Senate and the Consuls, and temporary dictatorship was resorted to in times of emergency. Of course the Roman model had a profound influence on future Republican

Thomas Jefferson.

A typical product of the Enlightenment, Thomas Jefferson (1743–1826) studied and wrote on an astonishing variety of subjects, but it was on America's political development that his influence would be greatest. A Virginian, he first came to public attention as the author of the 1776 Declaration of Independence, which articulated the principles for which the American revolutionaries were fighting. From 1785 to 1790 Jefferson was the US Ambassador in Paris, where he developed a strong sympathy for the French revolutionaries. On his return Jefferson served as Secretary of State under George Washington, but resigned in protest at Hamilton's economic policies and Washington and Hamilton's generally pro-British diplomacy. Jefferson feared that Hamilton's measures would concentrate economic and political power among a narrow manufacturing elite, and erode the basis of the decentralised agrarian republic of yeomen that Jefferson believed the revolutionary war had been fought to preserve and protect. In opposition, he formed his own political party, the Democratic–Republicans, and was elected Vice-President in 1796. Four years later Jefferson was elected the third President of the United States (1801–09), the most noteworthy achievement of his presidency being the Louisiana Purchase, which dramatically extended the territory of the US.

thinkers, and it is interesting to note the extent to which the framers of the US Constitution used Roman pseudonyms in their political writings (the authors of the *Federalist* used the name 'Publius').

The Republican tradition of political thought was revived in the Italian city-states of the Renaissance, most notably in Machiavelli's *Discourses*. Italy also furnished the finest example of successful Republican government at this time. Venice – 'the most serene Republic' – had dominated the entire Mediterranean, again owing much of its internal political stability to a mixed constitution.

Despite the examples of Rome and Venice, however, most Republics had tended to degenerate into tyrannies, or become absorbed by other republics and empires. The central question for the authors of the *Federalist*, therefore, was how best to preserve the infant American Republic from these dangers? In their view the sorry history of most attempts at Republican government was due to the fact that the framers of most previous Republican constitutions had been naive about human nature. They saw human beings as essentially virtuous and believed this would naturally come to the fore, the more government was based directly on the popular will of the citizenry. Hamilton and Madison thought this was dangerously misguided thinking. They shared the Scottish Enlightenment conception of Man, not as inherently virtuous but as inherently corrupt. As humans were governed not by their reason but by their passions, if they became virtuous in a republic they had to learn to be so the hard way. Too often Republican government had failed because the framers of Republican constitutions had failed to take human depravity into account:

> But what is government but the greatest of all reflections on human nature? If men were Angels no government would be necessary. If Angels were to govern men, neither external nor internal controls on government would be necessary. In framing a government which is to be administered by men over men, the great difficulty lies in this: You must first enable the government to control the governed; and in the next place, oblige it to control itself. A dependence on the people is no doubt the primary control on the government; but experience had taught mankind the necessity of auxiliary precautions.[12]

This then is the fundamental premise of the *Federalist*: a republic is to be established that takes account of human corruption rather than denying it or trying to eliminate it.

One of the major problems which any Republican form of government has to face is the issue of 'faction': 'The friend of popular governments, never finds himself so much alarmed for their character and fate, as when he contemplates their propensity to this dangerous vice.'[13] Factions undermine the republic from within, placing their personal interests before that of the republic as a whole and thus providing the enemies of popular liberty with their principal argument against free government. Madison defines factions as follows:

By a faction I understand a number of citizens, whether amounting to a majority or minority of the whole, who are united and actuated by some common impulse of passion, or of interest, adverse to the rights of other citizens, or to the permanent and aggregate interests of the community.[14]

In short, 'factions' are equivalent to interest groups as we understand them in the modern world. Madison did not believe that it was possible to eliminate factions without destroying liberty itself, hence this solution would be worse than the disease it was trying to cure, and would undermine the entire purpose of Republican government. It is also impossible. Men have an inherent tendency to form themselves into 'factions': 'The latent causes of faction are thus sown in the nature of man; and we see them every where brought into different degrees of activity, according to the different circumstances of civil society.[15] Thus the causes of faction cannot be removed and the framers of a system of government must content themselves with controlling their effects. Madison sees the real danger of factions arising when they are in the majority among the citizenry:

When a majority is included in a faction, the form of popular government on the other hand enables it to sacrifice to its ruling passion or interest, both the public good and the rights of other citizens. To secure the public good, and private rights against the danger of such a faction, and at the same time to preserve the spirit and the form of popular government, is then the great object to which our enquiries are directed.[16]

How did Madison and Hamilton hope to prevent this potential tyranny of the majority in the American Republic? They thought that majority tyranny would be preventable in the US for two main reasons. First, America was not to be a 'pure democracy'. In such a society consisting of a small number of citizens who govern themselves directly through a popular assembly there is no 'cure for the mischiefs of faction':

A common passion or interest will, in almost every case, be felt by a majority of the whole; a communication and concert results from the form of government itself; and there is nothing to check the inducements to sacrifice the weaker party, or an obnoxious individual. Hence it is, that such democracies have ever been spectacles of turbulence and contention; have ever been found incompatible with personal security, or the rights of property; and have in general been as short in their lives, as they have been violent in their deaths.[17]

So much, then, for direct democracy. This was the last thing which the pessimistic and conservative framers, America's social and political elite of the time, had in mind as a system of government. Madison distinguishes between a

'democracy' and a 'republic', and it is the latter which the framers are seeking
to create in the United States. By a 'republic' Madison means a representative
system of government rather than a direct democracy, and with a representative system also comes a potential cure for the mischiefs of faction:

> to refine and enlarge the public views by passing them through the medium
> of a chosen body of citizens, whose wisdom may best discern the true interest
> of their country, and whose patriotism and love of justice, will be least likely
> to sacrifice it to temporary or partial considerations. Under such a regula-
> tion, it may well happen, that the public voice, pronounced by the repre-
> sentatives of the people, will be more consonant to the public good, than if
> pronounced by the people themselves, convened for the purpose.[18]

Another defining characteristic of a Republican form of government is its
greater size. Representatives will be chosen from larger constituencies and
there is less chance of them being controlled by any one faction. The federal
principle ensures, however, that the government does not become too remote
from the citizenry. A larger population also means greater internal diversity
and a greater number of competing interests. Even if a faction dominates in
a particular state it will be unlikely to be able to dominate the Union, and the
greater number of factions makes it much less likely that any one faction will
come to dominate the government at the national level.

But these features might still be inadequate to prevent tyrannical behaviour
on the part of the government itself. To address this problem Madison intro-
duces his version of the separation of powers and the checks and balances:

> it is evident that each department should have a will of its own; and conse-
> quently should be so constituted, that the members of each should have as
> little agency as possible in the appointment of the members of the others.
> Were this principle rigorously adhered to, it would require that all the
> appointments for the supreme executive, legislative, and judiciary magis-
> tracies, should be drawn from the same fountain of authority, the people,
> through channels, having no communication whatever with one an-
> other . . . Ambition must be made to counteract ambition. The interest of
> the man must be connected with the constitutional rights of the place.[19]

Thus we see the fundamental governmental theory that underlies the principles of representative government and the separation of the legislative
powers in the United States. Yet despite the separation of powers, Madison
also states that the among the branches of government he expects the legislature to predominate because it is the branch closest to the people:

> In republican government the legislative authority necessarily, predomi-
> nates. The remedy for this inconveniency is, to divide the legislature into

different branches; and to render them by different modes of election, and different principles of action, as little connected with each other, as the nature of their common functions, and their common dependence on society, will admit.[20]

In addition to a bicameral structure, Madison states that 'further precautions' may be necessary to curb the legislature and this provides his rationale for the presidential veto, although he rejects an absolute veto on the grounds that it is too susceptible to abuse (with the experience of British monarchs in mind). He then discusses the federal principle (the division between the federal government and the states) and argues that this gives the US an additional defence against tyrannical government at the centre and helps guard against one faction predominating by keeping society fragmented into different states.

One final aspect of the new federal government remains to be discussed: the judicial branch. Hamilton discusses the judiciary and the framers' conception of its role in the political system in *Federalist 78*. He argues that the judiciary is likely to be the least potentially tyrannical part of the new governmental framework:

Whoever attentively considers the different departments of power must perceive that, in a government in which they are separated from each other, the judiciary, from the nature of its functions, will always be the least dangerous to the political rights of the constitution, because it will be least in a capacity to annoy or injure them . . . It may truly be said to have neither force nor will but merely judgement; and must ultimately depend upon the aid of the executive arm even for the efficacy of its judgements.[21]

But why was a separate judicial branch of the federal government necessary in the first place? The framers could have confined the judiciary to interpretation of statutes passed by the legislature (as in Great Britain). But in the US the legislature is not sovereign as it is in Britain, and in *Federalist 78*, Hamilton produces a defence of the power of judicial review – the right of the judiciary to declare acts of the legislature unconstitutional and therefore void. In a republic, where the people rule, giving the branch of the government most removed from the popular will – the federal judiciary – such power appears to violate the whole principle on which the American Revolution had been based. Hamilton nevertheless defends judicial review on the grounds that the Constitution is a fundamental law that expresses the real will of the people of the US, as opposed to what may be only the transient will of their representatives in the legislature:

Nor does this conclusion by any means suppose a superiority of the judicial to the legislative power. It only supposes that the power of the people is

superior to both and that where the will of the legislature declared in its
statutes, stands in opposition to that of the people, declared in the Constitution, the judges ought to be governed by the latter rather than the former.
They ought to regulate their decisions by the fundamental laws rather than
by those which are not fundamental.[22]

So Hamilton uses a conception of the fundamental will of the people similar
to Jean-Jacques Rousseau's concept of the 'General Will' as an argument to
defend judicial review. It must be conceded however, that an independent
judicial branch also fits in with the overall thrust of the *Federalist's* theory of
government, providing one more effective check against factions and governmental tyranny.

In the *Federalist* Hamilton and Madison are wrestling with the problem of
how to provide a Republican government that is stable and energetic, but not
at the expense of the freedom and essential liberties of its citizens. In adopting
Scottish Enlightenment ideas on human nature and human government, they
thought that they had found the answer to that age-old political problem in
the following essential precepts: Republican (i.e. representative) government;
the federal system; the separation of powers; and Judicial Review.

Having discussed the political theory underlying the *Federalist*, we can better
understand the essential provisions of the 1787 US Constitution, which has
come to define not only the framework of America's political institutions, but
also American nationality itself. Let us now examine the articles of the Constitution to see how these principles are manifested in the document that
emerged from the Philadelphia convention in 1787.

The 1787 Constitution

The Preamble establishes the Republican basis of government – 'We the People' – and lists the basic functions of government as the framers saw them:
'[to] establish justice, insure domestic tranquillity, provide for the common
defence, promote the general welfare, and secure the Blessings of Liberty' (note
the mixture of liberal and Republican precepts).

Article I discusses the legislative branch, and we should note that it is given
precedence over the other branches. The legislature is to be bicameral –
according to the framers' theory of checks and balances. The House is elected
by the people directly every two years, in single-member districts that are
allocated to the states according to the population as reflected in the decennial
census (with the proviso that no state shall have less than one district and
districts cannot cross state lines). The Senate represents the states. Each state
(regardless of population) has two Senators, chosen by the state legislatures
(until 1913) for six-year terms in staggered elections, with one-third of the
chamber coming up for election every two years. The House is given the power
to impeach executive and judicial officials (from the old English practice of
parliament impeaching miscreant Crown officials), and the Senate is to try all

impeachments. Section 7 stipulates that all money bills are to originate in the House, and this section also gives the President the power to veto legislation, which Congress can override by a two-thirds vote of both Houses. Section 8 specifies the powers of the Congress, and section 9 some restrictions on those powers.

In *Article II* the framers rejected any temptations of monarchy and established the executive power in a President of the United States, who together with his Vice-President is given a four-year, renewable term of office. The first section of this article also spells out in laborious detail the convoluted system of election of the President, which came about as a compromise between those at the constitutional convention who were bitterly opposed to either selection by the Congress (which would violate the separation of powers) or selection by the people directly (too democratic and thus potentially tyrannical). The cumbersome electoral college, with each state having a number of electors equal to its congressional delegation (the states' Representatives plus the two Senators) and the method of choosing the electors being left up to the states, and the even more awkward fallback procedure with the House choosing the President (the Representatives vote as states, with one vote per state), remains a major oddity in the US Constitution, but it accords with the anti-democratic instincts of most of the framers.

Section 2 of Article II lists the presidential powers. Only two are given to the President without qualification: Commander-in-Chief of the armed forces, and the power to grant reprieves and pardons. He can make treaties, but the Senate has to ratify them by a two-thirds majority. With the 'advice and consent of the Senate' (this time only a simple majority is required), the President appoints the federal judiciary and the other executive officers. Section 3 gives the President the power to 'take care that the laws be faithfully executed', and Section 5 provides for his removal by impeachment for 'Treason, Bribery or other high Crimes and Misdemeanors'.

Article III establishes the judicial power in the Supreme Court, but it does not clearly establish the principle of judicial review in the way Hamilton does in the *Federalist*. Congress is given the power to establish the jurisdiction, composition, and structure of the federal judiciary. Article II has already given the President the power to appoint the federal judges with congressional consent. Does the phrase 'The judicial power shall extend to all cases, in law and equity arising under this constitution' imply judicial review? The principle was not definitively established until the famous case of *Marbury* v. *Madison* struck down an Act of Congress as being in violation of the Constitution in 1803.

Article IV provides some restrictions on the powers of the states and procedures for admitting new states to the Union. Perhaps its most important phrase is in Section 4: 'The United States shall guarantee to every state in this Union a Republican form of Government.'*Article V* provides the procedures for amending the Constitution. Congress can propose amendments that have been approved by a two-thirds majority in each House, or alternatively two-thirds of the states can call a constitutional convention to propose amendments. In any case any such amendment must be approved by three-quarters of the state legislatures (or by conventions in three-quarters of the states if Congress prefers) before it can take effect. All the amendments to date have begun in Congress and then proceeded to the state legislatures for ratification (except for the Twenty-first Amendment repealing prohibition, where Congress stipulated that state conventions be used for ratification). All this means that amending the US Constitution is a very difficult process indeed, requiring a truly remarkable degree of national consensus. Again this is perfectly in line with the cautious, conservative, Republicanism of the framers.

Article VI makes it clear that the Constitution and the laws of the US shall be the supreme law of the land, and that there will be no religious test for members of Congress, the executive or judicial branches. *Article VII* provides that the Constitution shall take effect once nine states have ratified it.

The Bill of Rights and subsequent amendments

This, then, is the original 1787 document. Brief and very Madisonian in its design, all of its provisions are clearly in alignment with the theory later set out in the *Federalist*. But in the state legislatures anti-federalist sentiment was strong, and to allay this suspicion of government *per se*, the framers had to concede certain guaranteed rights in the Constitution as further safeguards. Hence the first ten amendments to the Constitution, the 1791 'Bill of Rights' where Lockean beliefs are much more evident than in the original seven articles.

Amendment I prohibits the establishment of religion and guarantees freedom of speech, the press, assembly, and the right to petition the government. *Amendment II* establishes the right of the people to bear arms for the purposes of a militia. *Amendment III* prevents quartering of troops in private homes. *Amendment IV* prohibits 'unreasonable' searches and seizures. *Amendment V* establishes some rights for those accused of crimes, and prevents the seizure of a person's life, liberty, or property without 'due process of law'. This amendment also enables defendants to resist being tried twice for the same offence and from being witness against themselves (when this occurs it is referred to as 'taking the Fifth'). *Amendment VI* grants the accused in criminal trials the right to a jury trial and to counsel for his defence. *Amendment VII* provides for a jury trial in all civil suits where the value in controversy exceeds $20. *Amendment VIII* prohibits 'excessive' bail, 'excessive' fines and 'cruel and unusual punishments'. *Amendment IX* states that the enumeration of these rights is not to be construed to mean that other rights 'retained by the people' are denied. Finally *Amendment X* states that 'The powers not delegated to the US by the Constitution nor prohibited by it to the States, are reserved to the States respectively, or to the people' (a vague and curious formulation).

Since 1791 a further seventeen amendments have been added to the Constitution. The most significant of these are: the *Twelfth*, passed in 1804, which provided for the separate election of the Vice-President (who was automatically the runner-up in the presidential contest in the 1787 document); *the Thirteenth, Fourteenth,* and *Fifteenth,* passed after the Civil War, which respectively abolished slavery, established the right to 'due process of law' and the 'equal protection of the laws' for all US citizens, and established the right to vote irrespective of race or colour; the *Sixteenth* (ratified in 1913), which allowed Congress to levy a federal income tax; the *Seventeenth* (ratified in 1913) which changed the method of electing US Senators from the state legislatures to popular election; the *Nineteenth* (ratified in 1920) which gave women the right to vote; the *Twenty-second* (ratified in 1951), which limited presidents to two terms; the *Twenty-fifth* (ratified in 1967) which allowed Presidents, with congressional approval, to appoint a new Vice-President should the office fall vacant, and provides some procedures for the removal of an incapacitated President; the *Twenty-sixth Amendment* (ratified in 1971) which lowered the voting age in federal election to eighteen; and, most recently, the *Twenty-seventh Amendment* (originally advocated by Madison), which prevents a congressional pay increase taking effect until after the following congressional election.

Conclusion

The bases for American political culture (and American exceptionalism more generally) were laid very early in the history of the US and were determined by the kind of people who settled there in the colonial period. This culture, rooted in the British political disputes of the seventeenth century and reinforced by the experience of the revolutionary war, has changed remarkably little in the 200 years since. The immigrants from other racial, ethnic, religious backgrounds who have numerically surpassed those of white Anglo-Saxon Protestant (WASP) descent, have generally assimilated to the various aspects of the old WASP political culture as set out in the Declaration of Independence and the Constitution, although this process did not take place without a prolonged political and cultural struggle. The surprising thing is, nevertheless, that the fundamentals of American political culture have changed so little from the period in which the Revolutionary War took place and the Constitution was written.

The US Constitution provides a set of natural rights guaranteed under a Republican system of government. Locke grafted on top of, or coexisting with, the revised Republicanism of the Enlightenment. Why has the system endured for so long? Part of the answer is that the US Constitution is brief and vague, and this ambiguity has allowed its clauses to be consistently adapted and reinterpreted to deal with changing circumstances. This adaptability has been the Constitution's greatest strength, but it leads to the obvious question: who is to interpret the Constitution? This would appear to be the role of the Supreme

Court of the US, although the Constitution is not explicit on this point. The acceptance of the Court's *Marbury* decision in 1803 indicates, however, that judicial review was found to accord perfectly with the principles expressed in the Constitution.

For all the differing interpretations of the document that have prevailed throughout US history, the basic framework of American government is still much the same as it was in the 1780s. The fundamental principles of the 1787 Constitution and the 1791 Bill of Rights – limited government, checks and balances, judicial review, and the protection of guaranteed human rights against governmental encroachment – are still the fundamental principles that underlie modern American government. In the next part of this book we examine the various components of the American political system to see how they have evolved since the 1780s and how they function in the more complex political universe of today.

Notes

1 See Hartz, *The Liberal Tradition in America* and Lipset, *The First New Nation*.
2 On the influence of the Republican tradition see Wood, *The Creation of the American Republic*, pp. 46–90.
3 Hofstadter, *The Paranoid Style in American Politics*.
4 Hartz, *The Liberal Tradition in America*.
5 On Puritan society see David Hackett Fisher, *Albion's Seed: Four British Folkways in America* (New York: Oxford University Press, 1989), pp. 3–205.
6 On southern culture see *ibid.*, pp. 207–418.
7 On the Scots–Irish see *ibid.*, 605–782; and James G. Leyburn, *The Scotch–Irish: A Social History* (Chapel Hill, NC: University of North Carolina Press, 1962).
8 See A. James Reichley, *Religion in America Public Life* (Washington, DC: Brookings Institution, 1985).
9 On the 'Whiggish' political outlook of American colonial society see Wood, *The Creation of the American Republic*, pp. 3–45.
10 On the influence of the Scottish Enlightenment on the framers see Wills, *Explaining America*.
11 On the failure of the Continental Congress see Hugh Brogan, *The Pelican History of the United States of America* (London: Penguin, 1986), pp. 192–222.
12 Hamilton, Madison, and Jay, *The Federalist Papers*, p. 322.
13 *Ibid.*, p. 57.
14 *Ibid.*, p. 78
15 *Ibid.*, p. 79.
16 *Ibid.*, p. 80.
17 *Ibid.*, p. 51.
18 *Ibid.*, 82.
19 *Ibid.*, pp. 321–2.
20 *Ibid.*, p. 322.
21 *Ibid.*, p. 465.
22 *Ibid.*, pp. 467–8.

Part Two

Political institutions

4

The presidency

The contemporary American presidency is a paradoxical institution. On the one hand the President is widely, and in many senses rightly, viewed as the apex of the American political system; on the other, most literature on the fate of individual presidencies stresses the disappointment and failure most endure. There seems to be a chasm between the expectations invested in the presidency and individual presidents and their capacity for fulfilling them. Furthermore, those writing about the presidency, even in the same era, have frequently disagreed about both the level and the sources of presidential power.

That presidents are expected to perform many and different functions is indisputable. The scale of them can be seen in Clinton Rossiter's description of the President's role: Chief of State, Chief Executive, Commander-in-Chief, Chief Diplomat, Chief Legislator, Chief of Party, Voice of the People, Protector of the Peace, Manager of Prosperity, and World Leader. From beyond the shores of the United States, the President has frequently been hailed as the most powerful man in the world, and during the Cold War era the President's control of the vast American nuclear arsenal gave him an apparent hold over the life or death of every single member of the planet.

Yet if Rossiter's portrayal suggests the President-as-Emperor, most detailed studies of the office in practice indicate an emperor with few clothes. Examining and explaining this difference between popular perception and frequent reality – especially in American domestic politics – will be the primary objective of this chapter.

Table 4.1. *The Presidents*

Years	President	
1789–1797	Washington	(F)
1797–1801	Adams	(F)
1801–1809	Jefferson	(D–R)
1809–1817	Madison	(D–R)
1817–1825	Monroe	(D–R)
1825–1829	J. Q. Adams	(D–R)
1829–1837	Jackson	(D)
1837–1841	Van Buren	(D)
1841–1841	Harrison	(W)
1841–1845	Tyler	(W)

1845–1849	Polk	(D)
1849–1850	Taylor	(W)
1850–1853	Fillmore	(W)
1853–1857	Pierce	(D)
1857–1861	Buchanan	(D)
1861–1865	Lincoln	(R)
1865–1869	A. Johnson	(R)
1869–1877	Grant	(R)
1877–1881	Hayes	(R)
1881–1881	Garfield	(R)
1881–1885	Arthur	(R)
1885–1889	Cleveland	(D)
1889–1893	Harrison	(R)
1893–1897	Cleveland	(D)
1897–1901	McKinley	(R)
1901–1909	T. Roosevelt	(R)
1909–1913	Taft	(R)
1913–1921	Wilson	(D)
1921–1923	Harding	(R)
1923–1929	Coolidge	(R)
1929–1933	Hoover	(R)
1933–1945	F. Roosevelt	(D)
1945–1953	Truman	(D)
1953–1961	Eisenhower	(R)
1961–1963	Kennedy	(D)
1963–1969	L. Johnson	(D)
1969–1974	Nixon	(R)
1974–1977	Ford	(R)
1977–1981	Carter	(D)
1981–1989	Reagan	(R)
1989–1993	Bush	(R)
1993–	Clinton	(D)

(F)	Federalist
(D–R)	Democratic–Republican
(N–R)	National Republican
(W)	Whig
(D)	Democrat
(R)	Republican

The issues that need to be addressed include:

o Why have interpretations of presidential power varied so widely amongst historians and scholars, particularly over the last forty years?

o How much power, and from what sources, does the President really have?

o What factors have created and sustained what will be described here as the 'Post-Reform presidency', visible since the late 1960s?

o How can outside observers measure presidential success?

o What determines presidential success?

o What is the current status of presidential power?

Put together, the answers to these questions offer a picture of a complex office and institution whose fate is largely determined by a struggle between constitutional constraints, political assets, and the pressing needs of modern government. It will also be argued that these informal political assets that make up the toolkit of the contemporary presidency have been badly shaken by a large number of institutional changes, pursued in the name of reform, that have complicated the operation of the presidency even more in the very recent era, changes that require considerably more than political skill to overcome.

Interpretations of the presidency

Perceptions of presidential power have varied enormously and the office itself seems to have evolved way beyond the original intentions of those who created it. Broadly speaking, seven periods of presidential power have been identified, the overwhelming majority of which have been christened in the last sixty years.

The first and longest period was that of the traditional presidency. From 1789 until 1933 the President acted largely within the rather limited specific role that the Constitution laid down for him. There were notably vigorous presidents during this period – George Washington (1789–97), Thomas Jefferson (1801–09), Andrew Jackson (1829–37), Abraham Lincoln (1861–65), Theodore Roosevelt (1901–09) and Woodrow Wilson (1913–21) – but they owed their elevated stature to periods of domestic and foreign disturbance (usually war) that led to large amounts of authority being thrust into their hands. Most presidents during this period were either just one of a number of political actors in a system of government where national office-holders raised little money and conducted very basic expenditures (such as William Taft (1909–13) or Calvin Coolidge (1923–29)). Other presidents were largely inconsequential to the practice of politics (Chester Alan Arthur (1881–85) or Benjamin Harrison (1889–93)).

The President's role changed dramatically after 1933 with the tenure of Franklin D. Roosevelt, whose New Deal role at home and conduct of the Second

The popular view of presidential–congressional relations. Cartoon by Mike Keefe from *P.S*, December 1993 (originally published in the *Denver Post*).

World War abroad fundamentally altered the role of the federal government in American society and the position of the President. The era of the *modern* presidency was ushered in with the President now seen as the pivot of American politics. However, the unresponsive attitude of Congress, due to institutional differences and jealousies, towards much of the domestic agenda of Truman, Eisenhower and Kennedy led that view to be amended somewhat. Scholars now contrasted the limitation that the President faced at home with the enormous discretion granted to him over foreign policy, and the idea of the *restricted* presidency came into vogue. This attitude had barely achieved a consensus behind it when it too was challenged. Based on presidential conduct of the Vietnam War, and the personal conduct of Lyndon Johnson and Richard Nixon, the concept of an over-mighty *imperial* presidency swept in.

This vision of the office was to have an even shorter tenure than its predecessor. After Richard Nixon's ousting from the White House as a consequence of the Watergate scandal, with Congress asserting itself again at home and abroad, and given Gerald Ford and Jimmy Carter's apparent failure to govern effectively, the *imperilled* presidency entered the arena. Once Ronald Reagan demonstrated, by his stunning victories on economic policy in Congress in 1981, that it was possible for presidents to enact their agendas, and through his landslide victory in 1984 that it was possible to gain re-election, the *restored* presidency suddenly became popular. Finally, the deadlocked second term of the Reagan Administration and George Bush's difficulties in domestic policy

Table 4.2. *Party support in Congress, 1932–94*

	House					Senate				
				Gains/losses					Gains/losses	
Year President	Dem.	Rep.	Other	Dem.	Rep.	Dem.	Rep.	Other	Dem.	Rep.
1932 Roosevelt (D)	313	117	5	+97	−101	59	36	1	+12	−12
1934	322	103	10	+9	−14	69	25	2	+10	−11
1936 Roosevelt (D)	333	89	13	+11	−14	75	17	4	+6	−8
1938	262	169	4	−71	+80	69	23	4	−6	+6
1940 Roosevelt (D)	267	162	6	+5	−7	66	28	2	−3	+5
1942	222	209	4	−45	+47	57	38	1	−9	+10
1944 Roosevelt (D)	243	190	2	+21	−19	57	38	1	0	0
1946 Truman (D)	188	246	1	−55	+56	45	51		−12	+13
1948 Truman (D)	263	171	1	+75	−75	54	42		+9	−9
1950	234	199	2	−29	+28	48	47	1	−6	+5
1952 Eisenhower (R)	213	221	1	−21	+22	47	48	1	−1	+1
1954	232	203		+19	−18	48	47	1	+1	−1
1956 Eisenhower (R)	234	201		+2	−2	49	47		+1	0
1958	283	154		+49	−47	64	34		+17	−13
1960	263	174		−20	+20	64	36		−2	+2
1962 Kennedy (D)	258	176	1	−4	+2	67	33		+4	−4
1964	295	140		+38	−38	68	32		+2	−2
1966 L. Johnson (D)	248	187		−47	+47	64	36		−3	+3
1968	243	192		−4	+4	58	42		−5	+5
1970 Nixon (R)	255	180		+12	−12	55	45		−4	+2
1972	243	192		−12	+12	57	43		+2	−2
1974 Nixon (R)	291	144		+43	−43	61	38		+3	−3
1976 Ford (R)	292	143		+1	−1	62	38		0	0
1978 Carter (D)	277	158		−11	+11	59	41		−3	+3
1980	243	192		−33	+33	47	53		−12	+12
1982 Reagan (R)	269	166		+26	−26	46	54		0	0
1984	253	182		−14	+14	47	53		+2	−2
1986 Reagan (R)	258	177		+5	−5	55	45		+8	−8
1988	260	175		+3	−3	55	45		+1	−1
1990 Bush (R)	267	167	1	+9	−8	56	44		+1	−1
1992	258	176	1	−10	+10	57	43		0	0
1994 Clinton (D)	204	230	1	−52	+52	47	53		−8	+8

Note Gains and losses are taken from the situation immediately before the election.
For example, in 1994 the Republicans gained two seats in special (by-)elections due
to a death and resignation. They thus had 178 seats going into the November
1994 elections at which they added another 52 seats.

again altered outlooks on the presidency, and the new fashion stressed the importance of divided party control of government and emphasised how this *constrained* the presidency.[2]

This is an astonishingly varied set of opinions to have held sway in such a short period of time. Much of this turnover results from the tendency of observers to equate the strengths and successes (or not) of individual presidents with the strengths and successes (or not) of the presidency as a political institution. This over-personalisation of the office is compounded by the instinctive sympathy with the White House as a power-centre that many presidential observers have, alongside a deep-seated conviction that only the presidency can provide genuine national leadership and in some heroic sense embody the common good. Thus, to such people, the performance of the presidency is the barometer of the performance of the entire political system.

Individual presidents and the institutional presidency are not one and the same thing, although both clearly have the capacity to affect each other. Any institutional appraisal of the presidency has to stress the basic formal advantages and disadvantages the office obtains, along with identifiable informal advantages. Only then should one try and devise some yardstick for presidential success and analyse what determines presidential success, limited success, or failure.

Constitutional powers and constraints

The formal constitutional powers granted to the President are modest, restricted, and vague. The 1789 Constitution created by the Founding Fathers spent considerably more ink outlining how the President should be chosen than what the incumbent would actually do once selected. The President was to be chosen by means of an electoral college (Article II, Section I) in which each state would have as many members as they had Senators and Representatives (although neither type of office-holder could actually be an elector). The means of selecting electors was delegated to the state legislatures, but it was assumed that they would either chose amongst themselves or pick other notable dignitaries within the state. Thus the President would emerge from a distinctly indirect method which avoided either nomination by congressional caucus or popular election.

In domestic policy the Constitution stated that 'The executive power shall be vested in a President' (Article II, Section I) but, rather unhelpfully, did not state explicitly what it understood executive power to mean. The President was given the right to nominate other members of the executive (Article II, Section II), although no other executive officers were actually named. The same right was extended to the nomination of Supreme Court judges (Article II, Section II). More usefully, the President gained the power to recommend measures to Congress (Article II, Section III) and convene an emergency session of Congress if that was thought necessary. Added to this, the President was entitled to give regular information to the legislature on the state of the

Union (Article II, Section III). Perhaps the most potent domestic weapon given to the President was a negative one not granted under the section dealing with presidential powers at all. A presidential right of veto was outlined (Article I, Section VII) that allowed the President to reject an Act of Congress, a veto which could only be overturned by the very high threshold of a two-thirds margin in both branches of Congress. It was, though, assumed that the President, lacking any electoral legitimacy, would only deploy this weapon on an infrequent basis.

In foreign policy, the Constitution offered a number of limited but helpful functions. The President became Commander-in-Chief of the Army and Navy (Article II, Section II). The President was identified as the nation's senior diplomat and given the right to negotiate treaties with other nations (Article II, Section II). Furthermore, the President's ability to conduct such relations on a day-to-day basis was enhanced by his power to nominate Ambassadors (Article II, Section II).

Table 4.3. *The constitutional position of the presidency*

According to the Constitution the President has the following powers

o the right to veto congressional legislation (Article I: Section 7)

o to be Commander-in-Chief of the US Armed Forces (Article II: Section 2)

o the power to grant reprieves and pardons (Article II: Section 2)

o to make treaties for the United States (Article II: Section 2)

o to appoint Ambassadors (Article II: Section 2)

o to appoint judges (Article II: Section 2)

o to appoint members of the executive branch (Article II: Section 2)

o to comment on the State of the Union (Article II: Section 3)

o to recommend legislation to Congress (Article II: Section 3)

o to call special sessions of Congress (Article II: Section 3)

All appointment matters require majority support in the Senate. All Treaties require two-thirds support in the Senate.

This rather short and ill-defined set of functions came with several important constraints and caveats. The first was that none of the powers granted to the President were given exclusively. The President had the right to nominate members of the executive and candidates for the Supreme Court but only if he could command majority support in the Senate for them. The President could recommend measures to Congressmen but could not force them to be accepted. The ability to outline the state of the Union appeared to have little practical application. The veto was a potentially significant resource but it was fundamentally negative, should only be employed sparingly, and could be overturned if Congress was sufficiently united and determined to do so. Similarly, the President's role as Commander-in-Chief was checked by Congress being given the sole right to declare war. Any treaty agreed by the President had to be submitted to the Senate where the hurdle of a two-thirds vote of approval was needed. The ability to nominate Ambassadors again necessitated majority backing by the Senate. Richard Neustadt's famous dictum that the Founding Fathers created separated institutions sharing powers thus applies.[3]

Compared to the role of the executive the tasks allocated to the legislature by the Constitution were substantial, were far less ambiguous than those offered to the President and Congress was restrained solely by their own ability to legislate and the presidential veto. Legislative powers were outlined in Article I of the Constitution (itself an implication of legislative superiority over the executive) and consisted of a lengthy list of areas where Congress could act, as well as setting out the basic internal features of the House of Representatives (which was to be popularly elected) and the Senate (selected by state legislatures).

The Constitution gave Congress exclusive control over matters pertaining to its own composition, rules, agenda, internal structure and timetable, with the President completely frozen out of any control of these areas. In other nations it has been precisely the ability of the executive to seize control of these matters that has presaged relative legislative decline. Furthermore, the Constitution created separate elections for the House and Senate, gave the President no right to dismiss Congress and call fresh elections, and provided a genuinely bicameral system, thus doubling the number of effective chambers the executive had to deal with. Finally, the Constitution also created a Supreme Court that swiftly developed the means of striking down executive and legislative acts as unconstitutional.

Taken overall, the Constitution of 1789 distributed authority in such a way as to render the President a modest political figure except in times of dire national emergency.

Since the original draft was ratified there have been only six amendments affecting the President's standing. The Twelfth Amendment (1804) reformed the precise means of voting for the President within the electoral college in a way that assisted presidential power. The Sixteenth Amendment (1913) allowed the federal government to collect a national income tax, and this proved critical to Franklin Roosevelt's drive towards the New Deal in the 1930s. Another two amendments affect procedural aspects of the presidency and are basically neutral in their practical application. The Twentieth Amendment (1933) brought forward the inauguration date for the President by six weeks and established 3 January as the time for a new Congress to assemble. The Twenty-fifth Amendment (1967) dealt mostly with the issue of presidential incapacitation due to illness or injury, and with vice-presidential vacancies. Two other amendments would appear to have harmed the interests of the White House. The Seventeenth Amendment (1913) created direct elections to the Senate which quickly enhanced the standing of that institution, further entrenching bicameralism. The Twenty-second Amendment codified the precedent that presidents could serve a maximum of two terms.

Thus the constitutional text is hardly weighted in favour of the executive. This was the quite deliberate result of the convention of 1787. Whilst there were a few influential figures who favoured a strong executive – such as Alexander Hamilton – the majority felt that having suffered under one over-mighty executive (King George III) they were in no hurry to create another one in the form of the presidency. Nor were there many precedents for such a strong figure in pre-revolutionary America. In most states the Governor was a predominantly ceremonial figure whose term rarely exceeded two years. Governors were invariably selected by the state assemblies and dependent on them. In most cases, the chief executive had to share what role he had with an inner council nominated by the legislature. Governors rarely possessed a strong veto and in only one state, New York, could they really be described as a central political figure. Even here important restrictions applied.

Given this background, and given that many convention delegates wanted no single executive at all, but a rotating executive council, what is surprising about the American Constitution is not how weak it made the President but that it gave the office any authority of note.

Faced with constitutional constraints that were usually much more significant than their formal constitutional powers, and with the national government playing a small role in a political system based on dual sovereignty between the centre and the states, it is hardly shocking that most nineteenth century presidents were figures of only marginal importance. The creation of a much more central figure in the twentieth century was the product of a new, informal, political authority that rose to close the constitutional gap.

The political powers of the presidency

Constitutional arrangements did not create the presidency that has been displayed in this century. Rather, evolving political circumstances did. Virtually all of the formal provisions relating to the office have witnessed a *de facto* expansion as the result of changes in the demands placed on – and the reactions of – the American political system.

The first and most significant change involved the selection of the President. As stated in Chapter 1, the Founding Fathers' vision of an indirectly selected individual, chosen by dint of personal qualities by an elite cross-section of American society, only happened at the election and re-election of George Washington. From 1796 onwards, political factions or parties grouped around presidential aspirants and campaigned within state legislatures for the selection of electors specifically committed, not open-minded, to a particular candidate. By 1832 democratic pressures strongly associated with the candidature of Andrew Jackson saw the creation of presidential electors move to a popular vote rather than elite choice. As the 1840 contest approached much of what we would now recognise in the modern presidential election – political parties, nominating conventions, national campaigns – were already in place.

Although the formal electoral college mechanism remained in place, the presidency had become, for all practical purposes, a directly elected office. This altered the character of the post, bestowing greater political legitimacy and creating one sole person who could claim a national constituency. Possession of the presidency became more important to the political parties that chose candidates, not least because of the tendency of the public to cast their congressional votes in the same direction as their presidential ballot – the so-called coat-tail effect. Between 1856 and 1956 (exclusive) there were just two occasions (1876 and 1888) when the winning presidential candidate did not see his party capture both wings of Congress, there were no instances when at least one House was not taken.

With the cataclysmic political crisis created by the Depression of the 1930s and Franklin Roosevelt's evident willingness to act on it, the domestic policy provisions of the Constitution changed meaning dramatically. The ambiguous notion of 'the executive power' being granted to a President began to be seen expansively and triggered a process where the White House staff grew and a vague theory of executive privilege evolved. The right to 'recommend measures' was transformed into the President as chief legislator and (after a major skirmish with the Supreme Court) chief economist. This move had been signalled by developments in the previous thirty years, notably by the willingness of the national government to regulate at least some aspects of the now rampant industrial–capitalist system by the establishment of an executive-based budgetary system in 1921, and by the forceful examples set by Theodore Roosevelt and Woodrow Wilson. Franklin Roosevelt's willingness to move the federal government into such areas as banking regulation, agricultural price support, job creation schemes, and social security represented a quantum leap. Initial congressional support for Roosevelt's plans meant that with this extension of the national government came an extension in the tasks of the President.

Table 4.4. *Veto power*

Years	President	Regular vetoes	Vetoes overridden	Pocket vetoes	Total vetoes
1789–1797	Washington	2	0	0	2
1797–1801	Adams	0	0	0	0
1801–1809	Jefferson	0	0	0	0
1809–1817	Madison	5	0	2	7
1817–1825	Monroe	1	0	0	1
1825–1829	J. Q. Adams	0	0	0	0
1829–1837	Jackson	5	0	7	12
1837–1841	Van Buren	0	0	1	1
1841–1841	Harrison	0	0	0	0
1841–1845	Tyler	6	1	4	10
1845–1849	Polk	2	0	1	3

Years	President	Regular vetoes	Vetoes overridden	Pocket vetoes	Total vetoes
1849–1850	Taylor	0	0	0	0
1850–1853	Fillmore	0	0	0	0
1853–1857	Pierce	9	5	0	9
1857–1861	Buchanan	4	0	3	7
1861–1865	Lincoln	2	0	5	7
1865–1869	A. Johnson	21	15	8	29
1869–1877	Grant	45	4	48	93
1877–1881	Hayes	12	1	1	13
1881–1881	Garfield	0	0	0	0
1881–1885	Arthur	4	1	8	12
1885–1889	Cleveland	304	2	110	414
1889–1893	Harrison	19	1	25	44
1893–1897	Cleveland	42	5	128	170
1897–1901	McKinley	6	0	36	42
1901–1909	T. Roosevelt	42	1	40	82
1909–1913	Taft	30	1	9	39
1913–1921	Wilson	33	6	11	44
1921–1923	Harding	5	0	1	6
1923–1929	Coolidge	20	4	30	50
1929–1933	Hoover	21	3	16	37
1933–1945	F. Roosevelt	372	9	263	635
1945–1953	Truman	180	12	70	250
1953–1961	Eisenhower	73	2	108	181
1961–1963	Kennedy	12	0	9	21
1963–1969	L. Johnson	16	0	14	30
1969–1974	Nixon	26	7	17	43
1974–1977	Ford	48	12	18	66
1977–1981	Carter	13	2	18	31
1981–1989	Reagan	39	9	39	78
1989–1992	Bush	29	1	17	46
Total		1,448	104	1,067	2,515

Note A pocket veto occurs if Congress goes out of session without the President having signed the particular piece of legislation. A veto can be overridden by a two-thirds vote in both chambers of Congress. Generally, Presidents use the veto power most often when the opposing party controls Congress. None the less Franklin Roosevelt had 635 vetoes against Congresses of his own party.

One further by-product of the enhanced federal role was that many more positions in the executive were devised for the President to fill and Congress, broadly speaking, allowed those posts to be filled by the President's first choice. The President continued to make nominations to the Supreme Court and for a considerable period did so with the minimum of congressional interference. Between 1933 and 1968 no presidential nominee was rejected by the Senate. Furthermore, from 1936 onwards, that Court became increasingly deferential to the presidency.

The President's right to inform Congress of the state of the Union became under Roosevelt the President's premier opportunity to lay out his legislative programme. Whilst earlier presidents had generally been cautious in their use of the veto power, Roosevelt saw it as his chance to strike down any and all laws that he disapproved. He formally vetoed 372 measures and pocket vetoed (failed to sign before a congressional session ended, thus killing the legislation) another 263 for a grand total of 635, of which only 9 were reversed by Congress. Such a generous use of veto authority happened despite the existence of Democratic party majorities in Congress throughout his tenure. Roosevelt's successors have followed his broad use of the veto mechanism to shape (primarily) domestic policy.

In foreign policy, the enormous American commitment to the Second World War, the subsequent decision not to retreat into isolationism, superpower status, the invention of nuclear weapons, and the coming of the Cold War revolutionised the United States' role in the world and with it the status of the President. The Commander-in-Chief portfolio gained greater and greater standing as an inevitable result. The same was true of the presidential position of Chief Diplomat which flowed from the task of treaty-making. Presidents found it increasingly convenient and possible to minimise the amount of diplomacy by formal treaty (which would require senatorial scrutiny and approval) and to conduct business through less formal arrangements with other heads of government, called executive agreements, which did not need Senate scrutiny. Although less legally binding, these agreements had many practical features similar to those of treaties and the distinction between the two blurred. For twenty-five years after Pearl Harbor Congress was willing to devolve vast influence over foreign policy to the White House in the name of Cold War efficiency.

The 'Roosevelt Revolution' in the American presidency was further assisted by an utterly extra-constitutional development (indeed one the founders could not have conceived of) – the emergence of nation-wide mass communication and its application to politics. In Roosevelt's case the medium was radio, which he utilised through his 'fireside chats' to the population. His successors would swiftly embrace the new medium of television, which from the Eisenhower Administration onwards, became the premier presidential communication method.

To sum up, five major factors shaped the modern presidency.

First, the enforced abandonment of the original means of presidential selection and the relegation of the electoral college to the symbolic elements of the Constitution enabled the President to emerge as the dominant electoral figure in American politics.

Second, the widespread reinterpretation or recasting of the original domestic policy provisions of the Constitution, largely as a response to the economic collapse of 1929–33, allowed the President to become the dominant policy initiator.

Third, the continuation of existing constitutional authority in foreign policy against the backdrop of entirely different circumstances allowed the President to evolve into the dominant foreign policy actor of the premier nation of the international system.

Fourth, this entire process was assisted by the communications revolution brought about by radio and then television. Such media found it far easier to focus on one man than on a 535-person Congress or a secretive 9-person Supreme Court. In addition, the media's sympathy for the valiant presidency fighting for the national interest and leading the nation through the Cold War gave an even greater emphasis on the White House.

Finally, and critically, there was no constitutional revolution to accompany the political one. The presidency gained no extra constitutional ammunition and none of the constitutional constraints that formerly restricted the Oval Office were withdrawn.

This final point should be stressed vigorously. The modern presidency which, in its original form, lasted from 1933 to 1968 did not create a quasi-dictatorial or even overwhelming political figure. The amount of actual authority a President could wield was determined by that struggle between the political powers that had evolved and the constitutional constraints that remained. On some occasions the former factor would win the struggle, on others the latter would prevail. The balance tended to lean against the White House in strictly domestic policy but move towards it in foreign policy. Even in the course of the same presidency the balance between the two elements could vary substantially in both domestic and overseas issues.

The position of the President, and the balance of strength between these two forces, does seem to have altered since the late 1960s, although both the extent of that shift and its permanence have been hotly disputed. The broad trends that can be identified seem to have weakened the informal political assets that the presidency relied on to boost its authority. As the pre-existing constitutional constraints have remained unamended in that period, the net effect of that change has been to complicate and weaken the presidency as an institution. That alteration was the often unintended result of various reforms triggered by the events of the 1960s. The imperial presidency identified by some represented the zenith of presidential dominance, not a new era in presidential supremacy. Indeed, its chief offshoots – the Vietnam War and Watergate – were to strengthen the forces conspiring against presidential pre-eminence. Therefore a new set of factors can be traced that eroded the political assets of the White House to move from the modern presidency of the Roosevelt to Johnson era to the 'Post-Reform' institution from Nixon onwards.

The making of the Post-Reform President

The advantages held by the President because of political evolution have been sharply diminished in many areas as a consequence of reforms not always intended to weaken the executive. Those reforms include: the move to a primary-based presidential nominating system; divided government; an increasingly assertive Congress at home and abroad; internal change within Congress that has complicated life for the White House; greater problems in co-ordinating the executive branch; and a less sympathetic media. These changes are spelt out in chapters throughout this book. Together these changes constitute a Post-Reform presidency.

One of the most striking developments has been in the nature of presidential selection. Before 1968, aspirants for a party's presidential nomination sought election by persuading party leaders in Congress and the fifty states to support them. There were some primary contests but these were of secondary import-ance to the independent assessment of a candidate by the various party chief-tains. Nominees gained favour by bargaining within the party and beyond it. Any candidate unknown to or unpopular with the party leadership in Congress was very unlikely to prosper. Thus bargaining skills (vital to presidential prac-tice) and an element of peer-group review were built into the selection process.

The shift away from party-based nominations to primary-based nomina-tions emerged out of the bitter struggle between pro- and anti-Vietnam War forces at the 1968 Democratic party convention. The former (under Vice-President Hubert Humphrey) had won the nomination whilst the latter (under Senators Eugene McCarthy and Robert Kennedy) had lost it, despite winning all the primaries. Since then campaigning and presentational skills, the build-ing of a personal political organisation, and the ability to appeal to that most politically active sub-set of the electorate who participate in primary contests, have replaced party brokerage as the means of nomination. The electorate now screen presidential hopefuls (aided by the media) at the expense of con-gressional party opinion.

Critics contend that by making the process longer, more expensive, and more intense, certain types of possible candidate are at a disadvantage. Those weakened candidates might be anyone with a senior job in the congressional leadership (witness the dire campaigns of Senator Howard Baker in 1980 and Senator Robert Dole in 1980 and 1988) and serving governors of large states (Mario Cuomo's refusal to run in both 1988 and 1992). Yet these are two fields from which one would hope and expect to find the sort of candidates who could effectively serve as presidents. What it now takes to become Presi-dent is seriously disjointed from the qualities and experience that common sense might suggest produce good presidents.

The move to primaries has also augmented an ongoing process whereby political parties have become less relevant as voting cues to the general public. In the hundred years from 1856 to 1956 one-party dominance of all branches of government was the norm because of consistent party-based voting. For a majority of the period since then, split-party control of government with one party holding the White House and the other at least one and usually both branches of Congress has been the norm. This divided government obviously complicates life for the President as he is forced to co-operate with party opponents. This is modestly mitigated by the relatively non-ideological nature of American political parties, although in many ways the post-New Deal party system has encouraged greater ideological cohesion within the two main parties.

In domestic policy, the willingness of Congress to defer to the presidency, which was always limited, has collapsed further. In reaction to the abuse of presidential power by Nixon, Congress regained much of its hold over the budget-making process through the Budget Control and Impoundment Act of 1974. It has shown greater enthusiasm for denying presidents their preferred appointments to their own administrations, as Jimmy Carter found with his nominees to be Budget Director (Bert Lance) and CIA supremo (Theodore Sorenson) and as George Bush discovered with his initial choice of Defence Secretary (John Tower). Congress threw out two of Richard Nixon's nominees to the Supreme Court (Clement Haynsworth and G. Harold Carswell), another of Ronald Reagan's (Robert Bork), and came within three votes of rejecting one of George Bush's suggestions (Clarence Thomas). In its overall approach to public policy Congress strongly disputed the idea that only the President can act in the public interest or that the executive has some unique expertise worth respecting. Presidents Nixon, Ford and Bush saw most of their domestic proposals mauled by the opposition party, and presidents Carter, and to some degree Clinton, had the indignity of seeing policy mauled by their own party.

As Chapter 14 expounds, increasing congressional assertiveness in domestic affairs has been matched by a similar concern in foreign policy. In response to the presidentialisation of the Vietnam War, and the shadowy conduct of foreign policy by Richard Nixon, Congress reacted with a torrent of legislation including the Case Act of 1972 (which regulated the use of executive agreements) and the War Powers Resolution of 1973 (which regulated presidential use of the armed forces). Congress cut off funds to South Vietnam over the protest of Gerald Ford. It came within one vote of denying Jimmy Carter his Panama Canal Treaty in 1978 and would have denied him his SALT 2 arms agreement in 1980 had it not been withdrawn in the light of the Soviet invasion of Afghanistan. Congress and President Reagan also clashed over arms control, El Salvador, the Lebanon, the MX missile, Nicaragua and South Africa. Although relations under President Bush were calmer, the Senate came within three votes of denying him the authority to retake Kuwait in 1991.

Table 4.5. *Success in the House of Representatives, 1953–92*

President (political party)/year	House Victories (%)	Number of votes	President (political party)/year	House Victories (%)	Number of votes
Eisenhower (R)			Ford (R)		
1953	91.2	34	1974	59.3	54
1954	78.9	38	1975	50.6	89
1955	63.4	41	1976	43.1	51
1956	73.5	34	*Average*	51.0	
1957	58.3	60	*Total*		194
1958	74.0	50	Carter (D)		
1959	55.6	54	1977	74.7	79
1960	65.1	43	1978	69.6	112
Average	68.4		1979	71.7	145
Total		354	1980	76.9	117
			Average	73.1	
Kennedy (D)			*Total*		453
1961	83.1	65			
1962	85.0	60	Reagan (R)		
1963	83.1	71	1981	72.4	76
Average	83.7		1982	55.8	77
Total		196	1983	47.6	82
			1984	52.2	113
Johnson (D)			1985	45.0	80
1964	88.5	52	1986	33.3	90
1965	93.8	112	1987	33.3	99
1966	91.3	103	1988	32.7	104
1967	75.6	127	*Average*	45.6	
1968	83.5	103	*Total*		721
Average	85.9				
Total		497	Bush (R)		
			1989	50.0	86
Nixon (R)			1990	32.4	108
1969	72.3	47	1991	43.2	111
1970	84.6	65	1992	37.1	105
1971	82.5	57	*Average*	40.2	
1972	81.1	37	*Total*		410
1973	48.0	125			
1974	67.9	53			
Average	68.2				
Total		384			

Note These support scores are calculated by *Congressional Quarterly* and have some limitations. None the less they indicate that Presidents' support scores in the House tend to vary according to whether their own party controls that chamber.

Table 4.6. *Success in the Senate, 1953–92*

President (political party)/year	House Victories (%)	Number of votes
Eisenhower (R)		
1953	87.8	49
1954	77.9	77
1955	84.6	52
1956	67.7	65
1957	78.9	57
1958	76.5	98
1959	50.4	121
1960	65.1	86
Average	70.7	
Total		605
Kennedy (D)		
1961	80.6	124
1962	85.6	125
1963	89.6	115
Average	85.2	
Total		364
Johnson (D)		
1964	87.6	97
1965	92.6	162
1966	68.8	125
1967	81.2	165
1968	68.9	164
Average	79.7	
Total		713
Nixon (R)		
1969	76.4	72
1970	71.4	91
1971	69.5	82
1972	54.3	46
1973	52.4	185
1974	54.2	83
Average	61.5	
Total		559

President (political party)/year	House Victories (%)	Number of votes
Ford (R)		
1974	57.4	68
1975	71.0	93
1976	64.2	53
Average	65.0	
Total		214
Carter (D)		
1977	76.1	88
1978	84.8	151
1979	81.4	161
1980	73.3	116
Average	79.7	
Total		516
Reagan (R)		
1981	88.3	128
1982	83.2	119
1983	85.9	85
1984	85.7	77
1985	71.6	102
1986	80.7	83
1987	56.4	78
1988	64.8	88
Average	77.9	
Total		760
Bush (R)		
1989	73.3	101
1990	63.4	93
1991	67.5	83
1992	53.3	60
Average	65.6	
Total		337

Note Regardless of which party controls the White House, these tables indicate that the Senate is usually more sympathetic to White House requests than the House of Representatives. In part this is because the Senate deals more heavily in foreign policy, on which there are usually fewer disagreements than over domestic issues.

As Chapter 5 notes, a series of internal changes to the committee system voted through by Democrats in the House of Representatives between 1971 and 1973 means power within the House has moved. Before the 1970s control of the House of Representatives lay with a small number of party leaders and committee chairmen whose support was vital to the passage of White House proposals but who could at least be identified and bartered with. Since the 1970s that control has been dispersed in a fragmented and highly fluid way between the party leadership, the party caucus, committee chairmen, the party caucus on any given committee, sub-committee chairmen, the floor of the House of Representatives, and congressional staff. This change has substantially contorted the process of legislative liaison and persuasion for every President who has had to co exist with the new system.

These difficulties have been reinforced by the multiplication of various interest groups, think-tanks, Political Action Committees, and lobbying firms that have descended on Washington, DC in the last two decades. They have frequently allied with congressional institutions as well as with individual Congressmen and committees to oppose presidential proposals.

None of this has been helped, from the President's viewpoint, by the changing attitude of the media. Radio and television were once *de facto* allies of the White House in its effort to control the political scene. Favourable coverage for presidential initiatives was almost guaranteed provided that the minimum of public relations competence was available. The Vietnam crisis and to an even greater extent Watergate produced a new mood of scepticism towards the executive from the print and visual media and spawned a generation of investigative reporters determined to expose wrong doing at every level of government.

All four areas of political advantage that the modern presidency acquired – electoral, policy, foreign, and public dominance – have been reduced by varying levels over the past three decades. The combination of all these factors has dramatically affected the position of the President regardless of whether his party possess congressional majorities or not. If one tries to judge the success or failure of a President then the size of the task that the institution faces has to be realised and reasonable criteria adopted to assess performance.

What constitutes presidential success?

Deciding what guidelines to use for establishing some sense of presidential success is not as easy as might first appear. Yet evaluation of presidential performance happens continually, despite wildly different interpretations about how this should be done. The first dilemma is that presidents themselves differ in how they see their role. In the modern era the notion of the President as a dynamic figure reaching out beyond strict constitutional powers, the idea of *stewardship*, has become broadly accepted and presidents are ranked according to how they perform in this regard. However, this is not the only possible conception of the President's proper function. Several presidents have held a *constructionist* view of their office, believing they should remain within their constitutional boundaries. Others, arguably President Eisenhower, have seen the presidency as a sort of *protectorate*, reaching outside his constitutional limits only when some clear case of the national interest requires it. Should presidents in the last two categories be regarded as unsuccessful when, in their own terms, they may have been highly effective?

Even within those presidents that subscribe to the stewardship theory measurement is problematic. One approach might be to compare the promises made before election – in the party platform (manifesto) and elsewhere – with what actually happened. However, such campaign promises are invariably vague, they rarely give a strong sense of priority, and many issues not anticipated in the campaign come up during a presidency and have to be dealt with.

Another widely touted method is to compare the proportion of legislative measures supported by a President that actually passed. The journal *Congressional Quarterly* has been keeping such records since 1954 and they are often cited by journalists and political scientists alike. Such scores are highly imperfect. A 75 per cent success rate is much less impressive if most of what the President really wanted enacted is in the remaining 25 per cent (as is the case for Kennedy and Carter). The measure takes no account of the degree of compromise and concession a President makes to get his proposal passed. Not all presidential life is based around laws. The Watergate burglary and cover-up, for example, involved no public legislation but its handling was critical to President Nixon's subsequent reputation. Attempts to circumvent these problems by only investigating success in the major parts of an administration's agenda have also proved extremely hard.

That leaves two other possibilities: whether or not what a President did was right. Or as Richard Neustadt puts it, 'what were his purposes and did these run with or against the grain of history?'[4] This is an appealing measure but one that is inevitably amorphous, retrospective, and subjective. Alternatively, one could evaluate the impact or legacy of a President on the political system he left behind. This again has attractions but is open to many of the criticisms of ambiguity and subjectivity mentioned previously. Inevitably, perhaps, strict methodology is abandoned by presidential observers in favour of some kind of 'feel' for presidential success, but feel is very much in the hands of the feeler.

What determines presidential performance?

Having outlined the constitutional and political elements the contemporary presidency has to live with, and having noted the ambiguous concept of success, what determines presidential performance? There appear to be four broad schools of thought: presidential skill; presidential popularity; congressional composition; and congressional deference.

Impressions of presidential skill have dominated evaluations of presidential performance. In Richard Neustadt's highly influential book *Presidential Power*,[5] the argument is made that presidents face a difficult institutional terrain in which their major asset is the power of persuasion and bargaining. Whether or not a President realises his goals is therefore the product of their skill in presidential persuasion. Neustadt's work has inspired hundreds of books written from the same perspective which use comparative case-studies across many presidencies to make judgements about individual office-holders. A common assumption of these investigations is that whether or not a President is successful comes down to his own individual political skills, with some element of luck allowed for.

This stance has some obvious advantages. American politics is about bargaining, especially given the limited formal assets of the presidency and the checks and balances of the Constitution. Any President who does not display high-quality political skills is, in all probability, doomed to failure. This approach does carry certain presumptions that might be debatable. It is a very presidential view in that it presumes that providing a President displays the necessary skills he will get his way. One might wonder whether, with all the persuasive skills possible, presidents can constantly get results from legislative chambers that are either in no mood to be led or are dominated by the opposition party. The use of case-studies, which this method constantly employs, is itself disputable. Why use some case-studies and not others? Should we exclude Kennedy's failure during the Bay of Pigs fiasco (Cuba, 1961) but include his handling of the missile crisis involving the same country just eighteen months later? Was Ronald Reagan a genius because of the passage of his economic proposals in 1981 or an incompetent because of the failure of his New Federalism package in 1982? Some issues are inherently easier to deal with than others – tax reductions are generally more popular than tax increases, for instance.

A different attitude is displayed by those, like Samuel Kernell,[6] who stress presidential popularity. This thesis asserts that presidents with very high public standing as measured by opinion polls are more likely to get their programme supported by the public and other politicians. Therefore, presidents should concentrate on those presentational matters that help build up popularity and use that as a battering-ram to force a fearful Washington, DC into line. This has an intuitive charm. Unpopular presidents surely command less respect on Capitol Hill than popular ones. Again, this is a very presidency-based approach. If only presidents can gain high poll ratings, political pay-offs are assured. It is also uncertain – given the weakness of the electoral coat-tails of presidents in recent decades – whether individual Congressmen should be concerned about crossing a President just because he is popular. A second-term President can have virtually no electoral threat at all. There have certainly been presidents – Eisenhower consistently, Reagan for part of his second term, Bush for much of his only term – who have possessed impressive poll ratings without equally impressive legislative victories.

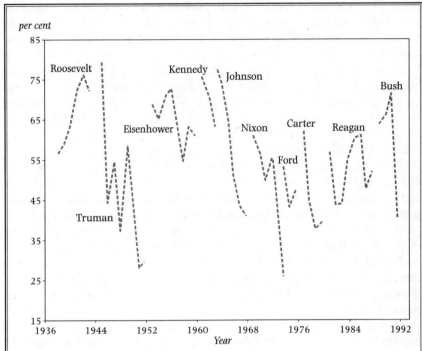

Public opinion ratings, 1938–92.

Source Vital Statistics on American Politics, 3rd edn (Washington, DC, Congressional Quarterly Press, 1992).

Note As this graph indicates, retaining presidential popularity is not an easy business. The general pattern is to start off with a good deal of public backing with erodes progressively. Dwight Eisenhower and Ronald Reagan are exceptions to this trend.

Other observers have approached the question from the other end of the avenue – the congressional perspective. Jon Bond and Richard Fleishel[7] have argued that what a President can achieve is largely predetermined – especially in domestic policy – by the party composition (Democrat/Republican) and the ideological make-up (liberal/conservative) of Congress which presidents cannot affect much any more in the short-term. Such observers would not claim that Congressmen are fixed on all issues, but would state that party and ideology lay out the parameters within which presidents move. This congressional-based view could be supplemented by similar notions based on the internal procedure and outlook of Congress, which also colours executive–legislative relations.

Such an analysis would grant a role to presidential skill and popularity where the party and/or ideological balance of Congress is evenly weighted, and on congressmen whose ideological views differ somewhat from their party label, such as centrists in either party. These are secondary, if sometimes vital, assets. Certain presidents, George Bush in the House of Representatives, for example, face such difficult party/ideological odds that all the skill and popularity in the world are unlikely to help them.

This theme has been pushed further by Charles O. Jones.[8] He argues that the American political system's distinguishing feature is not that it is a presidential system restrained by an unusually awkward legislature, but that it is a genuinely separated and equal division. Hence to analyse presidencies without regard to the Congress with which they serve is to fundamentally misread the real dynamic of modern politics.

Overdeterminism should be avoided. The possession of a party and ideological majority in Congress (actually a rather rare event) cannot guarantee presidential triumph. Congress must be willing as well as able to help and presidents must display some bargaining ability. There have been presidents with very weak positions in Congress who have received support for major pieces of policy – Truman and the Marshall Plan, Bush and Gulf War authorisation – but these instances are not overnumerous and tend to be in foreign affairs. Certain shock events can galvanise even a hostile Congress behind the President, although again most of such surprises involve international action.

All of these factors have their pros and cons. They can each be utilised to explain instances of unmistakable presidential success. Ronald Reagan's economic victories in 1981 could be accounted for by personal skill, his high popularity rating, the ideological conservative (but not party) majority in the

Table 4.7. *Presidential press conferences*

President	Average number of press conferences per month	Total number of press conferences
Roosevelt (1933–45)	6.9	998
Truman (1945–53)	3.6	334
Eisenhower (1953–61)	2.0	193
Kennedy (1961–63)	1.9	65
Johnson (1963–69)	2.2	135
Nixon (1969–74)	0.6	39
Ford (1974–77)	1.3	39
Carter (1977–81)	1.2	59
Reagan (1981–89)	0.6	53
Bush (1989–93)	1.3	64

Note Since television has been the primary medium for press conferences (from Eisenhower) they have been used less frequently. Both Richard Nixon and Ronald Reagan were often accused of avoiding the press, a view this table seems to vindicate.

House of Representatives or congressional willingness to back him because of the economic malaise he inherited. Every suggestion may be true. Nevertheless, some sort of weighting has to be made between them. On balance, earlier scholars of the President may have overstated his room for action and understated the extent to which he is the prisoner of the Congress that serves beside him. Observers of the contemporary President might make a considerable effort to avoid repeating that error.

The contemporary President – some concluding thoughts

This chapter has made four, hopefully complementary, key points. Perspectives of presidential standing have been over-influenced by the standing of individual presidents. The President's capacity is decided by a trade-off between mostly constitutional constraints and mostly political advantages. A set of identifiable factors have arisen over the last thirty years to restrict those political advantages to varying degrees. Presidential success is not derived autonomously but is highly correlated to congressional circumstances. The great unanswered issue in all this relates to divided partisan control of government. How much does its existence or not weaken the political assets of the President? Instinctively, we assume it must matter enormously. Some scholars though, notably David Mayhew,[9] say it matters far less than that. As five of the last six presidents have had to operate under divided government, the degree of its impact is obviously critical to assess.

All these arguments should be approached with caution. Party majorities are not the same as ideological ones, and the relative performance of presidents Carter and Reagan sit uneasily with this argument. Furthermore, divided government was only one of a host of recent changes that have compromised the political assets of the contemporary presidency. Assuming that divided government is not the sole predictor of Oval Office output, some tentative conclusions can be offered.

First, presidential power is increasingly shaped by the actions and predispositions of others. At home, while presidential skill and popularity do count for something (sometimes a lot), it is congressional factors that often come first. Abroad, whilst the United States remains the world's only economic, political, military, and cultural superpower, relative economic decline and increasing global interdependence have a considerable influence on presidential options.

Second, Richard Neustadt's 'power to persuade' has also changed. There are many more people, not only within Congress but in the wider political system, who presidents need to persuade today than was the case for 1960 when Neustadt's work was first published. The same is true – to a slightly more manageable extent – for international policy, where not just other governments but transnational institutions such as the UN and the IMF, as well as more disparate constituencies such as the foreign exchange markets are involved. Indeed, the assets of the President and the vast number of contacts

President Clinton talking to the media at Thanksgiving.

that he needs to make may mean that persuasion as Richard Neustadt used it is an inappropriate word. Perhaps the power to negotiate would be more appropriate.

Third, precisely because bargaining is now so complex, presidents have increasingly abandoned it as a direct tool in favour of appealing to public opinion as the indirect route to political glory. The cult of presentation initiated by the Reagan Presidency may be a permanent aspect of American political life – President Clinton certainly seems attracted to it. Whether such a strategy is either appropriate or profitable is hard to know, given experience thus far. It is an approach with limitations as well as strengths.

The exact role of the contemporary presidency is highly sensitive to short-term institutional and political developments. The model of the President-as-Emperor is surely misplaced, just as the President-as-weakling is a misleading picture. There are distinct features that shape the Post-Reform presidency. Most of those features look unlikely to be reversed in the near future. Those factors set upper and lower limits to presidential authority but do not necessarily ensure any particular outcome. They do, however, power-fully influence what the presidency can achieve.

Notes

1 Clinton Rossiter, *The American President* (New York, Harcourt Press, 1957).
2 For fuller versions of these various views see (in order): Woodrow Wilson, *Congressional Government* (Boston, Houghton, 1913); Edward Corwin, *The American Presidency* (New York, New York University Press, 1957): Richard Neustadt, *Presidential Power* (New York, Wiley & Sons, 1960); Arthur Schlesinger Jr., *The Imperial Presidency* (Boston, Houghton, 1973); Thomas Franck, *The Tethered Presidency* (New York, New York University Press, 1981); Fred Greenstein (ed.), *The Reagan Presidency: an early assessment* (Baltimore, Johns Hopkins Press, 1983); and Richard Rose, *The Post-Modern President*, (Chatham, New Jersey, Chatham House, 1988).
3 Neustadt, *Presidential Power*, p. 29.
4 *Ibid.*, p. 167.
5 *Ibid.*
6 Kernell, *Going Public*.
7 Bond and Fleisher, *The President in the Legislative Arena*.
8 Jones, *The Presidency in a Separated System*.
9 David Mayhew, *Divided We Govern* (New Haven, Connecticut, Yale University Press, 1991).

5

Congress

While the presidency has become the major focus of attention in modern American government, it is the legislative branch that is mentioned first in the US Constitution. The two Houses of Congress were also given many more specific powers than the president, including the two most important powers of all: the power of the purse, and the power to declare war. As far as the framers were concerned, it seemed obvious that the legislative branch would be the predominant branch of the federal government. According to Madison in *Federalist* 51: 'But it is not possible to give to each department an equal power of self-defense. In Republican government the legislative authority, necessarily, predominates.'[1] Indeed, so fearful were the framers of the dominance of a popularly elected legislature in the new federal government, that they divided the legislature into two chambers and established the presidential veto as an extra check.

Of course, there were other reasons to justify the division of Congress into two Houses apart from checking and balancing. The Senate, with its longer term (six years) and smaller membership, was intended to both represent the states (who were wary of the proposed new federal government) and (since its members would be indirectly elected by the state legislatures) to provide an 'aristocratic' element in the federal government less responsive to the popular will. The Senate was also given special prerogatives over foreign policy since the assent of two-thirds of its membership is necessary to ratify treaties. A simple majority of Senators is also required to confirm presidential appointments to the judicial and executive branches.

The only prerogative reserved to the House of Representatives, following British parliamentary practice, was that all financial legislation was to start there. The House can impeach presidents and federal judges, but the power to try impeachments is given to the Senate, with a two-thirds majority of the membership required for conviction and removal from office.

Despite its predominant position in the Constitution, the US Congress is the most troubled institution in the federal government today. As the twentieth century has progressed Congress has forfeited many of its constitutional prerogatives to the presidency, the bureaucracy, and the federal judiciary. Efforts to reverse the imbalance through a combination of internal reform and a more combative attitude *vis-à-vis* the executive since Vietnam and Watergate have not improved Congress's public image. By the mid-1990s Congress had become the most despised and disparaged institution in American government: widely blamed for policy 'gridlock' in Washington, and popularly regarded as being in thrall to lobbyists and unrepresentative of the concerns of everyday citizens.

In this chapter we shall discover how Congress has come to this pass, and to what extent the popular disparagement of Congress is deserved.

The golden age of Congress: the nineteenth century

For most of the nineteenth century Congress was undoubtedly the dominant branch of the federal government. There were two essential factors underlying this dominance. The first was the very limited size of the federal government at this time, and the second, that power inside the Congress was highly concentrated and centralised under a powerful party leadership.

In the very early decades of the Republic (1789–1820) the House was the dominant chamber (as the framers had feared) because the Senate then was very small (due to the smaller number of states), and the House dominated the congressional caucuses that effectively chose the President up to 1825. After the Jacksonian revolution in the 1820s and the emergence of national parties, however, the Senate began to rise in status. Its membership rose as the number of states admitted to the Union grew; the great debates over slavery tended to take place in that chamber where the slavery and anti-slavery forces were deliberately balanced; and the Senate's constitutionally designated speciality – foreign affairs – became more important as the century advanced. Finally, because the Senators were selected by the state legislatures, powerful party bosses often secured US Senate seats for themselves from pliant state legislatures, so that they could direct federal patronage back to their local party organisations.

After the Civil War power in the House became more and more centralised under the Speaker.[2] This was particularly true in the period from 1890 to 1910 when the House was dominated by two very strong Speakers, Thomas 'Czar' Reed of Maine, and 'Uncle' Joe Cannon of Illinois. The Speaker's control came mainly from his dominance of the majority party caucus, through which he was able to control committee assignments, the Rules Committee, and the scheduling and debate of legislation on the House floor. Members went along with the Speaker because that was the key to success in the House, and conciliating the Speaker was also critical in delivering the federal patronage that kept the local party organisation happy. As a consequence the loyalty of members to their parties was remarkably high by modern congressional standards (see diagram).

The Progressive era (1900–16) brought about momentous changes in the nature of both Houses of Congress and Congress's role in the governmental structure, however. With the widespread climate of opposition to party machines and 'bossism' and the introduction of the direct primary, members of the House began to find that going along with the Speaker was no longer necessarily the best guarantee of a lengthy House career. Even in the most reliable congressional districts for their party, an unwary incumbent might be challenged in the primary by a dashing reformer if he did not take care to carve out a personal, as opposed to a partisan, constituency of support.

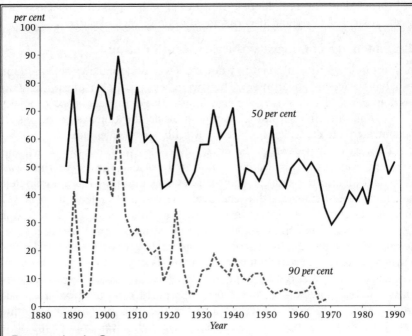

per cent

Party voting in Congress.

Note Figures shown by Congress. A party vote occurs when the specified percentage (or more) of one party votes against the specified percentage (or more) of the other party. Figures for 90 per cent party votes are generally unavailable after 1970. In 1987–88 the proportion of 90 per cent party votes was 7 per cent.

Sources 1887–1969: Joseph Cooper, David William Brady and Patricia A. Hurley, 'The Electoral Basis of Party Voting: Patterns and Trends in the US House of Representatives', in Louis Maisel and Joseph Cooper (eds), *The Impact of the Electoral Process* (Beverly Hills: Sage, 1977), 139; 1970–88: Congressional Quarterly, *Congressional Quarterly Almanac* (Washington, DC: Congressional Quarterly, annual volumes); 1989–90: *Congressional Quarterly Weekly Report* (1990), 4185, 4188.

Reproduced from Harold W. Stanley and Richard G. Niemi, *Vital Statistics on American Politics*, 3rd edn (Washington, DC: Congressional Quarterly Press, 1992), p. 213.

In 1910 these wider changes in the political universe of American electoral politics also led to a major change in the rules of the congressional game.[3] In that year progressive Republicans joined with the Democratic minority to strip Speaker Cannon of his power over committee assignments, the House rules, the legislative agenda, and floor debate. In the Senate the age of the party bosses' dominance was ended by the introduction of the direct election of Senators in 1913, and the impact of the direct primary.

These changes were also symptomatic of a broader change in the roles and the balance of power between the federal legislative and executive branches. Progressive reformers sought to expand the scope of federal government activity, but had little time for legislatures which they regarded as entirely dominated by parochial concerns and irredeemably corrupt, instead placing greater faith on a powerful presidency and a bureaucracy of experts chosen on merit. The expansion of the federal government and the sudden emergence of the presidency under Roosevelt and Woodrow Wilson from its late nineteenth-century hibernation began the gradual reversal of the roles of Congress and the presidency in the political system during this century. Congress ceased to be the active and dynamic element in the federal government, and instead became increasingly reactive and passive, responding to stimuli from the executive and judicial branches and ceding control over the political agenda to the White House. The events of 1910 set in motion the long, slow decline in power, authority, and prestige that has characterised Congress during this century.

The committee–seniority system: 1910–70

After 1910 the strong leadership model of Congress was replaced by the committee–seniority system. Instead of control lying in the hands of the party leadership, it rested in the hands of the chairmen of the powerful standing committees of the House and Senate. In order to scrutinise adequately the expanding, increasingly expert federal bureaucracy, Congress had to specialise. Each congressional committee became sovereign in its own policy domain, and naturally enough, members gravitated towards committees that were likely to help them electorally back home. Committee chairmen controlled the agenda of their committee, committee staff, and assignments to subcommittees. Once a president got a committee chairman on his side, for example, he knew that his legislation was likely to get through the committee and the floor of the chamber. In the face of the determined opposition of the relevant committee chairman even a powerful incumbent President would get nowhere.

Chairmen were selected according to seniority, that is, their length of service in Congress. There were two reasons for this: first, seniority meant the most experienced and (hopefully) most expert member of the committee would become chair; secondly, the seniority system prevented party leaders or presidents from trying to influence the selection of chairs and therefore reduce the independence of the committee as a whole. Strict adherence to seniority after the New Deal, however, meant that the committee chairs were invariably southern Democrats (since the Democrats controlled Congress most of the time, and the safest Democratic states and districts were in the southern states), who were much more conservative than the totality of House Democrats and even most of the Republicans up to the mid-1960s.

In such hands it was not surprising that the whole congressional power-structure was designed to produce conservative outcomes except in exceptional circumstances such as the early New Deal (1933–37) and LBJ's 'Great Society' Congress (1965–66). The key budgetary committees in the House – Ways and Means (which deals with taxation) and Appropriations (spending) – were deliberately stacked with members of both parties from very safe, very conservative, small-town and rural districts, so that they would be largely immune from inflationary spending pressures.[4] Indeed the Appropriations Committee had been deliberately created in 1921 in order to remove the appropriation of federal funds from the 'authorising' committees, thereby placing a powerful additional constraint on federal government expenditure.[5] Moreover, the Democratic members of Ways and Means handled the committee assignments for their party in the House, and thus could keep 'big spenders' (i.e. northern urban Democrats) away from key committees.

The Senate, with its smaller membership (100), has always been a more individualistic and less rule-bound body than the 435-member House, but in the heyday of the committee–seniority system, it too came under the control of an 'inner club' of senior members: generally southerners with powerful committee chairmanships such as Richard B. Russell of Georgia. Junior members were expected to keep a low profile and serve an apprenticeship before they were admitted to the inner circle of Senate power. Lyndon Johnson, for example, on election to the Senate in 1948, immediately set out to become Russell's protégé so as to gain admittance to the inner club, and was so good at it that by 1953 he had become the Democratic leader in the Senate. Southern gentility, excessive courtesy and deference also became habitual in the Senate to such an extent that journalist William S. White described that body in 1955 as 'the South's revenge for Gettysburg'.[6]

Another peculiarity of the Senate is the tradition of unlimited debate. In the nineteenth century, talking a bill to death was not a very effective strategy because the legislative calendar was relatively uncluttered, and moreover, such conduct was generally regarded as ungentlemanly. As gentility declined somewhat, however, the 'filibuster' was used to destroy legislation that President Woodrow Wilson believed was necessary to fight the First World War. In reaction to this the Senate introduced Rule 22, which provided for the closure of debate if two-thirds of the Senators voted for a 'cloture' motion. This still presented a formidable hurdle for advocates of legislation to surmount, however, and during the era of southern dominance on Capitol Hill southern Senators resorted (usually successfully) to the filibuster if all else failed, particularly on measures that might threaten racial segregation in the South (such as federal anti-lynching legislation in the 1930s).

By specialising rigorously and sacrificing strong centralised partisan leadership Congress also sacrificed much of its power within the federal government.[7] From the Progressive era onwards Congress looked more and more to the presidency for the initiative on major issues. The 1921 Budget Act gave the President the authority to submit an executive budget (and created a Bureau of the Budget to help him), which set the agenda for congressional action on taxing and spending legislation. During the New Deal era the power of the presidency and the federal government was further expanded into many areas of economic and welfare policy. Congress's attempt to tie the President's hands on foreign policy in the late 1930s was ultimately discredited by Pearl Harbor, and after that the Congress surrendered most of its national security prerogatives completely to the presidency. In the 1950s Truman (in Korea with the loss of over 50,000 American lives) and Eisenhower (the Lebanese intervention of 1958) committed US forces to major foreign conflicts without even asking Congress for a declaration of war. Presidents conducted foreign policy by executive agreements (that did not require congressional consent, or even notification) rather than by treaties. Chastened by the experience of the 1930s and impressed by the advent of the nuclear age and the need for instantaneous reactions to crises abroad, Congress tended to give the President the benefit of the doubt in national security matters, while neglecting its own constitutional prerogatives.

By the early 1960s Congress was generally regarded as an outmoded and increasingly irrelevant institution in American government. Liberal, educated opinion saw Congress as a perpetual stumbling-block to reforming legislation. Presidents helped the poor, defended the free world, and supported civil rights for southern blacks. Congress, generally dominated by a conservative coalition of Republicans and southern Democrats (first forged in opposition to FDR's 'court-packing' bill in 1937), dragged its feet on all these matters, and gained a not entirely undeserved reputation for obstructionism, bigotry, and reactionary attitudes. The legislative branch became the chief culprit in what historian, commentator and liberal Democrat James Macgregor Burns described as 'The Deadlock of Democracy'.[8]

Backlash: congressional reform and resurgence in the 1970s

The Vietnam War and Watergate finally made Congress fully aware of how weak it had become *vis-à-vis* the White House. The Gulf of Tonkin Resolution that gave congressional sanction to the Vietnam War sailed through the Congress in one summer afternoon in 1964 with only two maverick Senators in opposition. When it became clear that the US had become involved in a quagmire, Congress also found that it was not easy to disengage in defiance of presidents who wanted to sustain the US military commitment. LBJ had claimed that he did not even need the authority of the Gulf of Tonkin Resolution to commit US forces (he believed that he could do so under his Commander-in-Chief powers), but merely sent it to Congress as a courtesy. Richard Nixon adopted the same rationale when he extended the conflict into neutral Cambodia in 1970, without any congressional consultation or even notification. With foreign policy being conducted through executive agreements, CIA covert operations, and Congress's war power having fallen by the wayside, the legislative branch appeared to have been excluded from national security policy altogether.[9]

On the domestic front the Democratic Congress and the Nixon White House were at loggerheads on a whole series of issues, ranging from Supreme Court nominations to the budget.[10] Nixon began to unilaterally 'impound' (i.e. instruct the Treasury not to release) funds appropriated by Congress: a direct assault on Congress's power of the purse. Frustrated at the influence of congressional committees over the domestic departments Nixon, in his second term, also planned an 'administrative presidency' that would govern as much as possible through executive orders from the White House while ignoring Congress. If Nixon had not been impeded by the onset of the Watergate scandal in 1973–74, he might well have succeeded in effectively closing Congress out of the national government and in establishing important precedents for his presidential successors to follow. The fall of Nixon, however, finally gave the supine Congress the opportunity to reassert its role in the national government.

Much of the impetus for this reassertion of congressional power came from a new generation of liberal Democratic members (particularly after the 'Watergate' election of 1974) that finally brought an end to the grip of the conservative coalition and the committee–seniority system. By reviving the moribund Democratic party caucus in the House, the Democratic 'Young Turks' succeeded in changing the House power-structure quite dramatically. Probably the most significant change was that committee chairs were made subject to a possible confirmation vote by the caucus regardless of their seniority. In early 1975 the three elderly conservative southern Democratic chairs of the Agriculture, Armed Services, and Banking committees were removed by a caucus vote, and one of them was replaced by the fourth-ranking Democratic on the committee.

In addition to the end of strict seniority, the committee chairs lost their absolute control over the committee agenda, staff, and subcommittees.[11] The latter became much more autonomous from the major committees with their chairs being chosen by 'mini-caucuses' of the Democrats on the full committee. The authority of the Speaker was also enhanced as he gained the power to nominate the Democratic members of the very important House Rules Committee, and to act as chairman of a new Steering and Policy Committee of the caucus that was to set party policy and take over the task of making committee assignments from the Democratic members of Ways and Means.

In the Senate there was less of a direct assault on the old power structure than in the House, but the impact of generational change in that body during the 1960s and 1970s saw the emergence of a new generation of ideologically motivated liberal (and later also conservative) Senators who were less willing to defer to their seniors, or 'go along to get along'. The number of votes required to end a filibuster was also reduced from two-thirds (sixty-seven Senators) to three-fifths (sixty) in 1975.[12]

As a result of these internal changes and the lopsided Democratic congressional majorities of the post-Watergate period, Congress finally began to reassert its prerogatives in opposition to the so-called 'Imperial Presidency'.

In 1972 Congress passed the Case Act, which instructed presidents to notify the Senate Foreign Relations Committee and the House Foreign Affairs Committee of all executive agreements concluded with foreign nations. Over Nixon's veto and in an attempt to prevent future Vietnams Congress passed the 1973 War Power Act, giving themselves the power by concurrent resolution (which the President cannot veto) of both Houses to recall US forces committed overseas by the President. Under the Act presidents must also consult Congress before making such a commitment and report to Congress within forty-eight hours. Finally, sixty days from that time the US forces must begin to disengage unless both Houses of Congress have specifically authorised that the commitment continue.

Congress began to display its new-found teeth on other areas of foreign policy. In 1974 it slapped an arms embargo on Turkey after the invasion of Cyprus, and passed the Jackson–Vanik amendment which made the extent of trade with the USSR conditional on the right of Soviet Jews to emigrate. In 1975 Congress finally cut off military aid to Cambodia and South Vietnam, and also to UNITA forces in Angola. The House and Senate Intelligence committees also began an extensive and embarrassing investigation of the CIA. During the Reagan Administration Congress continued to assert its authority by cutting off supplies to the Nicaraguan Contras in defiance of the Reagan Administration, and passing strict economic sanctions of South Africa over Reagan's veto. President Bush was also compelled by political exigencies to obtain specific congressional authorisation to fight the 1991 Gulf War although, like Lyndon Johnson, he denied that it was constitutionally necessary.[13]

In the domestic sphere, Congress reacted to Nixon's attacks on its profligacy and the threat of presidential impoundments by passing the 1974 Congressional Budget Control and Impoundment Act. This Act gave Congress the authority to override presidential impoundments by concurrent resolution, and established congressional budget committees in each House, and a congressional Budget Office, to draw up a congressional budget resolution and reassert congressional authority on fiscal matters over the President and his Office of Management and Budget (OMB). During the 1980s Congress used this process to thwart attempts by the Reagan and Bush administrations to extend Reaganomics beyond the tax and spending cuts in the 1981 budget.[14]

Both the War Powers Act and the Budget Act included a device called the legislative or congressional veto. This device allows Congress to delegate some specific task to the President (for example, the power to commit forces abroad or to impound funds) while giving Congress (in some cases one House or even a congressional committee) the right to overrule that action by concurrent resolution (which since it is not legislation, the president cannot veto). Despite the obvious problem that the legislative veto encroached on the constitutional prerogatives of the executive branch, dozens of congressional veto clauses were written into bills authorising or re-authorising new federal programmes and agencies during the 1970s.[15]

How effective has the reassertion of congressional power been in practice? While there can be no question that Congress has become better informed and less deferential to the executive on foreign and national security policy, the President's greater resources, the Commander-in-Chief power, and the need for rapid responses to overseas crises, still gives the White House the upper hand. Presidents have chosen to ignore the War Powers Act (on grounds of its dubious constitutionality) and Congress has been reluctant to risk being perceived as undermining US forces by putting it into effect (with the exception of the stationing of marines in Lebanon in 1983).

After Carter's abortive hostage rescue mission in Iran in 1979, Reagan's invasion of Grenada and bombing of Lebanon, and Bush's invasion of Panama, Congress huffed and puffed but did nothing to restrict or rescind the intervention, although they had not been consulted in either case. Similarly, President Clinton committed US forces to restore Haitian President Jean-Baptiste Aristide in October 1994 despite evident congressional scepticism. In 1990 President Bush had committed a vast American force to the Persian Gulf region without congressional approval, although, as mentioned above, he did request and was granted a congressional resolution authorising the use of force prior to the commencement of hostilities against Iraq in January 1991.[16]

On the domestic front, Congress had never relinquished its prerogatives to the same extent as in the military–diplomatic sphere, and the budget reform certainly made Capitol Hill less reliant on the OMB and the presidential budget. However, the congressional budgetary process proved unable to contain the record budget deficits of the 1980s or to enhance Congress's reputation for fiscal probity. Congress could dismantle or ignore presidential budgets, but lacking the co-operation of the Oval Office, it could not, by itself, deal with America's fiscal crisis.

The legislative veto proved to be a useful device in restraining the executive and enabling Congress to perform its oversight functions, but since the *Chadha* v. *INS* Supreme Court decision of 1983 outlawed many instances of its use and called its constitutionality into question as a possible violation of the separation of powers, it has become a much less effective weapon.

The essential problem that Congress has been unable to resolve in attempting to reassert its constitutional authority has been that it tried to do so at the same time that it was pursuing the internal reforms that further fragmented its internal power-structure, and thus made it less capable of playing a leading role in the federal government. Despite some strengthening of the authority of the Speaker, the overall result of the reforms in the committee system implemented by the House Democratic caucus was a move from committee government to subcommittee government, and an even greater dispersion of power within the Congress. Such an atomised body is very good at articulating grievances and catering to the narrow material interests of the individual states and districts. It is even less capable, however, of formulating a national programmatic strategy either at home or abroad, and this role of setting the national political agenda by default continues to be held by the executive branch. As long as this situation persists Congress will continue (despite its important prerogatives) to play second fiddle to the White House, even when the branches are controlled by different political parties, as has so frequently been the case in the last quarter-century.

A large part of the reason for Congress's weak and disaggregated power structure lies in the politics of congressional elections to which we now turn.

Congressional elections: 1954–94

With the decline in importance of party identification, incumbency became the decisive advantage in congressional elections. Not only were incumbents invariably re-elected, but they were being re-elected with larger and larger margins of victory. Table 5.1 shows how the victory margins of members of Congress grew after the Second World War, and the number of marginal districts drastically declined. Increasing electoral security for incumbent members also largely explains the Democratic party's forty-year control of the House from 1954 to 1994. After 1930 the Republicans controlled the chamber for only four years (1947/8 and 1953/4) until the political earthquake of the 1994 mid-term elections. It is now necessary to examine the factors underlying incumbency protection and how these affected the internal structures of the House of Representatives.

During the nineteenth century, congressional elections hinged on partisanship and national partisan swings. Single issues and the attributes of individual candidates counted for little. Party bosses chose candidates and voters made their choices on the basis of the national party that they supported. With the decline of party and party identity in this century, incumbency has replaced party as the most essential cue for voters in House elections. House candidates are no longer chosen by party hierarchs but in primary elections, where candidacies are generally self-generated. In presidential election years voters have become adept at splitting their tickets between candidates of different parties at different electoral levels, and recent presidential election winners have possessed notably short 'coat-tails' in comparison to their predecessors of a century ago (see Chapter 12). To the extent that party has come to matter so little in the calculus of contemporary House elections, name-recognition of the candidates on the part of the voters has come to play a decisive role, and for reasons that will become apparent below, incumbents are likely to have far higher name recognition that their challengers.[17]

The security of incumbents (and particularly Democratic incumbents) has also been enhanced by the means employed to draw the boundaries of congressional districts. In most states these are drawn by state legislatures, and when a party controls a state's governorship and both Houses of the legislature, it invariably attempts to 'gerrymander' the congressional district lines to favour its own candidates. Where control is divided between the parties the easiest compromise districting plan to adopt is one that protects incumbents

Table 5.1. *Victory margins in congressional elections, 1972–92*

Year	House % of districts won with 60% and over	% unopposed	total
1972	59	12	71
1974	46	14	60
1976	56	12	68
1978	53	16	69
1980	60	8	68
1982	63	6	69
1984	61	14	75
1986	64	17	81
1988	67	18	85
1990	58	15	73
1992	58	3	61
Mean 1972–1992	59	12	71
Senate			
1972	33	0	33
1974	35	6	41
1976	30	6	36
1978	36	6	42
1980	21	3	24
1982	43	0	43
1984	58	3	61
1986	47	0	47
1988	52	0	52
1990	49	14	63
1992	32	0	32
Mean 1972–1992	40	3	43

Source Data in Roger H. Davidson and Walter J. Oleszek, *Congress and Its Members*, 4th edn (Washington, DC: Congressional Quarterly Press, 1994).

of both parties. As the Democrats traditionally controlled more legislative chambers and had more incumbents, the norms of the redistricting process as traditionally practised obviously favoured them.

In the 1990s, however, two significant developments in the congressional distracting process have complicated the situation and enhanced the prospects of challengers and Republicans. The first are the 1982 amendments to the

Voting Rights Act, which instruct those drawing district lines to ensure blacks and Hispanics are represented in the congressional delegation roughly according to their proportion of a state's population. Secondly, partly as a result of the first factor, the federal courts have become much more involved in the re-districting process. Partisan re-districting plans are now open to court challenges by minorities on the grounds that they fail to meet Voting Rights Act requirements. More minority districts also help the Republicans, since they pack the most solidly Democratic electoral constituencies into overwhelmingly black or Hispanic districts while leaving more 'lily-white' districts that Republican candidates can win. Under the court-ordered plan implemented in Georgia after the 1990 census, for example, the state's US House delegation went from consisting of eight white Democrats, one black Democrat, and one white Republican in 1990, to one white Democrat, three black Democrats, and seven white Republicans after the 1994 elections. Similar effects were apparent in North Carolina and Florida.

The re-districting process has also led to the creation of bizarrely shaped districts, the most notorious recent example being the infamous North Carolina 'bugsplat' depicted below. This district, drawn to encompass the maximum number of minority voters, became the subject of a federal lawsuit by aggrieved white voters in the case of *Shaw* v. *Reno* (1993), where the Supreme Court for the first time recognised the appearance of districts as grounds for a legal challenge, and thus appeared willing to delve further into the re-districting process. The overall consequence of all this is likely to make it harder, though by no means impossible, to gerrymander for exclusive partisan or incumbent advantage.

Another factor that contributed to the protection of incumbents was that members of the House became extremely adept in utilising the perquisites of their office for electoral advantage. Incumbents regularly bombarded their constituents with newsletters and other mailings through use of the congressional free-mailing or 'franking' privilege. They also consistently increased their numbers of personal and committee staff, which, of course, enabled them to perform their constituency casework more effectively. Generous telephone and travel allowances were additionally valuable in this regard, particularly for members whose districts were far from Washington. None of these advantages were available to challengers.

The system of financing congressional campaigns also worked to the advantage of incumbents. After the Federal Elections Campaign Acts of 1971, 1974 and 1976, individuals were allowed to contribute a maximum of $1,000 to a congressional candidate in both the primary and general elections, while Political Action Committees (PACS) could give up to $5,000. (PACs are basically the fund-raising arms of interest groups, and can be formed by corporations, professions, labour unions, or single-issue 'cause' groups.) Due to a loophole in the law opened by the Supreme Court in its 1976 *Buckley* v. *Valeo* decision, PACs may also spend an unlimited amount

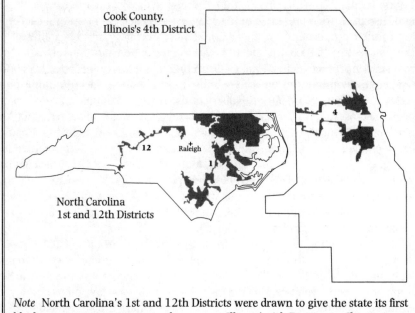

Cook County.
Illinois's 4th District

North Carolina
1st and 12th Districts

Note North Carolina's 1st and 12th Districts were drawn to give the state its first black representatives in ninety-three years. Illinois's 4th District, in Chicago, was drawn to maximise Latino voters.

Reproduced from Roger H. Davidson and Walter J. Oleszek, *Congress and its Members*, 4th edn (Washington, DC: Congressional Quarterly Press, 1994), p. 57.

'on behalf of' a chosen candidate, as long as this spending is not directly co-ordinated with a candidate's campaign. (The direct contribution limits for political parties are the same as for Political Action Committees, though like PACs, state and national parties can channel money to candidates by indirect routes.) Incumbents have been the biggest beneficiaries of direct PAC contributions, and House incumbents on average get over 40 per cent of their total funding from PACs. This is because PACs – particularly the corporate PACs – have placed a priority on protecting ties that they have built up with favourable incumbents over the years (even if that meant supporting Democrats over the ostensibly more pro-business Republicans). The PAC system also allowed incumbents to build up such fearsome electoral arsenals that they effectively discouraged strong challengers from filing against them.[18]

An additional factor that enhanced the electoral advantage of incumbent members of Congress was the post-New Deal system of distributive politics in Washington that enabled incumbent members to claim credit for federal programmes or projects that affected their district.[19] In an age of weak parties, House elections turned into 435 referendums on the performance of individual incumbents, and if a member had consistently 'delivered' for his district, it

Table 5.2. *Distribution of PAC $: 1988 congressional elections*

Category	% total PAC contributions ($99.2m)
House	
Democratic incumbents	54
Republican incumbents	29
Democratic challengers	7
Republican challengers	2
Democratic open-seat candidates	5
Republican open-seat candidates	3
Total incumbents	83
Total Democrats	66
Senate	
Democratic incumbents	34
Republican incumbents	30
Democratic challengers	10
Republican challengers	7
Democratic open-seat candidates	8
Republican open-seat candidates	10
Total incumbents	64
Total Democrats	52

Source Norman J. Ornstein, Thomas E. Mann, and Michael J. Malbin,
Vital Statistics on Congress, 1989–90 (Washington, DC: Congressional
Quarterly Press, 1990).

made little sense to dislodge him for a newcomer with no seniority. The fact
that the news media has become the principal intermediary between voters
and government also provided yet another advantage to House incumbents,
since given their position, they have had many more opportunities to generate
favourable media coverage on local television stations and in newspapers than
their challengers.

A significant factor in retarding Republican prospects in House elections
was that party's grip on the presidency after 1968, which meant that they
suffered from a succession of typical mid-term election swings against the
White House party. Another problem was the relatively poor quality of
Republican House candidates. This was in a large part a further consequence
of the Republicans' presidential success, which naturally led able young Republicans to concentrate on political opportunities in the White House or in
the Executive Branch rather than run for the House back home. Moreover,
the rewards of a House salary were not particularly attractive to an aspiring
Republican businessman or lawyer. Finally, since the New Deal, Democrats

have generally believed that government should be put to work for people, and thus they effectively localised House elections into contests over who was more likely to put more federal dollars into the district. Republicans, by contrast, dislike government and thus felt uncomfortable with the whole tenor of House politics in the 1970s and 1980s. Voters expected their Congressman to look after their interests in Washington, and other things being equal, this factor worked massively in favour of Democratic candidates, even in open-seat contests where there was no incumbent on the ballot.[20]

Interestingly, Senators were significantly more vulnerable to defeat than House members. Indeed unlike the House, the Senate actually changed hands twice between the parties during the 1980s, and did so again with the House in 1994.

One factor that is important here is that Senate races became more national contests than those for the House, because the Senate deals with national and foreign policy issues such as Supreme Court confirmations and treaties, where incumbents have to take clear positions. In relation to this factor the 100 Senators have a far higher level of visibility in the media than the 435 House members, and thus could not so easily control how they were perceived by their constituents. The larger populations of the states and their more heterogeneous electorates also made it impossible for a Senator to 'service' them in the way that an effective House member could service his district. Finally, the higher profile of Senate races and the greater focus on national issues made it somewhat easier for challengers and Republicans to raise money and thus fight a competitive race.

The requirements of re-election thus entailed that members of both Houses had to seek a greater piece of congressional turf so as to service their districts, raise funds, and control their media visibility. This, in turn, led to a highly decentralised Congress, with a good deal of power for individual members, but institutionally weak. The electoral process also encouraged the voters' tendency to love their Congressman, but increasingly despise Congress as an institution. Popular enthusiasm for congressional term limitations and the Republican takeover of the House in 1994 indicated, however, that the American public had finally connected its discontent with Congress to the workings of the congressional elections process.

The legislative process

Bills can be introduced in either House (with the exception of finance bills, which must begin in the House). In the Senate the sponsor of a bill must be recognised by the presiding officer in the chair (a role usually rotated among the junior Senators), while in the House bills are dropped into a box or 'hopper'. The bills are then referred to a committee or committees by the Speaker or the Senate presiding officer.

Both chambers also pass resolutions to set their own rules and to express their sentiments on topical issues. These lack the force of law and do not

require the President's signature, except for Joint Resolutions, which
in all but name and do require the presidential signature. Joint Re
are also used to pass constitutional amendments (although the President has
no role in the amendment process) and a two-thirds majority in both Houses
is required.

Most bills die at the committee stage. After a bill has been referred to one
of the permanent Standing Committees of the House or Senate, the committee
generally refers it to one of its subcommittees. The subcommittee may hold
hearings and take testimony on the bill. Finally, the bill is 'marked up' or
written and voted on line by line. After the subcommittee has reported the bill
the same procedure takes place in the full committee. The committee may
report the bill favourably or unfavourably, or it may vote to 'table' the bill,
thereby allowing it to die in committee.

Getting a tabled bill out of committee in the House is notoriously hard,
requiring a 'discharge petition' to be signed by over half of the members of
the House (218) and then voted on. Very few of these succeed. In the Senate
this is not a problem since there is no 'germaneness' requirement, and bills
tabled in committee can be brought to the floor as amendments to a completely
different bill (except finance bills).

Once the bill is out of committee its chances of ultimate passage are excellent. In the Senate bills go directly from committee to the floor. In the
House most non-routine bills (except for finance bills) have to go through
the Rules Committee, since unless a bill gets a 'rule' for floor debate it will
generally die. It is possible for a majority of members on the floor to get a
bill out of the Rules Committee either by using a discharge petition or passing
a motion to 'suspend the rules' (which needs a two-thirds majority), but it
is very difficult to do. Rules given by the Rules Committee vary, but they
generally fall into two broad categories: 'open' rules permit amendments on
the floor, while 'closed' rules set a strict timetable for debate and allow few,
if any, amendments.

The norms governing floor debate are quite different in each chamber. In
the House the chamber generally turns itself into 'a committee of the whole'
for the purpose of floor action because the quorum for that (100) is smaller
than for the House proper (218). The chair of the committee sponsoring the
bill initiates the debate, giving equal time to supporters and opponents. If
amendments are permitted, they must be relevant to the subject of the bill.
No member may generally speak for more than five minutes on an amendment. For the final vote the committee of the whole then reports the bill back
to the House proper (i.e. itself) and the final vote is taken.

In the Senate, there are no closed rules and amendments can be offered at
any time. Except for appropriations bills, these need not even be germane to
the subject of the bill. The Senate also has a long tradition of 'unlimited' debate
(again, with the exception of appropriations bills), which allows a determined
Senator or groups of Senators to 'filibuster' or attempt to talk a bill to death.

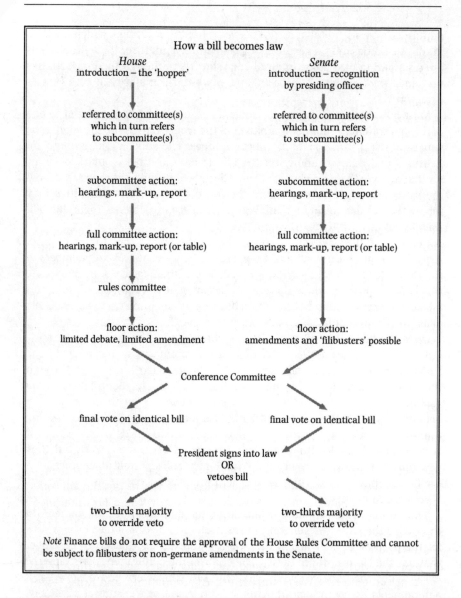

How a bill becomes law

House
introduction – the 'hopper'

Senate
introduction – recognition
by presiding officer

referred to committee(s)
which in turn refers
to subcommittee(s)

referred to committee(s)
which in turn refers
to subcommittee(s)

subcommittee action:
hearings, mark-up, report

subcommittee action:
hearings, mark-up, report

full committee action:
hearings, mark-up, report (or table)

full committee action:
hearings, mark-up, report (or table)

rules committee

floor action:
limited debate, limited amendment

floor action:
amendments and 'filibusters' possible

Conference Committee

final vote on identical bill

final vote on identical bill

President signs into law
OR
vetoes bill

two-thirds majority
to override veto

two-thirds majority
to override veto

Note Finance bills do not require the approval of the House Rules Committee and cannot be subject to filibusters or non-germane amendments in the Senate.

The filibuster can only be limited by invoking Rule 22 which permits 'cloture' (closure of debate and an immediate final vote) if sixty Senators (three-fifths of the total) vote for it.

If the House and Senate have passed different versions of a bill then a conference committee of the two chambers is necessary to iron out the differences. These committees are composed of an equal number of members from each chamber picked by the chairs of the House and Senate Standing Committees that dealt with the bill. Any decisions taken in conference committees must be approved by a majority of each chamber's delegation. Identical versions of the bill are then passed on the floor of each chamber.

The bill then goes to the President's desk for signature. If he vetoes the bill, it must be re-passed by a majority of two-thirds in each House to override his veto and become law (except for 'pocket vetoes', where Congress adjourns during the ten-day period that the President has to consider a bill, and all the bills on the President's desk automatically die). Although presidents are sometimes overridden, the occurrence is rare enough to make the veto a very effective weapon indeed.[21]

Committees

Most of the important business of the Congress is conducted in committees. The most important committees are the Standing Committees with permanent memberships that deal with the various areas of government and administration (see Table 5.3). There are also Select Committees – appointed for limited or *ad hoc* purposes, such as the Senate Watergate committee or the Iran–Contra committees in each House – and joint committees of the two houses, the most important of which, of course, are Conference Committees. House members have only one major committee assignment and Senators have two or more – the division between major and minor being shown in Table 5.3. Chairmen now have to elected by a secret ballot in the conference (or caucus in the case of the Democrats) of the majority party, although in most cases seniority still obtains. No member in either chamber can chair more than one full committee.

These days much of the real legislative action takes place in subcommittees rather than in the full committee. Subcommittees have become more important because members have powerful electoral motivations to control their own small piece of legislative turf, particularly if there is a significant constituency interest involved.[22] At one time a president knew that if he got the full committee chair on his side his measure would get through. These days chairmen no longer control the Standing Committees or their subcommittees to such an extent.[23]

In the House there is still something of a hierarchy among the committees although it is not as rigid as it once was. Fifty years ago the three most important committees – Ways and Means, Appropriations, and Rules – virtually dictated to the rest of the House. These were the committees for the members who sought a long House career and saw their job as restraining upward pressure on the public purse. Since the congressional revolution of the 1970s the situation has changed. These are still the three most important committees, but they no longer dominate to such an extent. The House floor has become more important and the new Budget Committee has taken on some of the financial watchdog functions of Appropriations and Ways and Means. Ways and Means Democrats also lost control over the Democratic assignments to the other committees.

Table 5.3. *Standing committees of the House and Senate, 1990*

House *	Senate
Exclusive	Major
Appropriations	Agriculture, Nutrition and Forestry
Rules	Appropriations
Ways and Means	Armed Services
Major	Banking Housing and Urban Affairs
Agriculture	Budget
Armed Services	Commerce, Science, Transportation
Banking, Finance, and Urban Affairs	Energy and Natural Resources
Education and Labor	Environment and Public Works
Energy and Commerce	Finance
Foreign Affairs	Foreign Relations
Judiciary	Governmental Affairs
Public Works and Transportation	Judiciary
Non-major	Labor and Human Resources
Budget	Minor
District of Columbia	Rules and Administration
Government Operations	Small Business
House Administration	Veterans' Affairs
Interior and Insular Affairs	Select
Merchant Marine and Fisheries	Aging
Post Office and Civil Service	Ethics
Science, Space, and Technology	Indian Affairs
Small Business	Intelligence
Standards of Official Conduct	
Veteran's Affairs	
Select	
Aging	
Children, Youth, and Families	
Hunger	
Intelligence	
Narcotics Abuse and Control	

Note * These classifications are from the rules of the House Democratic caucus, but are basically adhered to by the Republicans. After taking control of the House in 1994 however, the House Republican Conference abolished some of the minor committees and renamed several of the others.

Source James Q. Wilson, *American Government*, 4th edn (Lexington, MA: D. C. Heath & Co., 1992).

The Rules Committee, which operated as an independent power centre during the heyday of the committee–seniority system in the 1950s, had its authority and independence reduced by an early 1970s decision by the House Democratic caucus to allow the Speaker to name the Democratic members of the committee. These days Rules operates as an arm of the majority party leadership in the House.

In the Senate, which is less focused on budgetary matters than the House, there is less of a clear-cut hierarchy among committees. Because of the Senate's foreign-policy prerogatives, however, the Foreign Relations and Armed Services committees are much more important than they are in the House. Judiciary is also important because it deals with presidential nominations to the federal judiciary, but it is not an assignment eagerly sought by senators, since there is little electoral reward and much potential embarrassment, as the members found after the tawdry public interrogations of Clarence Thomas and Anita Hill in 1991.[24]

The party structure

As we have seen, the nineteenth-century Congress tended to be rather partisan. Most votes were party-line votes and the party leadership held control over their members through discipline and patronage inducements. In this century, party has become less important because declining party identification and the direct primary have meant that members increasingly rely on their own resources to get elected and re-elected. Inside the Congress that has meant assiduous attention to one's constituency and when the party leadership got in the way, it was the leadership that had to back down. As former Speaker Tip O'Neill said, 'All politics is local.'

Yet the party leadership positions are still the most important and visible positions inside Congress. The leadership structure in each House is illustrated in the diagram below. At the top of the ladder in the House is the Speaker – not an impartial presiding officer, but very much the leader of the majority party and third in line to the presidency – effectively chosen in the caucus of the majority party. Below that are the floor leaders of the majority and minority parties, who count heads and try to mobilise their members on particular issues. In recent years the position of Majority Leader has effectively become that of the Speaker-in-Waiting, while the Minority Leader becomes Speaker if his party should control the House. Beneath the floor leaders come the positions of Majority and Minority Whip, who act as the eyes and ears of the leadership, assessing just what the general opinion of the congressional party is likely to be. All these positions are elected by the caucuses of the majority and minority parties.[25]

In the Senate there is no position equivalent to that of Speaker. In theory the Vice-President presides but he only appears when his vote is likely to matter. The next highest position, President *pro tempore*, is largely ceremonial and by tradition goes to the longest-serving Senator of the Majority party. The really important positions are those of Majority and Minority leader. Between them the two party leaders attempt to set the Senate agenda and keep business flowing through a notoriously unruly body. Of course, the greater flexibility of Senate rules gives much more power to the Senate Minority Leader than his House counterpart, who lacks effective weapons such as the filibuster to thwart the will of an overbearing majority party.

Newt Gingrich, Speaker of the House of Representatives, is sworn in.

The first Republican House Speaker since 1954, Newt Gingrich (b. 1943), is also the most visible and powerful holder of that office in the modern era. Unlike most of his Democratic counterparts of recent years, Gingrich did not reach this position by keeping his head down and working his way slowly up the party hierarchy. Indeed, since his election to the House from a suburban Atlanta, Georgia, district in 1978, he has made his reputation as a gadfly, and his rise to leadership among the House Republicans was a consequence of relentless self-promotion, determination, and the desperation of a party that seemed to be stalled in a permanent minority status. After his ascent to the Speaker's chair, Gingrich immediately took control of the national political agenda away from the Clinton White House, as he passed most of the 'Contract With America' – the programme on which he fought the 1994 elections – through the House on party-line votes. He also restructured the House committee system and inaugurated a highly partisan and confrontational style of leadership. If the Gingrich Speakership, which violates all the norms of the pre-Gingrich House, is perceived as a success, it may set the pattern for a much more partisan and centralised House of Representatives in the early decades of the next century.

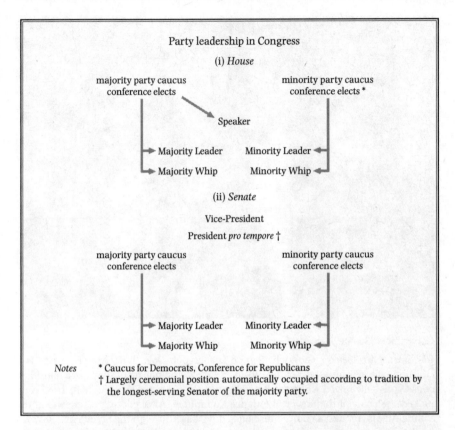

Party leadership in Congress

(i) *House*

majority party caucus
conference elects

minority party caucus
conference elects *

Speaker

Majority Leader   Minority Leader

Majority Whip   Minority Whip

(ii) *Senate*

Vice-President

President *pro tempore* †

majority party caucus
conference elects

minority party caucus
conference elects

Majority Leader   Minority Leader

Majority Whip   Minority Whip

Notes   * Caucus for Democrats, Conference for Republicans
† Largely ceremonial position automatically occupied according to tradition by
the longest-serving Senator of the majority party.

The leadership can still play some cards if it wants to get members to go along with them: projects for the district, better assignments, and help with a pet piece of legislation. Threats are rarely effective these days, however, and the leadership knows that in a pinch a member will always vote for his district ahead of his party, since this is the cardinal rule of survival in the modern-day house. Yet Congress has been more partisan in recent years. We saw that the rate of party voting has risen from Figure 5.1. The two parties in each chamber are also now pretty internally consistent in terms of ideology. Liberal Republicans and conservative Democrats are becoming rarer and rarer in Congress. There are two basic explanations for this.

First, since the election of the ideologically conservative Republican Ronald Reagan to the presidency in 1980, congressional Republicans have felt obliged to mobilise on behalf of a radical conservative agenda, while congressional Democrats have felt duty-bound to resist such proposals.

Secondly, and perhaps more importantly, across the country members of Congress now have to appeal to very similar constituencies of activists in their primary electorates: blacks, feminists, peace activists, labour, and environmentalists for Democrats; the religious right, anti-abortionists, business

Robert Dole, Senate Majority Leader

In contrast to Speaker Gingrich, Senate Leader Bob Dole (b. 1923) of Kansas is a consummate Washington political insider. Dole's original reputation as a hard-line conservative mellowed when the Republicans took control of the Senate in 1981, and he became chair of the powerful Finance Committee. After piloting a renewal of the Voting Rights Act and a compromise budget package through the Senate in 1982, his stock as a deal-maker rose considerably, and he was easily elected to succeed Howard Baker as Majority Leader in 1984. Resuming this position in 1995, Dole became responsible for the passage of the Republican 'Contract With America' through a highly fragmented and individualistic chamber, far less amenable to partisan control than Gingrich's House. Since his election to the Senate in 1968, Dole has served as Republican National Chairman under President Nixon, was President Gerald Ford's Vice-Presidential running-mate in 1976, and ran for the Republican presidential nomination in 1980 and 1988, and again in 1996. His wife, Elizabeth Hanaford Dole, was a Cabinet member under Presidents Reagan and Bush, and the Doles have often been described as the ultimate Washington, DC 'power couple'.

groups, the NRA (National Rifle Association) for Republicans. As a reflection of facing a similar mix of local interests whether in Boston, Atlanta, or Los Angeles, Democrats and Republicans from around the country have come to resemble their fellow-partisans much more than they did fifty years ago.

Given the election of a Republican House under the Speakership of the outspokenly confrontational Congressman Newt Gingrich in 1994, the higher partisanship of recent years within Congress will likely persist into the next century.

Conclusion: Congress in crisis and a Republican Congress

In the last quarter-century there has been a clear transformation in Congress. The seniority system has been substantially broken and power in both chambers has devolved more towards junior members. Subcommittees have become more important; staffs have grown; and members no longer defer to the President but are increasingly likely to question the actions of the executive. Members are also generally better informed and more energetic than they were in the 1950s.

The legislative branch tried to regain important prerogatives lost to the executive in the Imperial Presidency phase. Since Vietnam, Congress has been very obstreperous on foreign policy, with the War Powers Act the most important symbol of its reassertion of power. In the area of the budget, Congress created the Congressional Budget Office (CBO) and its own budget committees in a successful attempt to take more of a role in the budget process. Congress also did not hesitate to use the legislative veto to rein in the presidency and the bureaucracy, despite its dubious constitutionality.

Yet other changes have meant that although Congress played a greater role in the governmental process than it did in the 1950s and 1960s, it was hard for the institution to play a constructive role. Internally it had become too fragmented and power was too evenly dispersed for Congress to be able to act quickly and effectively in a crisis. Indeed Congress has not been keen to assume more responsibility for day-to-day government, since that might jeopardise its pattern of relationships with various constituencies. What we have in the modern Congress, is, in a sense, power without responsibility.

The question of representativeness also became worrisome. The Democrats controlled the House of Representatives for forty years from 1954 to 1994, and it is hard to think of another major legislative chamber in a contemporary liberal Democracy that had been controlled by one party for so long. The immense advantages held by House incumbents also began to make a mockery of the electoral process.

In the early 1990s the unease felt by political scientists and commentators over developments in Congress began to be reflected at the mass level as popular opinion regarding Congress hit new levels of disgust. Congress's apparent inability to deal with pressing national problems such as the ballooning budget deficit, and a series of scandals regarding abuses at the House Bank and Post Office were the main contributors to this angry mood. By early 1994 Congress had a 14 per cent approval rating and strong public support existed for measures such as congressional term limitations (already approved in many states). Members of Congress themselves had become adept at denigrating the institution, while extolling their own personal abilities to their electors. For the last two decades such a strategy paid great dividends for incumbents although it added to public discontent with the institution in which they served.

But in 1994 the strategy failed to work as the national anti-Congress fever

---

The 'Gingrich Effect'

Committee	New Name
Agriculture	
Appropriations	
Armed Services	National Security
Banking, Finance and Urban Affairs	Banking and Financial Services
Budget	
Education and Labor	Economic and Educational Opportunities
Energy and Commerce	Commerce
Foreign Affairs	International Relations
Government Operations	Government Reform and Oversight
House Administration	House Oversight
Judiciary	
Natural Resources	Resources
Public Works and Transportation	Transportation and Infrastructure
Rules	
Science, Space and Technology	Science
Select Intelligence	
Small Business	
Standards of Official Conduct	
Veterans Affairs	
Ways and Means	

Committees eliminated: Post Office; District of Columbia; Merchant Marine and Fisheries

---

Since taking office after the 1994 congressional elections, House Speaker Newt Gingrich has introduced a number of significant changes in the House committee system. In addition to the changes illustrated above, Gingrich reduced the membership of most committees, altered the jurisdictions of several, and eliminated some 25 of the House's 115 subcommittees. He also breached the seniority rule in selecting the chairs of the Appropriations, Judiciary, and Commerce committees, preferring younger Republicans who were committed to the Republican legislative agenda. The power of committee chairs was further restricted by limiting them to no more than three two-year terms, prohibiting the chair's casting the 'proxy' votes of absent committee members, ending the practice of 'multiple referral' by which legislation could be sent to a number of committees whose chairs claimed some jurisdiction over the matter at hand, and reducing committee staffs by approximately one-third. Speaker Gingrich also cut the budgets of congressional support agencies such as the Library of Congress and the Congressional Budget Office, and ended congressional financing for the single-interest 'caucuses' such as the Black Caucus and the Women's Caucus. In terms of procedure the Republicans promised to allow more 'open rules' (permitting the submission of amendments to floor debate), introduced a rule requiring a three-fifths majority for tax increases, and fulfilled their popular campaign pledge to make Congress subject to his own laws.

The net effect of these changes and Gingrich's conduct of the office constituted a major reassertion of the power of the party leaderhip and the House Speaker, making Gingrich the most powerful Speaker since Joe Cannon at the turn of the century.

and the unpopularity of Democratic President Bill Clinton upset the usual rules for congressional elections and led to the election of a Republican Senate and the first Republican House since 1954. This change in partisan control of the House brings with it the possibility of the passage of congressional term limitations which would entail the complete unravelling of the seniority structure, and might lead either to Congress's complete eclipse as a national governing institution, or perhaps to a much more partisan and centralised leadership in both Houses. In Speaker Gingrich's 'Contract With America' the Republicans also committed themselves to reform of the committee system (primarily by reducing the number of committees and subcommittees); a loosening of the rules on floor debate; the line-item veto for the President on appropriations bills (giving the President the power to veto individual items rather than reject the bill *in toto*); a change in House rules requiring that all tax increases receive the approval of three-fifths of the House; and a balanced budget amendment to the Constitution.

The 1994 Republican landslide was a further indication of the vast public discontent with Congress, and perhaps provided a final opportunity for Congress to prove that it could still be an effective branch of the federal government, and not totally beholden to powerful private interests and parish-pump politics. Whatever transpires under Speaker Gingrich, in the absence of a serious effort by Congress to address pressing national economic and social concerns, the future for a powerful legislative branch in American national government in the twenty-first century looks rather bleak.

Notes

1 Alexander Hamilton, James Madison and John Jay, *The Federalist Papers* (New York: New American Library, 1961), p. 322.
2 See Peters, *The American Speakership in Historical Perspective* pp. 52–91.
3 On the revolt of 1910 see *ibid.*
4 On the old politics of the budget process see Aaron Wildavsky, *The New Politics of the Budget Process* (Glenview, IL: Scott, Foresman, & Co., 1988), pp. 1–119.
5 While the House and Senate Armed Services Committees, for example, might draw up a bill authorising the construction of a military base and pass it through both chambers, not a cent of the funds to build the base can be released unless or until separate appropriating legislation has been passed. Moreover, the amount of funds released may be more (unlikely) or less than the amount stipulated in the authorising legislation. The subcommittees of the Appropriations committees in each house (in this case the Armed Services Subcommittees) that write the thirteen annual Appropriations bills are therefore arguably more influential than the more visible authorising committees.
6 William S. White, *Citadel: The Story of the US Senate* (New York: Harper & Brothers, 1956. See also Donald R. Matthews, *US Senators and Their World* (New York: Vintage, 1960).
7 On Congress's decline of power *vis-à-vis* the presidency, see Sundquist, *the Decline and Resurgence of Congress*, pp. 37–195.

8 James MacGregor Burns, *The Deadlock of Democracy: Four Party Politics in America* (Englewood Cliffs, NJ: Prentice Hall, 1963).

9 On the erosion of the war power see Arthur Schlesinger, Jr, *The Imperial Presidency* (Boston: Houghton Mifflin, 1973).

10 On Nixon's deteriorating relations with Congress see A. James Reichley, *Conservatives in an Age of Change: The Nixon and Ford Administrations* (Washington, DC: Brookings Institution, 1981).

11 On the congressional revolution of the 1970s and the move to 'subcommittee government' see Sundquist, *The Decline and Resurgence of Congress*, pp. 367–414.

12 On the changes in the Senate see Sinclair, *The Transformation of the US Senate*.

13 On Congress's new-found assertiveness on foreign policy see Thomas M. Franck and Edward Weisband, *Foreign Policy by Congress* (New York: Oxford University Press, 1979).

14 On the new budget process see Sundquist, *The Decline and Resurgence of Congress*, pp. 199–237.

15 On the legislative veto see *ibid.*, pp. 344–66.

16 The resolution passed both Houses after heated debate, particularly in the Senate, where the margin of victory was only 52–47.

17 See Jacobson, *The Politics of Congressional Elections*.

18 See *ibid.*

19 See Mayhew, *Congress*; and Fiorina, *Congress*.

20 On the Democratic bias in House elections see Ehrenhalt, *The United States of Ambition*; and Gary Jacobson, *The Electoral Origins of Divided Government: Competition in US House Elections, 1946–1988* (Boulder, CO: Westview Press, 1990).

21 From 1789 to 1984 of the 1,393 presidential vetoes, only 96 (7 per cent) were overridden in Congress. Data from James W. Davis, *The American Presidency: A New Perspective* (New York: Harper & Row, 1987), p. 152.

22 See Mayhew, *Congress*, and Fiorina, *Congress*.

23 See Roger H. Davidson, 'Subcommittee Government: New Channels for Policymaking' in Thomas E. Mann and Norman J. Ornstein (eds), *The New Congress*, (Washington, DC: American Enterprise Institute, 1981), pp. 99–133.

24 Despite the fact that four Democrat women were elected to the Senate in 1992 by using the committee's treatment of Hill as an major issue, none of them were particularly keen to sit on Judiciary, although eventually Diane Feinstein of California and Carole Moseley-Braun of Illinois agreed to do so.

25 The Republican insist on calling their party meeting a 'conference'. On party leadership and leadership elections in Congress see Robert L. Peabody, *Leadership in Congress: Stability, Succession, and Change* (Boston: Little, Brown & Co., 1976).

6

The Supreme Court and the federal judiciary

The role of the judiciary in American politics and government is probably greater than in any other advanced industrial society. Issues affecting the everyday lives of American citizens, such as race relations, sexual morality, abortion, criminal procedure, the relationship between Church and State, that are invariably decided in the democratic political process in other liberal democracies, are resolved in the courts in the United States. The high degree of controversy over the nomination of Judges Robert Bork and Clarence Thomas to the Supreme Court in recent years has demonstrated how high the political stakes have become in Supreme Court appointments, as the Court has acquired the decisive voice on an ever-larger range of issues.

Courts play such a decisive role in contemporary American politics because they have the power of judicial review, that is, the power to declare acts of Congress, state legislatures, or any other official acts in violation of the US Constitution, and therefore invalid. This power is not explicitly granted by the 1787 Constitution. Article III, Section I of the Constitution merely states that: 'The judicial power of the United States, shall be vested in one Supreme Court, and in such inferior courts as Congress may from time to time ordain and establish' while Section II states that 'The judicial power shall extend to all cases, in law and equity, arising under this constitution.'[1]

There are good grounds, however, for believing that judicial review was intended by the framers. Firstly, judicial review fits very well into their generally patrician attitude towards government and their contempt for direct democracy. It also accords perfectly with Madison's checking and balancing scheme for the federal institutions set out in *Federalist* 51. Finally, in *Federalist* 78, Alexander Hamilton presents a strong argument for judicial review. He argues that the Court is the 'least dangerous' branch of the federal government because it has no forces directly at its disposal to enforce its decisions, and therefore must rely on the co-operation of the executive and legislative branches. Hamilton argues further that the power of judicial review is justified because the Constitution represents the real, permanent will of the people of the United States as opposed to the temporary will of the legislature:

A constitution is, in fact, and must be regarded by the judges as, a fundamental law. It therefore belongs to them to ascertain its meaning as well as the meaning of any particular act proceeding from the legislative body. If there should happen to be an irreconcilable variance between the two, that which has the superior obligation and validity ought, of course, to be preferred; or, in other words, the Constitution ought to be preferred to the statute, the intention of the people to the intention of their agents.[2]

Brief history of the Court

The Court did not immediately use the power of judicial review to strike down acts of Congress. The power was first asserted in the famous case of *Marbury* v. *Madison* in 1803, in defiance of President Thomas Jefferson, the dominant political figure of the age. *Marbury* demonstrated the formidable political skills of Chief Justice (and strong Federalist) John Marshall by giving Jefferson the short-term policy result he wanted (the replacement of several judicial appointees from the previous administration) while simultaneously striking down the 1789 Judiciary Act, and thereby setting a devastating precedent. Later, the supremacy of federal law over state law was established in the case of *McCulloch* v. *Maryland* in 1819. Marshall, the third Chief Justice of the United States, was unquestionably the greatest, since during his long reign at the Court (1801–35) he established the Court's authority and that of the supremacy of the federal government over the states.

The Court did not strike down another federal law, however, until Marshall's successor Roger Taney (1836–64) presided over a Court that was

Table 6.1. *The Chief Justices of the US*

Chief Justice	Appointed by	Term	Years
John Jay	Washington	1789–1795	5
Oliver Ellsworth	Washington	1796–1800	4
John Marshall	Adams	1801–1835	34
Roger B. Taney	Jackson	1836–1864	24
Salmon P. Chase	Lincoln	1864–1873	8
Morrison R. Waite	Grant	1874–1888	14
Melville Fuller	Cleveland	1888–1910	21
Edward D. White *	Taft	1910–1921	11
William H. Taft	Harding	1921–1930	8
Charles E. Hughes	Hoover	1930–1941	11
Harlan F. Stone *	FDR	1941–1946	5
Fred M. Vinson	Truman	1946–1953	7
Earl Warren	Eisenhower	1953–1969	16
Warren Bruger	Nixon	1969–1986	17
William H. Rehnquist *	Reagan	1986–	

Note * Already serving on the Court as an Associate Justice at the time of appointment.

bedeviled by the issue of slavery – as was every other American political institution of the time. That decision, the most disastrous in the history of the Court, was the case of *Dred Scott* v. *Sanford* in 1857. The runaway slave Dred Scott was residing in Minnesota, a free territory, but his former master claimed him back. The Court found against Scott, declaring that since slaves were not citizens of the US the 'Missouri Compromise' which prohibited slavery in the northern territories was unconstitutional. The Court's attempt to resolve the issue judicially failed completely, and the *Dred Scott* decision increased the national polarisation over slavery and probably accelerated the outbreak of the Civil War.

In the period from the end of the Civil War to the New Deal, the Court concerned itself with the issue of government regulation of the economy. During this time the Court was mainly preoccupied with the issue of private property rights. They interpreted the 'due process' and 'equal protection' clauses of the Fourteenth Amendment (passed in 1868 primarily to protect newly freed slaves from hostile state action) as also protecting private property and corporations from hostile state action, namely regulation: 'nor shall any state deprive any person of life, liberty or property, without due process of law; nor deny to any person within its jurisdiction the equal protection of the laws'.

Reflecting the *laissez-faire*, Social Darwinist public consensus of late nineteenth-century America, the Supreme Court treated business corporations as 'persons' and thus became committed to a very activist posture in the regulatory area, deciding what kinds of regulation of property were permissible and which were not. The Court proceeded to uphold injunctions against strikers, limited regulation of industry and application of the anti-trust laws, and struck down the federal income tax, child labour laws, and legislation limiting workers' hours. Nevertheless the Court did not dismantle all efforts at regulation and did permit safety legislation to pass constitutional muster. The justices could not resolve the issue of the constitutionality of the regulation of private property and so they vacillated, and thus entangled themselves more and more with detailed economic questions that were generally beyond their competence to resolve.

At the same time as it was tormented by the thought of violating the property rights apparently guaranteed under the Fourteenth Amendment, the Court showed very little interest in interpreting the Fourteenth and Fifteenth Amendments to protect black voting and civil rights in the southern states after the end of Reconstruction in 1876. In the case of *Plessy* v. *Ferguson* 1896, the Court decided that segregation could be upheld under the rule of 'separate but equal' (separate facilities for the races were constitutional so long as they provided equally for each race), and despite several challenges from the NAACP (National Association for the Advancement of Colored People) and others, they did virtually nothing to protect black voting rights until after the Second World War.

The Court adhered to its generally pro-business attitudes during the Progressive era, and although justices such as the legendary Oliver Wendell Holmes (appointed by Theodore Roosevelt) and Louis Brandeis (the first Jewish Justice, appointed by Woodrow Wilson) consistently challenged the court's pro-business judicial activism and its lack of concern for civil liberties, they were generally in a dissenting minority. Holmes's 'legal realist' jurisprudence, which challenged the Court's authority to strike down acts of Congress in the name of a higher law (his position came close to saying 'the law is what judges say it is'), reflected Progressive opinion's view of the conservative judicial activism of the time.

With the advent of Franklin Roosevelt's New Deal the Court, dominated by justices appointed by the conservative Republican presidents of the 1920s, proceeded to dismantle several of its key features, particularly the National Recovery Administration (NRA) and the Agricultural Adjustment Act (AAA). After his landslide re-election in 1936 a frustrated Roosevelt set out to deal with the obstreperous 'nine old men' of the Supreme Court. He proposed to Congress his infamous 'court-packing' bill that would have allowed him to appoint a new Supreme Court justice for every sitting justice over the age of seventy. Since six of the nine justices were in this category, he would have been able to appoint six new justices – enough for a New Deal majority.

Despite Roosevelt's popularity, his court-packing bill was unpopular with both the public and Congress, who were uncomfortable with such direct executive branch meddling with the independence of the federal judiciary.[3] The Court also defused the threat of the court-packing bill by an opportune change in its approach to New-Deal legislation. Justice Owen Roberts, a Hoover appointee, voted with the four justices more sympathetic to the New Deal to uphold the 1937 Fair Labor Standards Act, and after the so-called 'switch in time that saved the nine', the Roosevelt plan collapsed in Congress from lack of support from the President's own party, and the Court also ceased to interfere with New-Deal legislation. During the remainder of Roosevelt's presidency he was able to appoint all nine justices (including Hugo Black, William O. Douglas, and Felix Frankfurter) who took the Court out of the area of government regulation of the economy altogether, and began to move the federal judiciary gradually towards a greater concern with civil liberties.

The Warren Court (1953–69)

Under Chief Justice Earl Warren, appointed by President Eisenhower in 1953, the Supreme Court embarked on a course of liberal judicial activism unprecedented in its history up to that point. Despite Warren's background as the Republican Governor of California, during his time as Chief Justice (1953–69) the Supreme Court issued a series of landmark liberal rulings on a whole range of sensitive social issues. As a result the role of the federal courts in the American political process was expanded greatly, but its political profile was also raised to a dangerous degree. By the mid-1960s presidential candidates were openly campaigning against the Supreme Court, and one of the unfortunate consequences of the Warren years has been the intense politicisation of court appointments and the Senate confirmation process over the past quarter-century.

Nevertheless it can be argued that without the decisions of the Warren Court America would not have dismantled segregation so rapidly, nor instituted fair voting procedures. Court decisions did end the deadlock in the political process on these issues and also legitimised the demands by black Americans and other minorities for full civil rights. On the other hand, the Warren Court's liberal rulings in the area of sexual morality, criminal procedure, and Church/State relations, far from creating a consensus among the public and legitimising social change, actually contributed to prolonged national cleavages on these questions and made the Court a perennial electoral issue. On race the Warren Court was reflecting changing attitudes in American society and breaking a deadlock on the issue maintained by segregationist southern Democrats in Congress. On the other matters the Court got ahead of public opinion, and given its slender democratic credentials, that is a rather dangerous place for an elitist and unaccountable body to be.[4]

The Warren revolution first became apparent on the issue of segregation. In the case of *Brown* v. *Board of Education* in 1954, the Court overturned the *Plessy* v. *Ferguson* decision and ruled that separation of the races in education (and, by implication, transport and public accommodation) was unconstitutional. As we have seen in Chapters 1 and 2, the Brown decision ignited a political revolution in the southern states and in American society as a whole. Over the next decade the Court would gradually dismantle most of the infrastructure of segregation.

In another two celebrated cases – *Baker* v. *Carr* (1962) and *Reynolds* v. *Simms* (1964) – the Warren Court established the 'one man, one vote, one value' principle, which in practice means that within states electoral districts for state legislatures (and the US House) should have virtually the same number of voters. Suspected gerrymandering on racial or ethnic (though not partisan) grounds was outlawed. These decisions were massively important in changing the whole nature of state legislatures and state and local politics not just in the South, but throughout the US. Previously, minorities and urban and suburban residents had been grievously discriminated against in the districting process, as the grossly malapportioned legislatures had reflected the dominance of conservative rural and small-town interests.

In the area of Church/State relations, the Warren Court more or less outlawed organised prayer and Bible-reading in public schools, in two cases: *Engel* v. *Vitale* (1962) and *Abington School District* v. *Schempp* (1963). These cases were decided on the basis of the Second Amendment's prohibition of any establishment of religion, and Jefferson's concept of the 'wall of separation between Church and State'.

As far as sexual relations were concerned the Court in *Griswold* v. *Connecticut* (1965) struck down a Connecticut law preventing the sale of contraceptives – even to married couples! The Court's reasoning was based on Justice Douglas's concept of a 'right to privacy', not explicitly stated in the Constitution but implicit in the Ninth Amendment ('The enumeration . . . of certain rights, shall not be construed to deny or disparage others retained by the people') and in the 'shadows' of the First, Third, Fourth and Fifth Amendments. In addition, the Court in a series of cases began to relax obscenity laws, prompting the famous remark in an opinion by Justice Potter Stewart that he could not define obscenity but 'I know it when I see it.'[5]

In the case of *New York Times Co.* v. *Sullivan* (1964) the Warren Court eviscerated the libel laws of the fifty states by making it virtually impossible for 'public figures' to sue for libel. To succeed, such figures were required to prove that the libel – even though it might be proven false – had not been undertaken with malicious intent: an almost impossibly high standard, as it turned out.

The decisions of the Warren Court that probably created the greatest degree of public outrage, however, were in the area of criminal procedures. The Court made it harder for materials seized without a search warrant to be used as evidence in court in the case of *Mapp* v. *Ohio* (1961). In *Gideon* v. *Wainwright* (1963) the Court guaranteed access to a lawyer for all those to be put on trial.[6] In two cases, *Escobedo* v. *Illinois* (1964) and *Miranda* v. *Arizona* (1966), the Court established that suspects taken into police custody had to be informed of their rights to remain silent and to have an attorney present during questioning.

The Warren Court's actions created a great deal of controversy both politically and in legal circles. Justice Frankfurter (who remained loyal to the old Holmesian theory of judicial restraint) and the Eisenhower appointees, Justices Harlan and Stewart, were frequent dissenters from later Warren Court decisions, fearing that the Court's activism had perhaps gone too far. In 1968, the Court appeared to have become dangerously entangled in electoral politics, as two presidential candidates, Republican Richard Nixon and the segregationist George Wallace, ran campaigns directed against the Warren Court on the grounds that it was 'soft on criminals'. In this fervid political atmosphere, outgoing President's Johnson's failed attempt to replace the retiring Warren as Chief Justice with his long-time friend Associate Justice Abe Fortas further aroused the ire of the Republicans and southern Democrats in the Senate. In retaliation they submitted Fortas to gruelling confirmation hearings at which the nominee was forced to answer for all the 'sins' of the Court. Dogged resistance from Nixon's conservative allies in the Senate ultimately compelled Johnson to withdraw the nomination.[7]

At the time of Chief Justice Earl Warren's final retirement in early 1969 the Court over which he had presided had thus effected a revolution in American jurisprudence and politics. Given the controversy that the Warren Court's decisions had engendered, however, we must now consider how its successors have extended or limited the Warren revolution.

The Burger Court (1969–86)

President Nixon had the good fortune to name four justices to the Court, including the new Chief Justice Warren Burger. If Nixon believed that the Court would then turn sharply in a conservative direction he was to be greatly mistaken, however. Indeed in its early years the Burger Court went on to extend what the Warren Court had been doing in several important areas.

The first of these was abortion. In the 1973 case of *Roe* v. *Wade*, Justice Blackmun's opinion used the right to privacy established by Justice Douglas in the 1965 *Griswold* decision as the rationale for establishing the right to an abortion in the first six months of pregnancy. *Roe* turned out be probably the most controversial Supreme Court case since *Dred Scott* and, confirming the worst fears of the adherents of judicial restraint, it gave rise to a large nation-wide anti-abortion movement that has kept the issue at the forefront of American political debate ever since, and moreover, has exacerbated the politicisation of the Supreme Court and the entire federal judiciary.

In 1972 the Burger Court also continued the radicalism of Warren in the area of crime and punishment by striking down the death-penalty laws of all fifty states in the case of *Furman* v. *Georgia*, not, however, as a violation of the Eighth Amendment's prohibition of 'cruel and unusual punishment', but instead on the grounds that the arbitrariness and capriciousness with which the punishment was applied violated the Fourteenth Amendment's 'due process' and 'equal protection' clauses.

In the area of desegregation the Burger Court extended the *Brown* precedent to permit busing of schoolchildren within school districts to achieve racial equality in public schools in the 1971 ruling *Swann* v. *Charlotte-Mecklenberg Board of Education*. As with abortion, this decision engendered a great deal of controversy and social unrest in parts of the US, particularly in northern cities such as Boston, where desegregation orders had not hitherto applied. Unlike abortion, the anti-busing fervour proved to have less of a long-term political impact, although it did lead to the withdrawal of large numbers of white schoolchildren from the public-school system, without visibly improving the quality of education offered to inner-city minority children.

Finally, the Court found against the Nixon Administration in two crucial cases where President Nixon had attempted to extend the scope of presidential power. In *New York Times Co.* v. *United States* (1971), the Court invalidated the Administration's prohibition of the publication of controversial leaked documents (the so-called 'Pentagon Papers') on the conduct of the Vietnam War. More importantly, the Court voted 8–0 (with Justice Rehnquist, a former high-ranking official in the Nixon Justice Department recusing himself) against Nixon in the 1974 case of *US* v. *Nixon*, when Nixon attempted to withhold crucial tape-recordings pertaining to the Watergate cover-up from the federal grand jury investigating the case, on the grounds of 'executive privilege'. The Court's ruling was the final nail in the coffin of the Nixon Administration and precipitated the President's resignation.

Nevertheless, as stalwarts of the Warren Court such as Justices Black and Douglas were gradually replaced, the Burger Court did begin to drift towards a more cautious, centrist position on most issues.[8] Closely divided between liberals and conservatives, the jurisprudence of the later Burger Court was largely characterised by the 'swing' justice, Lewis F. Powell, Jr, who voted with the liberals (led by the Warren-era veteran Justice William J. Brennan, Jr) on abortion and religion cases, and with the conservatives (led by Justice William H. Rehnquist) on criminal procedure matters.

After the 1974 *Milliken* v. *Bradley* decision, where the Court refused to order busing across school district lines, the Court became less enthusiastic about busing as a means of desegregation. In *Gregg* v. *Georgia* (1976) the Court also voted to permit the death penalty once more after the states had rewritten their death-penalty laws to conform to the *Furman* requirements. The *Miranda* standards were also gradually relaxed in the criminal procedure area. In *Bowers* v. *Hardwick* (1986) the Burger Court curiously refused to extend the right to privacy, that had been used to uphold the right to contraception and abortion, to cover homosexual acts between consenting adults. Finally, in the 1978 *Bakke* decision, the Court straddled the controversial issue of 'affirmative action' (positive discrimination) in college admissions and hiring in general, by striking down the particular affirmative action programme at issue, while denying that affirmative action was *ipso facto* unconstitutional.

On the whole the Burger Court was a cautious, transitional court. Unlike the Warren Court, it did not follow a crusading activist jurisprudence by setting bold precedents on as many issues as it could find. Instead the Burger Court in its later years adopted a restrained, legalistic approach, seeking to avoid establishing precedents as far as possible and preferring to decide issues on a case-by-case basis. Of course this meant that the same issues kept coming back to the Court again and again, and the Court's work-load increased dramatically. The Warren Court's legacy of activism meant that the Court, once entangled in sensitive political issues, was not easily disentangled, even by a majority of self-consciously 'restrained' justices.

The Rehnquist Court (1986–)

In 1986 Burger was replaced as Chief Justice by Associate Justice William H. Rehnquist, the most conservative justice on the Court. Rehnquist's accession to the chief justiceship marked the Court's significant move to the right during the Reagan–Bush years. Between them Presidents Reagan and Bush appointed over half of the total number of federal judges, and also over half of the Supreme Court justices (including Sandra Day O'Connor, the first woman justice). All of the Reagan–Bush appointees were more conservative than the Justices that they replaced (see Table 6.2). Yet even in a court that seemed to be moving against them, the liberal veterans Brennan and Thurgood Marshall (the first black justice, appointed by President Lyndon Johnson) could still occasionally either win a case (as in the 1989 *Texas* v. *Johnson* decision that outlawed laws prohibiting the burning or desecration of the US flag), or dilute a conservative ruling. Moreover, as was the case with the Nixon appointees, the Reagan–Bush justices refused to march in conservative lock-step on every issue.

Table 6.2. *The Rehnquist Court, 1994–95 term*

Justice	Appointed by	Year	Age when appointed
William H. Rehnquist *	Reagan (R)	1986	62
John Paul Stevens	Ford (R)	1975	55
Sandra Day O'Connor	Reagan (R)	1981	51
Antonin Scalia	Reagan (R)	1986	50
Anthony M. Kennedy	Reagan (R)	1988	52
David H. Souter	Bush (R)	1990	51
Clarence Thomas	Bush (R)	1991	43
Ruth Bader Ginsburg	Clinton (D)	1993	60
Stephen Breyer	Clinton (D)	1994	54

Note * Originally appointed to the court by President Nixon in 1971, and promoted to Chief Justice by President Reagan.

By comparison with its predecessors, however, the record of the Rehnquist Court is indubitably conservative.[9] On criminal procedure, in particular, the Court has continued to adulterate the 1960s Warren Court rulings gradually without reversing them *in toto*. With Rehnquist taking the lead, the Court has also consistently reduced the restrictions on the use of the death penalty and expedited the process of execution. On abortion, the Rehnquist Court refused to reverse the *Roe* v. *Wade* decision, though in two cases, *Webster* v. *Reproductive Health Services* (1989) and *Planned Parenthood* v. *Casey* (1992), it upheld state laws restricting access to abortion for teenagers without parental or judicial consent, mandating waiting periods, and denying public funding of abortion. On race relations the Rehnquist Court has been much tougher than its predecessor in the area of affirmative action and preferential treatment for women and minorities in employment, although its most controversial decision, *Wards Cove Packing Co.* v. *Antonio* (1989), was largely reversed by the Civil Rights Act of 1991. On redistricting, the Rehnquist Court in the 1993 *Shaw* v. *Reno* decision for the first time called into question the creation of bizarrely shaped electoral districts guaranteed to elect minority members to the US House or state legislatures. As a result the districting plans of three states – Louisiana, Texas and Georgia – were invalidated by lower federal courts just weeks prior to the 1994 congressional elections. Finally, the Rehnquist Court has so far proved reluctant to relax the strict Warren Court standards against religion in public schools, despite the clear desire of a determined minority of the justices to do so.

Interestingly, one major accomplishment of the Rehnquist Court, in which the Chief Justice takes considerable pride, has been the reduction in the Court's overall case-load. As a matter of policy, Rehnquist and his conservative brethren have sought to reduce the number of cases on the Court's docket, and they have succeeded to quite a remarkable extent. In the mid-1980s the Court was issuing over 150 rulings a term, but the 84 cases decided in the 1993–94 term was the fewest number since 1955.[10] While this logically diminishes the Court's capacity for judicial activism, it has not hitherto reduced the controversy and political contention that continues to hover over the Supreme Court, particularly when a new justice is nominated. In this respect the Warren Court legacy has survived into the 1990s.

The structure of the federal judiciary

Article III of the Constitution only ordains that there shall be a Supreme Court, and grants it the power of original jurisdiction in some areas. Everything else regarding the federal judiciary is left to the discretion of Congress, including the judicial hierarchy, the numbers of justices, and the jurisdiction of the courts. The federal judicial system has three levels of courts: the *Federal District Courts*, the *Circuit Courts of Appeal*, and finally the *US Supreme Court*.

The lowest tier of the federal judiciary are the *Federal District Courts*. The US is divided into ninety-four federal districts, with each state having at least one Federal District Court (since districts cannot cross state lines) and the larger states several. Each District Court has at least one judge, but it may have as many as twenty-seven. These judges, appointed by the President with Senate confirmation, usually hear and decide the cases allocated to them individually. Senators of the President's party play a major role in District-Court appointments within their states, according to the doctrine of 'senatorial privilege' that dates back to the time of George Washington.

The *Circuit Courts of Appeal* constitute the next level of the federal judiciary. The US is divided geographically into twelve circuits (or eleven plus the *Federal Court of Appeals for the District of Columbia*), and each appellate court has six to twenty-eight permanent judges, depending on the case-load. These judges (again appointed by the President subject to Senatorial confirmation) normally hear and decide cases in panels of three, but in especially important cases they may sit *en banc* or altogether. The Courts of Appeal have *appellate* jurisdiction, that is to say they review decisions of district courts and federal Independent Regulatory Agencies within their circuit. Each of the nine Supreme Court justices is responsible for supervising at least one of the circuit courts, and bringing cases from that court to the attention of his or her colleagues. This power becomes particularly significant where a quick decision is needed from the Supreme Court, for example in death-penalty cases where the power to issue a temporary 'stay' of execution may be in the hands of the supervising justice. Because of the number of cases concerning the federal government, the *Federal Court of Appeals for the District of Columbia Circuit* deals with very high-profile cases, and is generally regarded as the second most important court in the land.

The Supreme Court consists of nine justices appointed by the President with the advice and consent of the Senate. (The number of justices is left to the discretion of Congress, but after moving up and down between six and ten before and just after the Civil War, the number has remained at nine since 1871). The justices sit as a court and hear oral arguments and issue decisions in public during their annual term, which runs from the first Monday in October to the end of June.

In addition to these courts of general jurisdiction Congress has also created some additional constitutional courts with special jurisdiction, including the *US Court of International Trade*, the *Foreign Intelligence Court*, the *US Court of Appeals for the Federal Circuit* (patents and claims for damages against the US), and the *US Court of Military Appeals* (courts martial).

In addition to this system of federal courts, each state, of course, maintains its own judicial system to deal with cases arising under state law.

How cases get to the Supreme Court

There are two routes by which a case can get to the Supreme Court.

The first is if the case falls under the *Original Jurisdiction* of the Court. Article III, Section I of the Constitution specifies the areas of original jurisdiction of the Supreme Court. These include all cases involving foreign Ambassadors and diplomats, cases in which the United States is a party, and cases involving two or more states. All cases in these categories may begin and end in the Supreme Court.

The second category of cases that the Court must hear are cases that arise under the *Appellate Jurisdiction* of the Court, which Article III, Section II of the Constitution leaves to the discretion of Congress. During this century, however, Congress has allowed the Court more and more discretion over the cases it hears as the case-load has increased, and thus most cases (over 90 per cent) arrive at the Supreme Court today by petitions or *Writ of Certiorari*. If four of the nine justices agree that the decision of a highest state court or a federal appeals court involves a federal constitutional issue, then the case will be argued before the Supreme Court. Each term the court reviews thousands of petitions for *certiorari* ('cert' petitions in court parlance) filed by claimants, but accepts only about 5 per cent of them for oral argument.[11]

How the Court decides cases

With the assistance of their clerks, the justices individually review the cert petitions and vote in conference whether or not they will hear the cases. If four justices vote to hear a case then it will be heard (in *certiorari* cases the justices are not obliged to give reasons for accepting or rejecting a petition).

Before a case is argued in court, the justices receive printed briefs – sometimes hundreds of pages long – in which each party to the case presents its arguments. The Court will also occasionally receive *amicus curiae* ('friend of the court') briefs. These are submitted by individuals, organisations, or government agencies who have an interest in the case and claim that they have information of value to the Court. This procedure is regularly used by the US Justice Department in the hope of persuading the Court to rule in a particular direction. For example, in the *Webster* and *Casey* abortion rulings the Bush Administration submitted *amicus* briefs asking the Court to repeal the 1973 *Roe* decision on abortion.

The next stage is for the case to be argued openly before the full Court. Oral arguments take place every two weeks on Mondays, Tuesdays, and Wednesdays during the Court's term. In making their presentations the attorneys are generally allocated a maximum of thirty minutes. During this time the justices are free to interrupt and interrogate the attorneys at any point.

The justices meet in conference on Wednesday afternoons and all day Friday. The Chief Justice is in the chair and the members of the Court discuss the cases before them and then vote. If the Chief Justice is in the majority, he assigns the opinion of the court. If he is in the minority, the senior justice in the majority assigns the opinion. Drafts are then circulated and justices agree whether to join the opinion, submit a concurring opinion, or circulate a dissent. Votes can still change at this stage, but once agreement on an opinion is reached these are 'handed down' in public sessions of the Court in the final weeks of the term. A summary of the opinion of the Court will be read by the justice who wrote the opinion, and brief summaries of concurring and dissenting opinions may also be read.

As the work-load of the Court increased dramatically during the Warren and Burger Courts, the role of the justices' law clerks became increasingly important. Justices hire the best recent graduates of the most prestigious law schools (such as Harvard, Yale, Columbia, Chicago, and Stanford) to serve as clerks for a year or two. Each justice is entitled to a maximum of four law clerks, although several make do with less than their full allocation. The clerks do a great deal of the legal research for the justices and assist in the drafting of opinions. Justices vary as to the extent to which they author their own opinions, and there have been members of the Court in recent years whose opinions have been substantially drafted by clerks. Finally, the clerks sift through the huge pile of cert petitions that land in the lap of the Court, and bring interesting cases to the attention of the justices. As the Court (like all other American political institutions) has become more bureaucratic in its operations, so the role of the clerks has become that much more significant.[12]

The Chief Justice

The only power which the Chief Justice has over his fellows is that of presiding over the Court's oral arguments and conferences, and assigning opinions when he is in the majority. In fact, however, the chief's influence is usually considerable.[13] He is the head of the federal judiciary and acts as their spokesman and as a spokesman for the legal profession as a whole. In this regard, both Chief Justices Burger and Rehnquist have spoken out about the need to reduce the case-load of the federal courts, and Rehnquist has been active and vocal on the issue of federal judges' salaries.

Within the Court the Chief Justice can exercise his personal authority in such as manner that he defines the essential nature and philosophy of the Court. This was particularly true of Earl Warren, who led from the front. Warren Burger, by contrast, while a superior administrator to Warren, tended to wait for a consensus to emerge within the Court and then joined it, thus evoking much less respect from his fellow justices than his predecessor. Rehnquist is a more genial and more straightforward (if more conservative) figure than Burger, but since becoming Chief Justice he has not exercised intellectual leadership, and has not been successful in forging a consensus between the conservative activists and the moderates on the current Court.

The politics of judicial nominations

The entire federal judiciary is appointed by the President with the advice and consent of the Senate. These appointments are for life, and federal justices can only be removed by the cumbersome process of impeachment, and conviction by the Senate. At the lower levels presidential nominations normally go through with little opposition, but Supreme Court nominations are often bitterly contested. Presidents seek to appoint justices who reflect their own judicial philosophy, and for this reason Senators in the opposing party fear that presidential appointments might pack the court with 'liberal' or 'conservative' justices. This has been a particular problem when the White House and the Senate are controlled by different parties, as has frequently been the case since the mid-1950s.

Since the Court has become more activist and more intimately involved in the everyday lives of Americans, the stakes involved in judicial appointments have become higher. Usually presidents still get their nominees approved, nevertheless. Of 142 Supreme Court nominees in US history, the Senate has rejected only 27, or 19 per cent. The seven failed nominees in this century are listed in Table 6.3.

For a nomination to be withdrawn or rejected there usually must be something suspicious in the nominee's background – Parker was a segregationist, Fortas and Thornberry were too close to Lyndon Johnson and the nominations with a presidential election impending outraged the Senate Republicans, Haynesworth belonged to clubs that excluded blacks and had some conflict-

Table 6.3. *Rejected or withdrawn Supreme Court nominations since 1900*

Nominee	President	Year	Reason for rejection/withdrawal
John J. Parker	Hoover	1930	Segregationist/anti-Labour background
Abe Fortas *	Johnson	1968	Lame-duck President/financial impropriety
Homer Thornberry †	Johnson	1968	Lame-duck President
Clement Haynesworth	Nixon	1969	Alleged segregationist/financial impropriety
Harrold Carswell	Nixon	1970	Incompetence/segregationist
Robert Bork	Reagan	1988	Conservative jurisprudence
Douglas Ginsburg	Reagan	1988	Smoking marijuana

Note * Fortas was nominated for Chief Justice while already sitting on the Court. The financial allegations stemming from this aborted promotion eventually forced his resignation from the Court in 1969.

† Nominated to fill the vacancy created by Fortas's elevation to Chief Justice.

of-interest trouble, while Carswell was widely regarded as incompetent. Ginsburg, President Reagan's first choice after the Senate had rejected Judge Bork, withdrew from consideration after he admitted having smoked marijuana with his students while a college professor. In many of these nominations the role of the American Bar Association's (ABA) Standing Committee on the federal judiciary, which rates nominees as 'well-qualified', 'qualified' or 'not qualified', is crucial.

Even when a president's nominees are confirmed, they often disappoint the presidents who appoint them by turning out to be much more liberal or conservative than intended. President Eisenhower did not intend his nominees Earl Warren and William Brennan to be liberal judicial activists; liberals were generally disappointed with the voting record of Kennedy appointee Byron White; President Nixon's appointees (with the exception of William Rehnquist) confirmed the Warren revolution; while conservatives have been perplexed by the moderate stance of Bush nominee David Souter. Yet a President's judicial appointees are likely to reflect the politics and ideology of those who appointed them to a major extent, and over time this will have an impact on the federal judiciary. Presidents Reagan and Bush filled over 50 per cent of the federal judgeships during the twelve years of Republican occupation of the White House from 1981 to 1993, and they unquestionably turned the federal courts in a much more conservative direction, although the impact of their Supreme Court appointments was perhaps somewhat less than expected.

The often brutal politics of judicial nominations was fully exposed during the battle over the confirmation of Judge Robert Bork to the Supreme Court in 1987.[14] Bork seemed eminently well-qualified to sit on the Court. He had been a distinguished law-school professor, a solicitor-general of the US (the Justice Department official who prepares and argues the federal government's case before the Supreme Court), and was a sitting judge on the District of Columbia Court of Appeals. Normally his nomination would have sailed past the Senate. But the circumstances of 1987 were not normal. President Reagan was weakened by the Iran/Contra scandal and looked increasingly like a 'lame duck' as the end of his second term approached. The Republicans had also just lost control of the Senate.

Perhaps most importantly, on a number of very sensitive issues – Church/ State relations, affirmative action, and abortion – the Court was very finely balanced between liberals and conservatives, and the justice who retired, Lewis Powell, had been the decisive 'fifth vote' for the liberal side on those issues. Bork's very conservative jurisprudence thus posed a real threat to some of the most critical decisions of the Warren and Burger Courts. Liberals were determined to stop the nomination at all costs and feminist and civil rights groups also mounted a militant national campaign against Bork. Ultimately the Bork nomination was defeated 58–42 on the Senate floor.

President Bush's first nominee, David Souter, who lacked the academic 'paper trail' left by Judge Bork and refused to reveal his views on established precedents before the Senate Judiciary Committee as Bork had done, was easily confirmed. But Bush's second nominee Clarence Thomas, a black con-servative judge, only forty-three years of age, was bitterly opposed by the same forces that had defeated Bork. The Thomas nomination was even more threatened by accusations of sexual harassment from Thomas's former aide Anita F. Hill, and the Senate Judiciary Committee's public investigation of Hill's accusations, conducted before a national television audience, did not reflect well on any of the participants or the process of selection for members of the nation's highest court. Ultimately Thomas was confirmed by the full Senate by a narrow 52–48 margin.

President Clinton had the good fortune to fill a Supreme Court vacancy in each of his first two years in office. After a tortuous process of selection in each case, Clinton eventually selected two highly respected, moderate, Demo-cratic federal appeals court judges: Ruth Bader Ginsburg in 1993, and Stephen Breyer in 1994. Both revealed little in their confirmation hearings but came to the Court with excellent judicial credentials, and incurred little opposition during the confirmation process. In return for an easy confirmation process Clinton sacrificed the opportunity to place a strong liberal voice on the Court, but at least the civil tone of the Ginsburg and Breyer hearings brought a semblance of sanity and respect back into the confirmation process for Supreme Court nominees.[15]

Conclusion: liberalism/conservatism and activism/restraint

Much of the debate over the Supreme Court's role in American politics in this century has centred over the issue of judicial activism: that is, whether the least democratically accountable and representative branch of the federal government should be deciding so many sensitive political questions. Many have feared that the enhanced rule of the Supreme Court as effectively a 'super legislature' undermines popular faith in both the democratic process and the legislative process in America.

In the early decades of this century the progressive justices Holmes and Brandeis argued this position against the conservative, *laissez-faire* judicial activism of the time. They believed that the Court should let the legislature get on with passing laws to reflect changes in society and not try to foist its own 'outdated' opinions on contemporary society. The Court's formidable power to strike down state and federal laws as unconstitutional should only be exercised in the most extreme circumstances.

Liberals generally held to this view of judicial restraint through the New Deal era in opposition to the court's assault on Franklin Roosevelt's measures, but during the Warren Court period, the Court embarked on a phase of 'liberal' judicial activism. This discomfited old-fashioned liberals like Justice Frankfurter, who still adhered to the old Holmesian doctrine of self-restraint. Nevertheless, by the late 1960s the liberals had become the judicial activists and the conservatives the exponents of judicial self-restraint. Nixon appointed four, apparently conservative adherents of judicial restraint, but most of them were all too consistent in their belief in restraint for the liking of conservatives, and although perhaps unhappy with Warren Court precedents, Nixon's appointees proved generally unwilling to overturn them. By the 1980s conservatives had gone much further and now seemed to be demanding a new phase of conservative judicial activism to reverse most of what the Warren Court had done. In doing so they demanded that the Constitution should be interpreted 'strictly' or according to the 'intent' of the framers: a view associated with Judge Bork and Reagan's Attorney-General Edwin Meese. Liberal jurisprudents, led by the veteran Warren Court Justice William Brennan, continued to argue for a 'living constitution'; vague and unspecific enough to allow for adaptation to changing circumstances.[16]

Many commentators now feel that the Court has become too important in American politics; that by developing an 'imperial judiciary', the Court has indeed become a 'dangerous branch'. In addition, they argue, Supreme Court activism may undermine faith in the Congress and in the democratic process generally. By becoming entangled in so many complex political issues, some not very susceptible at all to legal reasoning or decision-making, the Court may be undermining representative government in the US.

In defence of judicial activism it can be argued that the Court sometimes reflects the popular view better than Congress or the President. Judicial activism has shown its utility in breaking legislative deadlocks on crucial issues (such as segregation) where it was apparent that a change in popular opinion was not being reflected in the more 'representative' elected bodies. Activists can also argue that the Court is needed to protect minorities (such as atheists, communists, or criminal suspects) who have little chance of getting a fair hearing from the executive or legislative branches which by their very nature are more beholden to majority opinion.

As far as an 'Imperial Judiciary' is concerned, it might also be pointed out that the Court never gets too far out of step with public opinion on a particular issue, and if it does it tends to backtrack rather quickly (the example of the Burger Court's retreat on several Warren Court precedents in the criminal procedures area comes to mind). If the Court does stray too far from the popular consensus, the executive branch can always refuse to enforce its decisions, and under Article III of the Constitution, Congress can always adjust the structure and much of the jurisdiction of the federal judiciary.

This perennial debate between judicial activism and restraint in twentieth-century American jurisprudence is no nearer resolution than it was half a century ago. What is not in doubt, however, is the continuance of the uniquely important and prominent role played by the federal judiciary in American politics and government.

Notes

1 In the case of *Marbury* v. *Madison*, where the Supreme Court first asserted the power of judicial review, Chief Justice John Marshall's opinion also relied heavily on the 'supremacy' clause of Article VI: 'This constitution . . ., shall be the supreme Law of the Land; and the Judges in every state shall be bound thereby, any Thing in the Constitution or Laws of any State to the Contrary notwithstanding.'

2 Alexander Hamilton, James Madison, and John Jay, *The Federalist Papers* (New York: New American Library, 1961), p. 467.

3 On the defeat of the 'court-packing' bill see James T. Patterson, *Congressional Conservatism and the New Deal* (Lexington: University of Kentucky Press, 1967).

4 On the Warren Court see Alexander Bickel, *Politics and the Warren Court* (New York: Harper & row, 1973).

5 Quoted in Hodder-Williams, *The Politics of the US Supreme Court*, p. 10.

6 For a vivid account of the *Gideon* case and the internal dynamics of the Warren Court see Lewis, *Gideon's Trumpet*.

7 As a result of alleged financial improprieties that first came to light during the confirmation battle, Fortas was forced to resign from the Court altogether the following year.

8 For an account of the early years of the Burger Court see Woodward and Armstrong, *The Brethren*; and Martin Shapiro, 'The Supreme Court: From Warren to Burger' in Anthony King (ed.) *The New American Political System*, (Washington, DC: American Enterprise Institute, 1978), pp. 179–211.

9 On the Rehnquist Court see Savage, *Turning Right*.

10 Joan Biskupic, 'Lifting the Veil On Life Inside the High Court', *Washington Post National Weekly Edition*, 29 August–4 September 1994, p. 33.

11 See O'Brien, *Storm Center*, p. 191.
12 On the clerks and the court bureaucracy see Hodder-Williams, *The Politics of the US Supreme Court*, pp. 82–93; and O'Brien, *Storm Center*, pp. 124–35.
13 On the role(s) of the Chief Justice see O'Brien, *Storm Centre*.
14 On the battle over the Bork nomination see Bronner, *Battle for Justice*.
15 For a critique of the confirmation process see Carter, *The Confirmation Mess*.
16 For a good collection of opposing viewpoints on the judicial activism/restraint debate see Mark W. Cannon and David M. O'Brien (eds), *Views From the Bench: The Judiciary and Constitutional Politics* (Chatham, NJ: Chatham House Publishers, 1985).

7

State and local government

The continued powers and importance of state and local governments is prob-ably the single most underestimated element of modern American politics. Given the focus on Washington, DC that is represented in the media (most of which is concentrated in Washington or New York) this is perhaps under-standable, yet it is still fundamentally true that most government activities and services that touch the daily lives of individual citizens are provided either uniquely or substantially by the states and sub-states.

This concentration on so-called 'national' politics at the expense of the states could perhaps have been justified, as for most of this century political authority appeared to be ebbing ever more substantially towards the centre and away from the periphery. At various points that process has seemed so strong and irresistible that serious observers of the United States predicted that the states would be reduced to a status little greater than symbolic. Developments gather-ing pace in the last fifteen years have produced substantial reform and re-energising of state and local governments, whilst the federal system has been crippled by an enormous budget deficit and policy inertia. This renders any excuse for ignoring sub-federal politics inadmissible.

This chapter will look at the evolution of American federalism in distinct stages. First, the constitutional status, history, and role of the states will be sketched. Then, the institutional revival of the states over the last thirty years will be outlined and explained. Next, the financial revival of the states will be examined. From this an analysis of state politics and prospects in the 1990s can be drawn. Finally, an analysis of sub-state governments – the cities, towns, and hamlets – will be offered. From this it can be concluded that in political terms (if not necessarily constitutional terms) the revived states and local government should be given a higher position in any evaluation of the Ameri-can political system than has often been popular.

The evolution of national–state relations

The United States was, as its name implies, the creature of the states in that its constitutional legitimacy and national standing came from sets of decisions made across and between representatives of state political authorities. To what extent state sovereignty was surrendered by the creation of the USA and the adoption of a national constitution has remained a matter of enormous con-troversy since 1787. However, it is reasonable to suggest that the states were and are the basic building-blocks of American life, and they remain highly individual and distinctive – although the arrival of a national mass media may have moderated some of these differences.

The Constitution was a political treaty between representatives of the various states. It was also an attempt to find a balance between the retention of state sovereignty and the creation of a national authority. In the eyes of those who drafted the constitutional provisions it was always a balance that would lean in the direction of the states. Before the American Revolution the then thirteen colonies had all been administered separately by Britain and had acquired very different qualities. It is only a slight overstatement to suggest that the United States was created by the incompetence of King George III and Lord North as much as by any pre-existing national American sentiment.

Federalism runs throughout the text of the Constitution. The states are mentioned explicitly or implicitly some fifty times. Along with the separation of powers, federalism represents a pillar on which the rest of the constitutional superstructure is built. Despite this the number of explicit guarantees that the states are given is quite small. Their territorial integrity is upheld, they are promised protection from foreign invasion and domestic violence, they are offered a Republican form of government, they gained equal representation in the Senate, and immunity from lawsuits by private citizens.[1] In part this list is so short because it was presumed that, as the Constitution was the creation of the states, few formal safeguards were necessary.

This lack of explicit protection for the states was unpopular at the time, and in order to ensure the passage of the Constitution the first ten amendments – the Bill of Rights – were passed in 1791 to placate critics of the original draft. The tenth of those amendments stated: 'The powers not delegated to the United States by the Constitution, nor prohibited by it to the States, are reserved to the States respectively, or to the people.'

Since 1791 there have only been five further amendments that had a major impact on states. The Eleventh (1798) prevented citizens of one state suing another state. The Fourteenth (1868) came to be the vehicle by which the national Bill of Rights – initially believed to only restrict the federal government – was made obligatory on the states. The Fifteenth (1870) evolved into the means by which national voting rights were created. The Sixteenth (1913) enhanced the national government by allowing a federal income tax. Finally, the Seventeenth (1913) ended the selection of Senators by state legislatures in favour of a popular vote in each state.

Despite this there remains uncertainty about where the Constitution draws the line between the states and the centre. Whilst strong supporters of the states can point to the language of the Tenth Amendment, those who prefer an expanded role for Washington, DC look to Article I, Section VIII which says that Congress may make laws for the 'general welfare of the United States', regulate interstate commerce, and do whatever is 'necessary and proper for carrying into execution the foregoing powers'. As will be outlined shortly, clashes between these rival interpretations of the Constitution have run through the national–state debate for the better part of 200 years.

State issues: Education

Education is highly decentralised in the United States, with power really held by some 15,000 school boards. In 1992 state and local governments provided some 93.6 per cent of all funding, leaving the federal government to contribute the remaining 6.4 per cent. The major issues facing virtually all states are:

o Radical variations in the level of funding provided across school boards. This has the usual effect of relatively affluent areas providing generous resources while poorer areas also have poorer-financed schools.

o Falling academic standards, as shown by tests which have been sat in states for over forty years. Some 25 per cent of young Americans leave school without the basic High School Diploma, and about 20 per cent of young Americans are believed to be functionally illiterate (unable, for example, to make sense of a daily newspaper).

Most states are taking broadly similar measures to tackle these sorts of problems. Money given by state governments towards local education budgets is often targeted at the least well-supported districts (often at the insistence of the local courts). Meanwhile, a variety of (quite familiar) reforms have been adopted to raise standards. These include encouragement of the adoption of a common curriculum, regular testing of both students and teachers, greater parental choice, more involvement of the local business community, and delegation of many administrative decisions directly to the individual school. The government in Washington, DC, has encouraged this process.

At a practical level the states and local governments are responsible for a number of important services. The 50 states and over 86,000 local governments are almost exclusively responsible for education (where together they cover over 90 per cent of expenditure) and crime and law enforcement (again over 90 per cent); they dominate public health services and transport, and are a major partner with the federal government in agriculture, conservation services and welfare. In this last category three of the major welfare programmes – Foodstamps, Aid for Families with Dependent Children (AFDC) and Medicaid (health care for the poor and disabled) – are organised and financed jointly by the federal government and states.[2] It is hardly surprising, then, that for many ordinary Americans their states and localities are the governments that matter most, while Congress and the presidency deal with distant issues such as macro-economic policy and foreign relations.

Nevertheless, virtually from the creation of the Republic, there has been an ongoing struggle between those who support greater power for the national authority and those who uphold states' rights. Indeed, the first party-system division between Federalists (led by Alexander Hamilton) and Democratic– Republicans (led by Thomas Jefferson) was over precisely this question. The nineteenth and early twentieth centuries have been labelled the era of 'dual federalism', where most political clout lay with the states and the national government had an extremely modest standing. However, even then there were movements towards the centre. In the early years of the nineteenth century the Supreme Court under Chief Justice John Marshall (1801–35) extended the rights of national political institutions in a set of key rulings.[3] The question of whether or not any state had the right to leave the Union and abandon the Constitution was brutally settled by the American Civil War (1861–65). The financial balance between the rival systems was tilted heavily in favour of the centre by the creation of the federal income tax in 1913.

This last change had an immediate impact. Until 1913 national grants to the states to support various projects had been minuscule, less than $5 million. With its enhanced revenues Congress could afford to be more generous and aid increased sharply after the passage of the Federal Roads Aid Act of 1916. Aid averaged around $100 million between 1918 and 1930, or about 3 per cent of the national budget.

The political relationship between the centre and the states was transformed during the New-Deal presidency of Franklin Roosevelt (1933–45) and his 'co-operative federalism'. In response to the Great Depression Roosevelt massively expanded the pre-existing grants system to assist the states, but critically made much of that help conditional on states following certain guidelines about how to spend that money, which were drawn up and enforced in Washington, DC. The states found themselves politically and financially dependent on Congress and the White House.

At first this process was resisted by the Supreme Court, which emasculated many of the New Deal provisions that extended federal government power. After Roosevelt's landslide re-election in 1936 the Court capitulated and reversed its previous opposition in a set of landmark decisions.[4] From here the Court became a positive ally of the New Deal. By 1941, in the case of *United States* v. *Darby*, it was willing to dismiss the Tenth Amendment as a mere 'truism' rather than a bulwark of states' rights. On a different level, the same 'Roosevelt Court' in *Palko* v. *Connecticut* (1937) enhanced the degree to which the Bill of Rights was obligatory on the states.

This process was taken much further under President Johnson (1963–69) and his Great Society programmes described by Johnson as 'creative federalism'. Johnson's supporters – overwhelmingly liberal Democrats – had come to see the states as old-fashioned, reactionary, racialist, and insensitive or incompetent towards the poor. They sought and obtained a huge increase in federal grants to deal with particular local problems. National grants-in-aid doubled between 1965 and 1969 (from $10.9 billion to $20.2 billion), this rise being concentrated in health programmes, education, training, employment opportunities, and urban renewal. The major beneficiaries were American cities and those who lived in them (by now disproportionately ethnic minorities). Over the wider time-period of 1960–80 federal aid to states and local governments rose from 7.6 per cent of the national budget to 15.5 per

---

State issues: Welfare reform

The provision of welfare to the poor and disadvantaged is shared between the national and state governments, but the states have increasingly been in the forefront of reform efforts. Issues of welfare are especially sensitive in the United States because they are often linked to socially explosive issues such as family structure and race.

The major policy problems in this area are:

o The increasing costs of provision. Some 13.5 million Americans collect monthly benefits. The costs of state spending on welfare have risen considerably – an average of 7 per cent since 1990.

o The emergence of a permanent welfare class. the American welfare system is really designed to provide temporary relief, yet in recent years over 90 per cent of welfare recipients have been on rolls for at least two years. Most of these citizens are single unmarried women (frequently black) with children. Often they are completely unprepared for the labour market.

Many states have adopted similar measures to deal with this crisis. During the early 1990s cuts in benefits and restrictions on eligibility by cash-strapped states have been common. To try and move people off welfare there has been greater emphasis on making benefits conditional on the citizen entering some form of education or re-training (so-called 'workfare'). However, with so many unmarried mothers with small children on welfare there are practical limits to how far this can go.

---

cent, a rate of growth some 250 per cent faster than the overall growth of the US economy.[5]

The Great Society followed the New Deal by concentrating its help in the form of categorical grants. That is, the money was given for a specific task, the rules as to how the money would be spent were created by officials of the national government and were vigorously monitored by those officials. Most money was given directly to local groups, not state governments, where it was tightly supervised. Once again the national government was backed by the Supreme Court. Under Chief Justice Warren (1953–69) the Court specialised in further increasing the standing of the national Bill of Rights and making virtually all of its provisions compulsory for the states.[6] The shift towards the federal government had been of such a dramatic and comprehensive nature that the states and localities appeared to have been rendered redundant as independent and influential units.

That analysis was to prove mistaken largely as a consequence of internal change amongst the states themselves. It was also in part because of a change in approach at the national level as well. The euphoria created by the Great Society dwindled as it became evident that poverty could not be eradicated merely by establishing a government programme. Many of the new projects proved ineffective in practice and the level of bureaucratic

---

> ## Proposition 13
>
> The revolt against the skyrocketing costs of Property Tax, particularly important
> to local governments, came to a head in dramatic fashion in California in 1978.
> These taxes were pegged to rapidly increasing house prices and values had been
> rising far more briskly than income and were concentrated on middle-class,
> middle-income (mostly white) voters. Anti-tax enthusiasts, led by businessman
> Howard Jarvis, successfully raised enough signatures to force a statewide ballot
> on the issue. Proposition 13 proposed to slash property taxes in half and then peg
> them. Virtually every participating politician in the state opposed the proposal,
> arguing that it would decimate government services if it were passed. Despite this,
> the voters approved the measure by a two-to-one margin. The vote was seen as
> a signal of middle-class insurrection against property tax in particular but gov-
> ernment taxation more generally. It is thus seen as a crucial landmark on the
> route to Ronald Reagan's election in 1980.

---

restriction associated with many categorical grants were widely condemned.
Taxpayers – locally and nationally – became unenthusiastic at the cost such
policy innovation entailed, as well as unconvinced about the quality of the
results it was producing.

The first President to react to these demands was Richard Nixon. Both out
of a belief that it was wrong to bypass state administrations and out of a
conviction that greater flexibility was required in the system, Nixon set out to
create a 'new federalism'. Nixon's efforts concerned replacing categorical
grants with block grants, whereby money would be given out under loose
headings such as 'public health' with the states given substantial autonomy
over detailed implementation. He then proposed to go further down that route
by suggesting general revenue-sharing, a straightforward cash subsidy to state
and local governments with no strings attached. The Democratic-controlled
Congress adopted both ideas, but only at a very low level.

Hence when President Carter restored the Democrats to power, categorical
grants still dominated the federal aid system. Carter did not greatly expand it.
Both his instincts as a fiscal conservative and his experience as a former
Governor of Georgia (1971–75) cautioned against that. Federal aid peaked in
real terms in 1978, the same year as the revolt against local Property Tax
signalled by Californian voters through Proposition 13.[7] The federal role was
thus in relative decline even before the arrival of Ronald Reagan, a former
Governor of California (1967–75), who was committed to a much greater
reversal of the trend towards national dominance over the states.

As the bulk of this chapter will illustrate, the combination of institutional
reform in the states, financial reform that increased the states' revenue-raising
capacity, and the Reagan effect both on federal assistance programmes and
through the impact on national governmental capacity of the federal budget
deficit have all engendered a revival of state and local government.

The institutional revival of the states

At the outset of the 1960s many outside observers, especially those of a centre–left political persuasion, held a very dim view about the institutional capacities of the states. As a rule they appeared to be governed by antiquated and inefficient constitutional arrangements, and the basic organisation of government was primitive. The Chief Executive – Governor – was rarely a serious political figure, restricted by rules that often prevented them from seeking re-election, and often granted formal powers that were little more than ceremonial. The state legislatures were grossly unrepresentative and unprofessional, unrepresentative because their electoral boundaries had deliberately not been adjusted to match changing population movements. This process of election-fixing or gerrymandering generally worked in favour of rural areas and against urban areas. Unprofessional, because the legislators rarely met, possessed poor staff resources, and were frequently bought by major commercial interests. The state judicial system was under-financed by a parsimonious state government, lacked imagination, and often failed to meet the most elementary standards of justice. All of these adverse tendencies were most blatant in the states of the American South.

Given this very unflattering picture of how politics worked inside most states, it should come as little shock that most reformers believed that they were incapable of serving the public good via political innovation. Logically, therefore, if one wanted to pursue such policies only the national government could serve as the appropriate forum. A political generation was raised for whom 'federalism' was a code-word for corruption, inefficiency, and racialism rather than being a high political and constitutional principle.

State governments have, over the last thirty years, moved a long way from the (largely accurate) picture painted here, and that shift has led outsiders to rethink their worth and ability as political actors. Since 1965 about half of all state governments have witnessed fundamental reorganisation and virtually no state has bypassed the reform movement altogether. One facet of this is that some four-fifths of the states have either ratified completely new constitutions or dramatically amended new ones.

This activity has occurred because of a number of major reforms at the national level during the 1960s which had an enormous effect on the states. They included:

o The Supreme Court's decisions in *Baker* v. *Carr* (1962) and *Reynolds* v. *Simms* (1964) to rule gerrymandered state legislative boundaries unconstitutional and insist on mathematical equality between state electoral districts. This provided a very strong motive for change inside states.

o The passage of the Civil Rights Act (1964) and the Voting Rights Act (1965), which revolutionised southern politics.

o The challenge of the Great Society process itself, which made it clear to many state governments that they faced an 'adapt or die' choice.

o Increasing demands for higher quality government services from state voters, coupled with a greater willingness to throw out state politicians who fail to deliver.

The political office to have experienced most dynamic change has been that of Governor. Belatedly, this office has followed the presidential trend at the federal level and seen a sharp increase in its position. Once derided as inept 'Good-Time Charlies',[8] Governors have been transformed by constitutional change since the 1960s. Certain basic constitutional amendments have helped their status. In 1955 only twenty-nine states offered their executive a four-year term, whilst twenty-one gave only a two-year tenure. Now forty-seven of the fifty states (New Hampshire, Rhode Island and Vermont being the exceptions) have a full four-year term. Again, forty years ago, only thirty-five of the fifty states allowed their Governor to serve more than one term of office (and these were concentrated amongst those with two-year term executives). Now forty-nine states permit this (the exception is Virginia).

The authority of Governors has historically been diluted by the tendency of states to elect to various other executive posts large numbers of other political figures (often of different political parties) rather than allow the Governor to appoint their people to such posts. The number of these other elected state-wide office-holders has fallen by over two hundred across the United States. In response to the rising status of Governors, their staff resources have also increased considerably, from an average of eleven in 1956 to an average of over fifty in the 1990s.[9]

The new role of Governors has attracted a more impressive type of candidate to contest the post. Once elected, the average Governor has more power than in the past. In forty-seven states the Governor is responsible for creating a state budget that is then put before the legislature (in Mississippi, South Carolina and Texas this is done jointly between the Governor and legislative leaders). In the 1950s only two states allowed their executive to order government reorganisation subject to legislative confirmation: nineteen now allow their Governor such sweeping authority.

Governors have taken on the role of chief economic salesmen for their states both at home and abroad. Some forty states have opened liaison offices in Washington, DC which operate as thinly disguised lobbying organisations. Almost all states have established trade offices abroad, with Tokyo having as many liaison offices with American states as exist in Washington, DC. The rise of individual Governors has transformed the National Governors' Association (NGA). Having been a rather sleepy holding body that did little more than organise an annual – and lightly attended – gathering of the nation's chief executives, which only moved its headquarters from Chicago to Washington in 1967, the NGA has gained real vitality in the 1980s. Its central

---

State issues: crime

The overwhelming proportion of crimes committed (95 per cent), expenditure on fighting crime (90 per cent), and the prison population (90 per cent) occur at the state rather than federal level. Although statistics indicate that the overall rate of crime in the United States is falling (while it is still at extremely high levels), public anxiety has increased through the 1990s. Opinion polls indicate it was the most important issue to voters in the 1994 congressional elections.

Given the strength of public concern most states have responded by taking a tougher line on crime, although without much stress on crime prevention. Capital punishment is increasingly used in the thirty-eight states that permit it. Longer sentences are being imposed on the persistent offenders. For example, California voters approved a measure in 1994 that imposed life without parole on those who committed three notable offenses. There has been an urgent programme of prison building. The United States has an amazing one million people in jail and that number will grow by much more before the year 2000. Many states and cities have expanded police numbers. With the exception of a modest push in some states towards gun control on the most dangerous types of weapon, efforts at prevention have generally been less popular in elections than tougher punishment.

---

headquarters organises a number of regional meetings between Governors as well as the national conference, and chairmanship of it was a launching pad for Bill Clinton's presidential bid.

State legislatures have followed the pattern of Governors. Supreme Court-ordered redistricting broke up their previously unrepresentative nature and active steps have been taken to meet the accusation of amateurism and petty corruption. The length of sessions and the work-load taken on have risen sharply. One manifestation of this is the length of time spent at work. As late as 1962 thirty-one of the fifty state legislatures only met every other year. Only six are now not required to meet annually. Legislatures are also spending more of each year in session. The California state legislature is a rather extreme example, meeting for about as many days each year as Congress, but it illustrates a trend. Salaries for legislators have increased, so that in most states they are genuine professionals rather than part-time politicians. To serve these new bodies a larger and more expert staff has been required. By the early 1990s over 15,000 people were working for state legislatures nationwide, an increase of well over 200 per cent since the mid-1960s.

The third branch of state government – the judiciary – has also witnessed renewal. Every state has its own Constitution, Bill of Rights, and State Supreme Court. The states deal with 99 per cent of civil law cases, 98 per cent of criminal law cases and house 93 per cent of the million-strong total prison population. Historically, neither state Supreme Courts nor the wider state judicial system had inspired much confidence, often being institutions packed with political appointees of debatable legal experience. Increasingly the

---

State rules on Governor's powers

The exact authority of state Governors is laid out in state constitutions. In every state except North Carolina the Governor has a veto. In forty-seven states (bar Mississippi, South Carolina and Texas) the Governor presents his own budget to the state legislature as the President does at the national level. In forty-four states (not Indiana, Maine, Nevada, New Hampshire, Rhode Island and Vermont) the Governor can veto individual elements of a state budget – a line-item veto. Finally, in forty-one state the Governor may reduce parts of the budget without legislative approval, the exceptions being Arkansas, California, Illinois, Kentucky, Maine, Michigan, Nebraska, New Hampshire and Wisconsin.

---

process of nominating judges has become more meritocratic. State courts have responded to the challenge to reform made by the Warren era and have taken on a more activist role in interpreting state constitutions, especially in the field of individual rights.

In the majority of states and virtually all of the larger ones (Texas has developed rather less fully than others) the new politics is unrecognisable from its predecessors. This superior level of organisation in both the legislative and executive branches has made it much harder for advocates of a stronger central government to base their arguments on the incompetence or corruption of the states. Having established more effective political institutions, the other major defect that needed to be tackled was the traditionally weak revenue-base of most states. A weakness that, even with much more impressive executives and legislatures, clearly limited their capacity to provide impressive public services without federal government assistance and control.

The fiscal revival of the states

To some extent the reinvigorated political institutions apparent in the states were bound to turn their attention to their limited financial base at some point. The historic problem of state governments had been their unwillingness to raise the sort of revenue levels necessary to sustain viable levels of services. Given that in virtually all states (not Vermont) there is some form of constitutional provision obliging the state to produce a balanced budget each year, states could not circumvent this revenue gap by borrowing. Traditionally states had received a little from, and local governments depended on, Property Tax (similar to the British rating system) as income. Property Tax has the difficulty that it is not a buoyant source of income (i.e. takings from it do not automatically increase with economic growth), so the rate of Property Tax had to be raised each time the government wanted to raise more money. This had been resisted by voters. If the states were to match the challenge of policy innovation they would have to find a wider range of tax measures.

The political incentives to do just that were enhanced by the events of the late 1970s and early 1980s. The first was the evidence of constituent revolt against increased levels of Property Tax, signalled by the passage of the radical Proposition 13 in California which was thought representative of a wider hostility.

Far more dramatic was the impact of the Reagan Administration. Reagan came to office armed with a philosophical commitment to return programmes (and the cost of implementing them) to the states and localities plus the desire to cut the level of government spending. Although his most grandiose plan for a new federalism – a welfare swap whereby the federal government took on the whole cost of Medicaid and the states accepted the whole cost of Aid to Families with Dependent Children (AFDC) and foodstamps – failed to make any political headway, he succeeded in radically altering national–state relations in a number of ways.

In 1981 he persuaded Congress to place fifty-seven existing categorical grants (and one block one) into nine block grants and at the same time got a further sixty categorical programmes eliminated altogether. Between 1980 and 1984 the total number of categorical grant schemes fell from 539 to 404. Although Reagan only saw one further block grant adopted after 1981 this set of cuts amounted to a radical reduction in government support. On top of this real spending on AFDC and foodstamps were also cut. The states were left with a stark choice. If they wanted to see the programmes eliminated by the national government continue, or if they believed the real value of AFDC or foodstamps should be maintained, then they would have to find the additional money.

This problem was compounded by cuts in the direct provision of aid by the federal government. In 1981 there was an actual dollar decline in federal aid (the first for three decades). From 1980 to 1985 grants-in-aid expenditure fell by $10.4 billion. Under the Reagan Administration grant expenditure fell from 3.4 per cent to 2.7 per cent of GNP, bringing spending nearly half-way back to 1965 levels. Grants sank from 15.5 per cent of federal expenditures to 11.2 per cent.[10] In 1986 Reagan eradicated what was left of Nixon's general revenue-sharing. The Tax Reform Act of the same year weakened state revenues further by reducing their ability to use tax-exempt debt – bonds – to cover the costs of major infrastructure repair and expansion, thus increasing the cost of borrowing for capital projects.

The new mood in Washington, DC saw an emphasis on deregulation. The *Federal Register* (a daily publication of all rules and regulations from national administrative agencies) fell from over 87,000 pages in 1980 to 55,000 by 1987. Much of this deregulation effectively transferred responsibilities to state governments. In the same spirit Congress increased the authority of the states over Medicaid spending by enlarging their control over the scope, coverage, and operations of their Medicaid programme.

In a very short period of time the states had seen national programmes cut, national fiscal aid reduced, and responsibilities increased. This inevitably

---

State issues: Medicaid

Health care is a major policy problem at both the federal and state levels. The particular concern of state politicians is Medicaid – a joint federal–state health insurance programme aimed at the poor and disabled. As the costs of medical provision have escalated the costs for the state for the 6 per cent of the population that rely on Medicaid has been rising at the rate of 10 per cent a year in the 1990s – three times the general rate of inflation. This rapid increase is squeezing resources that otherwise would be used for crime, education and training. Added to this the costs of health insurance for state government employees have also escalated. More frustrating still for the states is that the precise design of Medicaid is largely out of their hands, being regulated by an Act of Congress.

Given that any major move towards comprehensive health-care cost control at the national level seems unlikely at present, states are tempted to look to themselves for a solution. Some states notably Oregon, have tried to escape the federal system and set up their own system. The state of Hawaii has had a British-style government-run scheme for two decades, although the voters of California rejected a similar plan by a three-to-one margin. To control their own costs states have become more assertive in negotiating with the employees' health plans via large co-operatives called Health Maintenance Organisations (HMOs).

---

placed very sizeable strains on their resources, exacerbated by the deep recession of 1981–83 which cut state revenue and increased state expenditure. Put together, this Reagan shock forced the new state institutions to deal with their revenue difficulties at a somewhat greater speed then they had probably planned.

The immediate reaction of most states to their predicament was to raise taxes – thirty-eight did so in 1983 alone. The wider consequence of the Property Tax revolt and the Reagan Presidency was to bring a diversification of tax measures. By the 1990s every state bar four had introduced some form of local income tax. These taxes vary enormously across states, both in terms of their progressivity (five states have flat rates) and their level, but this represents a major shift since the 1950s. Between 1960 and 1990 Property Tax's proportion of all state and local revenues fell from three-eighths to one-fifth, while income tax increased from one-twentieth to three-twentieths. That shift has given much greater revenue flexibility.

Other forms of taxation have widened as well. Forty-six states now possess some form of corporation tax. Forty-five states now operate a sales tax. Only New Hampshire has neither a state income tax nor a state sales tax.

The largest single area of expansion has been in user fees for various government services and miscellaneous revenues. These now bring in about 15 per cent of state and local income compared with around one per cent forty years ago. The most spectacular example of such innovation has been the rapid expansion of state lottery schemes, which over thirty-five states now have.

The net effect of all this was that most states and many local governments were able to raise sufficient resources to meet the new demands placed on them. Total state spending rose from just over $200 billion to nearly $600 billion in the 1978–88 period. In contrast to much of the previous fifty years it was the states that engaged in many major forms of domestic policy reform – in employment promotion, training, education, health-care services, and welfare – while the federal government, paralysed by the vast federal budget deficit, appeared ossified and ineffective. By 1991 the state and local governments were spending more on domestic programmes than the national government ($1 trillion compared to $0.9 trillion) and had five times as many civilian employees (15.5 million compared to 3.1 million).

This reversal in fortunes was critically linked to the fiscal renewal of the states. Between 1981 and 1989 states' total general revenue increased by 96 per cent despite substantial cutbacks in help from the federal government. In 1990 sub-federal governments had total monies of nearly $750 billion, of which less than 20 per cent came from Washington, DC. This turnabout can be illustrated by the rise in state and local revenue (excluding federal grants) from 7.6 per cent of GNP in 1960 to 10.3 per cent in 1990, whilst federal tax revenue (excluding Social Security Tax) fell from 15.4 per cent to 12.0 per cent in the same period.[11]

The most pressing dilemma for state governments, now that they had acquired this tax bonanza, was how to resist the demands of voters for their money back in tax cuts or rebates once it became evident that many state budgets were in healthy surplus. In many cases these demands proved politically irresistible, particularly in election years.

This was perhaps unfortunate in that it left many states in a potentially vulnerable position should there be a sharp economic downturn. The recession of 1990–92 proved a severe test to the capacity of the states. Although federal aid had expanded a little during the Bush Administration, this increase was tied to new costs imposed by changing Medicaid regulations in 1990, the Clean Air Act of the same year and the Surface Transportation Act of 1991. These were so-called 'Unfunded Mandates' in that Washington, DC legally obliged the states to make certain reforms but did not offer the cash to pay for them. Twenty-nine states had to cut spending to balance their 1991 budgets, including seven states that cut actual (not just inflation-adjusted) expenditure. Some thirty-four states saw tax increases in 1991 and another thirty followed suit in 1992. The most dramatic example was California, which having closed a $14 billion deficit in 1991, could not find a political consensus on how to close an $11 billion gap in 1992, produced a budget four months late and was forced to issue registered warrants (basically IOUs) to cover its debts.

Generally speaking the states adjusted very competently to the unfortunate circumstances of the 1991–92 period, and made tough decisions of avoiding government deficits (partly because many had no choice, given their balanced budget provisions) that the federal government simply avoided. Before the extension of their tax base the states would have had their finances decimated by sudden recessions: in fact most services were protected. Given the likelihood of continued national budget deficits for the remainder of the twentieth century, the states are likely to be the source of many new political ideas.

State politics in the 1990s

Any analysis such as this runs the risk of generalising across a group as large and diverse as the fifty American states. In looking at the particular issues that Governors and legislatures will face over the next ten years one has to remember that diversity, as well as offering a broad critique. Although most states have seen dramatic improvements in the quality of their political institutions some states have not changed their constitutions, others retain relatively weak executives, a few legislatures meet once every two years and remain unprofessionalised. Although most states have a greatly improved tax base many individual states do not have one of the following: income tax, sales tax, corporation tax or a state lottery. Although the extreme exceptionalism of the southern states that was so evident forty years ago has largely disappeared, most of the states with the least advanced institutions do still come from that region. Bill Clinton became Governor of Arkansas in 1978, but that state did not adopt a four-year term for its Chief Executive until after the election of 1986. Even as he was leaving office the state legislature was still meeting two months in every two years.

Having noted that, the main difficulties facing virtually all Governors are financial, the formation of state budgets now being the primary function of the modern executive. In facing this certain state constitutional elements remain critical. In forty-two states the Governor is given the advantage of a line-item veto in budgetary matters. That allows the executive to veto individual items in a state budget he or she objects to rather than having to sign or reject the whole document. Six states follow the presidential example in giving their Governor a simple veto rather than a line-item one. The Constitution of North Carolina grants its Governor no veto whatsoever.[12]

An equally important constitutional element is whether or not provision is made for a balanced budget between current revenues and current spending (capital spending on infrastructure can usually be financed by state-issued bonds). In forty-four states the Governor must propose a balanced budget, in thirty-eight states legislators must pass one, in thirty-one states the Governor must sign one into law and nine states allow for a deficit to be carried from one year to the next. Allowing for states that require some form of balanced budget element over a two-year rather than annual period, only the state of Vermont emerges with no balanced budget restriction at all.

These are not the only constitutional aspects that make political life difficult. Certain states oblige supra-majorities to support a budget before it can become law. California, for instance, demands a 60 per cent vote of approval in both the State Assembly and State Senate before its financial arrangements can be agreed. Others place super-majorities on taxation powers. Arkansas law insists that three-quarters of state legislators' backing is required before the state income tax can be increased.

Matters are even more complicated in those states where the budget, and the wider political system, can be shaped by the voters through the use of the initiative (referendum) system. In many states items can be placed before the electorate by the collection of a certain number of signatures. This popular initiative can be used to amend the state constitution in seventeen states, demand new state legislation in twenty states and be used to reject measures passed by the legislature in thirty-five states. In every state except Delaware popular ratification is needed for amendments made to the state Constitution by the legislature. Initiative use reached record levels in elections of the 1990s.

An increasingly frequent trend in those states (mostly in the western United States) that regularly use this device has been for voters to cut their own taxes via an initiative or demand that tax increases of various types will only be admissible if backed in an initiative. California is probably the most initiative-centred of the major states. Its voters severely limited its revenues by their support for Proposition 13 and then in 1988 decided – through Proposition 98 – to shape expenditure by mandating that at least 40 per cent of the state's general fund budget is spent on education. That provision had the practical effect of insulating under-eighteen education from budget cuts in 1991 and 1992, but imposing reductions on higher education and welfare payments instead.

Governors are also faced with increasing demands for their basic services. In the 1970s Medicaid accounted for less than 5 per cent of state budgets, but by 1990 that figure was 14 per cent and estimates for the year 2000 run as high as 20 per cent. Increasing levels of crime have led to public demands for more law-enforcement officers and more prisons. The newly active state courts have also pushed up state costs by demanding that state education provision is equalised by greater expenditure in poorer school districts.

The role of Governor thus has the blessings and the curses of ever greater responsibilities. As Governors have become serious political figures making major public decisions their popularity as individuals has inevitably suffered. Only half of the thirty-three Governors eligible to run in 1990 were still in office in 1991; ten stood down (often under the threat of defeat) and six were defeated. Fifteen states saw the Governor's mansion change party hands.[13] The dramatic 1994 elections in which the Republicans gained a net increase of eleven Governors again saw a party switch in fifteen states. By January 1995 in only six states (Colorado, Indiana, Iowa, Nevada, West Virginia and Wisconsin) had the Governor started his term of office before January 1991.

State legislatures face two main contemporary problems, both of them imposed by their voters. The initial conundrum is that state-level voters have followed the national example in regularly electing different parties to the office of Governor and to the legislature and, in the forty-nine states which

---

State issues: term limits

Ironically, because of extreme voter dissatisfaction with the performance of Congress, citizens of those states which allow initiatives to be placed on a public ballot by a petition of the electorate have turned to limiting the numbers of terms their state legislators may serve (usually six or twelve). Although first passed in Colorado, it was the state of California – as so often – that blazed the trail. Here voters adopted, in November 1990, Proposition 140 that imposed draconian term limits and slashed back legislative perks such as staff. By November 1994, citizens in every state that permits the direct petition process (twenty-three), with the exception of Mississippi, had voted on term limits, and with the single counter-example of Utah, they had adopted them

The impact of term limits on these states cannot yet be assessed. There are real fears in some quarters that legislatures will be dramatically deprofessionalised, reversing much of the modernisation that has occurred at the state level over the last three decades. Others doubt the impact will be that drastic or believe that power will flow to Governors. Many states have imposed two-term limits on Governors, but the political impact of this is not great as few Governors sought to serve more than eight years anyway.

---

have two legislative chambers, producing alternative party majorities in these as well.[14] In the 1950s it was unusual for as many as ten states to have split-party control of government: by the early 1990s thirty was the norm. Most of those states which kept one-party government were in the south, where Republicans are still a rarity in most state legislatures. After the 1994 elections twenty-two states had a Governor and legislative majority of the same party while twenty-eight has split control. All of the five largest states – California, New York, Texas, Florida and Pennsylvania – had a Governor of one party and at least one legislative chamber of the other.

The other, more recent, alteration has come through the widespread impo-sition of term limitations on the number of years state legislators may serve. Initially a reaction to the incumbency advantages enjoyed by Congress, by 1995 voters had used initiatives in twenty-two states to limit the tenure of their local politicians. Predictably California – through Proposition 140 in 1990 – was the first big state to back term limits and equally predictably, others quickly followed. The impact of these limits on the efficiency of state legislatures, or on the power balance between them and Governors, cannot yet be assessed but it threatens to be one of the most important developments in state politics this century.

The final major concern for states is their continued constitutional vulner-ability. Ironically, whilst so many changes have moved in favour of the states in the last twenty years, the Supreme Court has been the one outstanding body that has moved in the other direction. In *Usery* v. *League of Cities* (1976) the Court appeared to have revived the Tenth Amendment and states' rights.

However, this decision was reversed in *Garcia* v. *San Antonio Metropolitan Transportation Authority* (1985) where a slim 5–4 majority again reduced the constitutional protection of the states to virtually nominal terms. The majority argued that the states' protection lie in their political representation, such as equal representation in the Senate, not in formal constitutional terms. This interpretation was reinforced in the case of *South Carolina* v. *Baker* (1988) where a narrow majority again backed this view. More recent Court pronouncements such as *Gregory* v. *Ashcroft* (1991) have seemed to indicate a retrenchment from this position, so that legally as well as politically and financially the restored standing of state governments may be recognised.

Sub-state governments in the 1990s

If making broad judgements across fifty American states is problematic, it is even more so in the case of the local governments that exist below the state level. There are over 86,000 sub-state governments, divided roughly evenly between general-purpose governments (such as city councils) and special-purpose governments (like school boards). The variation in size is also enormous, between New York City which has over 200,000 employees down to small hamlets that might employ twenty. The sort of social difficulties these governments face also varies by very wide margins. Cities such as New York, Los Angeles and Chicago have populations greater than many countries and face urban poverty, poor housing stock, weak infrastructure, high levels of crime, a drugs explosion, and an AIDS epidemic.

Constitutionally there is no mention of, or provision for, sub-state governments. In the eyes of the Supreme Court such units are the creatures of the states themselves.[15] As states are so different, and as each state has its own historic relationships between itself and sub-state governments as well as unique urban–suburban–rural mixtures, it is hardly surprising that the pattern of state–local governance is rarely the same across states. In virtually all states responsibility for certain vital services – education, law enforcement, transport – is shared between the respective levels of government, but the balance alters from place to place. The estimated national average of all internal state services provided by state governments in 1990 was 51.3 per cent. This masked a range from a high in Vermont where 78.6 per cent of services were provided by the state to a low of 38 per cent in Nevada.[16] Even across local governments the precise location of political authority varies. Although most American cities have an elected Mayor and a Council, the powers of the Mayor can range from quasi-dictatorial to ceremonial and the degree of political professionalism is diverse. Some local governments have significant political-party machines dominating their elections, and others are non-partisan.

Looking across this huge number of authorities certain patterns can be discerned. Like the state governments, local authorities did not have a glowing reputation for competence, financial security, or honest government forty years ago. Again, like the states, the 1960s saw a vast increase in federal grants allied to much greater regulation of their activities. In the case of local governments this dependency relationship on Washington, DC was extended by the enactment of Richard Nixon's general revenue-sharing which was specially targeted at them. In 1960 only 8 per cent of all national government aid went directly to general purpose local governments: by 1980 25 per cent did. The larger cities disproportionately gained from this expansion, so that by the late 1970s the fifty biggest cities had national grants totalling nearly half of what they themselves were raising in taxation. Even with this level of support the (white) population flight from the cities led to excruciating financial troubles best symbolised by New York City's near-bankruptcy in this period.

Having been so dependent on federal aid, the Reagan era cutbacks struck this level of governments hard. The scrapping of large numbers of categorical grants designed for them, the end of general revenue-sharing in 1986 and the recession of 1981–83 hit cities and towns much more severely than most states. The ten years after Reagan took office saw reductions in federal grants to local governments in the order of $30 billion. By 1992 only 5 per cent of the fifty biggest cities' revenues came from national grants.

Local governments did not collapse for two reasons. One was that the states used their new-found political and fiscal strength to help. Total state aid to the localities increased by more than 60 per cent in the Reagan tenure with real increases of 5 per cent per year being commonplace. This is another example of Reagan's ability to force responsibilities back on to the states. The other is that local governments also tried to expand their tax base, where possible reliance on Property Tax was curtailed by increases in other forms of taxation. The local bodies – especially the cities – did not have the same flexibility as the states to fully reform their finances, but some progress was made. Out of this combination local government revenues rose by 102 per cent between 1981 and 1989, although the pressure on costs was at least as great as those faced by Governors.

Much of that progress was offset by the 1990–92 economic downturn, which probably hurt local governments more than the states. Once again it was the major urban areas that were hit hardest with New York, Los Angeles, Chicago and many others forced to raise taxes and enact painful spending cuts. A few governments were taken to the brink of bankruptcy and the experience is likely to make many look to emulate the states' fiscal performance further over the coming decade. The capacity of the largest cities to do this is limited by the fact that their populations are now so overwhelmingly composed of the poor and ethnic minorities.

Given the financial impasse in Washington, DC most local governments will have to look to their own resources and help from their states in dealing with future political demands. It is a striking testament to the changing balance between national, state and local governments over the last fifteen years that

Political control of the ten largest states in 1995

State	Governor	Assembly	Senate
California	Republican	Republican	Democratic
Texas	Republican	Democratic	Republican
New York	Republican	Democratic	Democratic
Florida	Democratic	Democratic	Republican
Pennsylvania	Republican	Republican	Republican
Illinois	Republican	Republican	Republican
Ohio	Republican	Republican	Republican
Michigan	Republican	Republican	Republican
New Jersey	Republican	Republican	Republican
North Carolina	Democratic	Republican	Democratic

As this table indicates, the major states are either controlled entirely by Republicans or divided. Nationwide the only states outside the old southern confederacy (traditionally Democratic at the local level) where the Democrats are in complete control are Hawaii, Kentucky, Maryland, Missouri, and West Virginia. Four of these five border the South.

state capitals rather than the national capital should be looked to in this way. According to your view of the proper balance between these institutions, this is either a disgraceful abdication of national responsibilities by the federal government, or the welcome revival of the bodies best placed to provide local services for distinct types of need, and a proper reassertion of federalism.

Conclusion

The central theme of this chapter has been the political renewal of state governments and a changing balance in American public life in their favour. That shift has come largely out of an initial move by the federal government in the 1960s which spurred the states into long overdue political and financial reform. In recent years that process has been taken further by the federal government's own traumas of, paradoxically, political inertia and fiscal imbalance caused, at least in part, by insufficient tax revenues.

The United States seems destined to continue this new era of what has been christened 'competitive federalism', and in many senses the new-found vitality of the states is proving itself a worthy change. Certainly the rather arrogant supposition that 'Washington always knows best' has taken a beating. Contemporary political ideas are now at least as likely to be borrowed from state examples by national politicians as vice versa, an astounding turnabout from thirty years ago. The election of former Governors Carter, Reagan and Clinton to the White House has brought the perspective of the new states to the national arena with varying degrees of success. The enhanced status of state politics may not always be the most discussed element of American politics, but it is certainly one of the most important.

Notes

1 Zimmerman, *Contemporary American Federalism.*
2 Medicaid, AFDC, and Foodstamps are provided on a joint basis with matching grants. Medicare, the health-care plan for the elderly, is provided by the federal government.
3 The key Marshall Court decisions were *McCulloch* v. *Maryland* (1819), *Cohen* v. *Virginia* (1821), and *Gibbons* v. *Ogden* (1824).
4 The vital case here was *National Labor Relations Board* v. *Jones & Laughlin Steel Corporation* (1937).
5 Peterson and Rabe, *When Federalism Works.*
6 The critical Warren Court judgements were *Mapp* v. *Ohio* (1961), *Gideon* v. *Wainwright* (1963), *Malloy* v. *Hogan* (1964), and *Miranda* v. *Arizona* (1966).
7 Proposition 13 was a radical plan to cut Property Tax, opposed by virtually the entire Californian political establishment but backed by the voters in June 1978.
8 See Larry Sabato, *Goodbye to Good-Time Charlie: the American Governor Transformed, 1950–1975* (Lexington, MA, Lexington Books, 1978).
9 Rivlin, *Reinventing the American Dream.*
10 Peterson and Rabe, *When Federalism Works.*
11 Rivlin, *Reinventing the American Dream.*
12 Maryland allows its Governor a line-item veto in certain limited circumstances.
13 See Tim Hames, 'The U.S. Mid-Term Elections of 1990', *Electoral Studies*, June 1991.
14 Nebraska has only one chamber. It also does not allow candidates for it to stand under a party label.
15 Formally acknowledged by Iowa Chief Justice John F. Dillon in *Atkins* v. *Kansas* (1903), popularly known as 'Dillon's Law'.
16 Zimmerman, *Contemporary American Federalism.*

Part Three

Political organisation

8

Bureaucracy

Even by the standards of the rest of American government, the nature, history, organisation, and debates over the United States bureaucracy are marked by complexity. This chapter will outline the reasons for such complication and attempt to show how the nearly three million-strong federal work-force fits in to the political perspective. Bureaucracy in the United States suffers to an advanced degree the problems faced by bureaucracies in all western democracy. Their role is known to be critical to the operation of the modern state and yet, compared with explicitly political institutions such as the White House, Congress, parties and interest groups, their activities are shrouded in some mystery.

This chapter will begin by looking at the nature of the modern bureaucracy, noting its highly fragmented and internally fractured pattern. It will then examine two major sources and explanations for this state. Namely, the historical evolution of federal administration in the United States and the different motives of those involved in the various aspects of its expansion, and the awkward political position that it occupies between the President and Congress, both of whom strive to maintain political authority over it. Finally, two major issues of bureaucratic management that have emerged over the past twenty-five years – those of political accountability and managerial efficiency, which are in many senses the inevitable product of both the historical development and political position mentioned previously – will be outlined. A few concluding thoughts will then be offered.

The nature of the modern bureaucracy

The United States may technically possess one federal bureaucracy but that is not how matters operate in practice. In reality, the United States is blessed with many hundreds of different forms and layers of public administration, which might collectively be described as a national bureaucracy but which are characterised by extreme fragmentation and decentralisation.

The tasks of the American bureaucracy are multiple and generally expanding. They are also fundamental to the workings of government. These tasks generally fall into three types. First, bureaucracies are responsible for the implementation of public policies devised by the President and Congress. This is not as mundane as it may sound, for the quality of government services and legislation relies at least as much on its actual implementation as it does on the merits of its original design. Second, bureaucracies produce those detailed rules necessary to enforce the often insufficiently specific will of Congress. This secondary legislation usually involves producing detailed regulations which are outlined in the *Federal Register* (a government public-ation containing new rules). Third, bureaucracies are responsible for monitoring the success and consistency of their own implementation and regulation, via their own internal inspections and through a complex appeals procedure for aggrieved citizens.

Table 8.1. *The Cabinet departments*

Cabinet office	Year established
State	1789
Treasury	1789
War	1789
Navy	1798
Interior	1849
Justice	1870
Post Office	1872
Agriculture	1889
Commerce and Labor	1903
Commerce	1913
Labor	1913
Defense	1947
Health, Education and Welfare	1953
Health and Human Services	1979
Housing and Urban Development	1965
Transportation	1966
Energy	1977
Education	1979
Veterans' Affairs	1989

Note War and Navy became parts of Defense in 1947. The Post Office became an independent agency without cabinet status in 1971. Commerce and Labor were split in 1913 and Health, Education, and Welfare were divided in 1979.

Put together, this represents very important authority. It is little wonder therefore that questions of the public accountability and efficiency of federal employees are so frequently and passionately fought over. The instinctive cultural reaction of most American citizens, including their elective repre-sentatives, is to treat the bureaucracy with deep suspicion. Popular sentiment is sceptical about the practical competence of 'Big Government' and distrust-ful of the relative secrecy that surrounds its work. Yet this strongly ingrained attitude is somewhat ironic. By international standards the United States does not have a particularly huge administrative sector. If anything, the reverse is true. Nor is it valid to suggest that it is an ever-expanding machine. Total civilian federal government employees reached 2,600,000 by 1952 and only reached just over 3,130,000 by 1992,[1] much of this expansion being the result of a rise in the number of employees of the US Postal Service, which is the largest single sub-group of the civilian bureaucracy. Nevertheless, despite these facts the perception of the federal government as out of control persists.

Hostility to the bureaucracy also centres on its alleged inefficiency. Here, popular opinion may be on stronger ground, but once again with a paradox attached. The US system can be criticised on numerous efficiency grounds mostly because of its fragmented nature. However, the main reasons for those faults is that they were deliberately designed at the time that the legislation creating a government agency was enacted. Pure effectiveness has never been the dominant criterion considered by Congress or the White House when forming new, or reforming old institutions. That has always taken second place, sometimes at great distance, to considerations of political control.

This has all conspired to create an incredibly diverse and disparate bureaucracy. Some agencies, called independent regulatory commissions, such as the Federal Reserve Board or the Federal Trade Commission, are extremely powerful and virtually autonomous of political control. Other agencies are placed underneath one of the fourteen cabinet departments and are tightly controlled by that parent body. In other cases the agency may be placed within the orbit of a department but be granted virtual independence from it. Where this prevails the Cabinet Department (and its chief political figure, the Cabinet Secretary) may function as little more than a holding company for a set of virtually free-standing bureaucracies. In other cases, such as the Environmental Protection Agency, the agency may be attached to the White House rather than a Department. In many other situations still, for example the Civil Rights Commission or the Tennessee Valley Authority, an agency may exist on its own, not under the direct supervision of any other element of the executive. Unsurprisingly this all leads to much confusion about who is responsible for what and to whom.

This diversity is enhanced by varying levels of decentralisation within and across agencies. Many organisations conduct most of their activities not in Washington, DC but in the various states and localities. Their internal structure inevitably has to respond to this by delegating enormous amounts of authority to its operatives in the field. In addition, many others need the assistance of non-governmental organisations in order to fulfil their functions. There is consequentially enormous variance in the degree to which an agency head is really in charge of his or her own organisation.

There is a similar confusion about what we mean exactly by a bureaucrat. The largest such groups are those allied to the Pentagon and the Post Office. If we exclude those then what is left is a civilian non-postal federal work-force. This is divided between career operatives and explicitly political appointees,

Table 8.2. *Major US regulatory agencies*

Agency	Year established
Consumer Product Safety Commission	1972
Environmental Protection Agency	1970
Equal Employment Opportunity Commission	1965
Federal Communications Commission	1934
Federal Deposit Insurance Corporation	1933
Federal Energy Regulatory Commission	1977
Federal Reserve System	1913
Federal Trade Commission	1914
Food and Drug Administration	1906
Interstate Commerce Commission	1887
National Labor Relations Board	1935
Nuclear Regulatory Commission	1975
Occupational Safety and Health Administration	1970
Securities and Exchange Commission	1934

although the distinction can blur powerfully. The career civil service is based on the principles of selection by merit (usually through open competitive examination), tenure of office, and political neutrality. It consists of eighteen separate grades (divided into General Service (GS) levels 1–18) with ten distinct sub-grades within each full category. This civil service should thus be immune to partisan political manipulation. However, not all career civil service posts are acquired through competitive examination; others require only the achievement of a general educational level. This allows those making the final selection somewhat greater flexibility of appointment. Furthermore, since the passage of the Civil Service Reform Act (1978) the highest grades of the bureaucracy (GS 15–18) have been able to exchange their rights of tenure for more flexible salary conditions and promotion prospects as part of a new Senior Executive Service (SES). The same Act allowed for up to 10 per cent of the overall SES (and up to 25 per cent in any single agency) to be explicitly political.

On top of this career civil service is the political service. This consists of around 3,000 people who are expressly appointed by the President (normally called Schedule C posts) and usually require confirmation by the Senate. Here selection is not by merit – indeed, many political appointees have no detailed knowledge of the agency they will be heading. There is no security of tenure, the average period in office is regularly two years or less, and there is no expectation of political neutrality. To complicate matters further, there is nothing to stop the President asking a 'career' civil servant to take up a 'political' position and on 'political' terms.

In short, the United States has an administrative system where all bureaucracies are not the same, nor are all bureaucrats. To understand the present system it is vital to appreciate both its historical development and political circumstances.

Historical development

The range of activities covered by the US bureaucracy has increased greatly over the past 120 years. That process has been characterised by spurts of activity rather than by a continuous and consistent increase. In particular, three main periods – the Progressive era at the turn of this century, the New Deal, and the Johnson/Nixon Presidencies – stand out from the rest. It is important to note that although all three periods saw an enhanced bureaucratic presence, the attitude of those responsible for that increase towards the bureaucracy itself was not consistent.

Federal employment grew from a minuscule base at the beginning of the nineteenth century. Indeed the total numbers increased eightfold between 1816 and 1861, but over 85 per cent of this rise came from rapidly expanding numbers at the US Post Office, that was in turn caused by the rapid westward expansion of the country. The fact that numbers remained small did not prevent the branches of government disputing authority over the fledgling service. In 1867 Congress passed the Tenure of Office Act which precluded Presidents from sacking federal appointees without the express agreement of Capitol Hill. Most federal posts were regarded, at least by the political parties concerned, as legitimate instruments of partisan patronage and distributed to supporters of the President and the various wings of his party machine.

The ability of political parties to control bureaucratic appointments in this way repelled the modernisers and technocrats who constituted the Progressive movement. From the 1870s onwards they argued for an efficiency-orientated public service. Their arguments were enhanced by the unfortunate assassination of President James Garfield by Charles Guiteau (a disappointed office-seeker) in 1881. In 1883 they succeeded in forcing through the Pendleton Act. This Act introduced the notion of a politically-neutral career civil service with lifelong tenure, selected on merit through a set of rigorous public examinations, which then served a set of openly political appointees. It has remained the basic foundation for the organisation of American administration to this day. Once the Pendleton regime had been established, Congress felt at liberty to repeal the Tenure of Office Act.[2]

The particular bureaucratic method favoured by most Progressives during this period, given their preference for dispassionate expertise over party politics, was the independent regulatory commission. Such commissions were noted by the relative independence of both their career and political appointees. The latter served on long terms of office (over ten years was not uncommon) and these agencies were given maximum possible freedom from both Congress and the President. Virtually all major agencies created between 1881 and 1921 came in this form.

The next bureaucratic expansion was through Franklin D. Roosevelt's New Deal. The activity of the Progressives had forced a rise in overall federal employment numbers but this was to prove modest compared with Roosevelt's effect. Under the New Deal the national government greatly expanded its role as a regulator, particularly over big business, as an agent of national economic recovery through public works programmes, as a protector of farmers' incomes via agricultural price supports, in welfare via the Social Security Act of 1935, and as a partner with the states in various fields of public policy. All of this expansion required new or remodelled bureaucratic agencies to implement them.

New-Deal Democrats did not share the enthusiasm for independent bureaucratic expertise of the Progressives. Indeed, rather the opposite was true. As the bureaucracy had spent most of the previous generation operating under Republican presidents Roosevelt was suspicious – approaching hostile – towards it. Issues of political control mattered to him more than those of independent expertise. One of his first acts towards the bureaucracy was to fire a member of the Federal Trade Commission, despite his entitlement to serve out his full term. In this Roosevelt was overridden by the Supreme Court.[3]

Roosevelt placed as many agencies directly under his own supervision as Congress would let him. Those agencies that were not placed immediately beneath him were ordered to report to him. The difficulty with this approach was that Roosevelt's White House support staff was too small to allow him to play the supervisory role he wanted. A presidential commission was established under Louis Brownlow, whose recommendations in adapted form provided the Reorganization Act of 1939.

Brownlow largely reflected Roosevelt's own thinking. The independent regulatory commissions so beloved by Progressives were attacked as a 'headless fourth branch of government'. The Commission went on to argue that managerial direction and control of the executive branch and all its Departments should fall to the President and that Congress should permit the White House the resources to fulfil this vital co-ordinating role. Congress was somewhat suspicious of Roosevelt's ambitions and intentions but it did agree to transfer the Bureau of the Budget from the Treasury to the White House and to allow the creation of an Executive Office of the President (EOP).

Although Congress had not wanted to see the rise of a large personal presidential bureaucracy, once the EOP had been created Roosevelt and his successors used it for precisely that function. The total number of employees rapidly expanded (at an average of 5 per cent a year for thirty-five years) and the number of sub-units contained within the White House also blossomed. Although Roosevelt had felt obliged to create some independent regulatory agencies to monitor the Stock Exchange, along with the banking and insurance industries, the general trend was towards agencies tied to the White House itself as far as Congress would permit.

The third wave of bureaucratic advance came with a new round of government activity and regulation under Presidents Johnson and Nixon. The federal government took on new responsibilities for urban America, expanded health and welfare, environmental policy, and consumer protection. This all required new or reformed agencies to implement. Yet neither man had much enthusiasm for the traditional bureaucracy. Both attempted large-scale reorganisation of existing agencies, both tried to promote new management methods within the public service, notably Lyndon Johnson's zeal for the planning, programming and budgeting systems, and both tried to import outside expertise to shore up the federal civil service. Each administration bent to outside criticism and created new independent regulators with a much more aggressive attitude towards those who they were supervising.

Hence the modern bureaucracy has been created in various layers. The first layer strongly favoured bureaucratic efficiency and strengthened independent regulators, the second was more sceptical and favoured politically controlled agencies and the last was highly critical of traditional bureaucratic arrangements, at the same time as enhancing it. In all cases, but especially in the modern era, the struggle over the nature of the bureaucracy has been mirrored by a political struggle over who should control it.

The political position of the bureaucracy

The bureaucracy as a whole, and its individual components, have been heavily influenced by consistent political power-struggles over its form between the President and Congress, augmented periodically by the judiciary and assisted by various interest groups.

As is frequently true of such struggles in American government the role of the Constitution is deeply significant. In this instance it is more concerned with what the Constitution fails to say. There were virtually no civilian public employees at the time when the Founding Fathers deliberated, so matters of bureaucratic substance were largely ignored. What they did say was that Congress could create various departments and decide their funding, while the President could nominate the heads and staff the remainder of the bureaucracy.

As so often, this limited mandate based upon the principle of the separation of powers has left a legacy of inter-branch political struggle. Presidents suffer from the reality that what they regard as 'their' own executive branch is constitutionally not 'theirs' at all but shared with the legislature. The American bureaucracy is thus the servant of many masters, unlike its equivalents in western Europe which are unambiguously part of the executive.

Presidents, and many others, believe that bureaucratic power can only be given democratic justification if its actions are in response to White House orders. Yet in terms of creating agencies, locating them, deciding their political purpose and organisational structure, funding them and determining exact staffing levels, and scrutinising their performance, it is Congress who have the upper hand, to the deep frustration of many occupants of the presidency.

The CIA

The Central Intelligence Agency (CIA) was founded in 1947 and was the creation
of the Cold War. It had no real predecessors in American history. Its mission is
the collection and evaluation of foreign intelligence data, and conducting covert
operations. Organisationally it is an agency working directly underneath the
White House rather than any normal executive department. Unlike most White
House employees, its senior personnel do require confirmation by the Senate. It
stands at the apex of twelve intelligence-gathering agencies, a number that strikes
critics as overkill. By the 1970s the CIA's role in covert operations had given it
an increasingly murky reputation, prompting the creation of Intelligence committees in both houses of Congress. More recently, the end of the Cold War had
given it something of a crisis of purpose. Its budget is now estimated at $3 billion,
down nearly half since the 1980s, and it has 19,000 employees, also a reduction
from the Cold War heights. This it out of a total estimated budget for all intelligence activities of $29 billion. The agency was further rocked in 1994 by the
revelation of a major spy scandal centred on Aldrich Ames and widespread accusations of incompetence over the agency's failure to detect him earlier.

In the creation of new bureaucratic agencies Congress has many weapons
it can deploy to shape the administration to fit its, rather than the Oval Office's,
goals. Amongst its arsenal it can:

o Decide how much detail to place in the original law creating the agency.
   An extremely detailed approach can impose rigid conditions on the agency's
   mission and decision-making process.

o Decide what type of agency it will be and where in the governmental
   organisation it will fit. Congress can decide, particularly if it fears that if it
   did not the President would exercise disproportionate influence over the
   new body, to make the new agency an independent regulatory commission.
   This means that very substantial freedom from political interference will be
   granted to the agency and its key members will be given very long terms.
   This makes it unlikely (even assuming Congress did not notice) that any
   President will get enough appointments to radically change the direction
   of the agency.

Similarly, Congress can insist that a certain percentage of an agency's com-
missioners come from each party. This is true of the Federal Elections
Commission, the Federal Communications Commission and the Federal Trade
Commission. This again limits the ability of the White House to manipulate
the institution after its creation.

o If the agency is to be of the conventional, rather than independent, form
   Congress can decide which Department to locate the agency with, what the
   relative authority of the Department will be, or, alternatively, where the

---

NASA

The National Aeronautics and Space Administration (NASA) was founded in 1958, largely in response to the near-hysteria in the United States over the successful launching of Sputnik by the Soviet Union. In theory it reports directly to the White House, but in practice has a rather autonomous existence. The Administrator has to be confirmed by the Senate. The glory days for the agency were clearly the 1960s, when the Kennedy and Johnson administrations poured resources into ensuring that an American reached the moon before 1970. Even by the time Neil Armstrong met that target, the era of cuts was under way. In the last ten years NASA has suffered a set of embarrassing setbacks, including the Challenger tragedy, the initial failure of the Hubble telescope, and continuing arguments about the design of the Freedom space-station. These have led congressional critics to target its budget. NASA now has a budget of just over $14 billion and just under 24,000 employees, both well down on its golden period. Ironically, its best long-term prospect now seems to be co-operation with the similarly financially beleaguered Russian space agency.

---

agency should be free-standing of any Department. Such decisions are rarely made purely on the technical merits of the case, and are heavily influenced instead by where those who want to create the agency think it would be best placed to achieve congressional goals and be kept under congressional control.

Ironically, opponents of a new agency are also aware of the crucial importance of these factors. If they believe that an agency they disapprove of is likely to be enacted they often concentrate on reaching 'compromise' legislation which waters down an agency's mission statement or deliberately places it in a hostile part of the federal government. Thus as Terry Moe notes: 'American public bureaucracy is not designed to be effective. The bureaucracy arises out of politics, and its design represents the interests, strategies, and compromises of those who exercise political power.'[4]

Once an agency has been created Congress has very substantial powers to oversee it and, by this oversight, to determine its future direction. It will generally be very reluctant to allow the executive to implement sweeping reorganisations of an agency, regardless of the efficiency arguments, partly out of fear of the real intentions for such a change but also because such reforms are inconvenient to Congress, requiring a revamp of its own committee structure to supervise the new agency.

Congress may choose to be hostile towards an agency whose presidential appointee is running it in a manner Congress disapproves of, or it may attempt to protect an agency whose goals it strongly supports from a White House that may be less enamoured with the agency. Congress may feel obliged to support an agency like this even if it thinks it is not being particularly well-run because it fears that presidential demands for efficiency are often a code-word for cuts in programmes that the House or Senate approve of. This frequently happened during the Reagan Administration, where the President regularly appointed agency heads who were hostile to their own agencies (for example the Environmental Protection Agency under anti-Green Anne Gorsuch Burford), who would then engage in a power struggle with the agency-sympathising, supervising congressional committees.

Congressional oversight can take place in a number of ways:

o Where the head of an agency, or important divisions within it, require senatorial approval in order to take up their post (which is very common), the Senate can either deny such confirmation or be very difficult while granting it as a warning shot to the administrator concerned.

o Congressional hearings about some aspect of an agency's work can be scheduled, at which the agency will have to defend itself.

o Congress can ask its own watchdog, the General Accounting Office, to investigate some element of the agency's activity.

o Individual Congressmen or their staff can communicate their views on the agency's performance directly to the senior management.

o Most effectively of all, Congress can use the power it has over the funding of an agency to increase or decrease overall funds and staffing or to relocate funds and staffing within different parts of an agency or Department.

Put together, this is a formidable array of powers. Furthermore, Congress appears to be increasingly willing to use them, especially when the White House and Capitol Hill are in the hands of different political parties. The overall effect is to make even the most zealous political appointee realise that they are the servant of two masters and had better pay homage to them both. For the more cautious career appointee, aware that over the course of a lifetime they will serve administrations of different political stripes, the cross-pressures of dual loyalty are even more intense. This sets up a pattern whereby Presidents believe that their own appointees have 'gone native' in deference to Congress and the career bureaucracy is disloyal. This encourages them to build up their own immediate personal White House staff (generally not subject to legislative confirmation or funding) because they alone are the President's creatures. This bunker mentality has taken two Republican Presidents down the slippery slopes of Watergate (Nixon) and the Iran–Contra scandal (Reagan).

In order to maintain its position Congress has not only directed the executive bureaucracy but created its own as well. When the White House was first invited into the budget-making process in 1921 via the Bureau of the Budget, Congress created its own auditing institution, the General Accounting Office, to supervise executive departments. Seeing the general expansion of the White House staff from the New Deal onwards Congress rapidly increased its own staff and established the Congressional Research

Table 8.3. *White House sub-divisions under Clinton*

The following are the major sub-divisions of the White House:

Office of the President
Office of the Vice-President
Office of the First Lady
National Economic Council
Council of Economic Advisors
National Security Council
Central Intelligence Agency
Office of Management and Budget
US Trade Representative
Office of Science and Technology Policy
Office of National Drug Control Policy

The Office of the President has numerous sub-divisions such as:

Office of the Chief of Staff
Office of the Staff Secretary
Office of Cabinet Affairs
Office of the Counsel to the President
Office of Communications
Office of Public Liaison
Office of Political Affairs
Office of Intergovernmental Affairs
Office of Legislative Affairs
Office of Management and Administration
Office of Presidential Personnel
Office of Scheduling and Advance
Domestic Policy Council
Office of National Security
Office of Environmental Policy
Office of the United Nations Representative

Service to help members monitor federal agencies. When President Kennedy created an Office of Science and Technology within the White House in 1962 Congress eventually responded with its own Office of Technology Assessment. After President Nixon reorganised and enhanced the Bureau of the Budget in 1970, turning it into the Office of Management and Budget, Congress returned the compliment by first upgrading the General Accounting Office and then creating the Congressional Budget Office in 1974 as a powerful economic think-tank of its own.

In a sense it could be argued that not only is the federal executive bureaucracy the servant of two masters but that the United States possesses both an executive and a legislative bureaucracy, the latter designed to be on a permanent war footing with the former. Nor is Congress the only rival to the White House for bureaucratic control. There are two other main participators, the judiciary and interest groups.

Environmental Protection Agency

The Environmental Protection Agency (EPA) was established by the Nixon administrations in 1970 in response to the sudden emergence of the American ecological movement. It is responsible directly to the White House. Its official functions are broad, including regulation of air and water pollution, hazardous waste disposal and clean-up, pesticides, toxic substances, drinking water, noise and radiation, and conducting environmental research. Its political influence depends critically on the degree of environmental commitment of the incumbent President. The EPS has a budget of nearly $7 billion, and around 17,000 employees. The election of Bill Clinton was thought to mark a major breakthrough for the agency as he had pledged in the campaign to turn the EPA into a full cabinet department. In fact, when this proposal reached congress it was a victim of the deficit-cutting emphasis of the 1994 budget, and the change of status did not take occur.

Administrative law inevitably overspills into wider law. In theory a distinction was drawn between the two by the Administrative Procedure Act of 1946, which obliged the judiciary to respect bureaucratic expertise in such matters. For the better part of twenty-five years a truce, sometimes uneasy, held between the two. However, from the late 1960s, but with particular vigour from the early 1970s, border clashes between the courts and agencies broke out.[5] A set of important Supreme Court decisions expanded the meaning of the Fourteenth Amendment and what constituted a property right. Thus the courts increasingly obliged agencies to hold public hearings for those claiming mistreatment from the bureaucracy, particularly where denial of welfare benefits was involved. The judiciary showed an increasing willingness to hear appeals from the administrative system into the judicial process.[6] At the state level many judges also became more willing to challenge the competence and domain of administrative agencies.

Finally, there is a long history of bureaucratic interaction with interest groups. This is covered more fully in Chapter 10. Suffice to say that, as James Q. Wilson notes,[7] bureaucracies usually operate against one of four interest-group backgrounds: a dominant single group which supports its goals; a dominant single group that opposes its goals; two or more rival groups that disagree on its goals; no significant interest group. The life of a bureaucracy will be heavily influenced by which of these regimes it faces.

Not surprisingly – given the content of these last sections – two major issues have dominated American bureaucracy, especially from a presidential perspective, over the last two decades or so. These are political control of the bureaucracy and its managerial efficiency. Both of these major questions will be discussed in the last two sections of this chapter.

The quest for political control

Questions of bureaucratic control do not only obsess the White House, but they have produced an enormous outpouring in the academic world. The fact that much of that output has come from the public-choice school, which argues that bureaucrats try to exercise the maximum possible independent authority and have a disposition for ever-increasing budgets, may have had some influence over the heightened role the issue has recently had.

However, the primary explanations are political. As the last section illustrated, presidents simply cannot assume the absolute attention of the bureaucracy. White House hostility towards its own executive administration is built into the political system. The degree of that hostility and the willingness to take radical action about it appears to flow from three political elements. First, whether or not the President's party holds majority status in both branches of Congress. Where they do then, at least initially, there is a lesser tendency for inter-branch conflict over the direction of bureaucratic management and hence less White House suspicion. Second, whether the incoming President's party have been out of office for any significant period (more than one term). Generally speaking, the longer the period in opposition the deeper the suspicion of a bureaucrat's political loyalties. Third, whether a President considers himself a Washington, DC insider or not. Those who do are generally more comfortable with public administration than those who do not.

The attitudes of recent presidents towards their bureaucracies have largely followed those ground-rules. Richard Nixon and Ronald Reagan were the most concerned about bureaucratic control; Jimmy Carter and Bill Clinton occupy a middle position; Gerald Ford and (especially) George Bush were the most relaxed about the federal work-force.

Presidents keen to exercise firm political control over the bureaucracy tend to look at two particular strategies. One is to create a counter-bureaucracy within the White House. A counter-bureaucracy is an agency whose primary mission is to monitor, supervise, and control other government agencies. The other is the Administrative Presidency option. This relies on an unusually rigorous process for screening potential political appointments within the bureaucratic machine with absolute personal loyalty to the President, their policies and philosophy being the overwhelming grounds for selection rather than any specialist knowledge about a particular agency.

The use of these strategies can be illustrated by looking at those Presidents with the greatest initial distrust of the bureaucracy. Richard Nixon chose his initial Cabinet on the basis of incorporating potential party rivals into it and then allowing them to choose their own departmental subordinates. He almost instantly came to bitterly regret this as he felt that his appointees were unresponsive to his demands and allied with his enemies in the Democratic-controlled Congress, the bureaucracy, and various interest groups.

As a result Nixon moved to build up his own White House staff, which doubled in size between 1969 and 1972. Within the White House he invigorated the Budget Bureau, creating the new Office of Management and Budget (OMB) in 1970, and making it the political centre of the entire Administration. In other words, a counter-bureaucracy. To regain control of his own Cabinet in 1971 he asked Congress to implement the recommendations of the Ash Commission which had backed replacing the Cabinet structure with four super-Departments working closely with the White House. Predictably, Congress refused. Nixon then expanded the OMB and used Program Associate Directors (PADs) based there to monitor the work of his colleagues.

Unfortunately, as the White House staff grew larger, it became harder to manage and itself suffered from bureaucratic inertia. The same blockages led to gung-ho privatised operations such as the infamous activities of the Committee to Re-elect the President, culminating in the Watergate burglary. After his landslide victory in 1972 Nixon demanded the resignation of his entire Cabinet and fired those deemed insufficiently loyal to him personally. In their place he sought absolute Nixon loyalists. He then attempted to implement the Ash Commission in a looser form by executive order, creating four supervisory cabinet members sitting on top of the conventional structure. In short, an administrative presidency. An attempt was made to locate and remove hostile career appointees. Nixon's forced resignation in 1974 ensured this strategy barely got started.

Nixon's successor Gerald Ford was determined not to repeat his mistakes and adopted a much more consensual style towards the bureaucracy. His replacement, Jimmy Carter, was cross-pressured on the issue. As he possessed firm party majorities in Congress he could afford to be more open towards the agencies than his Republican predecessors, yet as a political outsider elected after eight years of Republican rule he was not entirely comfortable with the governmental machine. As will be outlined, most of his energy went into managerial reform, yet he followed Richard Nixon in one important respect. He too decided to pick independent political figures for his Cabinet and then allow them to choose their own political appointees. Like Nixon he came to deeply regret this, and in July 1979 he summoned his Cabinet members to Camp David where nearly half were fired or persuaded to resign while the White House was reorganised to allow Carter greater capacity to supervise the government.

In retrospect, the Nixon period was but a rehearsal for the Reagan Presidency which approached office with a distinct ideological distaste bordering on contempt for the civil service and a special dislike for burdensome government regulation for which most conservatives believed the bureaucracy displayed an enthusiasm. Reagan's contribution to political control strategy was to pursue both the counter-bureaucracy and administrative president strategy simultaneously.

Table 8.4. *The Federal Register, 1940–76*

Year	Pages	Year	Pages
1940	5,307	1977	63,629
1945	15,508	1978	61,261
1950	9,562	1979	77,497
1955	10,196	1980	87,012
1960	14,479	1981	63,554
1965	17,206	1982	58,493
1966	16,850	1983	57,703
1967	21,087	1984	50,997
1968	20,068	1985	53,479
1969	20,464	1986	47,418
1970	20,032	1987	49,653
1971	25,442	1988	53,375
1972	28,920	1989	53,821
1973	35,586	1990	53,618
1974	45,422	1991	67,716
1975	60,221	1992	62,919
1976	57,072		

Note The *Federal Register* outlines pages of new government regulations. As this table indicates, regulation exploded during the Johnson and Nixon periods (1963–74), reached a peak in the Carter tenure (1977–81) and was scaled back under Ronald Reagan, before seeing a resurgence under George Bush.

Reagan, like Nixon, centralised power in the White House staff, especially the OMB, which came to dominate government. Within the OMB the Office of Information and Regulatory Affairs (OIRA) was established as the primary means of attacking federal regulations. The OIRA was granted authority by Reagan under Executive Order 12291 (February 1981) to put all proposed regulations through its own version of cost-benefit analysis, in the belief this would screen out most of them. It was then granted power by Executive Order 12498 to vet all regulatory decisions emanating anywhere in the executive.

Meanwhile, the Reaganites also followed the administrative presidency route. A transition team was created seven months before Reagan was even elected that followed through into government. It made absolute devotion to the White House and conservative political ideology the touchstone for appointment. The Office of Personnel Management and the White House Office of Presidential Personnel became the institutional means of seizing control of the government. The Administration also used the Civil Service Reform Act of 1978 and its newly-created Senior Executive Service to extend the number of political appointees.

Needless to say Congress had little enthusiasm for Reagan's efforts. Whilst the Republicans maintained control of the US Senate their capacity to resist was limited to denying appointment of, or then harassing, some of the more virulently conservative of Reagan's appointments. When the Democrats re-gained the Senate after the November 1986 elections they counteracted vigorously. OIRA's staff and budget were slashed and the agency was threat-ened with extinction. During the Bush Administration the Senate refused to appoint anyone as permanent head of the agency so it ran for four years under the temporary supervision of a career civil servant. Similarly, the Senate attacked the Office of Personnel Management and refused re-nomination of its controversial conservative chief, Donald Devine, and again threatened the existence of the agency.

The Bush Administration found an alternative means of pursuing its bureaucratic goals. The White House Competitiveness Council – chaired by Vice-President Quayle – took on new regulations and old, scrutinising them to see how they measured up compared with free-market principles. The Council was especially hostile to environmental regulations and became im-mensely controversial. Bill Clinton abolished the body early in his presidency.

Questions of political control over the bureaucracy have thus come to domi-nate the presidential agenda. The Nixon and Reagan examples show that there are strategies that can be employed by the Oval Office in pursuit of control, but neither can be said to have fully succeeded.

The pursuit of managerial efficiency

Presidents who enter office with certain qualms about the bureaucracy (such as Carter and Clinton), but at a level lower than that displayed by Nixon and Reagan ultimately tend to concentrate on issues of managerial efficiency rather than those of political control. Administrations that display most com-fort with the bureaucracy tend to do so as well but in a more modest fashion. The Reagan Administration is a partial exception to this in that it expended energy both on political control and managerial efficiency but, as will become evident, its really major efforts and innovation went on the political side.

Presidential enthusiasm for managerial innovation has been assisted by one factor and restricted by another. It is helped by a widespread public mood that government is run inefficiently, and hence the political certainty that all at-tempts to increase administrative effectiveness will be popular with the public even if the voters are dubious about whether such plans will ultimately work. Congress, on the other hand, is often unenthusiastic about such schemes, preferring instead to concentrate energy on dealing with instances of outright fraud. This reluctance reflects a historic, and not entirely unjustified concern, that managerial reforms often mask the real presidential intention which is to make agencies less dependent on Congress.

Enthusiasm for managerial reform has its roots in the 1960s partly as the result of a new generation of agencies being created but also because of the rise of 'management science' in the corporate sector, which stressed the enormous gains that could be achieved by new managerial techniques and philosophies. That development led Robert MacNamara (Defense Secretary 1961–68) to introduce one such technique, that of Planning, Programming and Budgeting Systems (PPBS) that so enthused Lyndon Johnson he tried to introduce it throughout the federal government in one day with predictable failure. Under President Nixon notions of Management by Objective (MBO) became the rage, but with at best modest consequences.

A more systematic approach was taken by President Carter. He also adopted the latest fad from corporate management, this time Zero-Based Budgeting (ZBB) that does not in retrospect appear to have had any great benefit of note. However, he also displayed a wider enthusiasm for reform. He introduced the President's Reorganisation Project, which aimed at redesigning federal agencies to meet changing needs. Through the Inspector-General's Act (1978) federal inspectors were placed within all major federal agencies with the mission to seek out abuse, fraud and waste. More radically still, he pushed through the Civil Service Reform Act (1978) which aimed to give greater flexibility and incentives to senior administrators through the creation of the Senior Executive Service. He set up the Management Improvement Council in 1980 to import private sector know-how into the government. Finally, he backed the Paperwork Reduction Act of 1980, aimed against managerial overload, which created the Office of Information and Regulatory Affairs within the OMB to implement it.

The Carter legacy is a sad reflection on the difficulties facing those who aim at large-scale managerial reform. Although many of the individual components of Carter's proposals had much value, they did not secure any obvious major overall gain. Instead, two of his most significant innovations – the Office of Information and Regulatory Affairs and the new Senior Executive Service – were used by his successor, as has been outlined, as critical vehicles for imposing the counter-bureaucracy and administrative presidency concepts of political control. The fact that they were eventually used this way has, of course, enhanced congressional concerns about management reforms as a Trojan horse for political motives.

The Reagan Administration came to power firmly convinced that the bureaucracy was deeply inefficient. It proposed to deal with its shortcomings by several means. One was through privatisation, contracting-out, and New Federalism, none of which were fully utilised. Another was through cutting overall civil service numbers and attacking civil service pay and benefits. In the first case they did succeed in cutting over 100,000 workers from certain agencies in their first six years in office. Those cuts were cancelled out by increases at the State Department, the Defence Department, and the Justice Department, amongst others, to leave the overall numbers barely changed.

Table 8.5. *Numbers of civilian employees, 1901–93*

Year	Number
1901	239,476
1910	388,708
1920	655,265
1930	601,319
1940	1,042,420
1945	3,816,310
1950	1,960,708
1960	2,398,704
1970	2,981,574
1980	3,121,769
1990	3,503,550
1993	3,038,045

Note Despite popular belief, the number of federal bureaucrats
has not increased dramatically over the last thirty years.
Furthermore, considerable further staff cuts are planned before
the year 2000.

The Administration was rather more adept at curtailing bureaucratic pay and perks.

The major thrust of Reagan's campaign was the introduction of private-sector expertise to clear out widespread and expensive waste. This started with the President's Council on Integrity and Efficiency (PCIE) and continued with the President's Council on Management Improvement (PCMI). These were supplemented by the Presidential Private Sector Survey on Cost Control (PPSSCC), or Grace Commission (after its chairman, businessman J. Peter Grace). This enormous effort involved 161 top private-sector executives who produced in 1984 a 47-volume, 2,478-recommendation document which claimed it could save $424 billion. Somehow, as is so often the case with these grand plans, the savings were not realised.

The Clinton Administration has become the latest entrant into managerial reform. Inspired by *Reinventing Government*,[8] a best-selling book about the rise of private-sector methodology into public-sector management in many of America's states and cities, Vice-President Albert Gore Jr was put in change of a National Performance Review. Gore duly reported back that by new methods over $100 billion could be saved and 250,000 civil servants disposed of over a five-year period. This report focused mainly on the costs of internal regulations and urged internal procurement reform. It also supported widespread internal reorganisation of agencies, eliminating antiquated services, and a new national budgetary system.

Recent experience would suggest that any gains from the Vice-President's efforts will be incremental and modest. Regardless of the merit of his proposals, Congress is unlikely to implement many of the more far-reaching suggestions.

Conclusion

This chapter has stressed the complicated and fragmented nature of the American bureaucracy and noted that many of the quite legitimate complaints made about its effectiveness should be lodged with those who created the agencies and continue to oversee them, rather than at individual bureaucrats. The nature, history, and institutional position of the bureaucracy means that matters of political control and managerial efficiency have dominated and will dominate the agenda surrounding it. Given the nature of federalism, the separation of powers, and checks and balances, the ongoing struggle for control over the bureaucracy is unlikely to diminish and the frustration of Presidents unlikely to recede. The bureaucracy is likely to remain the unloved and unacknowledged fourth branch of American government caught in the crossfire of the executive–legislative battle. Whether in such a situation, debates over the nature of political control (be they by counter-bureaucracy or administrative presidency) and managerial efficiency (as a genuine goal or a surrogate for institutional politics) can ever reach consensual and satisfactory outcomes, must surely be very doubtful.

Notes

1 Source: H. W. Stanley and R. G. Neimi, *Vital Statistics on American Politics*, 4th edn (Washington, DC, CQ Press, 1993).
2 It was finally repealed in 1886 but the right to fire normal agency appointees was not as absolutely established until *Myers* v. *United States* (1926).
3 FDR was overruled in *Humphrey's Executor* v. *United States* (1935).
4 Terry Moe in J. Chubb and P. Peterson (eds), *Can the Government Govern?* (Washington, DC, Brookings Institution, 1987).
5 The most significant case being *Goldman* v. *Kelley* (1970).
6 The complications arising from this have led to a specialist lower court, the Court of Appeals for the Federal Circuit, being created to deal with this category of case.
7 Wilson, *Bureaucracy*.
8 Osborne and Gaebler, *Reinventing Government*.

9

Political parties

Political parties are essential to any modern liberal democratic political system, since it is only through political parties that electoral choices become meaningful and governments can be held accountable. Parties allow differences on issues to be accommodated and resolved; channel popular discontent and demands into the political system; and provide a means by which rulers can be removed peacefully and legitimately. Yet since the time of the Founding Fathers (Madison equated them with 'factions'), political parties have been the most disparaged and abused of America's major political institutions. In American political culture partisanship has never been highly regarded, since the culture stresses individualism, independence, and limitations on large concentrations of political power. Strong parties, by contrast, require collective endeavour, discipline, hierarchy, and concentrated power at the centre. In short, Americans have never felt comfortable with strong parties, and because of this, American parties have acquired several peculiar characteristics.

Unlike those in other liberal democracies, American parties do not control nominations for public office because of that uniquely American device, the primary election, where party candidates are chosen not by the party organisation, but by the voters.[1] Relative to the major parties in most other mass democracies, the American Republicans and Democrats have traditionally been non-ideological, and this is largely due to another uniquely American feature, the absence of a major socialist or labour party. American parties have also been highly decentralised (it used to be said that there were fifty different Democratic and Republican parties rather than one single national party), with no formal organisational hierarchy and little sense of party discipline. The US, moreover, has no concept of formal, 'dues-paying' party membership in the European sense. Finally, American voters no longer have strong loyalties to their major political parties.

In order to understand why American parties have turned out to be so different, we now have to examine the various party systems in US history since the days of the Founding Fathers, and see how the modern American party system evolved. In this survey the concept of partisan 'realignment' will be utilised. Realignment theory holds that American electoral history has been characterised by long periods of stability in electoral support, broken by sudden changes in the partisan balance ('realignments') at certain critical elections – 1828, 1860, 1896 and 1932. Each of these elections ushered in a new electoral era, and a major change in the direction of American politics and society.[2]

For a realignment to take place this sudden change therefore must be, firstly, durable; and secondly, reflected at all levels of electoral competition from the presidency down to the state and local level. Realignments also require political parties to serve as vehicles for electoral change and to consolidate the new balance, and thus realignment requires parties of sufficient organisational strength to channel voter demands and to build strong affective ties between voters and parties.

According to realignment theory there have been six party systems or partisan eras in US history: the era of the Federalists and Jeffersonian Republicans (1789–1824); the Jacksonian Democrats versus the Whigs (1824–60); the post Civil War era (1865–96); the Republican ascendancy (1896–1932); the New Deal (1932–68); and the era of party decline (1968-). Each will now be considered in turn.

The first party system: Federalists v. Jeffersonians

This was not a party system at all in the modern sense. The earliest American parties were more like loose legislative factions, based in the Congress and the state legislatures. There were real differences between them, however. The personal rivalry between Hamilton and Jefferson, Federalist sympathy for Great Britain as opposed to Jeffersonian support for revolutionary France, and Federalist support for a vigorous federal government contrasted with Jeffersonian support for states' rights. The Federalists eventually lost out after 1800 because their constituency of electoral support – wealthy New England families and urban commercial interests – was too limited in a country where democratising tendencies were creating an ever-larger electorate. After the Federalists had virtually died out, a non-party politics based on the Jeffersonian caucus in the Congress prevailed in the so-called 'era of good feelings'.[3]

The second party system: Democrats v. Whigs (1824–60)

American parties really became properly established in this period. The main reason why they developed was the breakdown in the framers' mechanism for electing the president: the electoral college. By the mid-1820s states were electing their electoral college delegates by direct popular election and voters could now choose between slates of electors pledged to particular candidates. After being robbed of the 1824 election in the House of Representatives, General Jackson and his political manager Martin Van Buren established a series of organisations in the various states to mobilise support behind slates of electors committed to vote for Jackson in the college. A look at the map of the 1828 election shows how successful the Jacksonians were.

It was the Jacksonian Democrats who adopted what came to be the classic features of American parties.

First, the Democrats emulated the small, short-lived, anti-Masonic party by adopting the national convention as the body that would make presidential nominations. Each of the various Jackson state organisations would send a

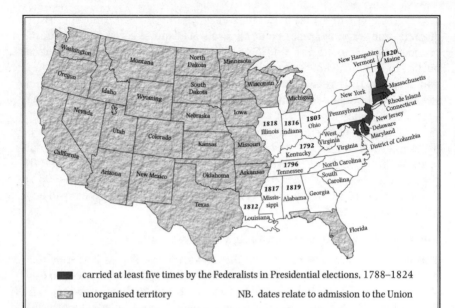

carried at least five times by the Federalists in Presidential elections, 1788–1824

unorganised territory   NB. dates relate to admission to the Union

The first party system, 1788–1824

The map shows the states that supported the Federalist candidates for President at least five times between 1796 and 1824. It can be seen that Federalist strength lay in New England and other pockets of the Northeast, and the Jeffersonian heartland was the southern and frontier states. Initially the Federalists were competitive in New York and New Jersey, but by 1812 their support was confined to their New England redoubts. As the electorate and territory of the United States expanded, the patrician Federalists became decreasingly relevant as a political force, while the constituency for Jeffersonian Republicanism was enhanced.

delegation to the convention, and the states would bargain with each other until an acceptable nominee could be found. The decentralised framework of the parties was also established during this period. Outside the quadrennial meeting of the national convention, there really was no national party, and the national party committee did little more than arrange for the time and place of the next convention. Party organisations were powerful only at the state and local level, and the national party had virtually no authority over them.[4]

American parties in the nineteenth century were all about patronage. To sustain the loyalty of the voters and their enthusiasm, the state and local parties had to provide jobs and favours once they gained office. This explains the development of that specifically American political institution, the party machine: a political organisation devoted wholly to winning office for the spoils that office brought with it. In addition to raw patronage, the machine also provided a sense of ethnic solidarity and social advancement for its

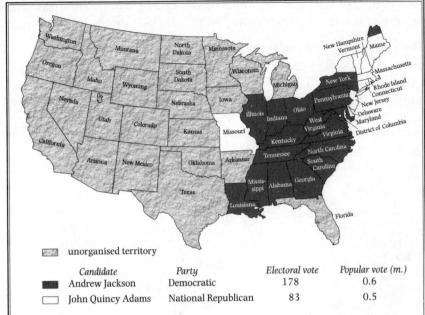

	Candidate	Party	Electoral vote	Popular vote (m.)
	Andrew Jackson	Democratic	178	0.6
	John Quincy Adams	National Republican	83	0.5

The election of 1828.

The map shows the states carried by Andrew Jackson in 1828: the election that set the contours of the Second American party system of Democrats *v.* Whigs (as Jackson's opponents later renamed themselves). Jackson and the Democrats, like the Jeffersonians, were strong in the South and on the expanding frontier. The Whigs, like the Federalists, were strongest in New England, although they were far more competitive than their forefathers in the Middle-Atlantic states and in the South. After the Whigs became fully established and organised in 1840, the second party system was very evenly balanced nationally until the slave issue tore both parties apart.

constituencies. Irish immigrants were the first to perfect the form, and later immigrant groups were then gradually absorbed into the organisation.[5]

The division between the Jacksonians and the Whigs (the opponents of Jackson, who by 1840 had organised themselves into a political party that emulated all the features of the Democrats) was mainly over the issues of states' rights versus a more powerful national government, epitomised by the conflict over the Second Bank of the United States during Jackson's administration. In terms of balance the two parties were fairly evenly matched across the country, although the Jacksonians did better the nearer one got to the western frontier, and the Whigs did better on the East coast and the older areas of settlement in the Northeast. As far as social support was concerned, frontiersmen, the lower middle class, workers, immigrants and artisans tended to support the Democrats, while the upper strata, Yankees, rich planters in the South, and northern Protestants tended to be Whigs. The Democrats favoured a stronger presidency; the Whigs preferred a stronger Congress.

The third party system: Democrats v. Republicans (1860–96)

The realignment of the 1850s occurred because of the slavery issue, which cut right through the electoral balance of the Whig/Democrat party system. As this issue came to predominate during the 1850s, the second party system disintegrated. The Whig party, fundamentally an alliance between southern planters and northern Yankees, could not survive once the consciences of the latter had become aroused by abolitionism. In the North the Whigs became

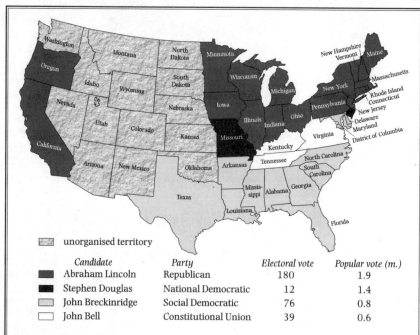

	Candidate	Party	Electoral vote	Popular vote (m.)
	Abraham Lincoln	Republican	180	1.9
	Stephen Douglas	National Democratic	12	1.4
	John Breckinridge	Social Democratic	76	0.8
	John Bell	Constitutional Union	39	0.6

The election of 1860.

The electoral map of 1860 reveals that the Whig–Democrat party system had broken down completely over the issue of slavery. Both major parties had divided into northern and southern wings, but the new anti-slavery Republican party showed a capacity to appeal to anti-slavery Democrats and the Great Lakes and frontier states that the Whigs had lacked, and Republican presidential candidate, Abraham Lincoln (a former Whig congressman) swept virtually all the northern states to win a landslide in the electoral college, although he secured only about 40 per cent of the popular vote. After the war and Reconstruction the reunited Democrats became dominant in the southern states and retained enough northern support to be competitive nationally, but this system was much more regionally polarised that its predecessor and the electoral legacy of the Civil War would pervade US politics for another two or three generations.

the new Republican party, and in the South most eventually joined the Democrats. The Democrats were also bitterly divided, and the northern section of the Jacksonian frontier constituency in states like Wisconsin and Michigan found itself more at home with the new Republican party as far as the slave issue was concerned.[6]

A glance at the map of the 1860 election shows how the system had fragmented. The new Republican party was dominant in the Northeast and the Upper Midwest: the trail of Yankee political settlement that extended as far as Oregon and Washington on the Pacific coast. In the South the Democrats were dominant. The Border and middle-Atlantic states were competitive. Once the Democrats had reunited after the Civil War and Reconstruction had finished in 1876, this became the general pattern of the third party system.

The Republicans were the party of northern white Protestants, and the Democrats the party of southerners, immigrants and Roman Catholics: a peculiar alliance of the northern immigrant machines and the segregationist white South, united only in their contempt for the Yankee Republicans. The fundamental cleavage between the parties in the third party system was based more on ethno-cultural lines rather than on socioeconomic grounds. Both parties constantly waved the 'bloody shirt' of the Civil War, and the difference between them was accurately (if insensitively) summarised in the famous description of the Democratic party by the Revd Samuel Burchard during the 1884 election campaign as the party of 'Rum, Romanism, and Rebellion'.

Presidential elections were very closely contested during this period with a slight Republican advantage due to three factors: firstly, reconstruction reduced the Democratic vote up to 1876; secondly, the Republicans stole the 1876 election; thirdly, the Republicans won in 1888 while losing the popular vote.[7] Thus although Cleveland in 1884 and 1892 was the only Democrat elected President during this period, the overall balance between the parties at all levels was very tight.

Perhaps because of this factor, this was the period of the most intense partisanship in US history. If we look at the turnout diagram we see that electoral turnout in the US in the late nineteenth century reached unprecedented levels. Nearly 80 per cent of the eligible electorate was participating in elections, since partisanship was intensely felt and the stakes involved in terms of jobs and favours were high. Electoral politics at this time was spectacle, hoop-la, and theatre, in which everybody could take part. It had a personal immediacy to the voter that modern election campaigns conducted on the clinical medium of television lack.[8]

Of course together with all the fun went an appalling degree of electoral fraud, intimidation (parties issued the ballots), and bribery. The machines grew more and more shameless in their corruption and many party organisations became little more than the political playthings of powerful industrial interests, such as railway corporations. America's moralistic political culture could only

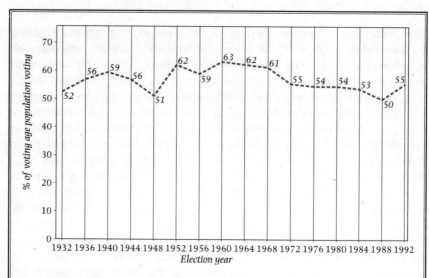

Turnout in presidential elections, 1932–92.

The figures shown in the graph represent the percentage of the estimated eligible electorate who actually showed up at the polls. Because America does not have automatic voter registration, the figures are not completely accurate. The pattern, however, is clear enough. Between 1960 and 1988 American electoral turnout dropped by 13 per cent – a powerful indication of voter alienation from politics and the party system. It seems that the sharp rise in turnout evident in the 1992 election was largely a result of new voters mobilised into the system by the Independent presidential candidacy of Ross Perot. If these voters stay mobilised for the rest of the 1990s they could have a decisive impact on the direction of the American party system.

Source The World Almanac and Book of Facts, 1993 (New York: Pharos Books, 1992)

tolerate corruption on such a massive scale for so long, and by the mid-1890s it was clear that another massive electoral shift was imminent.

The system of 1896: the Republican ascendancy (1896–1932)

The realignment of 1896 came about due to the crisis in American agriculture that had existed since the Civil War; a crisis, created by overproduction and the systematic exploitation of farmers by railroads and middlemen, that was exacerbated further by the great economic depression that hit the US in the mid-1890s. The agrarian crisis gave rise to the Populist or People's Party, which with a radical programme of regulation, public ownership, and currency reform aroused a great deal of support in the western and southern states. Eastern elites were terrified of the Populists, not only because of their 'socialistic' programme, but also because they regarded the Populist panacea for the nation's economic woes – backing the dollar up by silver rather than gold – as likely to lead to complete economic collapse. The fears of the business establishment were increased when in 1896, the Democrats repudiated the conservative incumbent President Grover Cleveland, and nominated the radical, young congressman from Nebraska William Jennings Bryan. Bryan argued that this was the classic opportunity for the Democrats to realign the party system in their favour by embracing the Populists and major elements of their platform – particularly free silver.* The famous peroration to his speech at the convention stated the issue in dramatic terms: 'You shall not press down upon the brow of labour this crown of thorns, you shall not crucify mankind upon a cross of gold.'[9]

The prospect of Bryan in the White House scared eastern businessmen and they flocked to the banner of the Republican nominee, William McKinley of Ohio, who ran on a platform that stressed the importance of the tariff and the gold standard. McKinley's political manager Mark Hanna used the threat of Bryan to extract vast sums of money from business corporations to finance the McKinley campaign.

In the end, despite Bryan's exertions, McKinley won the election quite handily. He also established a new partisan alignment that worked very much to the advantage of the Republicans.[10] The even partisan balance of the post-Civil War period was replaced by a Republican ascendancy that persisted until 1932 – with the exception of Wilson's victories in 1912 and 1916, when the GOP was split. They not only won, they won by landslides, because Bryanism, with its rural, western bias, alienated urban, middle- and working-class Democratic support. Labour could see little advantage in free silver – a policy oriented exclusively towards the interests of western agriculture – and McKinley seemed a much better bet for a return to industrial prosperity with his promise of a 'full dinner pail'. When economic recovery and the Spanish–American war followed McKinley's accession to the presidency, the Republican dominance was confirmed. The Republicans had now become the 'Grand Old Party' – associated in the public mind with reliability, nationalism, and prosperity. The Democrats were an unholy alliance of unsavoury elements – the racist South and the corrupt urban machines of the North. For most of the 1896–1932 period, they looked wholly unconvincing as a governing party. Almost all respectable and educated opinion was Republican in its politics.

The pattern of the 1896 election result illustrates the contours of the new Republican alignment in geographic terms. The Republicans were now dominant in the industrial and urban centres of the Northeast and the Great Lakes, and also on the Pacific coast. The Democrats had their solid South and the agricultural and silver mining states of the West. In electoral votes however, the Republican dominance in the metropolitan Northeast gave them a decisive

---

* Farmers, and others in debt to the banks, favoured basing the value of money on silver, not gold, because silver was cheaper and such a shift would reduce the level of their debts. Banks, predictably, favoured gold.

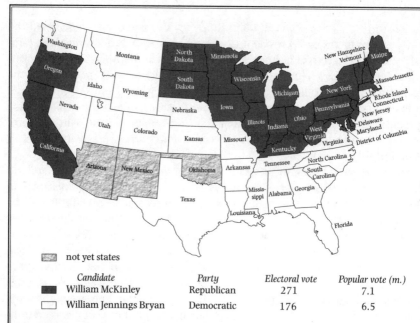

	Candidate	Party	Electoral vote	Popular vote (m.)
■	William McKinley	Republican	271	7.1
□	William Jennings Bryan	Democratic	176	6.5

not yet states

The election of 1896.

In 1896 William McKinley and the Republicans mobilised industrial America – the Northeast and the Great Lakes states – to defeat the southwestern, agrarian, Protestant Fundamentalist Democrat William Jennings Bryan. Although the 1896 election was not a Republican landslide the party system became lopsidedly Republican thereafter, as the Democrats – a party of southern reactionaries, agrarian populists and northern, urban machine bosses – were consistently divided, or (with the exception of Woodrow Wilson) failed to find presidential candidates with any significant electoral appeal to the nation's major population centres. The generally business-oriented Republicans remained more or less excluded from the southern states, but for the period of the Fourth Party System (1896–1928), their national predominance was so great that they did not need to compete there.

electoral edge, with the Democrats being confined to their southern and western electoral ghetto in presidential contests.

A further development of this system was that while the third party system had seen real competition between the parties in most areas of the country, the system of 1896 turned America into a nation of one-party states. The Republicans were virtually eliminated in the South, and the Democrats ordinarily had very little chance of victory in the Northeast. The end of regular alternation in partisan control in many areas meant that the excesses of political machines which had captured the label of the dominant party in an area became even more dangerous. This was one factor that inspired the growth of the Progressive movement after 1896.

The impact of the Progressives: 1896–1916

The Progressives sought to root out 'corruption' from the American political process at the turn of the century. They saw, correctly, that the parties had become vehicles by which powerful private interests such as railways had come to dominate the governmental process in many states. Outraged at the extent of venality in politics, and eager to curb the power and ambitions of the corporate moguls, the Progressives embarked on a series of reforms designed to strengthen American government and improve its quality.[11]

Progressives believed that government should serve as a countervailing power to oppressive private interests. But to get better people into government they needed to take nominations for elective office out of the hands of the parties, especially since, after 1896, there were so many one-party states. The Progressives' answer was to weaken the parties organisationally, so that the people would have direct control over political nominations and the influence of the special interests would thus be curbed. The most important of the Progressives' reforms were the introduction of the direct primary (where the voters chose the party nominees rather than party organisations) and the introduction of the 'Australian' ballot (the state government rather than the parties providing the electoral ballot). These measures were important because the primary reduced the control of the party machines over nominations, and the Australian ballot made electoral intimidation and fraud much more difficult, while also making it much easier for voters to 'split their ticket', that is, vote for the candidates of different parties for different offices. The Progressives further weakened the parties by prohibiting party labels from appearing on the ballot in local elections in many areas.[12]

These measures were introduced in several states – particularly in the South and West where party machines were not so well developed – and by mid-century the direct primary had become almost universal. At first it did not make that much difference in the machine-controlled eastern and Great Lakes states, because party machines simply organised their cohorts of voters behind the 'organisation candidate' in the primary. The long-term consequences of the Progressive reforms would be very momentous for American parties however, since it is from this point that the long-term decline of the US parties in the twentieth century commences.

The New Deal and after: 1932–68

After a Democratic interlude under Woodrow Wilson (1913–21), the Republican ascendancy returned with a vengeance in the 1920s. Harding, Coolidge and Hoover each won presidential election landslides and Congress remained solidly Republican. In 1924 the Democrats had taken 103 ballots and over two weeks to choose a presidential nominee, and at the same convention they *failed* to condemn the Ku Klux Klan by one-quarter of a vote. One year later their great hero Bryan ended up as a figure of ridicule after the infamous

'Monkey' trial in Tennessee.[13] In 1928 the Democrats nominated the first Roman Catholic to head a national party ticket, New York governor, Al Smith. Smith's candidacy raised the turnout somewhat as he drew out extra Catholic voters for the Democrats, but Republican Herbert Hoover still won by a landslide and even broke into the hitherto solidly Democratic South.

The onset of the Great Depression during Hoover's presidency (1929–33) finally gave the Democrats the opportunity to break the Republican grip on national politics. In Franklin Roosevelt they found exactly the right man for the hour. Roosevelt overwhelmed Hoover in 1932 on a platform that flayed the Republican incumbent for irresponsible spending and failing to maintain a balanced budget. Once in office, however, Roosevelt introduced deficit spending and expanded the scope of the federal government to an unprecedented degree. By 1936 FDR had turned his opportunity into a full-scale realignment in favour of the Democratic party.

The white South remained the basis of the New Deal Democratic majority coalition, but Roosevelt was able to solidify the ethnic, Catholic vote and the Jewish vote for the Democrats. Blue-collar workers and particularly those organised in labour Unions became a pillar of Democratic support, and the Democrats also dug deeply into the midwestern farm vote. Black voters in the North, where they were migrating in large numbers and where they could vote, also changed from overwhelmingly Republican to overwhelmingly Democratic in allegiance.[14]

The Republicans were left with the northern urban upper-middle class, and white Protestant voters in the smaller cities and rural areas of the Northeast and Midwest. In the 1936 elections they could win only Maine and Vermont in the presidential contest and were reduced to eighty-nine Congressmen and seventeen Senators. They came back after the War to control Congress in 1947/8, but their moderate candidate Thomas E. Dewey still lost to Democrat Harry Truman in 1948, even with the Democratic party split three ways! Only riding on the coat-tails of the personally appealing General Eisenhower in 1952 and 1956 were the Republicans able to get back in the presidential saddle, and even then they lost Congress after 1954, and had to wait forty years before controlling the House of Representatives again. Indeed the Eisenhower Administration confirmed the New Deal since it reversed none of the changes in domestic and foreign policy that the Roosevelt era had brought about.

During the New Deal era, the parties essentially divided on socioeconomic policy. Democrats believed in expanding the welfare system and in government management of the economy, while Republicans opposed these as detrimental to the free-enterprise system and to American individualism. On foreign policy the Republicans were isolationist and nationalist, while the Democrats were internationalist and Europe-oriented. On civil liberties matters the Democrats were pulled to the right by their southern wing, so the Republicans remained generally more supportive up to the mid-1960s. It was when civil liberties

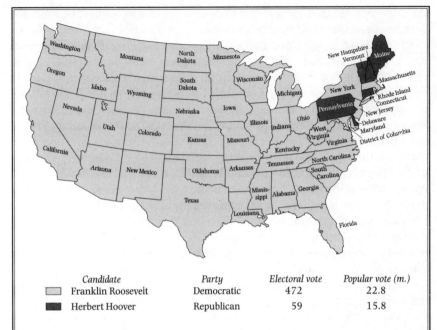

Candidate	Party	Electoral vote	Popular vote (m.)
Franklin Roosevelt	Democratic	472	22.8
Herbert Hoover	Republican	59	15.8

The election of 1932.

The election of 1932 ushered in the New Deal electoral realignment and dramatically changed the parisan balance. In 1932 the Repubican Herbert Hoover carried only six states, and four years later the Republican presidential candidate was reduced to only two. Elsewhere the Democrats were dominant for a generation. Under Franklin D. Roosevelt they held on to their southern base and ousted the Republicans from their dominance in the northern industrial and farm states. Although the Republicans came back in the Farm Belt and were competitive again in the major industrial states by the late 1940s, the staying power of the New Deal coalition enabled the Democrats to win five successive presidential elections, and the Republicans had to enlist the country's greatest national hero, Dwight Eisenhower, to oust them in 1952. During the 1950s and 1960s the Democrats actually enhanced their dominance in Congress and in state and local elections: a dominance that has only very recently been eroded significantly.

and foreign policy issues began to come to the fore and cut across the socioeconomic divide that the Democrats' New Deal coalition came under strain.

The first signs of fragmentation came in 1948. In protest at the inclusion of a civil rights plank in the Democratic platform, some of the southerners broke away and ran on a States' Rights or 'Dixiecrat' ticket (headed by Governor J. Strom Thurmond of South Carolina) in several southern states. On the Left flank progressive Democrats, angry at Truman's Cold-War policies, rallied behind the 'Progressive' ticket headed by FDR's former Vice-President Henry Wallace. Democratic strength was still such that Truman won despite these fissures. Wallace carried no states and Thurmond could carry only the Deep South – Alabama, Mississippi, Louisiana, and South Carolina.

But on the civil rights question the Democrats had already indicated what their choice would be. In order to gain the support of black voters in the North concentrated in big cities in key electoral college states, they would have to sacrifice some of their strength in the white South. The whole logic of their position in the party system since the New Deal also pushed them to the more liberal position on civil rights. To do this and hold the South ultimately proved to be impossible, however. During the 1950s the Republican party began to emerge in the South, and not only at the presidential level.[15] Kennedy's narrow win in 1960, and the 1964 Johnson landslide, served to disguise the under- lying decay of the New Deal coalition. But the latter election, although a Republican disaster, gave a clear indication that the party system was chang- ing. The states carried by the conservative Republican nominee Barry Goldwater in addition to his home state of Arizona were the Deep South states where Republican presidential candidates had invariably won only a derisory number of votes in elections since the Civil War: Alabama, Louisiana, Missis- sippi, Georgia, and South Carolina. Some of his worst showings were in northern states that had been kind to the GOP even in the darkest days of the New Deal, such as Maine and Vermont. Goldwater's opposition to the 1964 Civil Rights Act had completed the *volte-face* of the parties on race-related issues. Now the Republicans, in search of disenchanted white Democrats North and South, embraced the more conservative position on the race issue and the Democrats became more explicitly liberal.

Race alone was not sufficient to destroy the New-Deal party system, how- ever. In the mid-1960s it was joined by a host of other issues which tore the Democrats' presidential majority to pieces – Vietnam, the campus revolt, law and order, the decisions of the Warren Court, and the so-called 'counter- culture'. In 1968 the party was again split three ways. The most conservative southern and northern blue-collar Democrats were attracted to the Populist, law and order candidacy of southern segregationist George Wallace. Within the party the New Deal/Labor establishment led by the retiring President Lyndon Johnson and his Vice-President Hubert Humphrey were pilloried by younger, anti-war activists led by Senators Eugene McCarthy and Robert Kennedy. Roosevelt's conjuring trick of submerging deep cultural differences between the components of the Democratic coalition by stressing the socio- economic issues on which the party could unite on a liberal position had finally ceased to work. In the more affluent America of the 1950s and 1960s the politics of economic populism no longer worked so well. The campus gener- ation of the 1960s could afford peace, love, and moral outrage over Vietnam, as opposed to having to endure the economic hardships of their parents or grandparents. Blue-collar and southern white Democrats felt that the angry children of the anti-war movement were trying to take their party away from them, and they were fundamentally correct! Humphrey's narrow loss to

Republican Richard Nixon, with the 'white backlash' candidate Wallace winning 14 per cent of the vote, brought the New Deal era to a close.[16]

The emerging Republican majority? 1968–88

The big question underlying the Democratic crack-up in 1968 was whether the Republicans would take the opportunity to turn this into a partisan realignment in their favour. The signs looked auspicious: the country was bitterly divided over the Vietnam War and the majority coalition was in deep trouble; and there was the Wallace movement, serving as a way-station for Democrats moving towards the GOP.

After the 1968 election, a young Nixon campaign staffer named Kevin Phillips wrote a book entitled *The Emerging Republican Majority*, in which he added together the Nixon and Wallace votes of 1968 (43 + 14 per cent) to produce what he predicted would be a new Republican majority. This Republican majority would be based in the 'Sunbelt': the GOP would dominate the economically expanding West and would win over the South on the race issue. They would also pick up much of the Democrats' lower middle-class/blue-collar ethnic vote in the North. To do this they might have to forfeit black votes and some of their traditional upper middle-class white Protestant constituency, but the overall impact of the shifts in numbers would work to their advantage. The Democrats would be left only with blacks, Hispanics, and college communities.[17]

If we look at the map of Republican strength in presidential elections since 1968 we can see strong evidence for the Phillips thesis. From 1968 to 1988 the Republicans won five out of six presidential elections and four of those were landslides. The presidential coalition that they built had fundamentally the same ingredients as Phillips predicted. Republican presidential candidates united the western and southern states and won enough votes away from the Democrats' old middle-class/blue-collar constituency in the Northeast and Midwest to win easily at this level. Their only defeat in 1976 could be attributed to Watergate, and even then they nearly won, with a very weak presidential incumbent, Gerald Ford. Between 1960 and 1988 the Democrats lost support among men, whites, blue-collar voters, younger voters, Fundamentalist and Evangelical Protestants, Roman Catholics, and, of course, among white southerners.

Given the general shift away from traditional Democratic positions on the economy and expanding the size of government over the period since 1968, we then have impressive evidence of a realignment of American politics in favour of the Republican party that was consolidated by the 'Reagan Revolution' of the 1980s.

There are several problems with this hypothesis, however. First, realignments have always been linked to a sharp rise in electoral participation but from 1968 to 1988 the underlying trend in electoral participation in the US was continually downward. Most importantly, apart from controlling the US

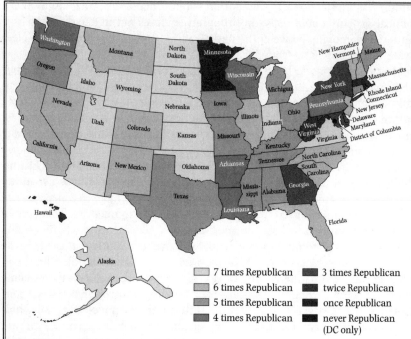

Republican strength in presidential elections, 1968–92.

After 1968 the New Deal system in presidential elections broke down utterly, and was replaced by a system of Republican dominance. The white South finally converted to the GOP (a century after the Civil War) due to the impact of the black civil rights revolution led by Democrat Presidents Kennedy and Johnson, and the booming sunbelt states of the South and West also became reliable presidential bastions of the GOP. With this formidable base of Republican support in the electoral college, the Democrats were able to win only in 1976, when the southern states defected to Jimmy Carter, the first Deep Southerner to be nominated for the Presidency since Reconstruction – and 1992 – where, with a little help from Independent Ross Perot, another southerner, Bill Clinton, swept the major north-ern states and California, while also picking off enough southern states to win handily in the electoral college. Whether Clinton's bi-coastal coalition is the harb-inger of a new electoral order remains to be seen.

Senate from 1981 to 1987, the Republicans were unable to extend their realignment beneath the presidential level. The Democratic party held on to the US House until 1994, and controlled the overwhelming majority of state and local offices during the Reagan–Bush years.

Until 1994 there thus appeared to be little evidence of a Republican rea-lignment at the other levels of government to match their presidential strength. And even in the wake of the 1994 Republican landslide in congressional and state elections, voters appeared to be motivated by antipathy towards the

Clinton Administration and the congressional Democrats, and disgust with political system in general, rather than an embrace of the Republican party. Rather than moving between the parties after 1968, it appeared the US electorate was disengaging from partisan politics altogether. The reasons for this will be discussed in the next section.

The decline of party

During the 1980s the US appeared to have different partisan alignments at different levels of electoral competition: the Republicans dominated presidential politics, while the Democrats dominated congressional and state and local politics. This situation was unlike any previous party system in US history and it is evident that the concept of party realignment is of little use in explaining it. To understand what has been going on we have to go back to the turn of the century and examine several long-term changes in the American political environment.

Realignment no longer works according to the conventional model because the relationship between voters and parties in the United States has been transformed. In the nineteenth century voter awareness about politics came almost entirely through the parties or the party-controlled press. Citizens related to politics through party loyalties that were grounded in family, community, ethnicity and favours. As America became a more advanced, urban, industrial society and a world power, so, like other industrial societies, it became bureaucratised. The new political class – the white-collar intelligentsia who led the Progressive movement – wanted to base government on 'rationality' and scientific expertise, rather than personal ties. For them the party organisations were inefficient and corrupt and their power over American politics had to be broken if America was to fulfil its promise at home and abroad. The story of American politics in this century has been that of the slow erosion of party organisations and party loyalties among the electorate, and the rise of technocratic politics, based on administrative rationality and expertise in its stead.

Keeping this general theme in mind we can discern several factors that have contributed directly to the decline of the parties. The introduction of the primary election for making party nominations during the Progressive era ultimately robbed the parties of control over their own nominations. The 'nationalisation' of American government in this century has also contributed, since the strong parties of the late nineteenth century were based on state and local politics and powerful local organisations. To the extent that the most important arena of political conflict in the US in this century has been the national arena, the parties have seemed decreasingly relevant. The replacement of the spoils system of the late nineteenth century by a professional corps of administrators selected according to merit and expertise was one of the great Progressive causes. Now the merit civil service generally prevails at all levels of American government, and the parties thus lost the political patronage that was the life-blood of their organisations. Moreover, the rise of a national, bureaucratically-administered welfare system, during the New Deal and later, took away the welfare function from party organisations.

The old party machines were based on urban, ethnic communities whose votes could be delivered *en bloc* through the influence of a few key community leaders. In this century many (though not all) of these ethnic ties have been eroded as voters moved from the inner cities to the suburbs. Suburban culture was less intimate and much more individualistic and ethnic and partisan ties meant much less there. Increasing levels of affluence and education also led voters to become more sophisticated in their political views, more ready to split their tickets and more politically motivated by single issues and ideology than inherited party ties.[18]

Finally, the rise of non-partisan political media, particularly television, took from the parties their crucial roles as intermediaries between government and citizen. In their late nineteenth-century heyday, the parties controlled all the channels by which the citizen related to politics. The advent of the telegraph services in the mid-nineteenth century, however, gave rise to the non-partisan, 'muck-raking' press of the Progressive period. Mass circulation newspapers now replaced the partisan broadsheets of old, and these newspapers sought to present the news in an 'independent' or at least less partisan fashion. This new journalistic ethic was transferred to radio and television when they came on the scene. The electronic media now dispensed political information to citizens everywhere, directly; without the intermediation of the parties. They also stressed issues and tended to disparage a politics based on blind party loyalty. The rise of the independent electronic media as the main intermediaries between citizens and government simply made the parties appear antiquated, untrustworthy, and irrelevant. By the 1970s Americans trusted CBS television anchorman Walter Cronkite more than they trusted any party politician.

In sum, the parties appeared decreasingly relevant to American politics and the voters were not oblivious to this. Candidates, interest groups, the news media, and bureaucrats were the new key actors in the game. American parties which had always been peculiar compared to those in other democratic nations became even more so. Instead of being the great ideological, organisational monoliths of Western Europe, they seemed to be disintegrating into bland and empty labels, useful only for structuring the vote at election time.

By the 1960s and 1970s the signs of party decline had become obvious. One of the most significant was the sharp decline in election turnout. After the Progressive era turnout fell precipitously from the 80 per cent level of the 1880s to a low of 49 per cent in 1924: a decline that was only partly reversed by the New Deal. Since 1960 US turnout has steadily declined to the point where only 50 per cent of the electorate voted in 1988. American electoral turnout is notably low by international standards, and this is surely related to the fact that America has the weakest party organisations of the major western democracies.

Walter Dean Burnham has argued that the Progressive reforms – particularly the Australian ballot, and the requirement that all eligible voters register themselves to vote – deliberately depressed turnout by effectively discouraging the less educated and the economically disadvantaged from voting.[19] Defenders of Progressivism have pointed out, correctly, that late nineteenth-century turnout figures were notoriously inaccurate and that the reforms eliminated a good deal of fraud. Electoral turnout figures in the contemporary US are also artificially depressed by the method of calculation which, in the absence of a national electoral roll, merely measures the percentage of the estimated eligible population voting (including the imprisoned, the insane, and illegal immigrants).

Yet despite the *caveats*, Burnham was on to something. The modern politics of single issues, ideology, and personality that replaced the old style party-machine politics nevertheless appeared less relevant and more alien to many voters, particularly those in the lower socioeconomic categories. Interest groups and the news media, who have taken on much of the parties' roles as political intermediaries, have also proven to be less effective in motivating idle or reluctant voters to go to the polls.

Table 9.1. *Declining party identification, 1952–88*

Year	Strong Democrat or Republican	Weak Democrat or Republican	Independent
1952	36	39	23
1956	36	37	23
1960	36	39	23
1964	38	39	23
1968	28	40	30
1972	25	39	34
1976	24	39	37
1980	27	37	34
1984	29	35	34
1988	31	32	36

Source National Elections Studies data in Harold W. Stanley and Richard G. Niemi, *Vital Statistics on American Politics*, 3rd edn (Washington, DC: Congressional Quarterly Press, 1992).

Another sign of party decline is the sharp fall in voters' self-identification with the political parties. As late as the 1950s political scientists discovered that these party identities grounded in the New Deal era, and passed on to the next generation by family and community, were still the main determinants of electoral choice. In the 1950s 75 per cent of Americans identified with the major parties, but by the late 1970s this had fallen below 60 per cent, and the number of 'strong' identifiers dropped below 30 per cent. Party appeared to matter much less in evaluating candidates, with personal attributes and issue positions becoming more significant.

The decline of party ID is obviously related to the fact that Americans are 'splitting their tickets' (voting for candidates of different parties for different offices at the same election) far more frequently in the modern era than they did fifty or one hundred years ago. A look at the graph below indicates that this trend has been under way since the 1920s. Voters have become so sophisticated at ticket-splitting between electoral levels, that during the 1980s it was not uncommon for Republican presidential candidates Reagan and Bush to carry a state or district with over 60 per cent of the vote, while a Democratic congressional incumbent on the same ballot was equally easily re-elected. The relationship between electoral levels has severely eroded in recent decades,

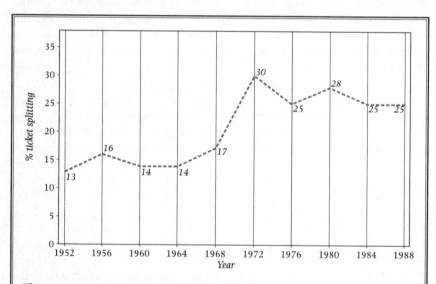

The emergence of 'split-ticket' voting.

The table reveals the dramatic increase in voting for different parties for President and Congress that has taken place since 1968. Split-ticket voting is part of the phenomenon of partisan dealignment that became evident in the United States during the 1970s: the troubled decade of Vietnam and Watergate and their aftermath. It is also a strong indication of the decreasing relevance of party ties, as voters make their electoral decisions on the basis of candidate personality, name-recognition, or simply hedge their electoral bets by dividing their votes deliberately between different parties for different offices. Although the rates of ticket-splitting declined slightly in the 1980s, they remain well above the pre-1968 levels.

and Presidents have short 'coat-tails'. For voters, the individual attributes and positions of the different candidates for the different offices mean much more than voting a straight party line.[20]

Perhaps the most obvious aspects of the party decline that became so evident in the US during the 1970s, however, was the virtually elimination of the parties from the presidential selection process after 1968. Prior to that year most of the delegates to both parties' national nominating conventions were still selected in closed processes by state and local party leaders who served as the real power-brokers on the convention floor. Presidential primary elections to choose convention delegates had been introduced in some states during the Progressive era, but they never really caught on in the major states (with the significant exception of ultra-progressive California), and were treated rather like opinion polls are today: interesting but not ultimately decisive. After the Second World War, primaries began to be taken more seriously, opinion polls and the electronic media became more important, and the nomination effectively began to move out of the convention hall. Yet in 1968 it was still possible for Hubert Humphrey to be nominated by the Democrats simply by courting state and local party bosses such as Mayor Richard J. Daley of Chicago, and without entering a single primary election.

In the 1960s climate of revulsion against the established order, however, the Humphrey nomination was not seen as legitimate by many in the anti-Vietnam War movement and the news media, and in an attempt to buy peace within the party, Humphrey conceded a reform commission to investigate the party's nominating process and recommend reforms. After Humphrey lost the election, this commission (named the McGovern–Fraser Commission after its two chairmen, Senator George McGovern and Congressman Donald Fraser) became dominated by figures from the radical, reform wing of the party, and its report in 1970 banned all reserved delegate places for party leaders and elected officials, and advocated that all delegate-selection processes in the fifty states should be governed by strict criteria of 'openness, representativeness, and maximization of participation'. These rules were enforced on the state parties, who found that moving to a presidential primary election was the easiest way to comply with the complex new rules.[21] As a result the number of presidential primary states grew from seventeen in 1968 to thirty-five by 1980, and the proportion of delegates chosen in primaries grew from about 30 per cent to over 80 per cent of the total. Although the Republicans did not formally change their national rules, as the minority party in most state legislatures they invariably had little choice in the matter when the majority Democrats opted to move to a presidential primary election, and so the GOP experienced a similar proliferation of primaries.

The intended consequence of the post-1968 reforms was to confirm the removal of the power over presidential nominations from state and local party leaders and office-holders, and to place it in the hands of the voters in primary elections. But the move to nomination in the primaries also enhanced the

Table 9.2. *Presidential primaries, 1948–88*

Year	Democrats		Republicans	
	Primaries	*% convention**	*primaries*	*% convention**
1948	14	36	12	36
1952	16	39	13	39
1956	19	41	19	44
1960	16	38	15	39
1964	16	41	17	46
1968	17	49	17	47
1972	23	67	22	58
1976	30	76	29	70
1980	35	81	36	78
1984	30	67	29	67
1988	37	81	38	81

Note * Proportion of the total number of national convention delegates chosen in primary elections.

Source Harold W. Stanley and Richard G. Niemi, *Vital Statistics on American Politics*, 3rd edn (Washington, DC: Congressional Quarterly Press, 1992).

influence of the news media and interest groups over the selection process, since they provided the only criteria by which the hapless primary voter might assess a plethora of unknown candidates. In the sequence of primary contests media assessments of how well or badly the various candidates were performing also governed the dynamics of the race. Success in the first primary in the small and unrepresentative (at least for the Democrats) state of New Hampshire thus took on an extraordinary importance. In 1976 the unknown former Georgia Governor Jimmy Carter was able to secure the Democratic nomination through a victory in New Hampshire, and a brilliant media strategy, and incumbent Republican President Gerald Ford almost lost the nomination to Ronald Reagan who had the endorsement of only one Republican incumbent Governor, and one Republican US Senator. Neither Carter nor Reagan would have come remotely close to nomination under the old rules.[22]

After McGovern–Fraser, parties appeared to have become marginal to the nominating process, confirming at the national level what had been taking place at the state and local level since the introduction of the Direct Primary at the turn of the century. Presidential candidacies were now largely generated by the candidates themselves or by a number of powerful interest groups within the two national parties. After the campaign finance reforms of the 1970s, candidates could raise money from small individual donors, Political Action Committees (the fund-raising arms of major interest groups), or if they surpassed a relatively modest threshold (candidates must raise $5,000 in amounts not exceeding $250 in twenty states) the federal government itself, but not from the parties. Presidential campaigns were conducted by media consultants and pollsters hired by the candidates, but not by party leaders. The nomination was invariably settled long before the national convention, and that body merely ratified the choice of the primaries, and served as a glorified launching rally for the campaign. In short, the parties had been effectively eliminated from the presidential nominating process.[23]

Rather than moving from one party to another, as in a realignment phase, in the 1970s and 1980s it appeared that the American electorate was moving away from parties in general. Instead of a realignment there appeared to be a 'dealignment' of the American electorate, created mainly by the decay of political parties as organisations and their decreasing relevance to the political concerns of the ordinary voter. The parties themselves became labels taken over periodically by particular candidate organisations, or by single-issue and/or ideological activists. As the bases of the old-style party organisations collapsed, so the old-style party professionals disappeared and were replaced by committed activists, more interested in the politics of principle and ideology than in the good of the party. These activists forced the parties into narrow ideological straitjackets that failed to reflect the complexity of the views of citizens or even party identifiers, and as a result more and more Americans became estranged from partisanship. During the 1970s US parties thus appeared to be trapped in an irreversible cycle of decline.

Party renewal?

The decline of US parties had several serious implications for the health of the political system as a whole. If the party system were no longer capable of realignment then the political system might become more unstable, with wild swings between the parties at different levels of government. In the vacuum left by the decline of the parties interest groups would expand their influence and aggregating interests would become virtually impossible. Sooner or later the governmental process might break down completely through inertia.

These were the sombre themes of much of the literature on US parties in the late 1970s, but we refuse to be as pessimistic with regard to their future development. Leon Epstein, a veteran scholar of US parties, interpreted the events of the 1960s and 1970s neither as a sign of the realignment or dealignment of the political parties in the US, but merely as the parties' continuing adaptation to their wider societal environment.[24] As the bases for the old party system – spoils and family–community ties – disappeared, the parties had to adapt to the new candidate-centred, issue-focused and bureaucratic environment of late twentieth-century American politics. Many of the parties' problems during the 1960s and 1970s arose because they had failed to adapt to this climate earlier, but, rather, had continued to operate on the basis of an organisational politics that had become irrelevant to most Americans.

After the upheaval of the 1960s had died down, some signs of revival became evident during the 1980s, that contradicted the general consensus on ineluctable party decline.

One sign of party renewal has been the rise in importance of the national party committees. Traditionally these concerned themselves largely with arranging the site of the party convention, and had little authority over the state parties. The national chairman of the party was traditionally responsible for dispensing patronage when the party held the White House, and liaising with important party leaders. In recent years the national chairman has become the most visible spokesman for the party whether the party is in or out of office, and directs a national party headquarters that is playing an unprecedented role in fund-raising and dispensing services to congressional and state and local candidates.[25] Direct mail and computer technology were pioneered by a succession of Republican National Chairmen after the Goldwater débâcle in 1964, as a means of raising national party finances from a wide small-donor base, and playing an active role in candidate recruitment and national campaigns. The results paid off as the Republicans were able to fight a national party campaign in 1980 that brought them the White House, the US Senate, and major gains in the US House. During the Reagan and Bush Administrations the Democratic National committee caught up with the GOP and became an equally formidable operation. Moreover, the Democrats' decision to enforce the McGovern–Fraser rules on the state parties, and the subsequent Supreme Court decision – *Cousins* v. *Wigoda*, 1975 – that upheld their right to do so, gave the national party committees sovereign authority over the state partes for the first time in US history. Recent evidence from congressional voting behaviour also indicates that the Republican and Democratic parties are now more ideologically coherent than they have ever been before. Liberal Republicans and conservative Democrats have become increasingly rare species, and in every region of the country the Democrats are clearly to the left of the Republicans, which was not the case as late as the 1950s.[26] Indeed, contrary to the scholarly wisdom that US parties are too weak and ideologically indistinguishable, it appears that the increased discipline and ideological coherence of the parties has contributed to the 'gridlock' in the US national government that characterised the Bush and Clinton presidencies.[27]

How should we explain the paradox of party renewal with the apparently strong evidence of party decline? The answer lies in Epstein's theory of party adaptation to circumstance. The growth in significance of the national party committees is a belated reflection of the nationalisation of American politics and government in general. The 'polarisation' of the parties is a result of the increasing importance of national single-issue groups and the national news media, who together have become the crucial agents of mobilisation in low-turnout congressional primary elections. To receive the endorsement of NOW (the National Organization of Women) or the NEA (the National

New-style party powerbrokers: Jesse Jackson and Pat Buchanan

Whereas power in old-style party politics depended on organisational control over a city or state, in the modern era other factors, such as media visibility and appeal

to a national activist constituency, have become decisive. Demoract Jesse Jackson (*left*) (b. 1941) and Republican Pat Buchanan (*below*) (b. 1938) both exemplify this new style of politics. Neither has ever held elected office, and both owe their prominence on the contemporary American political scene to a high media profile and a narrow but very committed popular following. An ordained Baptist Minister and long-time civil rghts activist, Jesse Jackson's campaigns for the Democratic presidential nomination in 1984 and 1988 established him as the most powerful black American political leader and a power in the national Democratic party politics. Pat Buchanan, speech writer for Richard Nixon and White House Communications Director under President Rea-

gan, established his appeal to right-wing Republican activists through regular appearances on television news shows as a conservative commentator. Buchanan's unsuccessful challenge to President Bush's re-nomination in 1992 earned him a prime-time address to the Republican convention that set the tone for the entire event. After the 1992 election Buchanan and Jackson both had their own talk shows on the Cable News Network (CNN).

Education Association, the largest teachers' union) for a Democrat, or the Christian Coalition or the NRA (National Rifle Association) for a Republican, guarantees campaign money, organisation, and a militant electoral constituency that is certain to show up at the polls. The entertainment requirements of television news, now the principal intermediary between government and voters, also prefers political polarisation and the politics of 'principle' to the old-style party politics of coalition-building and 'splitting the difference' on contentious issues.

None of this has made the parties more relevant to the voters. Survey data continue to demonstrate widespread discontent, and diminishing voter identification with both parties, whose new ideological concerns do not reflect the more pragmatic and material concerns of the electorate. Voters react by continuing to split their tickets on a massive scale, as if to encourage the increasingly polarised parties to work together to address their concerns.

At first glance the sharp rise in turnout from 50 to 55 per cent in the 1992 presidential election, and the election of the first single-party-controlled federal government since 1976 under Democrat Bill Clinton appeared as a harbinger of a partisan realignment in favour of a reinvigorated Democratic coalition. On closer analysis the 1992 result gave little encouragement to the parties, however. Clinton was elected as a minority President with a lower percentage of the popular vote than the losing 1988 Democratic candidate, and the turnout increase was largely generated by enthusiasm for Independent candidate H. Ross Perot, who won 19 per cent of the vote after an explicitly anti-party campaign. President Clinton's subsequent problems in passing major legislation through a Congress dominated by his own party, and the return of 'gridlock' in a new guise after the Republican takeover of both houses of Congress in 1994, are further indications that Americans are a long way from single-party government on the European model.

Conclusion

We are not convinced that American parties are about to disappear. Indeed in some respects they show some prospects of revival. What will not happen is that they will never again have the organisational strength (based on state and local machines) that they had one hundred years ago. Neither are they going to turn into European-style, mass party organisations (indeed a more convincing case can be made that European parties and party systems have recently been developing more 'American' features). With the demise of the last of the old-style patronage-based party organisations, the parties have adapted to late twentieth-century American society by becoming more national in organisation and more ideologically oriented and polarised than they have even been. At the same time, however, they have forfeited their roles as political intermediaries between citizen and government to television news and interest groups. American parties play a much less important role in the political system than they once did, but they are still necessary to organise legislatures and to structure vote choices and make them meaningful. Americans have never liked parties, but they have not found a way to make their political system work without them.

Notes

1 Eligibility to vote in primaries varies according to state law. In several 'open primary' states voters choose which party's primary to vote in, but in 'closed primary' states (which register votes by party) Democratic or Republican registrants may only vote in their party's primary, crossovers are prohibited, and those who register as Independents cannot vote. To add to the confusion, however,

several states permit those who register as Independent to vote in the primary of their choice.

2 For the most complete statement of realignment theory see Sundquist, *Dynamics of the Party System*.

3 On the first-party system see Ronald P. Formisano, 'Federalists and Republicans: Parties, Yes – System, No' in Paul Kleppner *et al.*, *The Evolution of American Electoral Systems* (Westport, CT: Greenwood Press, 1982), pp. 33–76.

4 On the Jacksonian parties see Reichley, *The Life of the Parties*, pp. 85–139.

5 On machine politics see John M. Allswang, *Bosses, Machines, and Urban Voters*, revised edition (Baltimore: Johns Hopkins University Press, 1986).

6 On the emergence of the Republicans and the Civil War realignment see Sundquist, *Dynamics of the Party System*, pp. 50–105.

7 In both the 1876 and 1888 elections the Democratic presidential candidate won a narrow plurality of the national popular vote for president, while the Republican candidate prevailed in the Electoral College. While this has not happened since 1888 it is a perfectly possible outcome. In 1960 John F. Kennedy won by a comfortable margin in the Electoral College, but only secured a very narrow plurality of 0.16 per cent of the popular vote.

8 See Michael E. McGerr, *The Decline of Popular Politics: The American North, 1865–1928* (New York: Oxford University Press 1986), pp. 3–41.

9 On the Populists, Bryan, and the 1896 election, see Richard A. Hofstadter, *The Age of Reform: from Bryan to FDR* (New York: Knopf, 1955).

10 On the 1896 realignment see Walter Dean Burnham, 'The System of 1896', in Kleppner *et al.*, *The Evolution of American Electoral Systems*, pp. 147–202.

11 On Progressivism see Hofstadter, *The Age of Reform*, pp. 130–328.

12 On the Progressive reforms and their impact on the parties see McGerr, *The Decline of Popular Politics*.

13 In 1925 schoolteacher John Scopes was put on trial in Dayton, Tennessee for teaching the Darwinian theory of evolution in violation of a Tennessee state law. Bryan acted as prosecutor for the state of Tennessee, and although he won the case, the 'Great Commoner' and his fundamentalist religious beliefs were ruthlessly derided before a huge national radio and newspaper audience by defence attorney Clarence Darrow and journalist H. L. Mencken. Bryan died the day after the trial was completed.

14 On the New Deal realignment see Sundquist, *Dynamics of the Party System*, pp. 198–297.

15 On the emergence of the Republican party in the white South see Earl Black and Merle Black, *The Vital South: How Presidents are Elected* (Cambridge, MA: Harvard University Press, 1992).

16 On the unravelling of the New Deal coalition in 1968 see Kevin P. Phillips, *The Emerging Republican Majority*. (New York: Anchor Books, 1970).

17 *Ibid*.

18 See Norman H. Nie, Sidney Verba, and John R. Petrocik, *The Changing American Voter*, revised edition (London: Harvard University Press, 1979).

19 Burnham, *The Current Crisis in American Politics*.

20 See Wattenberg, *The Decline of American Political Parties*.

21 See Shafer, *Quiet Revolution*.

22 On the effects of the party reforms see Polsby, *Consequences of Party Reform*.

23 On the marginalisation of the parties in presidential politics see Austin Ranney, 'The Political Parties: Reform and Decline' in Anthony King (ed.) *The New American Political System*, (Washington, DC: American Enterprise Institute, 1978), pp. 213–47.

24 See Epstein, *Political Parties in the American Mold.*

25 See Xandra Kayden and Eddie Mahe, *The Party Goes On: the Persistence of the Two-Party System in the United States* (New York: Basic Books, 1985). Although this phenomenon may have been overstated in the early 1980s, it is still in striking contrast with these organisations' historical role. For a more sober view of what national committees can achieve see Tim Hames, 'The RNC from Bliss to Barbour' in John C. Green (ed.), *Politics, Parties, and Professionalism* (University Press of America, 1994).

26 On the decline of the 'centrist' factions in each of the major parties see Rae, *The Decline and Fall of the Liberal Republicans*; and *Southern Democrats.*

27 On polarisation and gridlock see E. J. Dionne, Jr, *Why Americans Hate Politics* (New York: Simon & Schuster, 1991).

10

Interest groups

The United States boasts a vast array of interest groups who exercise very significant political influence both in Washington, DC and the individual states. Few accounts of American government fail to stress the central role played by organised interests and the particular characteristics they exhibit. To many observers of modern politics interest groups – or at least certain interests – seem more powerful than most politicians.

This chapter will concentrate on two major elements. First, the historic nature of interest-group authority in the US will be examined along with competing theories as to why these groups operate in the way that they do, what their overall effect on the political system is, and why they might be as effective as they are.

Second, interest groups, like so many other elements of American politics, have dramatically changed over the past twenty years. There are now many more groups, especially Political Action Committees, which are intimately involved in the financing of elections. There has been an explosion in political lobbying. The new world of interest groups has a massively different balance between various types of group. These groups are now more likely to be based in Washington, DC, and are lobbying the presidency, the judiciary, and the states as well as their traditional bases of Congress and the bureaucracy. Finally, the role of these groups has attracted increasing controversy in a nation that has traditionally regarded interest-group activity as essentially benign. A few concluding words about their future role and power will be offered.

Defining interest groups

Interest groups have a long history of political activity in the US. Indeed, the First Amendment to the Constitution (adopted in 1791) explicitly recognises the rights of the people 'to petition the government for a redress of grievances'. From the inception of the political system certain interests were clearly successful in promoting their special agenda: agriculture, large corporations and the railways being notable examples. De Tocqueville was one of many early nineteenth-century commentators to note the tendency of Americans to form interest groups and the striking impact that had on the political system.[1] Nearly a century later, on the verge of assuming the presidency, Woodrow Wilson complained that 'The government of the United States at present is a foster child of the special interests',[2] language that most if not all of his post-1945 predecessors have at some point echoed.

Before asking why interest groups play the role they do in the US it is worth noting what they are exactly. The term 'interest group' appears to cover a variety of sins. Entities might be described as interest groups, pressure groups, think-tanks, public interest groups, citizen groups, associations, special interests, lobby groups, and so on. Some interest groups are very explicit, maintaining a full-time political presence; others are not. The National (American) Football League (NFL) or Harvard University might not initially strike one as being groups in the same sense that Greenpeace or the United Automobile Workers appear to be, yet both the NFL and Harvard have proved capable of highly effective political mobilisation on issues that affect them. The problem of precise description is one that affects the study of organised interests in all countries, therefore an exact quantification is virtually impossible. In this chapter the working definition will be that offered by David Truman, namely 'Any group that, on the basis of one of more shared attitudes, makes certain claims upon other groups in society for the establishment, maintenance, or enhancement of forms of behaviour that are implied by the shared attitudes.'[3]

This is admittedly a fairly broad category, and one not entirely without ambiguity, but it seems less problematic than other attempts to be more precise.

Theories of interest-group power

There are a number of theories about the nature of American interest groups, all of which attempt to explain their importance but which differ widely about their desirability.

Traditionally, interest group theory has been dominated by the *Pluralist* viewpoint. Founded on the group-based view of politics offered by Arthur Bentley in 1908[4] but formalised and developed by David Truman in 1951, this school regards the role played by American groups as the natural by-product of American political life. To pluralists American groups are signs of a healthy democracy and their existence is critical to the operation of public life.

Pluralists such as Truman believe that interest-group activity is beneficial in several ways:

○ They are invariably bottom-up locally-based citizen-generated institutions whose concerns fairly reflect those of ordinary people who are entitled to offer such views.

○ They provide information and argument about issues of concern into the public arena which might not otherwise be there.

○ A critical objective in any genuine democracy is finding the correct balance between the rights of majorities and minorities. Election results, inevitably, stress majority power, groups allow minorities another form of political voice.

○ In a country as large as the United States, with such a heterogeneous population, it is quite impossible for political representation to be achieved solely on the basis of election by territorial unit through two large and amorphous political parties.

o Although interest groups obviously vary in size and political power there are enough of them and there is sufficient competition between them (business v. unions, agriculture v. urban, pro-abortion v. anti-abortion, etc.) to prevent any single group or block of groups exercising disproportionate control.

This pluralist perspective has thus seen interest groups as, on balance, a benign influence and an important addition to the overall quality of the political process. It has looked at efforts to regulate or reduce group authority with deep suspicion. However, there have always been significant minorities of academics, politicians, and voters alike who have disagreed with the pluralist perspective. They are particularly suspicious of the claim that interest groups are local, citizen-based, and spontaneous and/or that competition between interest groups prevents them possessing undue strength.

The question of how interest groups are created has seen an important disagreement between those, like Truman, who believe that they are the natural result of shared attitudes and circumstances and that the vast number of such groups in the United States is therefore utterly unsurprising, and those who approach interest-group analysis from a background in economic theory. In 1965 Mancur Olson wrote an extremely important book – *The Logic of Collective Action*[5] – which demonstrated that it was highly irrational for people sharing a set of beliefs to join a group in pursuit of collective goals that, if achieved, would be granted to both members and non-members of that group. In other words, a free-rider problem exists: individuals can gain whatever benefits a group wins without paying the costs in terms of money and time. There is also no reason why adding one more member to a group should make the difference between that group's success or failure.

From this Olson concluded that there were only two valid reasons why any individual should join a group. Either they had no choice owing to some form of coercion (such as a trade-union closed shop), or the group offers special selective benefits as part of its membership package (cheaper insurance, for example) that attract members. Nevertheless, Olson's argument is utterly rational. Despite the logic of his case, there are literally millions of Americans who, 'irrationally', do join groups without coercion and without special benefits to offset their membership costs. Olson may be strong in theory but Truman appears to be stronger in practice.

A more fundamental attack on the pluralist viewpoint comes from three different theories which have in common a scepticism about whether internal competition between groups prevents them from unduly dominating the political system.[6]

The economic power critique argues that American interest groups vary dramatically in their capacity to shape public policy. Specifically, interest groups are the means by which those who hold economic power in the United States, notably large corporations, are able to advance their own interests, block initiatives they disapprove of, and resist the will of the popular majority. Far from assisting American democracy as the pluralists claim, interest groups prevent the exercise of genuine popular expression.

The populist critique is also concerned about the role of larger interest groups. It, though, is hostile to all large institutions – big business, big unions, big campaign groups – on the grounds that the average citizen is ignored and excluded by these faceless organisations that dominate politics. Ross Perot's rhetoric in the presidential election of 1992 strongly echoed these popular concerns which are part of a wider view that Washington, DC procedures have become remote from, and hostile to, the rest of the country.

The rational choice/public choice critique believes that interest groups do not compete but collaborate. They are all basically after the same thing, unwarranted favours from public law and the public purse, and they generally succeed in wringing concessions from vote-hungry politicians. Interest groups primarily represent the wishes of those who run and work for them rather than their ordinary membership. The net effect of their efforts is the creation of a distorted and highly inefficient distribution of political goods, exaggerated levels of government spending and thus taxation and borrowing, a bloated regulatory bureaucracy, and an overburdened economic system, all of which are against the public interest.

These models now compete for favour and there is some justification in each one of them. An important item to note is the absence of one model – corporatism – which would be cited in any study of interest groups in western Europe. Corporatist political systems are structured by formal co-operation between government and certain major economic groups (notably business and unions) which together make the major political decisions affecting the country. Although elements of Franklin Roosevelt's 'New Deal' had a corporatist flavour, the model has thus far proved alien to the US.

The organisation of interest groups

All interest groups are not the same, not only in terms of size and effectiveness but also in the type of people and issue promoted. Although defining interest groups is a slippery process that makes a further division into types problematic, some distinctions can be drawn between economic/occupational, sectional, and advocacy bodies.

There are large numbers of groups associated with the nature of employment. These include American businesses, both individually and within joint groups such as the National Association of Manufacturers (NAM), and trade unions, again individually or through the national umbrella group, the American Federation of Labor and Congress of Industrial Organizations (AFL/CIO). These groups have an economic/occupation concern that makes them distinct.

The AARP

The American Association of Retired Persons (AARP) represents over twice as many members as the American trade union movement. It has almost thirty million members, up from one million in 1968 and ten million in 1978. After the Roman Catholic church it is the largest organisation in America. It started life in 1947 as the National Retired Teachers Association and gained a more independent role in 1958 as a marketing device for a large private insurance company. Its strengths lie in the significant discounts it can offer its members. It entered the political realm in support of Medicare – government-funded health insurance for the elderly – which was enacted in 1965. It has used this asset to recruit almost half of all citizens over fifty, it has a full-time lobbying and legislative staff of nearly 150 people, a total staff of 1,250, an annual budget of $250 million, a network of 35,000 volunteers, and its monthly magazine, *Modern Maturity*, has the highest circulation in the US. Unsurprisingly it is the most feared lobby in Washington, DC.

There are sectional groups which represent types of people, such as the National Organization of Women (NOW), the National Association for the Advancement of Colored People (NAACP), and the American Association of Retired Persons (AARP). Membership of these groups is limited to those within that section – in these examples being female, coloured, or elderly is a prerequisite for entry – and the objective is to advance the general condition of these groups across a broad array of issues.

There are other sectional groups which represent types of activity rather than types of people, such as the National Rifleman's Association (NRA) or Dog Owners of America. Again, membership of these groups is likely to be limited to those who share its concerns, gun-owners and dog-lovers, and the principal aim of such groups is to advance the preferences of their particular activity.

Finally, there are advocacy groups of citizens from wide-ranging backgrounds who agree on a particular issue or issues. These range from bodies with a wide political agenda, environmental groups such as the Sierra Club or consumer organisations, to single-issue groups such as the National Right to Life Political Action Committee (anti-abortion) and the National Abortion Rights Action League (pro-abortion). A particular sub-set of advocacy groups are the various research institutions or think-tanks such as the Brookings Institution (centre–left) and the Heritage Foundation (conservative) which offer new policy ideas across a variety of issues.

Whatever category any group falls into, money is essential to their operations. Funding for interest groups invariably comes from one or more of five separate sources: foundations; other associations; corporations; government grants; and individuals. The precise balance will depend on the nature of the individual group: pro-business bodies receive their backing from corporations, trade unions rely on their members' subscriptions, think-tanks tend to be supported by philanthropic foundations, advocacy groups by individuals, export-orientated trade associations frequently receive government grants. The division of financial backing across groups is far from uniform: certain groups find raising money easier than others, as supporters of the economic power critique are quick to point out.

The financial resources of a group, along with the nature of its membership and its precise aspirations, largely shape strategic decisions about how they operate. Interest groups adopt a variety of different tactics to promote their message. Three strategies are regularly employed. Direct persuasion techniques, whereby a group openly solicits an elected representative or bureaucrat on behalf of a particular policy; indirect persuasion, whereby a group tries to stimulate a local campaign on a measure which generates letters and other forms of publicity in a representative's district that then influences their actions. The creation of 'spontaneous' local campaigns and concerns has become a major cottage industry in modern-day politics. Public awareness – a more indirect method still – whereby interest groups use the mass media to air their viewpoint and hope to shape the political environment. Again, the precise formula deployed will depend heavily on money.

An overall assessment of American interest groups must conclude that while some are much stronger than others, in general the interest-group system is stronger than in most western democracies, especially when it comes to preventing hostile initiatives becoming law. There appear to be three major explanations for this relative success. The first is cultural: interest groups are strong because central government is weak, and central government is weak because of a highly individualistic political culture that is suspicious of strong central authority.

The NRA

The National Rifleman's Association (NRA) is perhaps the most famous (or infamous) of American interest groups. Founded in 1871, dedicated to shooting instruction, it became a lobbying powerhouse in response to moves to limit guns in the 1960s. It now has three million members, spends nearly $30 million on lobbying and legislative activities, spends a further $3 million in direct spending on congressional elections, and a similar amount indirectly through communications with its members. Thanks in large part to the NRA, there has been no comprehensive gun control legislation in the United States since 1968, when the Gun Control Act banned interstate sales of weapons and required gun dealers to maintain sales receipts. Indeed in 1986 Congress repealed the provision on interstate rifle sales. Politics became more challenging in the 1990s when two modest gun control measures were passed. The prospect for more radical reform was halted by the 1994 elections. Increasingly the NRA is looking to recruit groups it has traditionally ignored – women and blacks – and is focusing its efforts at the state level where gun control advocates now increasingly operate.

The other two explanations are based on institutional arrangements. One view has it that the nature of Congress, genuinely bicameral and divided into committees and sub-committees where real authority lies, is perfectly designed for interest groups, which can latch on to the particular part relevant to them. This is combined with a notoriously diffuse bureaucracy that is also easy to lobby. The second view gives greater weight to the weaknesses of American political parties and argues, not without some logic, that the consequence of a strong party system is weak interest group influence and vice versa,[7] so the strength of American groups is largely the consequence of the limitations of the party system.

The interest-group system is not static. As the remainder of this chapter will outline, the last two decades have witnessed dramatic change in the role of organised interests, in the relative balance between different types of group, and the relationship between groups and the wider governmental apparatus.

Trends in interest-group politics

A number of very important developments affecting the role of interest groups has occurred over the last twenty years, and the implications of them will be outlined in this section. Put simply, there are now more interest groups conducting more activity in a wider range of places and that trend is likely to continue. Whether the existence of more groups means that they exercise greater overall power or, instead, that they exercise the same amount of power but that it is now differently distributed, is one of the most important issues in contemporary government.

○ *While there have always been many interest groups there are now a great deal more.*

Because of the difficulty in precisely defining an interest group it is hard to give an exact statistic for the rise in interest group numbers, but all the measures that can be used indicate a major increase in numbers. Estimates range from 25 to 40 per cent over the last twenty years. The US now has at least 16,000 national voluntary organisations and close to 200,000 state and local organisations. If anything, these numbers probably underestimate the real number of bodies that are capable of acting as interest groups at any moment.

Four major explanations for this increase have been offered. The first, which will be explored further in an analysis of Political Action Committees, is that federal legislation (unwittingly) has created incentives for groups to form that did not previously exist. The second is that the expansion of the welfare and regulatory activities of the federal government in the 1960s and early 1970s created new interest groups affected by those activities. The third is that the changing distribution of power in Congress towards sub-committees, a theme to be explored later, offered new opportunities for groups. The fourth is that the continued, many would say accelerated, weakening of the political parties

opened the way to interest-group growth. The unheroic – but probably correct – explanation is that there is considerable merit in all four of these theories.

o *The major vehicle for interest group expansion has been the enormous boom in*
  Political Action Committees (PACs).

As a consequence of a series of scandals involving political donations and the
activities financed by those donations (most notably the Watergate scandal
that drove President Nixon from office in 1974), Congress passed a set of
Federal Election Campaign Acts in 1971, 1974, 1976 and 1979. The intention
of these laws was to limit financial contributions by individuals, political
parties, and groups to political candidates. A by-product of this was a reshaping
of the role of Political Action Committees which had existed previously but
had not been an especially important element in politics.

Table 10.1. *Growth in PACS, 1974–92*

Date	Corporate	Labour	Trade/ membership/ health	Co-operative	Corporation without stock	Nonconnected	Total
31 Dec. 1974	89	201	318	—	—	—	608
31 Dec. 1978	785	217	453	12	24	162	1,653
31 Dec. 1980	1,206	297	576	42	56	374	2,551
31 Dec. 1982	1,469	380	649	47	103	723	3,371
31 Dec. 1984	1,682	394	698	52	130	1,053	4,009
31 Dec. 1986	1,744	384	745	56	151	1,077	4,157
31 Dec. 1988	1,816	354	786	59	138	1,115	4,268
31 Dec. 1992	1,735	347	770	56	142	1,145	4,195

Under the 1974 Act groups could establish a federally registered Political
Action Committee which could solicit funds that it would spend on political
activities, notably campaign contributions. The maximum amount that a PAC
could give was set at a modest-sounding $5,000 in a primary election and a
further $5,000 in the election proper. No limits were set on the number of
candidates a PAC could have donations to or on the number of different PAC
contributions any individual could receive. The same act created a Federal
Election Commission whose role was to oversee the new regulations.

A set of decisions by the FEC and Supreme Court then made the formation
of PACs more attractive. The 1974 Act had allowed government contractors
to form their own committees, and the FEC then ruled in 1975 that corporations and unions could use their treasury funds to start PACs. The Supreme
Court, in the case of *Buckley* v. *Valeo* 1976, liberalised the process further. It
ruled that there were no limits on the number of local or regional PACs that
corporations or unions could form. It also said that there was no limit on the

amount of money PACs could spend for or against a particular candidate in any electoral contest, providing that money was not given in the form of a donation and that it was not spent in co-ordination with a candidate's campaign organisation.

The net effect of these decisions was to create an explosion in Political Action Committees. Their numbers increased from 608 at the beginning of 1975 to 4,009 exactly ten years later, since when it has levelled off. The PACs now dominate the process of campaign finance. For the 1992 elections they contributed $179.2 million to various candidates. PACs are extremely selective in where they spend money, making great efforts to focus it on those individuals most likely to be elected. In the modern era – especially in the House of Representatives – that has usually meant backing the incumbent member. Not just any incumbents however, but invariably the incumbents sitting on the committees and sub-committees relevant to the interests of the PAC. In 1992 only 11.7 per cent of PAC contributions went to candidates challenging sitting members.[8] Of winning candidates, therefore, 41.7 per cent of their campaign receipts in the House and 26.7 per cent in the Senate came from this particular brand of interest group.[9] For the then majority Democratic party those figures were higher still.

There has been a howl of protest from many quarters about this development, with widespread accusations that the PACs now buy the votes of members. This in turn has sparked several unsuccessful attempts at meaningful campaign reform. In fact it is unclear whether PAC money is a *de facto* bribe to politicians or whether politicians use their position to effectively blackmail PACs into giving the money. None the less, the overall effect has been to give some interest groups a radically different role in the political process.

o *There has been an enormous increase in the numbers and prominence of the lobbying industry.*

In tandem with the rapid growth of interest groups in general, and Political Action Committees in particular, the lobbying industry has witnessed an enormous growth. There are now some 15,000 officially registered political lobbyists in Washington, DC compared with only 4,000 in 1977. Some 2,000 law firms employ over 100,000 individual lawyers as lobbyists. Business groups and various individual corporations dominate those who have permanent lobbyists. There are now so many lobbyists in Washington, DC that they have formed their own lobbying organisations, three of them in fact – the American Society of Association Executives, the American League of Lobbyists, and the National Association of Business PACs. Depending on the issue, lobbyists try to influence congressional votes either by direct persuasion and argument, or, increasingly, by generating a political storm about the issue in the member's constituency by identifying and mobilising those who will be adversely affected by the proposed change.

This has led to the development of a secondary political industry in firms who specialise precisely in this technique of discovering those whose interests will be hurt, informing them of the possible impact on them, and directing them towards the local media and their politicians. This is an industry that can be politically subtle on issues where public opinion would normally seem to lean against it. In 1993 President Clinton proposed to reduce the proportion of business entertainment (mostly restaurant meals) that could be deducted as a legitimate corporate expense against tax. Restaurant owners feared a loss of custom so they brought in the lobbyists. Rather than demonstrate the industry's concerns by bringing their executives to Washington, the lobbyists found low-paid waitresses struggling to bring up families who testified to Congress about their fears for their jobs if the proposed measure was passed. It was ultimately watered down.

Whilst there has been an increase in lobbying at all levels, a significant factor is the number of foreign firms and overseas governments that now hire full-time lobbyists. Israel, Japan and Saudi Arabia have been prominent customers. The government of Japan spends upwards of $50 million annually – a five fold increase in a decade – and more than 250 Japanese companies, industries, and governmental agencies have lobbyists.

Explanations of this rise in lobbying tend to follow those used to explain the general increase in interest-group activity. The expanding role of the federal government has created more opportunities and concerns, particularly in the field of business regulation, changes in the structure of Congress, and the continued difficulties of the political parties have reinforced the impression that lobbying works.

The AIPAC

The American Israeli Public Affairs Committee (AIPAC) is the leading political pressure group on behalf of Israel and is thus the most significant foreign policy interest group on Capitol Hill. Founded in 1951, its influence increased in the 1980s due to an aggressively high-profile strategy. Its main objectives are the preservation and expansion of American aid to Israel and the representation of Israeli interests on Middle East issues more generally, for example by opposing arms sales to Arab states. By 1993 it had a budget of £15 million and 55,000 members providing a staff some 150 strong. Although small by the standards of the AARP and NRA, these numbers dwarf any other foreign policy-oriented group. Although, despite its acronym, it is not a Political Action Committee and thus does not give directly to congressional candidates, it is known to be highly effective in advising pro-Israeli contributors where to donate. Again, no other foreign policy group has such an ability. AIPAC enjoyed highly cordial relations with the Reagan Administration, had a much more rocky time with President Bush, but has had an exceptionally intimate courtship with Bill Clinton.

Table 10.2. *PACS* v. *parties in House elections, 1977–92*

	House of Representatives: General election campaign receipts		
Year	Total ($m)	Party donation ($m)	PAC donation ($m)
1977/78	92.2	4.1	22.9
1979/80	124.6	7.7	36.0
1981/82	183.9	11.8	57.9
1983/84	196.1	13.3	72.9
1985/86	228.4	9.4	85.2
1987/88	243.3	10.2	99.1
1989/90	249.7	9.2	104.0
1991/92	321.4	11.0	119.0

Note The ratio of PAC spending to Party spending has increased from about 5–1 to 10–1 in little over a decade.

Source Federal Elections Commission.

Money spent on lobbying might appear rather unproductive but it is perfectly rational. A relatively small amendment to the intricate American tax code could be worth, or cost, millions of dollars to the interests concerned. During President Clinton's attempt to pass his 1993 budget, lobbying by the American oil industry to turn the vote of one individual Democratic senator (David Boren of Oklahoma) on the powerful Senate Finance Committee killed the Administration's plans for a broad-based energy tax at a revenue cost of some $50 billion that had to be made up by cuts in Medicaid and Medicare (health programmes for the low-paid, the disabled, and the elderly).

Interest-group power was illustrated even more starkly in the battle over President Clinton's plan to ensure all Americans had health cover mostly paid for by their employers. The Health Insurers of America exploited the complexity of his proposals with a set of television commercials featuring a fictional middle-class couple, 'Harry and Louise', who bemoaned the (alleged) impact the Clinton plan would have on their health-care quality, choice, and cost. The Administration never really recovered the political initiative after these attacks.

These last examples illustrate the point that the increase in lobbying – rather like the rise of Political Action Committees – has the effect of dividing interest groups, and their probable political success, between those who can and cannot afford to employ these resources.

○ *The balance of interest-group power between business and the unions has shifted in the direction of corporations.*

Traditionally, interest group activity in the United States was dominated by the big three of agriculture, business (especially big business), and organised labour. This oligopoly has been shaken by the challenge from hundreds of sectional and advocacy groups, as the next section will outline, but there has also been a major change in the balance of power between corporations and unions.

To be fair, it was never a particularly equal struggle. Business has been involved in interest-group politics for a much longer period than unions, whose status was only formally recognised by the federal government in 1935. Nonetheless, the balance of power has, over the past two decades, swung significantly towards employers.

That switch has happened for two main reasons. First, the evolution of the present Political Action Committees has been better exploited by corporations. Between 1974 and 1989 the number of labour PACs increased by 83 per cent but corporate PACs shot up by 1,900 per cent.[10] By 1993 there were 1,735 corporate PACs, 770 trade/membership PACs (which include many business interests), and just 347 labour PACs. During the 1974–89 period the pattern of funding has switched from one where labour PACs spent over 20 per cent more than corporate PACs to one where corporate PACs spend 20 per cent more than labour ones. Pragmatic business contributors tend to assist important incumbents of both parties – giving them a foot in both camps – whereas virtually all labour PAC money goes to liberal Democrats. Business has also proved much more effective at co-ordinating its lobbying activities than has been true for labour.

The unions have also been hurt by economic trends that have undercut their strength. The proportion of the labour force holding union membership cards has virtually halved in the past two decades (down from 24.5 per cent

Table 10.3. *Percentage of the US labour force in unions, 1920–91*

Year	% unionised	Year	% unionised
1920	11.7	1983	16.6
1930	7.8	1984	16.1
1940	13.1	1985	14.5
1950	23.0	1986	14.2
1960	22.3	1987	13.9
1970	25.4	1988	13.8
1980	19.6	1989	13.5
1981	19.0	1990	13.2
1982	17.8	1991	13.1

Note As this table illustrates, the proportion of the American work-force unionised (never high) fell by almost half between 1970 and 1990 and is now back where it was in 1940, with every prospect of returning to 1930 levels.

to 13.2 per cent). That fall has been the consequences of more women in the work force, a major increase in Hispanic and Asian–American immigration, and rapidly rising numbers of part-time employees, all parts of the population where unions have consistently proved poor recruiters. In addition, the population shift from the traditionally unionised Northeast and industrial Midwest towards the traditionally non-unionised South and West, along with a change in the pattern of private-sector employment away from heavy manufacturing towards services have also hurt badly.

American unions are widely perceived to be stuck in a long-term process of decline. Their character has certainly changed as their traditional dominance by employees in blue-collar private-sector employment has moved towards white-collar public-sector employment. Probably the most politically significant unions today are the National Education Association (the main teachers' association) and the AFSCME (the American Federation of State, County, and Municipal Employees) which is a problem for their employers (various levels of government) but not for private corporations.

o *The greatest growth in interest groups has been amongst the sectional and advocacy types.*

The real expansion in interest-group numbers and activities has come amongst those groups outside the traditional economic/occupational strata. Sectional bodies – both those based on types of people and types of activity – and advocacy groups have all mushroomed. The development that has attracted most political attention is that of single-issue groups, particularly those on the right of the political spectrum concerned with issues of public morals. However, they are but one of a host of changes that have broadened the coverage of interest groups. The so-called Public Interest sector, a term that covers a broad swath of campaigning sectional and advocacy groups, now contains over 2,500 national organisations representing over forty million individuals and spending over $4 billion annually.[11]

Within this sector there has been a proliferation of groups concerned about consumer issues, environmental policy, and foreign affairs, as well as those associated with the religious Right. The number of policy institutes or think-tanks offering new ideas into the public domain has also grown rapidly. Not only has the number increased but there has been a general trend towards larger staff, especially on congressional relations, and a more aggressive pursuit of political goals. The most spectacular example of this has been the rise of the American Association of Retired Persons, which has exploited a rising proportion of older Americans and a set of membership services to grow to 34 million members, making it the second largest organisation in the United States after the Roman Catholic Church. The AARP is now arguably the most important single-interest group in America.

These bodies have either formed their own Political Action Committees or liaise with allied PACs. and hence are increasingly involved in financing congressional campaigns. This growth has been welcomed by some as bringing a much greater quality of diversity and genuine pluralism into American democracy and has been decried by others as producing a politics dominated by special interests over the national interest. Whichever side is right, the expansion of sectional and advocacy groups both of a single-issue and multiple-issue nature now seems well established and is unlikely to be reversed.

○ *Interest groups are increasingly basing their headquarters in Washington, DC.*

The number of groups located in Washington has risen sharply, largely as a consequence of the expansion of federal activities. The number of national associations has risen from just under 5,000 in 1956 to 12,900 in 1975 up to over 23,000 in 1990. Of those associations the proportion based in Washington has risen from one-fifth to one-third in twenty years. The number of health groups based in the capital have increased sixfold in fifteen years.

This rise has been rooted in a number of trends. Well-established groups have decided to relocate from their previous base to Washington, and consequently the cities of Chicago and New York have seen a relative fall in their standing. Groups previously based at a local level or with only minimal national organisation have decided they need such representation and that it was rational to put themselves near the institutions of government. Newly-formed groups have overwhelmingly chosen to base themselves in Washington.

One interesting example of this process has been the degree of inter-government lobbying. Various agencies of state and local government – the National Governors' Association, the National League of Cities, and the US Conference of Mayors – have located themselves in Washington and now actively lobby the federal government over their concerns – a move that reflects both the importance of Washington and the increased effectiveness of sub-federal governments.

As will be noted later, this tendency to locate interest-group headquarters in Washington should not be taken to mean there is less activity at the state and local level by the newly-located organisations. In fact the opposite is true. It is more of a response to changes in national political institutions, and their relationship with interest groups, that has encouraged them to base themselves in the capital.

○ *Changes in the internal organisation of Congress have affected the environment in which interest groups operate.*

Monumental changes in the internal organisation of the US Congress have had a fundamental effect on the relationship between that body and interest groups. Traditionally there was a cosy alliance between a few large interests and key congressional committees – under the control of a few powerful chairmen – mostly conducted behind closed doors. This led to the phenomena of

---

The BTU Tax, 1993

As part of President Clinton's 1993 budget package his Administration proposed a broad-based energy tax based on the heat content or British Thermal Units used. The industries affected, especially the oil lobby, instantly launched a major campaign against it, focused most directly at politicians from oil-producing states. Nearly $50 million was spent whipping up (and sometimes manufacturing) grass-roots hostility to the measure. The campaign succeeded in detaching oil-area Democrats from their party and aligning them with Republicans who were uniformly opposed to all tax increases. The switch of Democratic Senator David Boren of Oklahoma proved crucial as he held the deciding vote on the Senate Finance Committee. With his defection the BTU proposal was killed and with it the prospects for a broad energy consumption tax for the foreseeable future.

'iron triangles' which described the alliance between congressional committees, interest groups, and the federal bureaucracy all of whom favoured greater spending in their particular area.[12]

The most prominent examples of these 'iron triangles' came in the fields of agriculture and defence spending, where the close bond between elected representatives, groups, and bureaucracy often appeared to override the financial priorities of the White House. This alliance existed because Congressmen on committees such as Agriculture and Armed Services chose to sit on those bodies because they were major constituencies in their districts, and not unnaturally, they favoured higher government spending. The interest groups concerned also favoured more spending and so did the bureaucracy. To solidify this pact the large interests concerned usually rewarded elected representatives with campaign support.

These traditional arrangements have been disrupted by three important developments.

First, in the name of open government a Freedom of Information Act was passed and a set of laws and internal rules were adopted (collectively known as the 'sunshine' acts) which opened up the vast majority of congressional meeting to open hearings and public deliberations.

Second, power has shifted away from the hands of committee chairmen and has been redistributed (to varying extents) towards sub-committee chairmen and individual members.

Third, as previously noted, the new role of Political Action Committees has drawn many more interest groups into a more important role in financing congressional contests.

The net effect of these measures has been complex. The move towards open government has allowed interest groups previously excluded from the process to force their way in and has made matters more awkward for those who benefited from the previous system. As such it has forced the old oligopoly of interests to innovate and allowed the new sectional and advocacy bodies to advance their agenda. Open government enhances the importance of the media and has highlighted the need for slick public relations, hence the demand for lobbyists.

Broadly the same is true for the impact of a shift to sub-committees. There are now many more access points for groups who want to influence public policy and the barriers to entry are much lower. However, there is the disadvantage that this diffuse system makes manoeuvring proposals into public law much harder. Again this helped (and encouraged) the rapidly proliferating new interest groups and made life more complicated for the old guard.

These trends are partly offset by the explosion of Political Action Committees. Although the PAC system has meant that many more groups can involve themselves in funding congressional politics, there is a two-tier system between more affluent PACs (generally those with economic/occupational concerns and those representing very large or wealthy sectional groups) and all other institutions.

The nature of congressional–interest group interaction has thus been altered. As Hugh Heclo noted, the old 'iron triangles' based on the extraction of money from the public purse have been supplemented – and to some extent supplanted – by new 'issue networks'[13] reflecting the demands of the new sectional and advocacy entrants to the market. Government agencies, as well as congressional committees, have also shifted their focus and become more responsive to these groups. Heclo defined an 'issue network' as 'A shared-knowledge group having to do with some aspect (or, as defined by the network, some problem) of public policy'.[14]

These networks are much more sophisticated then the previous system, consisting of several (often competing and opposing) interest groups, technical specialists in the legislature, the executive, and experts from outside, administrators, political entrepreneurs, the White House (often via the Office of Management and Budget), interested office-holders, and the media.

Whether the total fallout of this set of dramatic alterations has actually made interest groups stronger or weaker is uncertain. More interest groups have access to Congress but a Congress that finds it harder to make authorative decisions. Some interest groups, previously outsiders or non-existent, have become insiders, others who used to dominate the process now face much more competition. It is a very different environment from three decades ago.

Finally, there is the hot dispute over the degree to which Congress has recentralised and restored authority to its leadership. In theory, greater centralisation in budgetary policy should have weakened domestic agencies, authorising committees, and appropriations committees, thus cutting the ground from under their interest-group allies. The experience of Presidents Bush and Clinton would suggest that if interest group authority has been undermined that decline is modest.

O *There has been an expansion of interest groups campaigning towards the White House and the judiciary.*

Historically, interest groups have concentrated their firepower on Congress and allied government agencies. Presidents felt able to distance themselves from such groups because the huge range of presidential activity allowed the White House to pick and choose interest-group allies issue by issue, and avoid groups when it wanted to. Interest groups in turn felt the White House was too big to successfully lobby. The Courts were virtually ignored by most groups.

The presidency has found the vast increase in interest groups impossible to ignore. This reality was formalised in the decision of President Ford to establish an Office of Public Liaison within the White House responsible for outreach to various lobbies. All his successors have maintained it. The presidential nominating campaign is partly financed by PACs, and, although theoretically interest groups have no role in the general election campaign, as the chapter on elections will show, several back-door means have been found to involve themselves here as well.

The federal courts have now been targeted by groups that previously saw no need for them. During the 1960s the Supreme Court made it much easier for interests to bring cases (called class action suits) and various bodies (notably environmental and civil rights activists) have done so. This is a particularly expensive route. A much cheaper option is to file *amicus curiae* (friend of the court) briefs in cases brought by others. Such a brief allows a group to offer its reasons why the Court should make a decision one way or the other. The number of *amicus curiae* briefs has sharply increased as interest groups have appreciated their value as a direct means of lobbying judges.

One further result has been an increased willingness of interest groups to sue (often successfully) federal agencies over the way they have implemented legislation. This success obliged Congress to pass the Negotiated Rulemaking

---

The Clinton health-care plan

In September 1993 President Clinton launched his long-awaited (and much de-layed) proposal to reform the American health-care system, in particular to guarantee that the thirty-nine million Americans without health insurance would get it. Initial opinion polls suggested the plan was reasonably popular. The interest groups adversely affected by the proposals (the current private insurance system, drug companies, and some doctors' groups) then campaigned against it. They were led by the Health Insurers' Association of America, which funded a set of television commercials featuring a fictional couple 'Harry and Louise', who lam-basted the plan for its alleged cost, bureaucracy and restrictions on choice. Although not widely aired outside the Washington region, these commercials were widely credited with stoking public and congressional anxiety about the proposal, concerns that other interest-group advertisements reinforced. President Clinton was forced to abandon his crippled proposal in August 1994.

Act of 1990, encouraging interest groups and bureaucracies to settle their differences out of court by direct bargaining.

o *Interest groups have expanded their activities towards state and local governments.*

The expansion of the federal government in the 1965–75 period produced a vast increase in the number of interest groups and led the headquarters of such institutions to be located in Washington. The last decade has seen major renewal of state governments and a shift in domestic political activity back to them. Interest groups have reacted to that phenomena by setting up regional offices, lobbying governors and state legislatures, and financing local campaigns. Even those groups primarily concerned with foreign policy – such as the American–Israeli Public Affairs Committee – have found it worthwhile to expand their campaigns into the states.

In many ways states resemble the shifts seen at the national level. An old order based on a few large organisations (usually agriculture, business, or unions) intimately involved in legislative politics has been replaced by a new order based on many more bodies attempting to exercise influence in a more open system. The extent of this process obviously varies according to the nature of the state. Larger, more populous states tend to be closer to the Washington model: southern states, as a whole, remain closer to the old system. Campaign spending in most states has skyrocketed under the influence of interest-group money. Lobbying has seen a quantum leap in its scale and scope. Every state has responded to this by enacting formal registration and restrictions on the lobbyists. Again, it is unclear whether the new state systems have made interest groups as a whole stronger or whether power has been redistributed within groups.

Conclusion

As this chapter has made apparent, there have been major changes within the interest-group community and in the political environment in which they work. Assessing the net effect is much more complicated. Many academic observers argue that more groups are sharing the same amount, or even a smaller amount of power. Yet popular sentiment, and to some extent intellectual opinion, seems far more sceptical about the pluralist explanation of an essentially beneficial interest-group system. Greater concerns have been aired about the inequality of resources and therefore influence between groups, about their internal democracy, and their impact on the capability of government to govern. The Reagan Administration came to office with a convinced hostility towards many sectional and advocacy groups and attempted to defund those politically hostile to them. By and large those efforts made little headway.

Despite increasing concern about their democratic credentials interest groups remain a vital element in American politics and society. The fact that their numbers continue to increase, and the range of their activities becomes ever more sophisticated, probably ensures that they will retain that role.

Notes

1 Cited in Christine Day, *What Older Americans Think* (Princeton, NJ, Princeton University Press, 1990).
2 Quoted by Graham Wootton, *Interest Groups: Policy and Politics in America* (Prentice-Hall, Englewood Cliffs, NJ, 1985).
3 David Truman, *The Governmental Process* (New York, Knopf, 1951).
4 Arthur Bentley, *The Process of Government* (Chicago, University of Chicago Press, 1908).
5 Mancur Olson, *The Logic of Collective Action* (Cambridge, MA, Harvard University Press, 1965).
6 These categories are used, but outlined rather differently, in David Mackay, *Power & Politics in the USA* (London, Penguin, 1987).
7 This relationship between interest groups and parties is not necessarily true. There are a number of European states such as Austria, Germany, and Sweden that appear to have a strong party system coupled with powerful interest groups.
8 The 1992 figure for challengers, poor as it was, was actually an increase over 1990.
9 Source: Federal Elections Commission.
10 Cigler and Loomis, *Interest Group Politics*.
11 *Ibid.*
12 Douglass Cater, *Power in Washington* (London, Collins, 1965).
13 Hugh Heclo in Anthony King, *The New American Political System* (Washington, DC, American Enterprise Institute, 1978).
14 Quoted by Jayne Mansbridge in Petracca, *The Politics of Interest Groups*.

11

The media

In this section of the book we have been discussing the crucial roles of intermediary institutions in American politics. It is only through intermediary
institutions such as parties and interest groups that citizens in a modern liberal
democracy can in any sense be said to influence the government of their
country. Only through representative intermediary institutions can a democracy's claim, that the views and interests of its citizens will be eventually
reflected in their government, be borne out.

We have already seen how in modern America, the political parties have
lost much of their traditional intermediary functions – educating the public
on the issues, setting the terms of national debate, providing basic political
information – to interest groups, and to the news media – particularly television news. Most Americans receive their basic impressions and ideas about
politics from the news media, and, in the absence of strong parties, the news
media play a more significant role in US politics than in any other contemporary democracy. Therefore in this chapter we shall examine the news
media's effects on American government and politics, and arrive at some
conclusions about the nature and extent of the media's political power.

The media occupies a unique position in American political culture, and
Americans have taken freedom of the press very seriously from the beginning.
Political journals and pamphlets were instrumental in the revolution against
British rule, and freedom of speech and of the press are guaranteed in the first
amendment to the Constitution. Americans tend to have a very positive view
of the media and in most conflicts between the media and politicians such as
the Vietnam War, the Watergate scandal, and the Iran–Contra affair, the
media has prevailed. Indeed, Americans give more credence and more trust
to journalists than politicians and elected officials. In European countries
governments can restrict the activities of the media by using tools such as
state-owned television, tougher libel laws, and draconian punishments for
civil servants who leak government secrets, that are not available to the
American federal government.

This is not to say that the power of the media in modern American politics
in uncontroversial. Many on the right of the American political spectrum
believe passionately that the national news media are biased against them,
and their ideas. They see the news media as part of a decadent, cosmopolitan,
liberal political elite, that has rejected the traditional values of American
politics. By contrast, writers and activists on the Left argue that the media
are servants of a corporate governing elite and reflect their view of the
world. Right, Left and Centre all deplore the media's increasing propensity

for sensationalistic journalism, its obsession with the private affairs of public figures, and its failure to address seriously the critical issues facing the country. We must now examine the media more closely to ascertain how much basis in fact, exists for these positions.

The print media: newspapers and magazines

For most of the nineteenth century the American press was ferociously partisan, but limited in its readership. Papers were usually started by a party or faction (for example, Alexander Hamilton's *Gazette of the United States*, or Andrew Jackson's *Washington Globe*) with the intention of mobilising their followers and whipping up their enthusiasm. Objective presentation of the news was not a priority for these journals. Due to difficulties in transport and high printing costs the circulation of newspapers was confined to the political and social elites who could afford a paper.[1]

All this changed with technological innovations in the mid- to late nineteenth century, and it is at this time that the rise of the independent, mass-circulation daily newspapers began. In addition to changes in printing technology that made production easier, the invention of the telegraph and the advent of the wire services meant that news could be quickly transmitted to all areas of the country. To attract as many subscriptions as possible from the local papers, the wire services had to develop a reputation for scrupulous objectivity in presenting the news, and this attitude soon became widespread. A paper's bias might show through in the editorial pages, but in the news section objectivity became a general criterion of success.[2]

With the growing population density of the US, a cheap daily newspaper was now available for a mass readership. This development also gave rise to so-called 'yellow journalism', as major publishers like Joseph Pulitzer and William Randolph Hearst sought to attract a large readership through a dramatic presentation of the news with particular emphasis on violence, scandal, and patriotism. To succeed in this climate newspapers thus not only had to inform but to entertain.

The new popular press was hardly unbiased and publishers such as Hearst explicitly used their papers to present their political views. Hearst, for example, deliberately whipped up anti-Spanish sentiment in his papers in the late 1890s, and contributed greatly to the outbreak of the Spanish–American war of 1898. Yet the bias was a personal one, not one based on partisanship, and indeed hostility or marked indifference towards political parties was a salient feature of the new popular press that Hearst and others created.

During the Progressive era (partly as a reaction by the professional middle class against the vulgarity of 'yellow journalism') national news magazines such as the *Nation*, the *Atlantic*, the *New Republic*, and *Harper's* appeared. These magazines were devoted to what became known as 'muck-raking' journalism: exposés of corruption in government at all levels with an intention of building a constituency for Progressive reforms. Famous muck-raking journalists such as Lincoln Steffens, Ida Tarbell, and Upton Sinclair were major contributors to the magazines.[3] Indeed Steffens's *The Shame of the Cities* and Sinclair's *The Jungle* were two of the most influential works of the period. Even more than the popular press, the tone of the journals was ferociously anti-partisan, as they explicitly set out to mobilise national constituencies of opinion to agitate for reform outside the existing structure of party organisations. By so doing they deliberately contributed to the parties' loss of their monopoly of inter-mediation in American politics.

By the 1950s, due to rising costs and the rise of the electronic media, newspapers and magazines were in a clear state of decline. The intense competition between big-city dailies that had given rise to 'yellow journalism' largely disappeared. New York had twenty-nine daily newspapers in 1880, but was reduced to three by 1969. Most US cities (98 per cent) were left with only one daily newspaper, and the overall circulation of the daily press has dropped from 35 per cent to 26 per cent of the population in the last thirty years.[4] Yet with the rise of new cities due to general population growth in the suburbs and in the southern and western states, the overall number of newspapers has declined only marginally. In 1950 1,772 daily papers were published in the US: in 1986 there were 1,657.

Table 11.1. *The largest circulation daily newspapers in the US, 1991*

Rank	Paper	Circulation
1	*The Wall Street Journal*	1,795,448
2	*USA Today*	1,418,477
3	*Los Angeles Times*	1,177,253
4	*New York Times*	1,110,562
5	*Washington Post*	791,289
6	*Newsday* (Long Island, NY)	762,639
7	*New York Daily News*	759,068
8	*Chicago Tribune*	723,178
9	*Detroit Free Press*	598,418
10	*San Francisco Chronicle*	553,433

Source *The World Almanac and Book of Facts, 1993* (New York: Pharos Books, 1992).

Most of America's major daily newspapers are strongly attached to individual cities, and only the Gannet Organisation's *USA Today* really qualifies as a national paper. The biggest national circulation is held by the business-oriented *Wall Street Journal*, followed by *USA Today*, with its mixture of brief stories and colour graphics. Although they are not at the top of the circulation list, the *New York Times* and the *Washington Post*, as the established papers of record, exercise a disproportionate influence over the remainder of the press.

Stories and columns from these papers are widely syndicated to the other daily papers. The *Los Angeles Times* has also become increasingly influential in recent decades. Because of competition from television and sensationalistic weekly magazines such as the *National Enquirer*, and the strong state and local ties of most newspapers, America does not have lurid daily tabloid newspapers to the same extent as Britain or Germany, although the *New York Post*, *New York Daily News* and the *Boston Herald* have been able to survive in cities with an established serious daily paper, by adopting something like the standard tabloid formula (unsurprisingly, two of these papers are owned by Rupert Murdoch).

Over 10,000 magazines are published in the US, and the magazine market is dominated by specialised journals such as *Modern Maturity*, *TV Guide*, and *Better Homes and Gardens*, and the gossipy tabloids. *Time*, *Newsweek* (owned by the same company as the *Washington Post*) and *US News and World Report* (2–4 million copies each) are the leading national news magazines, with the political bi-weeklies such as the liberal *Nation* and *New Republic*, and the conservative *National Review* enjoying only very limited circulation among the politically active.

The advent of the electronic media

Radio broadcasting was introduced in the United States in 1920, and within two decades 860 stations were being listened to in nearly 30 million American homes. So pervasive was the new medium that a particularly vivid 1938 radio dramatisation of H. G. Wells's *War of the Worlds* by Orson Welles's Mercury Theatre created a national panic as thousands of listeners who had accidentally tuned in became convinced that the Martians had actually landed! The formation of the national radio networks in the late 1920s also turned radio into America's first genuinely national news medium and made it possible for millions of Americans to hear President Franklin Roosevelt's so-called 'fireside chats' in the 1930s.

Roosevelt was the first President to comprehend the political possibilities of the new medium. While Woodrow Wilson had almost literally killed himself with the sheer physical effort of making a national speaking tour to try and persuade the public to support the League of Nations in 1919, Roosevelt simply had to sit before a microphone in the Oval Office to bring the New-Deal message to the masses. Thanks to radio it was now possible for Presidents and other politicians to go over the heads of the parties, Congress, and other political institutions and make a direct personal appeal to the citizenry. Roosevelt's skill at using the new medium demonstrated its awesome political potential.

The process was taken one stage further by the advent of television during the 1950s. In 1950 only 9 per cent of Americans had television sets, but there were already 98 television stations in existence. In 1951, the televised coverage of Senator Estes Kefauver's hearings into organised crime made the Tennessee Senator into a national figure and nearly got him the Democratic

Table 11.2. *Best-selling magazines in the US, 1991*

Rank	Magazine	Circulation
1	Modern Maturity*	22,450,000
2	NRTA/AARP Bulletin*	22,174,021
3	Reader's Digest	16,306,007
4	TV Guide	15,353,982
5	National Geographic	9,921,479
6	Better Homes & Gardens	8,003,263
7	Family Circle	5,152,534
8	Good Housekeeping	5,028,151
9	McCall's	5,009,358
10	Ladies Home Journal	5,002,900
11	Woman's Day	4,751,977
12	Time	4,248,565
13	Redbook	3,841,866
14	National Enquirer	3,706,030
15	Playboy	3,498,802
16	Sports Illustrated	3,444,188
17	Newsweek	3,420,167
18	People	3,235,120
19	Star	3,207,951
20	Prevention	3,109,562

Note * Given free with membership of the American Association of Retired Person (AARP).

Source The World Almanac and Book of Facts, 1993 (New York: Pharos Books, 1992).

party nomination the following year. Televised hearings also led to the downfall of Senator McCarthy in 1955, and Richard Nixon brilliantly exploited the potential of television in the celebrated address (referred to by his detractors as the 'Checkers Speech' because Nixon had referred to the Nixon family dog, Checkers, during the address) that kept him on the Republican ticket as Eisenhower's vice-presidential running-mate in 1952.

By 1960 87 per cent of US households had television and there were over five hundred stations. Most Americans now get their political information largely from television, and they overwhelmingly believe, moreover, that television is a more credible news source than radio or the print media.[5] Americans trust television news in a way that they do not trust newspapers or politicians. When he retired from the CBS Evening News in 1981, veteran anchorman Walter Cronkite was one of the most trusted and influential people in America.

In the US today there are about 970 local commercial television stations, roughly 70 per cent of which are 'affiliates' of the three major national commercial networks – CBS, Capital Cities–ABC Inc., and NBC (a subsidiary of General Electric Corporation). Due to high production costs the local stations concern themselves mainly with local news and programming, and broadcast the network 'feeds' of national and international news. Each major network also directly owns five stations (the maximum allowed by the Federal Communications Commission's Rules) in the nation's largest media markets.[6]

While the networks and their affiliates all rely on advertising to make their profits, there is also a non-commercial Public Broadcasting Service (PBS), financed partially by federal government funds and by viewer donations to its local affiliates. While PBS's audiences are small compared to those of the networks, it does produce the best evening news show (a full hour compared to the half-hour national news broadcasts on the commercial networks), excellent documentaries, and high-quality cultural and children's programming. To fill their schedules and keep down production costs, however, the perennially cash-starved local PBS stations rely heavily on imports (of variable quality) from British television.[7]

Recent technological developments and trends in the electronic media have loosened the grip of the national television networks on political information, however. During the 1980s the number of independent stations increased from 120 to over 400, and advances in satellite technology have enabled affiliated stations to cover national events directly and cut out the network intermediaries. Fox TV, owned by Rupert Murdoch, also emerged as a new national network with over 140 affiliates by 1990, although it does not possess a national news service.[8]

The advent of cable television in the early 1980s has provided another serious challenge to the networks. Over 60 per cent of US households had access to Cable by 1992, and Atlanta millionaire Ted Turner's CNN (Cable News Network) has emerged as a formidable rival to the major network news services. With its greater freedom to depart from daily schedules to cover breaking stories live, and with its capacity to cover topical issues in greater depth than the network news bureaux, CNN has already revolutionised American television news. Another almost universally available cable channel, C-Span, provides live coverage of both Houses of Congress and other major political events, and has a devoted following among the politically aware.

The networks' position is unlikely to improve in the next phase of the communications revolution, as the advent of fibre-optic cable, with literally hundreds of cable channels becoming available, will encourage the development of a multitude of alternative networks catering to specialised political audiences. Advances in telecommunications and computer information technology, most evident in the evolution of the Internet or 'Information Superhighway', will also provide a vastly greater number of alternative and specialised sources of news and information outside the established channels.

The Perot phenomenon

One of the most staggering aspects of recent American elections was the performance of Ross Perot in 1992. Perot is a Texas billionaire (b. 1934), based in Dallas, who was virtually unknown at the beginning of 1992 outside big business circles. He appeared on the CNN news talk-in programme 'Larry King Live', a forum particularly attractive to him, his Independent presidential candidacy emerging from his frequent appearances on the programme. Perot announced that if citizens would raise enough signatures in all fifty states (each of which have their own law for this) then he would run for President and spend $100 million of his own fortune on the campaign. It was largely this financial promise that made him a credible candidate, despite no prior political experience. By the summer of 1992 he was a household name and leading the race in some opinion polls. Press coverage of him became more serious and less favourable, focusing on his alleged megalomania. He then stunned the political work by announcing in July 1992 that he would not be a candidate. He reconsidered and entered the contest again in October 1992 and a participant in the three presidential debates. He spent about $60 million, mostly on 30-minute 'infomercials' to promote his candidacy. On election day he achieved 19 per cent of the popular vote, the second best performance by an independent candidate this century, a score that surely reflected the level of voter concern about the American political system, and the power of big money and media in modern elections. After he unsuccessfully opposed the North American Free Trade Agreement (NAFTA) in 1993, being outpointed in a debate with Vice-President Albert Gore in the process, his political profile dimmed.

Prime-time CNN talk-show host Larry King (b. 1934) featured prominently in the 1992 presidential campaign, as all the major party presidential candidates made high-profile appearances on his phone-in programme. King's gentle style of questioning was also far more congenial to the candidates than the abrasive style of the network news journalists and the national press corps. In general the 1992 campaign saw a clear move by all the presidential candidates away from the 'hard news' programmes on the major networks, and towards appearances on 'softer' forums with more specialised audiences on cable television and local stations.

The potential impact of these changes on electoral politics first became evident during the 1992 campaign, as all three major candidates devoted less attention to the major networks and concentrated more on local outlets (where interviewers were invariably less knowledgeable and aggressive). Cable TV also attracted an unprecedented degree of attention from the candidates, who were eager to reach its segmented markets. The Perot presidential candidacy was actually launched by the Dallas millionaire's regular appearances on CNN's nightly phone-in show *Larry King Live*, and presidential candidate Bill Clinton appeared on MTV (the rock-music cable station) to enhance (with some success) his support among the younger voters who constitute the MTV audience.[9]

The 1990s also witnessed the resurgence of radio as a major political force. The movement of the music stations to FM has left the local AM radio stations to subsist on a diet of news, sports, and talk (generally phone-in shows). Radio talk-show hosts, both local and nationally syndicated, have now become a major political force, providing an outlet for public discontent with the political status quo unavailable elsewhere. Large numbers of radio talk-show listeners have been mobilised for specific political causes. The impact of talk-radio first became apparent nationally in 1989, when a public outcry generated by a number of radio talk-show hosts around the country forced the members of Congress to postpone a pay-rise that they were about to award themselves (together with the federal judiciary and executive branch appointees, it should be added). The legislative branch has been a particular target of talk-show hostility, and the attacks on congressional privileges and perquisites, and the (widely popular) movement to limit the terms of state legislators and members of the national Congress, have been largely driven by radio campaigns.

Appearances on radio phone-in shows with sympathetic hosts also featured heavily in the media strategies of the 1992 presidential candidates. Both President Bush and Vice-President Quayle appeared as guests of the most notorious of all the radio talk-show hosts, the rabidly conservative Rush Limbaugh. The unremitting hostility of Limbaugh and other right-wing hosts towards the Clinton presidency was also widely believed to have contributed to the President's abysmally low popularity ratings and the Republican congressional landslide in the 1994 mid-term elections: another indication of the potential power of this new element in an increasingly variegated and complex American national news media.

Ownership and regulation

Private ownership of both print and broadcast media (very exceptional by international standards in the latter case) gives more potential freedom to the American news media than elsewhere in the world, but this freedom comes at a price. Less dependence on government means more dependence on advertising to cover costs, and because advertising rates are tied to audience ratings, the news media must appeal to the audiences that they serve. In such

a situation there is a danger that 'entertainment', rather than political significance or educational value, becomes the criterion for newsworthiness on
television. Ratings wars and the advent of competition from cable and talk-
radio had led to an increasing degree of gimmickry, sensationalism and
disregard for hard fact, even in the mainstream media, that gets in the way
of the media's obligation to inform the public.

Table 11.3. *The largest newspaper chains in the US, 1986*

Rank	Corporation	Total circulation (millions)
1	Gannet Co., Inc.	5.51
2	Knight-Ridder Newspapers	3.6
3	Newhouse Newspapers	2.9
4	Tribune Company	2.6
5	Dow Jones & Co., Inc.	2.5
6	Times Mirror Co.	2.4
7	New America Pub. Corp.	1.9
8	New York Times Co.	1.7
9	Scripps-Howard Newspapers	1.6
10	Thomson Newspapers	1.2
11	Cox Enterprises	1.2
12	Hearst Newspapers	1.1

Source Thomas R. Dye, *Who's Running America? The Bush Era* (Englewood Cliffs, NJ: Prentice-Hall, 1990).

There has been a decided trend towards more concentrated ownership of
all kinds of news media. More and more newspapers have been acquired by
chains such as Hearst, Cox, Knight-Ridder, Scripps-Howard, Murdoch, and
Gannet, some of which are very large indeed (Gannet has ninety papers,
including *USA Today* – the second biggest circulation daily in the country).
Of the daily newspapers, only 400 remain independent.[10] In television the
concentration of ownership does not seem to be a serious problem, as the
networks do not usually own their affiliates. However, like newspapers, television stations in different cities are sometimes owned by the same group.
In 1987, for example, the Cap-Cities/ABC group owned eight television stations in New York, Los Angeles, Chicago, Philadelphia, San Francisco,
Houston, Fresno and Raleigh-Durham – serving 24 per cent of the national
market. A group of stations owned by NBC/General Electric covers 22 per
cent of the market. Recently America has also begun to see ownership concentration across the division between the print and electronic media. The
Chicago Tribune Company owns the *Chicago Tribune* (Chicago's largest selling
daily), *The New York Daily News* (the third largest-selling paper in the US),

six television stations in major cities serving 19 per cent of the market, and several radio stations.

Regulation of the broadcast media is carried out by the Federal Communications Commission (FCC), consisting of seven members (no more than four from the same political party) chosen by the president for terms of seven years. The Commission grants licences to stations, and regulates the organisation of broadcasting companies and their inter-relationships.

In terms of regulating content, the FCC compels broadcasters to operate under several constraints, most notably the Equal Opportunity rule, the Reasonable Access rule, the Right-of-Reply rule, and the Political Editorializing rule.

Under the Equal Opportunity rule, if a station sells time to any candidate for public office, it must make the same amount of time available for sale to other candidates for the same office.

According to the Reasonable Access rule, stations must make their facilities available for the expression of conflicting views or issues from all responsible elements in the community. The Right-of-Reply rule states that any person attacked in a TV programme (other than a regular news programme) has the right to reply on the same station. Finally, the Political Editorializing rule stipulates that if a broadcaster endorses a candidate for office on the air, the candidate's opponents have the right of reply.

None of these restrictions is imposed on the print media, of course, and many broadcast journalists find them exceedingly restrictive and unfair. They argue that the broadcast media should be just as free as the print media to decide which candidates they endorse and which issues they support. For many years the broadcast media were also governed by the 'Fairness Doctrine', which held that broadcasters had to give time to opposing views if a programme on their station gave only one side of an important issue. In 1987 the FCC, acting on the advice of the Reagan Administration, repealed the Fairness Doctrine on the grounds that it chilled freedom of speech.[11] Democrats in Congress tried unsuccessfully to restore the doctrine by writing a federal law in the early 1990s.

The influence of the media

There can be no doubt that the media is particularly influential in American politics, primarily due to its sacrosanct place in the Constitution and American political culture, and the weakness of political parties. Commentators from all aspects of the political spectrum have attributed many of the malign characteristics of modern American politics to the undue influence of the media over political events. Let us now examine the merits of these criticisms in turn.

One accusation commonly made against the media is that it distorts the electoral process, particularly as it reports presidential primary campaigns. The American public relies on the media to interpret the results of primary elections and to tell them who has won or lost or done 'better than expected'. The disproportionate influence of the first presidential primary in tiny New Hampshire is largely explained by the extensive coverage provided by the media, and the media bandwagon effect (or 'big Mo') that a strong New Hampshire showing provides.[12] In the 1972 New Hampshire Democratic presidential primary, for example, Senator Edmund Muskie defeated Senator George McGovern 46–37 per cent, but the press and television reported the result as a 'worse than expected' showing for the Democratic front-runner from the adjacent state of Maine, and the bandwagon effect helped to propel McGovern towards the presidential nomination. In this instance we can legitimately ask whether the media were creating reality as well as reporting it.

The news media are also accused of simplifying and trivialising politics. This is not, perhaps, so true of the print media, who have the space to give a more comprehensive treatment to complex issues. But television evening news has only half an hour to present all the issues and stories of the day, and to maintain ratings it had to be entertaining as well. As a consequence issues get boiled down to the ludicrously simple level of 'soundbites' and 'photo opportunities' and the public is not really informed. In election campaign coverage the same constraints often lead the broadcast media to adopt a 'horse-race mentality' that places too much emphasis on who's winning or losing, rather than the fundamental issues involved.[13]

Another disturbing attribute of the media's role in contemporary electoral politics is that 'telegenic' qualities such as good looks and a warm delivery come to matter more than substantial issues. In other words: instead of reflecting reality, television begins to create its own reality.[14] John F. Kennedy 'defeated' Richard Nixon in 1960 because Kennedy looked better in the crucial first television debate (radio listeners gave the debate to Nixon). Ronald Reagan's phenomenally successful political career would only have been possible in a television age, where his skills before the cameras made such a powerful impact. Also, Bill Clinton's victory in the 1992 election was largely due to his poise and smooth delivery by comparison with his rivals in the television debates.

Another accusation levelled against the media from both right and left of the political spectrum is that it presents the issues with a pronounced liberal or conservative bias. Left-wing commentators believe that the media has a pronounced bias towards corporate interests, while the right inveighs against the media's social liberalism. A glance at Table 11.4 demonstrates that the right-wingers have a stronger case. Journalists are noticeably more liberal than the American public on almost all issues, particularly at the elite level. The issue may be less a question of left and right, however, and more one of different life-styles and attitudes towards authority. Conservatives respect authority, be it family, religious, or governmental. Journalists, by the very nature of their profession, are in an adversarial relationship with authority.[15]

On the other hand, as far as the print media is concerned, most newspaper endorsements in presidential elections invariably go to the Republican candidates.

Table 11.4. *Attitudes of the media elite*

	% agreeing with viewpoint		
Social issue and viewpoint	Business leaders	Newsmakers	Entertainment producers
Economic liberalism			
Government should redistribute income	23	68	69
Government should guarantee jobs	29	48	45
Big corporations should be publicly owned	6	13	19
Private enterprise is fair	89	70	69
People with more ability should earn more	90	86	94
Reformism			
Structure of society causes alienation	30	49	62
Institutions need overhaul	28	32	48
Social Liberalism			
Strong affirmative action for blacks	71	80	83
Women have the right to abortions	80	90	97
Homosexuals should not teach in schools	51	15	15
Homosexuality is wrong	60	25	20
Adultery is wrong	76	47	49

Sources Lichter and Rothman, 'Media and Business Elites', *Public Opinion* (October–November 1981), pp. 42–6; Lichter and Rothman, 'Hollywood and America: The Odd Couple', *Public Opinion* (December–January 1983), pp. 54–8.
Reproduced from Thomas R. Dye, *Who's Running America? The Bush Era*, 5th edn (Englewood Cliffs, NJ: Prentice-Hall, 1990), p. 130.

Several leading political scientists have argued that the prevalence of television has had an adverse impact on the presidency, since in an age of ineffectual parties, Presidents are compelled to try and manipulate their media image to generate public support.[16] The relationship is not a one-way street, however. The media is also obsessed with the glamour and power of the presidency, and literally everything done by the Chief Executive and his family is under a continual media spotlight. Presidents have tended to saturate the airwaves until the public becomes disgusted with them and their high media visibility turns into a diminishing asset.

Media obsession with the White House also comes at the expense of the legislative branch, which lends itself much less readily to the requirements of the media than the executive. Legislative activity is all about cutting deals, and making compromises to get the lowest common denominator of agreement and pass legislation. The arcane rules and mores of Capitol Hill are not looked upon sympathetically by the media, who view politics in terms of issues, principles and drama, rather than simply as a matter of getting something done. Congressional observers would probably concur than the full coverage of Congress's floor and committee sessions on television has not had a particularly positive effect on the institution. The intense and comprehensive television coverage of the Senate Judiciary Committee's examination of Anita Hill's allegations against Supreme Court nominee Clarence Thomas hearings in 1991 certainly did not reflect well on Congress.

It is further alleged that the media are too disrespectful towards public figures, and too obsessed with their conduct in their private lives. US libel laws are far more lax than those in other democracies, as public figures have to prove not only that something said or printed about them was factually incorrect, but also that it was done with 'malicious' intent, a standard which in practice has proven almost impossible to achieve. In search of scoops and ratings, the media now habitually intrudes upon the private life of public figures in a cruel and unfair manner, as in the cases of former presidential candidate Gary Hart, the late Senator John Tower, and candidate Bill Clinton in 1992. This is not only often hypocritical, but also lowers the average citizen's respect for government.

The final common indictment of the media is that its interests are fundamentally in conflict with those of the nation as a whole. The media's presentation of the Vietnam War certainly contributed to the anti-war movement and national disgust with the conflict. America's fanaticism about 'open government' may also entail that the overall interest of the US can be critically harmed. A powerful reason that some national security decisions remain secret is to give more flexibility in relations with foreign powers, and perhaps to save lives. In the domestic sphere it appears that greater openness in government has only provided more access points for powerful lobbies to influence the policy-making process. It can therefore be argued that the increasingly open nature of American Government (as demanded by the media) entails misgovernment or no government.

Conclusion

This sums up the case against the influence of the media over American politics today. It appears somewhat overstated. The media has great influence over US politics only because its adversarial role towards government and politicians accords with American political culture. Americans think that a powerful press is a healthy thing to keep government accountable and to keep the politicians on their toes. There is no question, moreover, that due to the rise of the news media as the principal vehicle of political intermediation in the United States, the American public as a whole is better informed about politics than it was a century ago.

The problems for the electoral process and government created by the growth in influence of the broadcast media in particular are intrinsic to modern journalism and communications, and are not easily remedied, given the very generous constitutional interpretations of the first amendment by the Supreme Court in recent decades. What is likely, however, is that computer technology, the information 'superhighway', and the continued growth of Cable, satellite, and other new forms of broadcasting, will together create an unprecedented number of news outlets, both local and national, and reduce further the power and influence of the major networks' news divisions. These new outlets will provide more diverse viewpoints and more 'in-depth' analyses of major political issues for those who want it.

The news media's relationship with American government is like that of an individual with his or her telephone or motor car. In some ways it makes everyone's life very tiresome and unpleasant, but given that we have such easy access to such devices, it is unlikely that we would seriously contemplate doing without them.

Notes

1 On the party press of the mid-nineteenth century see Michael E. McGerr, *The Decline of Popular Politics: The American North 1865–1928* (New York: Oxford University Press, 1986), pp. 3–41.
2 On the rise of the mass-circulation independent press, see *ibid.*, pp. 105–37.
3 On muck-raking see Richard A. Hofstadter, *The Age of Reform: From Bryan to FDR* (New York: Knopf, 1955), pp. 185–212.
4 See Thomas R. Dye, *Who's Running America? The Bush Era* (Englewood Cliffs, NJ: Prentice-Hall, 1990), p. 121.
5 According to Austin Ranney's data, in 1978 67 per cent of Americans named television as their principle news source, and 47 per cent found it to be the most credible source, compared with 23 per cent for newspapers. See Ranney, *Channels of Power*, p. 14.
6 Dye, *Who's Running America?*, p. 121.
7 PBS has come under regular attack from Conservatives on two grounds: first, alleged 'liberal' bias; and second, that the federal government should not be subsidising a service viewed by a relatively small, 'elitist', upper middle-class audience. The leadership of the Republican Congress elected in 1994 has singled out PBS for particular attention in their efforts to reduce federal spending, and thus the future for public, non-commercial broadcasting in the US appears bleak.
8 See Tim Hames, 'The Changing Media' in Gillian Peele *et al.*, *Developments in American Politics 2* (London: Macmillan, 1994).
9 *Ibid.*
10 See Dye, *Who's Running America?*, pp. 121–2.
11 On the abolition of the Fairness Doctrine see Entman, *Democracy Without Citizens*, pp. 102–24.
12 On the influence of New Hampshire see Orren and Polsby, *Media and Momentum*.

13 On the 'horse-race' mentality in campaign coverage, see Patterson, *The Mass Media Election.*

14 See Ranney, *Channels of Power*, pp. 3–30.

15 *Ibid.*, pp. 31–63

16 On the media and the presidency see Richard L. Rubin, *Press, Party, and the Presidency* (New York: Norton, 1981); Roderick P. Hart, *The Sound of Leadership: Presidential Communication in the Modern Age* (Chicago: University of Chicago Press, 1987); and Samuel Kernell, *Going Public: New Strategies of Presidential Leadership* (Washington, DC: Congressional Quarterly, Inc., 1986).

Part Four

Elections and public policy

12

Elections

Elections are the essence of American democracy and conducted in a manner emulated by few other nations. As this chapter will illustrate, the United States elects a greater number and range of public office-holders than any other country. Those elections take place under rules of candidate selection, lengths of campaigns, and expense of campaigns that are again virtually unmatched. American citizens are called upon to participate in the electoral process at a positively exhausting rate.

This enthusiasm for the ballot-box is somewhat paradoxical, given that neither the Founding Fathers nor the Constitution they created wanted it. The opening section here will trace how the cautious instincts of the founders and the fear of popular rule embedded in the Constitution were swiftly eroded and how the electoral principle has expanded in American public life. Having established this, the chapter will then examine five important trends in the conduct of American elections that have manifested themselves over the last thirty years with considerable consequence for the operation of American government. Those trends are: the changing role of political parties in election campaigns; the increasing ability of incumbent (serving) Congressmen to gain re-election; the spectacular increase in candidate spending in elections; the low and declining level of turnout; and the frequent tendency of the voters to elect differing parties for the White House and Congress. Such trends have led some observers to worry that the obvious quantity of American electoral democracy may not be producing a similar level of quality.

Having demonstrated the importance of these themes for elections – and public policy – in the 1980s, the concluding section will note that some of them were less evident in elections of the 1990s but also that one trend – increased campaign expenditure – was spectacularly reinforced during these contests and another, divided government, left the stage in 1992 only to return two years later.

History and procedure

The Constitution of 1787 said remarkably little about elections and in what it does say there is an enormous amount of delegation to the individual states. Article I Section II establishes elections every other year for the full House of Representatives but did not name any particular election system to be used, merely stating that the size of the electorate should be the same as for the lower chamber of a state's own legislature. The number of representatives any state receives is determined by population size. Section III of the same article ensures that Senators – two for each state regardless of population level –

would be selected for six years by the state legislatures (by whatever means they preferred) and that one-third of Senate seats would be contested every two years. This broad delegation is confirmed by section 4, which states that 'The times, places and manner of holding elections for senators and representatives shall be prescribed in each state by the legislature thereof.'

The election of the President was outlined in Article II, Section I which created an electoral college, with each state having a delegation the size of its total number of Senators and representatives combined. These presidential electors were to be chosen by whatever method state legislatures saw fit, with the presumption that the legislatures themselves would probably make the choice.

This relative disinterest in the details of public elections could well have sprung from the founders, deeply-cherished hope that there would not be too many of them and they would not decide very much. In the original draft of the Constitution only the House of Representatives was to be directly elected by whatever proportion of adult citizens states chose to permit the franchise. The Senate would be selected by state legislatures. The President would be selected by an electoral college whose members were themselves appointed rather than elected. To further display the Constitution's distrust of mass democracy, the unelected Supreme Court, whose members had life tenure, was to be nominated by the non-elected President and confirmed (or not) by the non-elected Senate. All in all, then, elections were granted a rather modest role in the theory of American government.

Despite the efforts of those who framed the original order, the history of the United States over the past 200 years has been of the ever-expanding use of elections to choose public officials and direct policy. Early elections to the House of Representatives saw an average of about half of all adult white male citizens granted the vote by their states, an astonishingly high proportion by the standards of the eighteenth-century world. By the election of 1840 virtually all of the remaining white male community had been enfranchised. This, at a time when the Great Reform Act of 1832 in Britain was expanding the suffrage, but left over 95 per cent of adults without votes.

Of the constitutional amendments passed since the adoption of the first ten (the Bill of Rights) in 1791, many have dealt with the expansion of voting rights. The Fifteenth Amendment (1870), theoretically – but alas not practically for nearly another century – enfranchised black citizens. The Seventeenth Amendment (1913) changed the selection of Senators from the state legislatures to popular ballot in all states. A number of states had held advisory ballots for some time in any case. The Nineteenth Amendment (1920) extended the ballot to all adult women. Again, some states had permitted women to vote for many decades previously. The Twenty-third Amendment (1961) gave the franchise in presidential elections to citizens of the District of Columbia.[1] The Twenty-fourth Amendment (1964) banned the use of the Poll Tax as a determinant of the right to vote. This had been frequently used in southern states to keep blacks off the electoral rolls. Finally, the Twenty-sixth Amendment (1971) lowered the voting age for all elections from twenty-one to eighteen.

As important as these formal constitutional changes was an informal one in the conduct of presidential contests. By the 1830s every state bar one (South Carolina, which changed two decades later) allowed its delegates to the electoral college to be chosen by its people rather than the state politicians. This means that while the President is still theoretically chosen by the electoral college in practice, their decision is predetermined by the voters, who choose between alternative lists of electors committed to their stated presidential candidate.

At the national level elections are therefore cast thus. In the House of Representatives all 435 members are elected every two years by the single plurality or first-past-the-post method. Senators are elected by the same method every six years, with elections staggered so that one-third of seats are filled every two years (the state of Georgia requires a run-off election if the winning candidate gets less than 50 per cent of all votes cast).[2] Any vacancies due to death or resignation are filled by special elections, the precise rules of which vary by state. Presidents are elected every four years by an electoral college consisting of party loyalists who, in every state bar Maine, are all given to whichever candidate wins the most votes in that state. Since 1967 Maine has awarded one each of its four votes to the two congressional districts within the state and has given the remaining two to the candidate who scores most votes overall.[3] The candidate who wins a majority of the 538 electoral college votes becomes President.[4]

At the state level, all fifty governors are directly elected by the same method as the national level (Georgia and Arizona requiring a run-off if a candidate is elected with a minority of the vote). In forty-nine states there are two chambers of the state legislature elected in the same way as the national legislatures. Nebraska has a single chamber and compounds its uniqueness by banning candidates from standing under a party label. At the local level there are over 86,000 forms of government with some 500,000 elected officials, with most cities vesting major power in a directly elected mayor. Once again, the single plurality system dominates.

There are three other facets of American electoral procedure worthy of comment. They are the sheer range of public offices chosen by election, the use of the direct primary as the technique for nominating each party's candidates, and the frequent deployment of the referendum or initiative to allow voters to choose their policies as well as their politicians. It is these factors which produce the unusually powerful role of elections in American society.

Many American states elect positions that in other nations would invariably be appointed. School boards – responsible for local education services – are hotly contested virtually everywhere. Other public boards, such as those responsible for state-owned land or railways, are often chosen by election. About half of all states elected their judges (unlike the national system, where none are directly elected) with a questionable effect on the quality of local justice. Then there are the well-known curiosities. Many southern states elect the local undertaker and dog-catcher as well as their sheriff. North Dakota elects its tax assessor. Just how one campaigns for such posts, or why one would stand for them, is a mystery to outside observers. Nevertheless, the breadth of offices decided by mass voting pays testament to the importance Americans attach to elections as a means of political legitimacy.

This eager use of elections extends to selecting party candidates as well as choosing between them. In the nineteenth century party nomination for Congress and most state elections were firmly under the control of party organisations, who would invariably select candidates loyal to the party leadership. This rule by party machines was bitterly resented by outsiders and would-be reformers who latched on to the idea of a direct primary, where ordinary party voters would choose between different candidates – by public ballot just like general elections – and award the party nomination. Starting at the turn of the twentieth century, the direct primary was rapidly adopted for choosing party candidates and is virtually universal for congressional and state-wide elections.

The actual rules for the primary vary by state law. Half of all the states ask voters to register themselves as Republicans, Democrats, or independents at the time they are placed on the electoral register, although this does not actually oblige them ever to vote for that party's candidates. In these states the usual practice is for 'closed' primaries whereby only registered supporters of the party can vote in its primary, although some states will allow registered independents to vote in a party primary as well. The remaining states hold 'open' primaries whereby any adult citizen may vote in either party primary. Hence a Republican voter faced with an unopposed candidate or obvious winner in his own primary might vote in the Democratic primary if that looked more interesting. Alaska holds the ultimate open primary in that it allows voters to participate in both party primaries, should they wish!

In most states the party primaries are separated. Some states, notably in the south, list all the candidates for an office together in one list and the top two candidates go on to fight out the general election. Therefore it would be possible for the final election to consist of two candidates from the same party. Louisiana law states that if any candidate wins more than 50 per cent of the total vote in their single list primary he or she is declared the outright winner and the general election is cancelled.

Although there have been presidential primaries since 1901 when Florida introduced one, primaries were not critical in deciding presidential nominations until the 1970s. Until then the choice of presidential nominee was basically the prerogative of congressional and state party leaders who sought an individual that united them and who had widespread electoral appeal.

Primaries, caucuses and state conventions

Candidates for public office can be nominated and delegates for national conventions chosen, in one of three ways. A *primary* is an all-day election (organised much like a general election) in which, varying with state law, either registered supporters of that party, those who are not registered supporters of the other party or (in most cases) any citizen may vote. A *caucus* is a public meeting which (usually) any citizen may attend, at the end of which a vote between the various candidates is taken. A *state convention* is a large formal party meeting that either only party officials or interested citizens may attend which, amongst other items of business, features a vote between candidates. Most delegates to national conventions which nominate presidential candidates, and virtually all other offices now use primaries. Turnout is highest (but not very high) in primaries and usually lowest (well under 1 per cent of party supporters) at state conventions.

Relatively few states held presidential primaries and those that did usually made them advisory and non-binding affairs popularly regarded as 'beauty contests'. From the late 1960s onwards (see Chapter 9) most states chose to acquire their delegates to the national convention which formally selects the candidates through primaries or caucuses (an open meeting which voters attend and at the end of which are asked to express a choice between the contenders).

This extension of the electoral process so that American citizens effectively decide who the major party candidates are, as well as which single individual wins office, is virtually unique in western democracies. It also means that in the United States voters are more powerful (provided they bother to use their franchise) and party organisations less powerful compared with other countries. Whether this produces better quality candidates is a matter of enormous dispute.

Not content with such wide authority over choosing politicians, many states allow their electorate even more impact through the widespread use of single-issue ballots. Some forty-six state constitutions allow either for regular referendum (where the state legislature asks citizens to vote on a matter), or initiatives (where people themselves, by achieving a required number of signatures on a petition, force an issue to a ballot), or for elected officials to be 'recalled' (thrown out of office) by a vote if a large number of signatures are raised to demand such a ballot. In about half of all states (disproportionately in the west of the nation) the initiative is very widely used to settle tax and spending issues which would normally be considered the province of state legislatures. In certain states, notably California (probably the most initiative-fixated), Colorado, and South Dakota (which introduced the device first in 1898), referenda are used so regularly and so widely that it is not really an overstatement to say that they, rather than elections to the state legislature, really decide policy.

Having outlined the basic procedure, the five key trends in elections from the 1960s to the 1980s – especially contests for national office – noted earlier, can be developed further.

The changing role of political parties

Political parties, and more specifically party organisations, once dominated American elections. They selected the candidates, they funded and ran the campaign, and most voters were clearly loyal to one major party or the other. They had few rivals in the electoral process and had a role not dissimilar to that which party organisations retain in Britain and Germany today. That role, probably at its pinnacle in the late nineteenth century, was battered by the so-called Progressive era reforms of the first two decades of this century, and has been severely mauled by changes in the last thirty years, so that by the 1980s parties were struggling to maintain any significant function in elections.

The parties have suffered from a three-pronged attack by interrelated factors. First, the electorate have become less loyal to the parties and much more willing to vote for different party candidates for different offices. Second, party organisations have declined, as witnessed by their loss of control over presidential nominations outlined above. Third, new rivals to the party in the funding and organisation of election campaigns have emerged.

Until the late 1950s the American voter was distinctly loyal to their preferred political party and would vote for all of that party's candidates for every office on the ballot-paper (known as straight-ticket voting). One sign of this was that the party which won the presidential election in any given year would invariably win control of both branches of Congress and make sizeable gains in the states and localities as well (the presidential coat-tail effect). Over the last thirty years surveys consistently show that Americans are much more inclined to describe themselves as independent of the two major parties, and those who retain party loyalties do so with less intensity. Explanations for these phenomena abound and there is no clear consensus on it, but one commonly agreed consequence is that it acts as an incentive for candidates in elections to emphasise their independence from their party organisations and run much more individualistic and personal campaigns.

This trend towards candidate-centred rather than party-centred elections was further fuelled by the wide adoption of the direct primary in non-presidential elections and its extension to presidential elections from the 1970s onwards. Individual politicians simply had less need of their party organisations and, in the majority of elections, literally anybody could enter a party's primary and get themselves nominated. As candidates did not need the party organisation to get nominated they had little incentive to use it in the actual election campaign.

This move in the direction of candidate-based elections has provided a stiff challenge to party organisations and produced new rivals to it.

The modern campaign

Few presidential candidates, or candidates for any other type of election, now allow their party organisations to run their campaign. The modern presidential campaign has a full-time campaign manager, a large salaried staff, and many volunteers, and employs professionals to deal with media strategy, television advertising, opinion polling, debate preparation, fund-raising and voter targeting. In many cases the professionals are more famous than the candidate when the presidential election season begins. Once elected, presidents usually retain their pollster and consult their favoured consultants. Virtually all contests for Senator and Governor, as well as many for the House of Representatives, have a similar structure. This professional structure leaves little for the ordinary volunteer political enthusiast to do and partly explains the expensive nature of modern American elections.

Parties no longer fund election campaigns. In presidential elections, whilst the law does allow the National Committee of each party to spend an allotted amount of money on behalf of their candidate, the majority of funding is provided by the taxpayer. In congressional elections party organisations do provide funds but come a poor third behind interest groups (known as Political Action Committees) and individual donors. That pattern is repeated in elections at the state level.

The actual running of an election campaign is dominated by the candidate's own personal organisation built up during the campaign for the nomination. Such teams usually consist of an inner core of close personal supporters and a cadre of hired professionals such as freelance political consultants, public opinion pollsters, media advisers such as the new breed of 'spin-doctors' who specialise in persuading the press that their candidate is running the superior campaign, and other assorted self-described experts at various aspects of campaign politics, such as fund-raising or preparation for television debates.

As that description implies, the mass media has become a major rival to the political party. Most elections for the Senate or for Governor and virtually all presidential primaries are fought out on television, both through paid television advertising and by coverage of the candidate's activities on news and current affairs programmes. This is often true for other elective offices as well. Critics contend that this pursuit of media attention deflects from the substance of democracy as campaigns struggle to get their message across in short media-friendly messages or 'soundbites'.

The major party organisations responded to this new environment in the 1970s and early 1980s by building up their National Committees (Washington, DC-based party bureaucracies). These began to solicit large amounts of money from party sympathisers via appeals through the mail, which was spent in donations to candidates and assistance in the form of their own political experts lent to key campaigns. The extent and value of this aid has been disputed,[5] but it has retained a role in election campaigns for at least the national party, even if these functions are something of a shadow of what the party organisations used to do.

In contemporary electoral politics, then, candidates and their own personally built and based teams are increasingly the dominant figures. This reinforces the tendency of voters to cast their ballots for individual politicians regardless of party, and treat each individual office as a separate contest.

The power of incumbency

The period from the mid-1970s to late 1980s saw a staggering improvement in the ability of elected officials to gain re-election, particularly in the House of Representatives. This, combined with lower rates of voluntary retirement in the same period, meant a collective ageing of the House along with a much higher average period served by members. This success in gaining re-election brought charges of corruption and a 'permanent Congress' from some quarters.

The existence of such high re-election rates is difficult to dispute. Although the average between 1946 and 1974 had approached 90 per cent (meaning between thirty-five and forty House members were beaten), that figure rose further in the 1980s. In the 1984 elections some 95 per cent of House incumbents were re-elected. This figure rose to 98 per cent in 1986 and 1988 before slipping back fractionally to 96 per cent in 1990. Across these four elections only thirty-nine incumbents in total – or an average of just ten a year – were defeated in general elections.

As Congressmen became more secure they increasingly decided to postpone the day of their eventual retirement. Whereas in the elections of 1974, 1976, and 1978, there had been a total of 139 voluntary retirements creating open seats where no incumbent sought re-election, the total for 1984, 1986, and 1988 was only 83 such retirements – a decline of 40 per cent. The combination of high re-election rates and low retirements meant that the average age of members of the House increased from 45.5 in 1983 to nearly 53 years by 1991. The average term served exceeded six (or twelve years) by the end of the 1980s.

The trend in the Senate was much more erratic, with re-election rates swinging between 55 per cent in 1980 and 93 per cent in 1982 or 60 per cent in 1986 and 97 per cent in 1990. Nor was the trend towards less frequent retirements always repeated. Although the Senate also aged, the degree was much more gentle.

Not only was the House member usually winning but the margin of victory was also increasing, to around two-thirds of the vote on average by 1988. However, there was another interesting development. In the three decades before 1974 it was relatively easy to predict which incumbents would lose by looking at who won by the narrowest margin in the previous election, with first-term incumbents being especially vulnerable. From the mid-1970s

Table 12.1. *Incumbency re-election rates, 1974–94*

Year/office	Number of incumbents			Incumbents winning election
	Ran	Won	Lost	
1974				
House	383	343	40	89.6
Senate	25	23	2	92.0
1976				
House	381	368	13	96.6
Senate	25	16	9	64.0
1978				
House	378	359	19	95.0
Senate	22	15	7	68.1
1980				
House	392	361	31	90.7
Senate	25	16	9	55.2
1982				
House	381	352	29	92.4
Senate	30	28	2	93.3
1984				
House	407	391	16	96.1
Senate	29	26	3	89.7
1986				
House	391	385	6	98.5
Senate	28	21	7	75.0
1988				
House	409	402	6	98.3
Senate	27	23	4	85.0
1990				
House	406	391	15	96.3
Senate	32	31	1	96.9
1992				
House	349	325	24	93.1
Senate	28	24	4	85.7
1994				
House	387	349	38	90.2
Senate	26	24	2	92.0

Note Incumbent (sitting) members of Congress have always had impressive re-election rates, with the House of Representatives more secure than the Senate. In the 1980s these re-election scores in the House of Representatives were consistently close to 98 per cent, leading to wide concern that challengers did not have a fair chance. These numbers decreased somewhat (although they were still high) in the House elections of the 1990s, although ironically the Senate has begun to look like a fortress for serving members.

onwards patterns amongst those Congressmen who were beaten became increasingly unpredictable, with first-term incumbents becoming rather competent at seeking re-election. This led to the paradox of elections to the House of Representatives in the 1980s: although virtually all incumbents were re-elected they became more obsessed about their re-election campaigns because almost any of them could be amongst the few incumbents who were destined to be defeated.

Why were members of the House so successful at ensuring their own re-election most of the time? The answer would seem to lie in a combination of two factors: the set of official perks that members of the House voted for themselves from the 1970s onwards, and the trend towards candidate-centred rather than party-based voting that assisted those candidates who were well known, invariably incumbents.

The House of Representatives' capacity to assist its own members is legendary. The very organisation of the place, with members serving on committees and sub-committees relevant to the interests of their district, and using these positions to push national expenditure towards their locality, helps the competent office-holder (failure to fulfil this function adequately is the largest cause – along with personal scandal – of an incumbent's defeat). This institutional bias was extended further, with a wave of new perks introduced in the name of better constituency service.

Such perks include taxpayer-funded newsletters to all constituents, allegedly as a public information exercise, but in reality an incumbent promotion exercise. This franked mail invariably increased as election day neared so that by the late 1980s over one billion pieces of mail a year were leaving Congress in the direction of constituents, the overwhelming majority of which was utterly unsolicited. The taxpayer also funds unlimited flights to return members to their districts, again in the name of good service but with clear political implications. The staffing levels of both the Senate and House have exploded, with the largest rise being amongst those staff members working in the incumbent's district office, those offices being thinly disguised permanent re-election machines churning out favourable publicity.

That publicity machine has been further enhanced by the free provision of radio and television facilities for members. The average Congressman now spends virtually every long weekend in his or her constituency, and many of the evenings they are obliged to spend in Congress are spent fund-raising. Most surveys estimate the commercial value of the services the average incumbent uses for free at substantially more than $500,000 a year.

Behind all this frantic self-promotion lies the assumption that with more voters casting ballots on a candidate basis then favourable name-recognition is the key to re-election. In the Senate, incumbency is less important because most challenger candidates tend to have run for elective office in the state before and are quite well-known, whereas few House challenger candidates can hope to match incumbents this way. The net effect of these factors is to

Table 12.2. *Congressional mail to voters, 1956–90*

Fiscal year	Millions of pieces
1956	58.2
1960	108.0
1966	197.5
1970	201.0
1974	321.0
1976	401.4
1980	511.3
1981	395.6
1982	771.8
1983	556.8
1984	924.6
1985	675.0
1986	758.7
1987	494.7
1988	804.9
1989	598.6
1990	564.2

Note The electoral success of incumbents is often blamed on the amount of 'informational' material they mail to voters at taxpayers' expense. As this table notes, the total amount of such mail has exploded since 1974. It is perhaps no coincidence that odd-numbered years (when there are no congressional elections) consistently see fewer mailings than even-numbered years (when there are always elections).

produce politicians who are hypersensitive to the concerns of their constituents and constituents who regularly complain about the collective failures of Congress but who usually support their incumbent.

The importance of money

Money has always been an important aspect of American elections, but its standing has increased dramatically over the last two decades such that it is frequently quipped by political operatives that 'money is the first primary'. Both the amount of money raised and spent and the sources of that money are unusual by the standards of western democracies. This section will attempt to make two points. First, that despite (because of?) an orgy of campaign finance legislation in the 1970s there is a significant gap between what the laws says happens and what actually happens. The second is that there has been a stark trend towards greater campaign expenditure and that funding has come from interest groups rather than political parties.

Before the 1970s political money was largely unregulated in the United States. The activities of Richard Nixon's Committee to Re-Elect the President (known as the CRP to him and CREEP to almost everybody else) in the 1972 campaign, especially the bungled break-in and subsequent hashed cover-up of the Watergate building, altered all that. A 1971 funding reform was compounded by further legislation in 1974, 1976, and 1979.

Table 12.3. *Challenger–incumbent spending ratios, 1976–92*

Year	House	Senate
1976	64	73
1978	67	52
1980	74	65
1982	57	65
1984	48	49
1986	37	60
1988	32	49
1990	32	48
1992	28	47

Source Norman J. Ornstein, Thomas E. Mann, and Michael J. Malbin, *Vital Statistics on Congress, 1989–90* (Washington, DC: Congressional Quarterly Press, 1990).

Note This table indicates the election expenditure of challenger candidates compared with incumbent members. This has shown a consistent downhill slide. In 1992 therefore the average House incumbent raised and spent nearly four times as much as their opponents, while Senators spent just over twice as much.

The system it produced works in theory like this. Presidential candidates in the primary campaign are limited in how much they can raise and spend both overall and in each state. An individual may donate a maximum of $1,000 and a Political Action Committee $5,000. If candidates are willing to accept taxpayer money to help subsidise their campaign (which all primary candidates bar Republicans John Connally in 1980 and Steve Forbes in 1996 have done), then they qualify by raising at least $5,000 in donations of less than $250 in at least twenty states. If they achieve this, and agree to be bound by federal law as to how they spend their money (not just the taxpayer component), then all donations received by candidates up to $250 will be doubled by the taxpayer. Once the primary season starts, failure to score 10 per cent in two successive contests leads to suspension of these matching funds.

Having received a taxpayer grant towards their national convention, the presidential nominees are even more tightly restricted in the November election. They may accept a taxpayer grant (in 1992 George Bush and Bill Clinton each received $55.24 million) but can raise and spend no more money if they do except for a grant that their National Committees may raise and spend on their behalf.

The regulation for congressional elections is less cumbersome, perhaps because it was drawn up by Congress itself, which chose to burden presidential contests with the most bureaucracy. There are no limits on what individual candidates may raise and spend on their campaigns and there are no donations (or regulations with it) from the public purse. Campaign finance legislation here is aimed at regulating those who donate the money, not those who spend it. Individuals may donate up to $1,000 in both the primary and final elections. Political Action Committees may donate a maximum of $5,000 in each election. In the course of any year an individual may give a maximum of $20,000 to all national party committees. The parties in turn are tightly limited in how much they can donate to candidates in House and Senate races.[6]

In practice, however, there are a number of ways by which the spirit of this legislation can be blatantly and legally flouted. Since 1976 (in *Buckley* v. *Valeo*) the Supreme Court has ruled that political expenditure in support of a candidate or opposing a candidate is constitutionally protected free speech, providing there is no formal collusion between the donor and the candidates' campaign organisation. Therefore if a Political Action Committee (PAC) such as the National Rifle Association wanted to spend vast sums of money 'independently' in an election then no law could stop them. It is this threat, rather than the $5,000 donation that can officially be made to a campaign, that gives certain interest groups real influence in American elections. The same case established that there was no limit on what an individual may contribute to his or her own election campaign.

A second loophole is that for presidential elections a number of activities at the state and local level (mass mailings, telephone canvassing, publicity materials) can be paid for by money raised by state rather than national laws, which are usually much more lax. This so-called 'soft money' means that presidential candidates often raise and spend double their theoretical limit.

None of this legislation has prevented the amount of money used in congressional elections rising from a total of $199.4 million in the 1978 elections to $472 million by 1986, where it levelled off for the remainder of the decade. In part this leap reflected increasing campaign expenses, especially in the price of television advertising. More broadly it is an unsurprising reaction to the willingness of voters to support candidates rather than parties. If very large numbers of the electorate might conceivably vote for you it makes sense to spend as much money on advertising yourself as you can raise. The spurt in campaign finance levelled off in the 1986–90 period when contributors realised how difficult it was for incumbents to get beaten and donations to challengers dried up.

Congressional election funding is dominated by (usually affluent) individual givers and interest groups. For the 1992 House contests 37.3 per cent of donations to all candidates came from Political Action Committees, compared with 3.5 per cent from party sources (most of the rest came from individuals).[7] If money buys influence, it is plain who has the influence.

The decline in electoral participation

Despite all the energy that goes into funding American election campaigns the rate of turnout amongst eligible adult citizens, always poor (only Switzerland compares) by the standards of western nations, has sunk to even lower levels over the past three decades. The presidential election of 1960 (in which John Kennedy narrowly edged out Richard Nixon) saw 61.9 per cent of eligible voters participate. That proportion had fallen to 55.4 per cent in 1972 and slid further to just 50.15 per cent in the 1988 contest. The decline in mid-term congressional elections have also slumped. Some 45.4 per cent of eligible voters went to the polls in the House elections of 1962, and that uninspiring number fell to only 33 per cent in the mid-term campaign of 1990 which, according to some calculations,[8] represents the lowest figure of the eligible public since the 1790s.

These astonishingly low turnout levels have obvious and disturbing implications for American democracy. There are also a number of proposed explanations which can be given varying degrees of plausibility.

Amongst the least credible is the notion that failing to vote represents public satisfaction with the status quo and therefore some kind of strange compliment to American society. If this were true then the happiest Americans would be the poor, racial minorities and young people who have the lowest level of turnout, whereas affluent elderly whites, who are most likely to vote, are truly miserable.

The most obvious cause of low participation is the process of registering to vote. Unlike western Europe, where citizens are automatically put on the electoral roll by the state, in the US the emphasis is on the individual adult to register themselves. The precise rules for this process are determined by the individual states, many of which do not seem to prioritise maximising turnout and who often employ bureaucratic and cumbersome procedures. A common difficulty is that, despite being a geographically mobile society, many states require voters to register six months before the election. Adults who move often find it impossible to cast their ballot.

Although such difficulties are a significant explanation of the historically low turnout levels they cannot explain the very poor figures of the 1980s. Restrictions on voting by southern blacks were swept away by the Twenty-fourth Amendment and the Voting Rights Act of 1965. The overwhelming majority of states have eased their rules over the last thirty years but despite that, non-voting has increased. As did the national government with the 1993 'Motor Voter' Act which encouraged voter registration with driving licences. Even those states with relatively benign registration rules, such as North Dakota, which requires no pre-registration, and Wisconsin, which

Table 12.4. *Electoral turnout (%), 1952–94*

Year	Presidential elections	House elections
1952	61.6	57.6
1954	—	41.7
1956	59.3	55.9
1958	—	43.0
1960	62.6	58.5
1962	—	45.4
1964	61.9	57.8
1966	—	45.4
1968	60.9	55.1
1970	—	43.5
1972	55.4	50.9
1974	—	36.1
1976	54.4	49.5
1978	—	35.1
1980	53.4	48.1
1982	—	37.7
1984	53.3	47.4
1986	—	33.4
1988	50.1	44.7
1990	—	33.0
1992	55.2	50.8
1994	—	38.1

Note As this table shows, voting in American elections has always
been light compared with those of other democracies. Turnout is
highest in presidential election years (House turnout in those years
due to unopposed contents and some voters abstaining) and lowest in
mid-term elections. Turnout in the 1980s appeared to be heading on a
continuous downward path. However this was reversed somewhat in
the 1990s.

allows voters to register at the polling booth, have seen a decline in participation.

If registration methods are not a sufficient explanation for the tumbling
turnout of the past few decades then alternative explanations have to be
considered and many have been offered. One such suggestion is that the trend
towards more and more elections and the wider use of initiatives has produced
a backlash amongst weary voters faced with ballot-papers containing dozens
of items. Sheer fatigue has driven turnout down. Although this in an innately

reasonable argument there seems to be no clear-cut relationship between the number of initiatives a state has and non-voting.

A more radical idea – popular on the left of the political spectrum – is that the lack of choice offered by the two major political parties, both of which lean towards the political centre, alienates certain voters, especially amongst the poor and racial minorities. A genuine radical party, or alternatively a leftwards shift by the Democrats, would thus ensure higher turnout. Again there is some possible truth in this argument but it is difficult to see why it has not happened in the last thirty years, when in many ways the two main parties have been getting more ideologically distinct.

A third candidate is the nature of modern campaigns. The declining hold of political parties over voters replaced by impressions gained of individual candidates might lead to weaker incentives to vote. Furthermore, it is argued, the typical American campaign – over-long, over-slick, and dominated by the mass media with a premium on character attacks on political opponents – may have turned off large numbers of voters. If the public is chiefly candidate-centred and all candidates succeed in doing some damage to the image of their opponents then non-voting might be a logical response. This idea also has a certain appeal but it is very difficult to evaluate the nastiness of different elections and compare them with the level of participation.

Whichever single explanation, or combination, is favoured this trend towards low turnout in elections is very disturbing, especially as it is being repeated in other elections such as presidential primaries and elections for big city mayors. Only about one-third of Americans are habitual ballot-casters and they are not an accurate cross-section of the wider adult citizens. If registration is the real answer it looks as if it results from a deliberate decision of potential voters not to register rather than being the result of burdensome laws. If so, then new rules easing registration requirements are unlikely to produce a huge surge in numbers. In 1988 the estimated proportion of adults registered was only about 70 per cent of whom about 70 per cent actually turned out, making the final figure of 50.15 per cent. How representative and legitimate elections or referendums are when they attract such limited backing from the public is troubling.

Divided government

Until the 1960s divided government, that is a situation where one party holds the presidency and the other holds at least one branch of Congress, was a rarity in American politics. It was not unknown in the dying years of a presidency for the other party to capture Congress, but that victory was usually followed by triumph in the next presidential election, thus re-unifying government. Hence the Democratic capture of Congress in 1910 was followed by the Democrats gaining the White House, under Woodrow Wilson, in 1912. The Republicans regained Congress in 1918 and retook the presidency, with Warren Harding, in 1920. To complete the pattern the

Democrats seized Congress again in 1930 and the presidency, via Franklin Roosevelt, in 1932.

Newly elected or re-elected presidents invariably captured both Houses of Congress at the same time. Between 1860 and 1964 there were only two occasions when the winning presidential candidate did not capture the House of Representatives (1876 and 1956) and another two occasions when the Senate was missed (1888 and 1956 again). With the election of Richard Nixon in 1968 this pattern changed. Nixon was the first newly elected President to win neither branch of Congress since Zachary Taylor in 1848. Between 1969 and 1993 the United States experienced divided government for twenty years (1969–77 and 1981–93). Far from being the great exception in American political life, divided government was rapidly establishing itself as the norm. Bill Clinton's victory in 1992 broke this pattern, although two years later Republican congressional victories restored it.

Table 12.5. *Split district outcomes, President and House, 1932–92*

Year	Total number of districts	Number of districts with split results	Percentage of total
1932	355	50	14.1
1936	361	51	14.1
1940	362	53	14.6
1944	367	41	11.2
1948	422	90	21.3
1952	435	84	19.3
1956	435	130	29.9
1960	437	114	26.1
1964	435	145	33.3
1968	435	139	32.0
1972	435	192	44.1
1976	435	124	28.5
1980	435	143	32.8
1984	435	196	45.0
1988	435	148	34.0
1992	435	100	23.0

Note It is possible to calculate how Americans voted by congressional district as well as by their state. This table shows that the number of districts that prefer a presidential candidate of one party but elect a House member of the opposite party has grown over the last forty years. Such splitting was at its strongest in elections such as those of 1968, 1972, 1980, 1984 and 1988 when a Republican won the White House but faced a Democratic House of Representatives. Such districts have been disproportionately in southern states.

It is a straightforward matter about how divided government occurs. With the electorate increasingly willing to vote for candidates of different parties for separate offices, then it is hardly surprising that the number of congressional districts that elect a representative (or Senator) of one party but back the presidential nominee of another has risen. In the period before the Second World War it was very unusual for the proportion of congressional districts that behaved this way to exceed 20 per cent of the total. Since 1952 it has been very unusual for that percentage not to exceed 25 per cent. When George Bush won the presidency in 1988 he carried 297 House districts, and of these just 162 simultaneously returned a fellow-Republican as their representative while 135 backed a Democrat. In Ronald Reagan's landslide victory of 1984 a majority of the congressional districts he won elected a Democrat to the House at the same time.

This trend towards divided government also showed itself in the states, where Governors of one party and state legislators of the other have become common. Since 1978 there has only been one state, Hawaii, which has always elected the same party to both its Senate seats, the Governorship, and to majority status in both its legislative chambers. Even the consistent state of Hawaii has elected a Republican to one of its two House seats during this period (Patricia Saiki, 1987–91) and voted Republican in a presidential election (Ronald Reagan in 1984).

If it is easy to see why divided government is more likely in a candidate-centred era it is much more difficult to explain why Republicans should so consistently win the presidency, and the Democrats usually win the Senate and regularly triumphed in the House of Representatives, where they were the majority party from the elections of 1954 until 1994.

Republicans would claim that the incumbency advantages mentioned earlier in this chapter robbed them of the opportunity of translating presidential victories into a majority in the House of Representatives. The difficulty with this claim is that the overwhelming majority of congressional districts (95 per cent) have had at least one 'open' election (with no incumbent seeking re-election) since 1968 and that until 1994 Democrats not Republicans had the most success in these incumbent-free elections.[9] Democratic partisans have argued that the new primary-based presidential nominating system has consistently left them with nominees too liberal for the party's moderate, especially southern, wing who promptly back Republican presidential candidates. This theory raises as many questions about the Democratic party as it answers.

Amongst political scientists seeking an understanding of divided government numerous theories flowed. In the aftermath of the 1988 election the most widely circulated was that proposed by Byron Shafer.[10] Shafer argued that as a consequences of the social and political strife of the 1960s a new political order dominated American elections. The public associated foreign policy and cultural values with the presidency, subjects on which most Americans are conservative and hence predisposed to Republicans. The voters associated economic provision and social programmes with the House of Representatives, subjects on which most Americans are liberal and thus biased towards the Democrats. The Senate could be affected by both sets of attitudes, but tended to be more like the House than the White House and leaned towards the Democrats. Although Shafer's argument was not universally popular it was certainly more credible than the alternatives offered by Democratic and Republican partisans.

Divided government seemed to have ended with Bill Clinton's defeat of George Bush in 1992, only to be reversed in 1994. As the concluding section will show, it was by no means the only theme of the 1968–88 period to be disturbed in that contest.

Electoral trends in the 1990s

The five trends that have dominated American elections since the 1960s and which have been outlined in detail here had a much more mixed record in the elections of the 1990s thus far.

The first, the tendency towards a weaker role for party organisations, did continue unabated. There was nothing in the way that Bill Clinton's campaign was run that signified any greater involvement for the traditional party organisation. Indeed, with his constant stress that he was 'a different kind of Democrat', there were times when Clinton seemed to be running against his own party as much as against the Republicans. One development in 1992 would imply that the plight of the political party has eroded further. The fact that Ross Perot, unknown to 98 per cent of the American public in November 1991, with no prior political experience, who did not formally enter the race until five weeks before polling day, could gain 19 per cent of the vote as an individual with no political party organisation whatsoever sends a powerful message about the relative strengths of money, media, candidate and party in modern American elections.

The second theme identified, the bias towards very high rates of incumbent re-election in the House of Representatives coupled with relatively low rates of voluntary retirement, was comprehensively shaken in 1992. Sixty-five House members retired of their own accord (a post-war high) and two others died before polling day. Forty-three incumbents were defeated (the highest since 1974), made up of nineteen defeats in primary contests (another post-war high) and twenty-four beaten in the November election. This produced a freshman class (new members) some 110 strong, the largest since 1948, and an incumbent re-election rate of 'only' 88.3 per cent.

There were four main reasons for this reversal. Having had nearly a decade of rather low voluntary departure it was inevitable, given age and infirmity, that at some point members who had put off retirement would have to accept it. They were given a further incentive by a campaign finance change. Before 1981 all members who retired could keep any surplus campaign funds as personal money after they left the House. This provoked a modest scandal so in 1981 the House voted that members elected before 1981 (i.e. all of them!) could retain this perk but all new members would lose it. This did not abate the opposition to this arrangement so by 1990 the House had decided this benefit would end for all members after the elections of 1992. Cynics have suggested this might have had some influence on the decision of certain members to quit in 1992 rather than later years.

In 1990, as is true every ten years, the United States held a census and as a result both the number of House seats a state has, and the boundaries within each state with more than one member, were radically altered. For example, population changes in the 1980s meant California gained another seven seats while New York lost three. These alterations shifted many district borders, devaluing the advantages of incumbency and name-recognition, producing some retirements: in other districts incumbents fought each other because their seats had been merged, and made others much more vulnerable to defeat.

Finally a set of scandals involving the House between 1989 and 1992 took their toll. In 1989 both the Speaker of the House, Jim Wright, and the Majority Whip, Tony Coelho, had to quit Congress in the wake of ethics scandals. In 1992 it emerged that scores of Congressmen had substantial unpaid accounts at the House restaurant, hundreds had used the House bank to write cheques that would have bounced if drawn on a normal bank account, and that the House post office had been a centre of petty and not so petty corruption. The

"...AND FINALLY, ALL THE POLLS SHOW THAT THE TYPICAL VOTER WILL NOT VOTE."

©Sidney Harris

The hard truth about American voting. Cartoon from *PS*, March 1994.

cheque-bouncing scandal was directly responsible for the defeat or retirement of at least two dozen members.

The 1994 congressional elections were more spectacular still. Here the combination of continued hostility to Congress and the unpopularity of the Clinton Administration produced the most striking results in half a century. The Republicans emerged with a 53–47 margin in the Senate and a 230–204 (with one independent) lead in the House of Representatives, controlling both chambers for the first time since 1954.

Republican gains were, however, concentrated in 'open' seats where no Democratic incumbent sought re-election. Despite the huge shift in House numbers 92 per cent of incumbent Senators were re-elected and 90.2 per cent in the House of Representatives.

Precisely because House elections were much more competitive in 1992 and 1994 the total amount of money raised and spent on them dramatically increased. After remaining relatively flat since 1986, spending shot up to some $678 million, easily a new record, and over 50 per cent higher than two years earlier. Estimates for 1994 suggested a new record for mid-term elections with a spectacular California Senate contest seeing $40 million spent, nearly $25 million of which came from the personal pocket of the losing candidate Rep. Michael Huffington (Republican). The hold of big money over American electoral politics is unlikely to weaken in the next decade.

More encouragingly, turnout appeared to reverse its long downward slide somewhat in 1992. An estimated 55 per cent of adult Americans cast ballots despite the fact that the proportion of all adults registered had barely changed since 1988. The 1994 mid-term elections also saw a modest upward move over 1990 with an estimated poll of 38 per cent.

Finally, of course, divided government first disappeared with the 1992 election of Bill Clinton alongside Democratic majorities in Congress, then re-appeared in 1994 as those majorities collapsed.

Conclusion

This chapter has outlined the way American elections work and identified five vital trends that have dominated them over the last thirty years. As this final section on elections in the 1990s has shown, some of those trends seem likely to persist into the twenty-first century (weak party involvement, expensive campaigns) one seems to have been notably altered (incumbency), and another moderately so (turnout). The remaining factor – divided government – arguably the most politically significant, first went, and then returned. The 1996 elections may well see the restoration of unified government, depending on perceptions of President Clinton and congressional Republicans, but it would be foolish to discount the continuing tendency of American elections to produce divided institutional outcomes.

Notes

1 Washington, DC is strictly speaking a territory of the federal government, not a state. Its citizens have no Senate seats and only a non-voting delegate in the House.
2 In 1992 this provision had a dramatic impact. Democrat Wyche Fowler 'won' the first election with only 49 per cent of the vote; in the run-off three weeks later he was beaten.
3 Since Maine adopted this law its two congressional districts have always voted the same way so it has cast its electoral college votes in the same manner as the other forty-nine states.
4 It is therefore possible that in a close election the candidate who gained most votes could lose in the electoral college. This happened in 1876 and 1888. If no candidate wins an electoral majority in the college the president would be elected in a complex process by the House of Representatives and the Senate would choose the Vice-President. This has not happened since 1824.
5 See Tim Hames in John C. Green (ed.), *Politics, Parties, and Professionalism* (Akron, OH, University Press of America, 1993).
6 In House elections political parties may contribute a figure equal to $10,000 in 1974 plus the rate of inflation since then. This worked out at around $30,000 in 1992. For the Senate the figure was set at $20,000 (plus post-1974 inflation) in smaller states and a figure of two cents for each voter in larger states. In California this figure would exceed one million dollars.
7 Figures calculated by Tim Hames from Federal Election Commission statistics.
8 See Walter Dean Burnham in Reichley (ed.), *Elections – American Style*.
9 See Jacobson, *The Electoral Origins of Divided Government*.
10 See Byron E. Shafer in Shafer (ed.), *The End of Realignment?*

13

Economic policy

The United States economy is by far the largest in the world. Yet, as this chapter will outline, the political decisions about the management of macroeconomic policy frequently possess a degree of chaos and confusion that might lead one to wonder how the American economic machine has survived it. During the 1980s that process encountered new and more disturbing difficulties that may have permanent consequences. The role of the federal government in economic policy-making has expanded enormously during this century. On the eve of the Great Depression federal expenditure amounted to about 3 per cent of GNP and had altered little since the Civil War. Furthermore, that low level of activity was underpinned by a widespread consensus that it was not the role of politicians to intervene in the operations of economic life. Both the level of spending and that assumption were shaken to the core by the Depression and the New Deal that emerged to combat it. Federal spending now amounts to just over 20 per cent of GNP and expenditure at all levels of government (including the states and localities) reaches 35 per cent. Politicians are held accountable for the nation's economic state and their popularity – plus re-election prospects – are heavily related to it.

However, by international standards that proportion of national income devoted to government activity is quite small. Indeed, of major industrial countries only Japan has a lower level. Whilst politicians are held responsible for the economic outcome, they possess fewer direct influences over it than is true in western Europe. *Laissez-faire* capitalism retains a large constituency and certain very common features of other economies – large-scale nationalisation for example – are completely outside the mainstream American agenda.

Economic policy in the last twenty years has been dominated by two major difficulties. The first is that the US economy, while still much bigger than any rival, has seen a relative decline. The particular problem has been an unimpressive productivity record. Output per worker has risen only modestly in the last thirty years (an annual average rise of 0.7 per cent since 1965). Economic growth has been largely fuelled by an expansion of the work-force, not an improvement in its quality. As a result real living standards have been flat, and only sustained for most families by the rapid increase in the number of married women in the work-place. The second difficulty, which will attract the lion's share of this chapter, is that of regular and extremely sizeable budget deficits (more government spending than revenues) which have placed an enormous strain on the economy and the political system more generally.

This chapter will start with an examination of how monetary policy (interest rates and the money supply) is made in the United States. It will demonstrate that this dimension of economic policy is conducted in a relatively ordered and structurally sound manner. The remainder of the chapter will look at fiscal policy (taxing and spending), which is much more chaotic. The history of the budget-making process will be outlined. The major post-war reform, the Budget and Impoundment Control Act of 1974, will be explained and analysed. The enormous growth in federal budget deficits will be highlighted and three recent attempts to control it – the Gramm–Rudman legislation of 1985, the Budget Enforcement Act of 1990, and Bill Clinton's deficit reduction of 1993 – and their very limited success will be explored. Finally, some proposed reforms to the whole process will be evaluated.

Monetary policy

Monetary policy in the United States is run in a relatively disciplined fashion. Cynics would suggest this is because neither the White House nor Congress control it. Policy is actually made by a semi-independent institution, the Federal Reserve Board, which is a unique mixture of both public and private influence. The Federal Reserve System consists of twelve regional reserve banks who are owned by the banking system. Each reserve bank has a president who is chosen by the bank's nine directors. Six of those directors are elected by the commercial banks. On top of this structure is the Federal Reserve Board, which has seven Governors. The Governors are nominated by the President and have to be confirmed by the Senate. They serve fourteen-year terms and can only be removed by their own resignation or for gross misconduct. The Chairman of the Federal Reserve Board, who has a great deal of influence over the general direction of policy, is appointed for shorter four-year terms.

The Board's major decisions are taken by its Federal Open Markets Committee (FOMC), which consists of the seven Governors plus five of the regional bank presidents who serve by rotation (except that the New York regional bank always has a seat on it). This committee takes the critical decisions on interest rates and the money supply. It controls this through the discount window at each of the twelve banks where commercial banks regularly borrow hundreds of millions of dollars to make up for temporary shortfalls in their supplies of cash. The interest charged for this privilege – the discount rate – is the benchmark for all other interest rates in America. The board can also affect the money market through its open market desk, where every day it buys and sells government securities on the Wall Street stock exchange.

This system was created in 1913, largely at the instigation of the private banking system, which had endured a decade of instability. Congress created the Federal Reserve Board which had within it two representatives of the President, the Treasury Secretary and the Comptroller of Currency. Although it was not formally given independence it was generally understood that it would not be subject to direct orders either from the White House or Capitol Hill. Nevertheless, as it was established by a simple act of Congress and has no other constitutional standing its functions and design can be altered by Congress. This did in fact happen during the New Deal era when, as part of a series of reforms to the badly battered American banking system, a set of changes to the Federal Reserve were made in 1933 and 1935. The consequences of these reforms were that power was centralised in the hands of the Governors and diminished amongst the twelve regional presidents via the institutionalisation of the FOMC. The political price of strengthening these appointees was that the two direct presidential influences on the Board (the Treasury Secretary and the Comptroller of Currency) were removed, thus asserting the independence of the system.

From the New Deal onwards, and especially under Franklin Roosevelt's choice of Chairman Marriner Eccles (1934–48), the Board has regarded its function as counter-cyclical. Thus when the economy is growing quickly and inflationary tendencies are observed interest rates should be raised to stop it, and when the economy is in recession interest rates should fall to breathe life back into it. The Board has taken its anti-inflation responsibilities very seriously over the last twenty years and was enormously controversial during the 1979–83 period, when it kept interest rates high to squash inflation, despite the fact that there was a recession and high unemployment as well, which high interest rates only worsened.

In general the Board has retained its independence rather well. There was a brief power struggle over the control of interest rates in the immediate post-war period between the Treasury Department (and in effect the President) and the Board (backed by Congress), which was settled by an accord in 1951 that broadly went in the Board's favour. Indeed, the general trend has been to increase the Federal Reserve's authority. Banking Acts of 1970 and 1976 saw Congress give the Board wide powers to regulate the banking industry. The Monetary Control Act of 1980 required all depositary institutions, member

---

The Federal Reserve Board

The Federal Reserve Board effectively controls both the money supply and interest rates in the US. It also supervises banks and bank holding companies and enforces laws designed to protect individuals involved in financial dealings. Founded in 1913, it has a modest budget of $140 million and a staff of 1,600, but its influence is much more profound than these numbers. It has seven governors – nominated by the President and confirmed by the Senate – who serve fourteen-year terms with the exception of its Chairman, who it appointed on a four-year basis. These extremely long terms, plus the political reality that all nominees must be acceptable to the financial markets, give the Fed an extraordinary degree of independence. These seven are joined on the key Federal Open Markets Committee by five of the twelve regional bank presidents whose appointment is completely outside presidential or congressional control – a factor which further reinforces its power.

and non-member banks and other bodies alike, to maintain reserves with the Board. By the standards of the world's central banks the US Federal Reserve is definitely amongst the most politically independent.

This does not mean that neither the President nor Congress try and influence the Board's decision, especially when the economy is in difficult straits, when both generally lobby for lower interest rates than the cautious Board are usually willing to concede. The White House has a number of ways it can apply pressure. The first is through the appointment of Governors. Although in theory board members have fourteen-year terms so that any individual President is unlikely to make many appointments, in reality resignation is far more frequent than that and so appointments are often made to fill out unexpired terms. Secondly, the Chairman only has a four-year term and hence has to be concerned about whether the White House will reappoint him. Having noted that, Presidents are not at liberty to hire and fire Chairmen that often because if a Chairman is thought credible by both Congress and the money markets he will prove difficult to replace. Finally, Presidents can use the moral authority that the electoral legitimacy of their economic preferences brings.

For Congress lobbying the Federal Reserve is more difficult. It can attempt to shape the general direction of economic philosophy by legislation such as the Full Employment Act of 1946, but this has not proved very successful. Its main weapon is through its committee's hearings. The Concurrent Resolution 133 of 1975 requested half-yearly appearances by Board officials, usually the Chairman, before its committees. This was made a binding obligation through the Humphrey–Hawkins Act of 1978. These question-and-answer sessions entail no policy obligations and are little more than an informational exercises. With its independent standing thus protected, the Federal Reserve is capable of running monetary policy rather as it wants to.

The history of the budget process

The relative calm of monetary policy is even more striking when compared with the strife of making fiscal policy. Since the establishment of the new nation, but especially in this century, there have been two ongoing power struggles over who controls the process whereby the nation gets a budget. The first is the struggle between Congress and the President, and the second is within Congress, between its ordinary committees (such as Agriculture or Armed Services) and its economic specialist committees (Appropriations, Ways and Means), over who controls government spending. These two contests heavily influenced the history of the budget process up to the landmark Budget and Impoundment Control Act of 1974, which redefined but did not settle those ongoing power disputes.

Constitutionally, the budget process lies with Congress. Under Article I Section IX no money may be legally spent by the Government of the United States unless it has been approved by Congress. The same section also requires a public statement of receipts and expenditures. The only detailed element beyond this general statement is that all revenue bills have to originate in the House of Representatives, which they still do, although the word 'originate' can be interpreted loosely. By tradition all spending or appropriations measures also start life in the House.

Congress has always been torn between allowing its ordinary committees to set spending in their individual area or instead giving that task to specialist economic committees. The advantage of letting individual committees do it is that it allows more members to shape spending decisions (with obvious political appeal): the attraction of centralising power is that the overall package would be better co-ordinated and some rather dubious spending proposals would be eliminated. In practice Congress has compromised by adopting a two-stage process. The ordinary committees are allowed to set guideline budgets based on what they would ideally like to spend (this is called the authorising process), but money can only be approved after further scrutiny

Table 13.1. *Economic growth, 1962–92*

Year	Annual percentage change		Year	Annual percentage change	
	GNP	GDP		GNP	GDP
1962	5.2	5.2	1978	4.8	4.8
1963	4.1	4.1	1979	2.8	2.5
1964	5.7	5.6	1980	−0.6	−0.5
1965	5.5	5.5	1981	1.6	1.8
1966	5.8	5.9	1982	−2.3	−2.2
1967	2.6	2.6	1983	3.8	3.9
1968	4.2	4.2	1984	6.0	6.2
1969	2.7	2.7	1985	2.9	3.2
1970	0.0	0.0	1986	2.8	2.9
1971	2.9	2.9	1987	3.0	3.1
1972	5.1	5.1	1988	4.0	3.9
1973	5.4	5.2	1989	2.7	2.5
1974	−0.5	−0.6	1990	0.9	0.8
1975	−1.1	−0.8	1991	−1.2	−1.2
1976	5.1	4.9	1992	2.0	2.1
1977	4.6	4.5			

Note The difference between Gross National Product (GNP) and Gross Domestic Product (GDP) is that the former includes imports and exports. Recent economic performance has been rather erratic, with a high of 6 per cent reached in 1984 (which greatly helped Ronald Reagan in the election of that year), to more modest rates in the 1990s (which largely sunk George Bush).

by the specialist committee (the *appropriating* process). Over time the relative strengths of these authorising and appropriating committees has varied widely.

For most of American history the federal government had so few functions and spent such little money that the budget procedure was not very important. Both Houses started by creating special committees to examine both taxing and spending, which is why the House Ways and Means committee was born in 1802 and the Senate Finance committee was established in 1816. Even at this early stage these bodies had to fight off attempts by other committees to claim jurisdiction over parts of the budget. The Civil War (1861–65) caused an explosion in federal government spending and left a large legacy of debt. To combat this, taxing and spending were split up and powerful new committees were created to organise spending decisions – the House Appropriations (1865) and Senate Appropriations (1867) committees. After the initial shock of government debt was overcome both committees found it harder to resist the attacks of other committees. In both chambers the appropriations power was largely decentralised, the House of Representatives in a gradual process between 1877 and 1885 and the Senate more directly in 1899. This division remained until the First World War.

Congress was not believed to have handled budgetary decisions well during that conflict and its decentralised spending structure was frequently blamed. Even before the war the passage of the Sixteenth Amendment in 1913 (allowing a federal income tax) had prompted calls for internal reform, and those demands were compounded by the extra spending and debt the war created. Two major reforms were instituted. In both chambers spending power was firmly re-centralised back into the Appropriations committees (the House in 1920 and Senate in 1922). More dramatically the President was brought into the budget process for the first time. Under the Budget and Accounting Act of 1921 the President was obliged to submit an annual budget. The Bureau of the Budget was created inside the Treasury Department (the executive's major economic wing) to help the President produce a budget, and the General Accounting Office was established as an impartial auditor.

From 1921 onwards the President would offer a budget that would be considered separately by both the House and Senate. Within each house taxation policy would be dealt with by the specialist revenue committees (Ways and Means in the House and Finance in the Senate). Meanwhile, spending policy would be determined by the authorising committees and the appropriating committees (the Appropriations Committee in both chambers), who would make thousands of alterations to the President's wishes. The two branches would usually produce different budgets, so their drafts would have to be reconciled by an inter-branch conference before a final agreed annual statement could be presented to the President for his signature.

Between 1921 and 1974 there were only two significant institutional innovations and two general political trends. Institutionally, the President became more directly involved in budgetary matters within the executive. The Bureau of the Budget was moved from the Treasury to the White House proper in 1939 and was renamed the Office of Management and Budget in 1970. To improve the quality of economic analysis Congress initiated a Council of Economic Advisors in 1946 who were to advice the President on economic matters. The second innovation was that in the wake of the Second World War and its impact on spending and debt Congress passed the Legislative Reorganisation Act of 1946 which created a joint budget committee drawn from both Houses and a streamlined budget process. This reform proved impossible to operate and was swiftly abandoned.

The major trends of this period were that the President became more influential over the budget-making procedure and that within Congress the Appropriations committees were being eroded by spending demands from other committees. The President's power increased for three main reasons. First, because Congress dealt with taxing and spending decisions separately only the White House could claim to have a fiscal overview. Second, armed with the Bureau of the Budget and the Council of Economic Advisors only the President could claim any economic expertise behind his budgetary priorities. Third, Presidents increasingly used the weapon of impoundment (refusing to spend money Congress had voted for) against projects they did not like in order to shape the budget.

Within Congress power was slipping away from the Appropriations committees. In the immediate post-1945 period Appropriations had been dominated by fiscal conservatives who limited government expenditure. This had been cemented by the so-called Cannon–Taber norm which meant that members were only assigned to Appropriations sub-committees that had nothing to do with the interests of their districts. Thus any attempt to use a seat on Appropriations to spend money on pet proposals back home would be frustrated. This rule broke down in the 1960s. Furthermore, liberal Democrats who wanted more spending found new ways to do it. Instead of going through the budget system they used ordinary law to establish certain social programmes that citizens who met the right requirements were entitled to receive. These obligatory entitlements circumvented the Appropriations committees and they mushroomed during the 1960s. They increased from 35.2 per cent of federal outlays in fiscal year 1967 to 53.6 per cent by 1974.[1]

The impression that Congress was incapable of constraining spending further emboldened the President to claim control over the budget. President Richard Nixon, a Republican facing a strongly Democratic Congress, needed little encouragement. He attacked congressional spending by using the weapon of impoundment more brutally than any previous chief executive. His efforts to kill much-loved congressional projects enraged both the Senate and House, who established a Joint Study Committee on Budget Control that used strong congressional sentiment in favour of changing the budget process, and

Nixon's rapid fall from grace in the aftermath of the Watergate scandal, to push through the biggest innovation in fiscal policy since 1921.

The Budget and Impoundment Control Act of 1974

The political coalition who supported the 1974 Act was an odd assortment. It included liberals who favoured change because they wanted Congress to have the means of spending more money, moderates who were simply outraged by Nixon's behaviour, and conservatives who wanted change so that Congress could control the budget deficits that were emerging because of the cost of the Vietnam War. The principal issues that the reformers had to tackle were those that had led to power drifting towards the Oval Office in the first place. These were the impoundment technique, Congress's lack of economic expertise, and Congress's inability to look over the entirety of the budget rather than slicing it up into spending and taxing.

Impoundment was dealt with by making it illegal for the President to delay any congressional expenditure (deferral) unless at least one branch of Congress voted to do that. Any permanent refusal to release money (recission) would require both wings of the legislature to agree. The expertise difficulty was tackled by founding the Congressional Budget Office, a lavish in-house economic think-tank that could rival the Office of Management and Budget. The fiscal overview dilemma was to be solved by having two budget resolutions passed by both Houses at the beginning and end of the budget process which would lay down overall targets for the authorising, appropriating, and revenue-raising committees to emulate. These resolutions would be enforced by new budget committees in both chambers.

The anti-impoundment provisions have worked, from a congressional perspective, extremely well. Unilateral impoundment by the President has been abolished and this weapon is virtually dead. Similarly, the economic ignorance factor has been effectively defused by the Congressional Budget Office. This has been a sparkling success and its economic projections have proved more accurate than those of the Office of Management and Budget.

The fate of the budget resolutions and the new committees has been far less satisfactory. The budget resolutions are not binding on anyone and hence have not been respected in many cases. The budget committees have not proved particularly effective at enforcing them and have not attained the high status that was hoped of them. In essence the pre-1974 system of taxing and spending committees feuding with each other has been retained, with the budget resolutions and committees uneasily trying to cope with it.

Part of this failure was almost built in. The failure to make the budget resolution legally binding doomed it from the outset. The House Budget Committee was deliberately sabotaged in that of its original twenty-five seats (there are now thirty-seven) ten were reserved for members of the Ways and Means and Appropriations committees, the very bodies that the Budget committees were meant to be policing. Additionally, the House committee's membership serves on a rotating basis. No member can sit on it for more than six years in every ten. This has weakened its standing as a committee and also means that as soon as a member has actually mastered their brief they leave the committee. These design faults were not accidental. Those who supported the 1974 change wanted to remove power from the White House, not recentralise it in a specialist economic committee which might prove anti-spending.

Thus spending decisions remained determined by the struggle between the authorising committees and the Appropriations committees. There are eighteen House committees involved in authorisation and their decisions then go to the Appropriations Committee (and its thirteen sub-committees), where they are generally scaled back. The House Appropriations Committee has such standing that its members serve on no other committee (except for its five slots on the Budget committee). Its authority continues to be attacked by the deliberately high and unrealistic bids put in by the authorising committees and the fact that, although the 1974 Act meant all new entitlements propositions

Table 13.2. *Unemployment rate (%), 1962–92*

Year	Civilian workers	Year	Civilian workers
1962	5.5	1978	6.1
1963	5.7	1979	5.8
1964	5.2	1980	7.1
1965	4.5	1981	7.6
1966	3.8	1982	9.7
1967	3.8	1983	9.6
1968	3.6	1984	7.5
1969	3.5	1985	7.2
1970	4.9	1986	7.0
1971	5.9	1987	6.2
1972	5.6	1988	5.5
1973	4.9	1989	5.3
1974	5.6	1990	5.5
1975	8.5	1991	6.7
1976	7.7	1992	7.4
1977	7.1		

Note With the exception of the two major recession years of 1975 and 1982/83, unemployment in the United States usually fluctuated in a relatively narrow range of 5–7 per cent. This was considered high by the standards of western Europe in the 1960s and 1970s but now has looked considerably more impressive than the European average in the 1980s and 1990s.

had to be voted through by it, the old entitlements projects of the 1960s did not. To maximise their impact authorising committees have taken to re-examining as much of their budgets annually as they can. Hence a large proportion of federal spending is pre-set and can only be altered by amending the original laws, not through the budget process. The Senate Appropriations Committee has to cope with the same conundrum. It is weaker than its House counterpart because its members do have additional committee assignments (frequently on authorising committees) and it falls foul of the generally looser and less rule-bound structure of the upper Chamber.

The taxing committees have the advantage of being both the authorising and appropriating committees for their domain. Since 1974 though, for reasons only partly related to the new procedure, they have been weakened. The House Ways and Means Committee had traditionally been extremely strong, functioning as the committee which decided on assignments to all other committees. It had also been dominated by fiscal conservatives, and so was an obvious target for more liberal Democrats. Its autocratic chairman, Wilber Mills (Democrat – Arkansas) became embroiled in scandal and was forced to resign in 1974. This served as a pretext to weaken the committee by expanding its numbers from twenty-five to thirty-seven and forcing it to use sub-committees for the first time. Its role as the committee on committees was also abandoned, and that function was transferred to the recently established Democratic Steering and Policy Committee. The Senate Finance Committee, rather like its Appropriations brother, is weaker than the House model and has never exercised the control Ways and Means once possessed.

Given the continued erosion of these specialist committees the budget process was based on fairly weak foundations, especially over spending control, from the very outset. The main reason why this did not immediately translate into high budget deficits was because of a phenomenon called bracket-creep. Income-tax bands were not index-linked in the 1970s. High inflation rates (and corresponding wage rises) therefore pushed many taxpayers up into a higher tax band because their nominal incomes had increased even though their real incomes (minus the inflation effect) had not. When Ronald Reagan's new economic proposals met the fledgling Budget Act in 1981 the implicit problem of deficit control became much more real.

Ronald Reagan, rising deficits, and the road to Gramm–Rudman

Ronald Reagan came to office in January 1981 committed to the most radical reshaping of American fiscal policy since the New Deal. Heavily influenced by the supply-side school of economic thought (who argue that lower tax rates do not lead to proportionately lower tax revenues because of the spur to economic growth such tax cuts generate), he initially proposed to cut tax rates by 30 per cent. On top of this he wanted a major increase in defence spending to counter the Soviet Union. This was to be paid for by cuts in domestic

Reaganomics

The economic policies of the Reagan Administration were heavily influenced by an economic theory called 'supply-side economics'. Pioneered (allegedly on the back of a napkin) by Professor Arthur Laffer, this held that radical cuts in taxation would not lead to a proportionate fall in tax revenue and could even lead to increased revenues because of all the extra entrepreneurial activity such a tax cut would stimulate. On this basis Reagan persuaded Congress to accept a 25 per cent cut in personal taxation in 1981, along with numerous tax benefits for business. To some extent the theory worked in that tax revenues did not fall by as much as conventional economics would predict. Nevertheless they did fall notably. To his supporters Reaganomics introduced the boom in the American economy that led to solid growth between 1983 and 1989. To his opponents Reagan was responsible for the vast increase in the American budget deficit.

President Reagan with his wife Nancy on an election tour, November 1980.

spending but not in anything as politically painful as social security. From the beginning these objectives did not appear to be compatible with Reagan's other stated goal – a balanced budget.

Although Reagan had to scale back his tax decrease to 25 per cent he none the less managed to persuade Congress to back him. Indeed, if anything, Congress outbid him by including a host of other tax cuts, notably on American business. In this orgy of tax-cutting the benefits of bracket-creep were eliminated by the decision to index-link income-tax bands. Reagan's Economic

Recovery Tax Act led to a $160 billion tax reduction in 1981 alone and meant a cumulative revenue loss of $750 billion over a five-year period. Reagan also succeeded in persuading Congress to back his military build-up. Real spending on defence increased by 17 per cent in Reagan's first year and continued to accelerate until 1985. In comparison to this the $37 billion domestic spending cuts agreed by Congress looked rather puny, and in fact many of these alleged savings never materialised.

The implications of an enormous tax cut, a vast rise in defence expenditure, modest cuts in domestic spending, and the high proportion of federal spending that went on entitlements and could not be easily checked, were quite clear. In the absence of extraordinary levels of economic growth (which did not materialise), the federal government's budget deficit was going to balloon. This is exactly what happened. The deficit increased from $79 billion in 1981 (itself a record high) to $208 billion two years later and threatened to stick at that level. Although economists argue about what the exact consequences of such a large imbalance are there are very few who would not accept that they are destabilising. In terms of the Gross National Product the deficit had risen from 2.6 per cent in 1981 to 6.8 per cent in 1983. The national debt was destined to virtually triple by the end of the Reagan era.

This massive increase in debt seemed unlikely to be easily cured. Although Reagan reluctantly accepted moves to increase government revenues in 1982 and 1984 he was unwilling to reverse his 1981 legislation. Nor was he prepared to accept sizable reductions in defence spending. The Democratic majority in the House of Representatives were not going to accept deep cuts in domestic spending, especially on entitlements. The two sides had reached an uneasy stand-off but it was hardly an understanding that was going to control the deficits. Some means had to be found to break the stalemate and make a serious attempt at deficit reduction.

It was against this backdrop that a novel suggestion was put forward by Republican senators Phil Gramm (Texas) and Warren Rudman (New Hampshire) who were supported by a leading Democrat Ernest Hollinngs (South Carolina). Their proposal was that a set of deficit targets should be set with the aim of achieving a balanced budget over five years. The opening deficit target would be $172 billion for fiscal year 1986 and it would fall to zero in 1991. If the projected deficit target was exceeded in any year and the President and Congress could not agree on how to reach it then automatic cuts would take place. These cuts, or sequestration, would be ordered by the Comptroller-General of the General Accounting Office (GAO) and would come half from defence spending and half from non-exempt domestic spending. An amendment was accepted to the effect that the process would be suspended during a recession. Gramm and Rudman hoped that the crude nature of these automatic cuts would be so unappealing that it would force the White House and Congress to find some compromise means of lowering the deficit to the stated target instead.

Booming budget deficits							
1976	66.4	1981	57.9	1986	220.7	1991	268.7
1977	44.9	1982	110.6	1987	149.7	1992	290.2
1978	44.8	1983	195.4	1988	155.0	1993	327.3
1979	27.7	1984	185.3	1989	153.4	1994	255.0
1980	59.6	1985	212.2	1990	220.4		\$ billion

There were numerous objections to Gramm–Rudman on both economic and constitutional grounds. Indeed in 1986 the Supreme Court (in *Bowsher* v. *Synar*) ruled that it would be unconstitutional for the Comptroller-General of the GAO to order such cuts. The legislation returned to Congress who amended it to allow the Office of Management and Budget to authorise these cuts instead, thus delaying the whole deficit reduction process by two years. None the less, there was no serious alternative being offered and it did appear to be an effective means of breaking the political log-jam. Without much enthusiasm, both the House and Senate voted to support it.

Gramm–Rudman was, in effect, a major amendment to the 1974 Act and a *de facto* admission that the procedure in that legislation was unworkable. It was also a deeply damning comment on the President, Congress, and the entire budgetary system. It was basically an admission that, left to their own devices, none of these characters were capable of producing a responsible budget. The only way one would emerge, Gramm–Rudman implied, would be if the gun of enforced sequestration was held to the collective heads of the President and Congress. Although Gramm–Rudman was an unappealing way of achieving deficit reduction – one of its supporters described it as a 'bad idea whose time has come' – it did at least seem to offer an orderly route towards a more sensible fiscal outcome. Gramm–Rudman was ultimately destined to fail in its noble objectives and be superseded by the Budget Enforcement Act of 1990.

George Bush, more deficits, and the Budget Enforcement Act

The adoption of the Gramm–Rudman targets did not lead to a wild outbreak of fiscal responsibility throughout American government. The legislation was instantly challenged in the courts and the political system waited nervously to see how much damage the Supreme Court would do to their offspring. As noted above the Court was relatively benign, only striking down the provisions about who should order sequestration rather than declaring the whole principle of sequestration unconstitutional, as many had feared and some had hoped they would do. The only major innovation in the two years between the passage of Gramm–Rudman and its amended version (Gramm–Rudman II) was the Tax Reform Act of 1986, which slashed income tax rates further and immensely simplified the US tax system which paid for itself by closing loopholes traditionally exploited by American business. If Reagan's 1981 reform helped the rich and the corporate sector, the bi-partisan 1986 effort largely reversed that as far as the corporate component was concerned. As the measure was basically revenue-neutral it had little effect on the deficit problem which continued undisturbed. The 1986 deficit hit $221 billion and the repayment of national interest became the third largest item of federal expenditure after social security and defence.

It fell to George Bush to be the first President who really had to work with the Gramm–Rudman arrangements. Bush had been elected in 1988 with the campaign promise that he would not raise taxes or radically alter defence arrangements to tackle the budget deficit but would instead meet it through a rather vague 'flexible freeze' on government spending. The new Congress he faced was heavily manned by the Democratic party whose priority (especially in the House of Representatives) was to reach the Gramm–Rudman figures by a combination of sharp decreases in defence spending and increased taxation on the wealthy. Once again, in the absence of outstanding economic growth (which did not materialise) a conflict was absolutely inevitable.

In George Bush's first year that conflict did not emerge. The Gramm–Rudman target was a deficit of $136 billion. The end of the Reagan defence spending boom and higher than average economic growth in 1988 meant that this goal could be reached by relatively modest and easy spending cuts. Bush could keep his infamous 'Read my lips, no new taxes' pledge that had proved so effective in the 1988 election contest. This good fortune would not spill over into 1990. Now the Gramm–Rudman target was a deficit of $100 billion. Initial estimates of economic growth suggested cuts of $30 billion would be required to avoid sequestration, a difficult target but not impossible to reach without tax increases. As the year went on it became obvious that the economy was slowing down and heading towards recession. The Congressional Budget Office estimates that every one per cent fall in GNP produces a 0.33 per cent increase in the deficit as government revenues fall and certain social expenditure increases. The Office of Management and Budget produced rapidly increasing estimates of what the budget deficit would be and how much would be required to match the Gramm–Rudman obligations.

By the middle of 1990 it was universally obvious that the Gramm–Rudman targets could not be met and that any significant deficit reduction deal would have to include new taxation. Bush agreed to enter negotiations with the congressional leadership and to drop his 'no new taxes' promise. After protracted discussions an outline agreement was reached that would reduce the deficit by $500 billion over five years through a mixture of increased petrol tax, more savings on defence, and some cuts in social programmes (notably Medicare, the health-care plan for the elderly). Conservative Republicans opposed the deal because of the tax increase element; liberal Democrats were unenthusiastic about the spending cuts. The two groups allied, and in an astonishing rebuke for both sets of party leaders the House of Representatives

---

The Budget Enforcement Act 1990

George Bush had campaigned on the slogan 'Read my lips – no new taxes': once President he faced the reality that by 1990 the economy was slipping into recession and the budget deficit numbers were crashing towards the $300 billion level. He had to swallow his original stance and agree to a budget package with congressional Democrats that included tax increases on the wealthy, an increase in the gasoline tax, and some spending cuts. To ensure this deal the Budget Enforcement Act 1990 was passed alongside it. This divided spending into three categories for three years – domestic, defence, and international – which would merge into one group for two more years. Each category had a spending cap which could not be exceeded. Any increase in spending within a category could only occur if offset by a spending cut in the same category (pay-as-you-go). It was illegal to pay for spending increases in one category by cuts in a different area (the firewall principle). Although it did not prevent rising deficits, this has proved a highly effective way of contraining spending.

---

threw out the package on a 254–179 vote, with a majority in both parties rejecting it. The President, now completely abandoned by much of his own party, had to renegotiate the deal with the chastened Democratic leadership, who demanded and successfully won a higher proportion of tax increases in the new package which was finally passed by both chambers.

The price of the Democratic party's victory over the details of the deficit reduction package was the Budget Enforcement Act of 1990 passed to regulate it. The deficit targets envisaged by Gramm–Rudman had proved so implausible that they were abandoned and replaced by new means of deficit control.

The 1990 Act aimed to control government spending and thereby discipline the deficit. For the period 1991–93 it established three separate categories of spending: defence; international aid; and domestic. For the period 1994–95 all three would be merged. Total spending caps for 1991–93 were established in law for all three categories. Any exceeding of these ceilings would result in automatic sequestration supervised by the Office of Management and Budget. Only in declared emergencies – such as the Gulf War – could any extra spending be made. Within each category any proposed new spending had to be matched by equivalent cuts within that category (the pay-as-you-go principle). The law prevents proposed new spending in one category being paid for by cuts in another (the 'firewalls' principle). Finally, a set of non-binding deficit targets were outlined which would lead to a reduction in the deficit from $327 billion in 1991 to $83 billion by 1995, when the Act itself would expire. Institutionally, by pre-setting these spending ceilings the Act virtually made the budget committees and resolutions redundant. More subtle than Gramm–Rudman, the Act of 1990 surely guaranteed significant deficit elimination in the 1990s? Unfortunately it did not.

Bill Clinton, more deficits, and a five-year plan

In terms of deficit reduction the 1990 budget agreement was a complete flop. Although the new rules initiated by the Budget Enforcement Act remained in place, none of the great savings promised were actually made and this failure became very clear very quickly. Between December 1990 and August 1992 the Congressional Budget Office revised upwards its cumulative five-year estimate of the Budget Deficit by an enormous $655 billion, more than offsetting the $496 billion deficit reduction promised by the 1990 agreement. By January 1993 they had revised that figure upwards again so that it exceeded $700 billion. Far from inheriting a smooth passage to relative fiscal ease, newly-elected Bill Clinton was instantly confronted by the worst deficit estimates yet produced.

This stark difference between what the 1990 package promised and what actually happened came from three sources. Only 3 per cent of it came from excess spending on various emergency needs largely produced by freak weather conditions (the Gulf War technically qualified here, but contributions from America's allies meant that it paid for itself). Another 33 per cent or $220 billion was the product of slower economic growth than had been anticipated with predictably negative consequences for the deficit. A further $420 billion (or 64 per cent) was caused by so-called 'technical re-estimates' of both the costs of spending programmes (notably Medicare and Medicaid) and tax revenue. In other words, the original figures were inaccurate by almost the same amount as the proposed deficit reduction.

The longer-term numbers were equally disturbing. Government spending on health-care programmes which had increased from 1.7 per cent of GNP to 2.7 per cent during the 1980s were estimated to rise further during the 1990s. Best predictions suggested it could rise as far as 4.5 per cent of GNP by the year 2000. That level of increase, and the general cost of entitlement benefits, would erode any defence savings achieved by the end of the Cold War. The consequence for the deficit in the absence of extremely strong rates of economic growth (which on past form will not materialise) was obvious.

It was against this worrying picture that Bill Clinton launched his contribution to deficit reduction. As a candidate he had pledged to halve the budget deficit over four years. The revised numbers for future deficits meant that commitment had to be shelved. Reducing the budget deficit became the major test of credibility for the new President.

Clinton's version was outlined in his State of the Union address to Congress only four weeks after taking office. In it he backed reducing the deficit by 38 per cent over four years and warned Congress that if no action were taken the budget deficit (driven by the costs of entitlements) would hit $650 billion by the end of the century. Clinton proposed a $493 billion programme of deficit reduction offset by $169 billion of new spending, leaving a net reduction of $324 billion by 1997. His package contained an increase in the top rate of

---

The Clinton plan, 1993

President Clinton entered office having promised a tax cut for the middle class, a substantial increase in 'investment' spending, particularly aimed at high-technology areas, and a pledge to halve the federal deficit. This was always an optimistic combination, and he was forced by economic reality and the depth of the deficit crisis to abandon the middle-class tax cut and drastically reduce the investment element. His proposal for a new broad energy consumption tax based on British Thermal Units (BTUs) was defeated, but ultimately and by very narrow margins (218–216 in the House of Representatives; 51–50 in the Senate) a $500 billion deficit reduction plan, at least resembling parts of the Clinton blueprint, was passed. This should ensure a short- to medium-term decline in the deficit but in the longer term the costs of entitlements (especially Medicare) are projected to force the deficit upwards.

---

tax for individuals and business, a new energy tax, alterations in the taxing of social security benefits for wealthy claimants, accelerated cuts in defence expenditure, and various small cuts in domestic outlays. Although the package was advertised as containing an equal mixture of tax increases and spending cuts, a more detailed examination suggested it leaned towards more tax rises than expenditure reduction. Allied to this, Clinton proposed an immediate $30 billion stimulus to the sluggish American economy, to be financed by further borrowing.

Initial reaction to the Clinton initiative seemed encouraging. The sheer scale of the deficit crisis had convinced most congressional Democrats that they had to do something about it. The 19 per cent vote scored by maverick anti-deficit independent presidential candidate Ross Perot in the 1992 elections implied that the public were genuinely concerned about the issue. Indeed the first opinion polls taken showed that a majority of Americans approved of the basic outlines of the Clinton plan. It was adopted virtually in its entirety by both the Senate and House at the first (but not binding) budget resolution, and the prospects of relatively speedy and painless enactment seemed quite good.

However, the cause of deficit reduction has rarely proved that smooth. Clinton's putative 1993 fiscal stimulus ran into the united opposition of Senate Republicans who used that chamber's rather free-wheeling rules to kill it. The public, although they backed deficit reduction in principle, quickly lost enthusiasm for specific tax increases and they indicated their displeasure with tumbling poll-approval ratings for Clinton, who became the least popular President after three months in office since public polling began.

That opposition encouraged conservative Democrats to demand a different balance between tax increases and spending cuts. The strength of that position almost led to the defeat of the entire plan when it passed through the House of Representatives on a 215–209 vote. The Senate version passed 50–49 on Vice-President Gore's casting vote but only after the whole energy tax and much of Clinton's plans for high-technology investment were removed. The final package would produce nearly $500 billion in deficit reduction over five years (if its economic assumptions and estimates proved valid) but after that rising health-care costs would see the deficit rise again. This ultimate compromise passed 218–216 in the House (41 Democrats rebelling) and 51–50 in the Senate (6 Democrats rebelling). In the absence of striking levels of economic growth, the United States will be living with bloated levels of government debt throughout the 1990s and further attempts to control it will occur.

The future of the budget process

The contorted pattern of fiscal policy over the last twenty years has, unsurprisingly, led to numerous demands for fundamental reform. Throughout American history, as this chapter has illustrated, it has been the presence of large-scale new debt that has acted as the pivotal incentive for institutional change. The major difference between those past debts and the present climate is that uniquely the 1980s and 1990s have seen enormous increases in public debt in peacetime rather than war.

Few would disagree with the proposition that the 1974 Budget Act, while successful in reorientating the process back towards Congress, failed to establish a sensible structure for evaluating national financial priorities. For many in Congress the budget is not viewed as a national document but as a set of cherished political programmes to be defended or expanded depending on the political climate. Few would also disagree with the proposition that President Reagan's economic priorities were not compatible with orthodox financial prudence and that he has to take major responsibility for the explosion of deficits from 1981 onwards.

Five major reform proposals have been aired over the last two decades and are worth brief consideration. They are presented here in ascending degree of radicalism.

The first suggestion is the recentralisation of spending power in the House and Senate Appropriations Committee. As was previously shown, this has frequently been the internal solution favoured by Congress during eras of high debt. Most supporters of this idea would probably end the current confusion over who makes fiscal policy by abolishing the budget committees. The advantage of this notion is that it is a relatively simple administrative exercise; the disadvantage is that history suggests it only works temporarily.

The second argument is that the first budget resolution, which currently lays down non-binding targets for revenue, expenditure and deficit, should be made legally mandatory and that it should require the presidential signature (or veto). The advantage of this is that the resolution is the only time in the procedure when Congress looks at the budget numbers as a whole. The disadvantage is that it is unlikely (especially under divided party government) that the White House, Senate, and House of Representatives will come to an easy agreement. Hence, months could be taken up in deadlocked negotiations between the parties. When agreement on the resolution was finally reached this would leave little time for detailed scrutiny of the individual components of the budget.

The third reform is to move to a two-year budget cycle. Ever since the 1974 Act deliberations about the budget have swallowed a greater and greater proportion of congressional time and deadlines are frequently missed. The move to a two-year cycle would allow for more intelligent analysis of the budget (which contains nearly 200,000 accounts). The advantage of this scheme is that it probably would produce a better quality procedure; the disadvantage is that it is unclear why that should produce a much lower budget deficit.

The fourth proposal is much more radical. Strongly supported by Ronald Reagan and George Bush (and more quietly by Bill Clinton), this would intro-duce a line-item veto for the President. At present the President has to accept or reject the entirety of any spending bill. He cannot veto individual projects that he considers wasteful. Governors in forty-two of America's fifty states have such authority.[2] Enthusiasts for the line-item veto say it would allow the Oval Office to produce lower deficits by chopping out the large chunks of the budget which Congressmen insert for no nationally good reason. Opponents claim that the line-item veto is little more than re-legalised impoundment (which is probably true) and a fundamental assault on the separation of powers. They also dispute how much of the budget consists of improper spend-ing items. A highly modified version was passed in 1996.[3]

Finally, and most dramatically of all, the idea of a balanced budget amend-ment to the Constitution. Again, this an idea borrowed from the states where all bar Vermont have some sort of constitutional obligation to submit a budget where current revenues and current expenditures are equal. At one stage in the early 1980s thirty-two states (out of a necessary thirty-four) had gone as

---

The entitlements problem

The longer-term health of American public finances depends critically on entitle-ments. This spending made on commitments enshrined into law which can only be changed by altering that law. Its major components are Medicare (the federal government programme of health insurance for the elderly) and Medicaid (the joint federal–state government provision for the poor and disabled). The costs of these two programmes – especially Medicare – have escalated far ahead of infla-tion because of expensive developments in medicine and an increasing level of life expectancy. On current trends they will drive the national deficit over $1 trillion a year unless tackled. This is clearly not an acceptable situation but major cuts in either programme will cause a political storm. Yet reform must happen if any balanced budget amendment or programme is to have credibility. Bill Clinton and Congress fought over this issue throughout 1995.

far as to call for a constitutional convention to discuss a balanced budget amendment (the first such convention since 1787). In 1992 the House of Representatives fell just nine votes short of the two-thirds margin needed to approve such an amendment. In 1994 the margin was twelve votes, with every Republican bar one in favour. Proponents claim this is the only guaranteed way of forcing fiscal responsibility on to the political system. Opponents dispute that a balanced budget every year is good public policy and ask how on earth the United States can get from $300 billion deficits to balance in any kind of reasonable time-scale. It fell short again in 1995.[4]

It is unclear that any of these reforms will be adopted wholesale in the very near future, although the rising popularity of the balanced budget amendment in Republican circles (especially given the 1994 election results) is improving its political prospects. For the immediate future the 1974 Budget Act, despite its battering at the hands of Reaganomics, is likely to remain the basic model of American fiscal policy.

This chapter has highlighted the difficulties of making economic policy in the contemporary United States. In particular it has noted the difference between monetary policy (made outside the political system by the Federal Reserve), which is broadly coherent, and fiscal policy (the product of inter-branch and intra-branch strife), which has never been especially coherent but has become recklessly misaligned. United States politics at all levels – economic policy, social policy, foreign policy – has been dominated for fifteen years by the consequences of a huge and seemingly uncontrollable deficit. That pattern is unlikely to be altered in the coming decade.

Notes

1 Figures from White and Wildavsky, *The Deficit and the Public Interest*, p. 5. Budget authority is the amount of money that may be spent on a project over a number of years (e.g. a missile system) budget outlays are what is spent in that particular fiscal year. American fiscal years run from 1 October of one year to 30 September of the next. So fiscal year 1967 started on 1 October 1966.

2 In addition to these forty-two, the state of Maryland grants its Governor the line-item veto in certain limited circumstances.

3 Under a scheme called 'enhanced recissions' passed in 1996, the President, for an eight year period only, could list individual items in appropriations bills he did not want to happen. Congress would have to accept his view or pass the items again as a separate law. This could be vetoed by the President with a two-thirds vote needed to override him.

4 It passed the House 300–132 but in the Senate the margin was only 65–35.

14

Foreign policy

If one way of examining the nature of a country's political system is by looking at the way it approaches other states – foreign policy – then the impression gained by looking at the particular and peculiar foreign policy-making process of the United States reinforces the themes of individuality and complexity that have run throughout this book.

This chapter will try to outline five main themes. First, the historical background to contemporary foreign policy, where it will be argued that the frequent description of pre-1941 American policy as isolationist is highly simplistic, with the notion of selective engagement being more appropriate. Second, the impact of the Constitution and the separation of powers which leads to open conflict between the presidency and Congress over who controls foreign policy – a conflict that has generally deepened over the last thirty years. Third, the reasons for internal dissent amongst the various branches of the executive itself – the White House, State Department, Defence Department, National Security Council and others – and why this too has generally increased since the 1960s. Next, an examination of the international environment against which American foreign policy takes place. This will lead to an argument that presidents from and including Lyndon Johnson (1963–69) have faced a more complex external situation and that since the American failure in the Vietnam War consensus in the pursuit of Cold War aims became progressively more difficult to achieve.

These three factors: rising executive–legislative tensions; internal incoherence; and greater policy complexity and dissensus will establish why American foreign policy decisions have often seemed, in the words of former Secretary of State Dean Acheson (1949–53), 'unknown and unknowable'.[1] Finally, there will be a brief set of thoughts about how the end of the Cold War will provoke a fundamental review of American international policy and its perceived world role entering the twenty-first century.

The historical background

As Chapter 1 noted, the United States has always seen itself as a different kind of nation–state. In particular, different from the states of Britain and continental Europe from where most American citizens (especially in the nineteenth century) were drawn. This sense of the United States as a missionary society, expressed by John Kennedy as her being 'the last best hope for mankind' and by Ronald Reagan as 'a shining city on a hill', has led to two notable traits in external policy. One is a certain distaste bordering on repugnance for European ideas of foreign policy, based on concepts such as balance of powers (the pursuit of stability at almost any price) and hence a deep suspicion of the motives of European states. The other is a certain zest for wrapping moral principles around international policy decisions as if the mere promotion or protection of national interests were not in itself a sufficient justification for any action. Neither of these tendencies are universal. At certain times, notably when Henry Kissinger was the premier foreign policy actor in the Nixon and Ford administrations (1969–77), US thinking has appeared far less distinct from Europe's. The Vietnam War dealt a severe blow to the moral crusade against communism.

Nevertheless, these traits, coupled with the country's geographical location, did lead to its international outlook prior to the Second World War being distinctly selective. As the feuds of continental Europe were not normally inside that range of selectivity, European commentators have tended to label it as isolationism.

Dealing with foreign policy questions has always been a problematic exercise for American leaders. During the War of Independence the Continental Congress of the thirteen states delegated external affairs to a five-member committee. It was not a notable success. Indeed, it was the consistent failure of the Continental Congress and the states to cope with issues of national defence and international trade that, as much as any other factors, brought the Constitutional Convention of 1787 and the subsequent relaunch of the United States as a nation.

The Founding Fathers were divided over foreign policy management and, as the next section will illustrate, the Constitution reflects that division. They were also split on what America's world role should be, especially with regard to the ongoing Franco-British wars of the 1790s and 1800s. There were factions in favour of supporting either side and another group that backed strict neutrality. More generally there was a division between those who favoured an expansive world role (verging on imperialism), who tended to ally with the Federalist party and Alexander Hamilton (the first Secretary of the Treasury) and those who supported a much more limited role, who gravitated towards the Democratic–Republicans and Thomas Jefferson (the first Secretary of State).

The electoral triumph of Democratic–Republicans such as Jefferson (1801–09), James Madison (1809–17) and James Monroe (1817–25), plus an unfortunate mauling at the hands of the British in the War of 1812, led to a clear victory for the more limited world role. However, complete isolation from the world was impossible even in the 1820s. Concern about the actions of European powers led in 1823 to the promulgation of the so-called Monroe Doctrine – that America would intervene to keep hostile outsiders from Latin America. That doctrine remains one of the fundamental dictums of American policy, as the governments of Grenada and Panama discovered in the 1980s.

From the 1820s onwards the United States expanded rapidly westwards towards the California coast, either buying or seizing that land from European nations or indigenous Indians. In 1848 Texas was grasped from Mexico. Generally speaking, the trend was still towards hostility to the affairs of Europe and (the Americas themselves excepted) isolation from other countries. First the Civil War, and then America's rapid industrialisation after it, provided plenty of alternative distractions.

However, sets of occasional but very sharp economic depressions in the last three decades of the nineteenth century led to a greater emphasis on international trade, which in turn led to a creeping internationalism. Asia became an increasingly important outlet for American commerce. This process exploded with the Spanish–American War of 1898 which, whilst initially about Cuba, led to the American annexation of Hawaii and the Philippines. The United States could now hardly avoid becoming a major player in Asian affairs. This widening of American selective engagement further manifested itself in the presidency of Theodore Roosevelt (1901–09). Roosevelt had the Panama Canal project built for the United States, asserted a new dominance in Caribbean affairs, and negotiated the end of the Russia–Japan conflict of 1905/6. China was crucial to American trading interests and through its 'Open Door' policy the US had every intention of assuring its economic position. To deter others (notably Japan) he sent the entire sixteen-battleship navy around the world in 1907.

By 1914 American foreign policy was thus active in the Americas and East Asia but remained limited as far as Europe was concerned. This was ended temporarily by US intervention in the First World War (beginning in 1917) and Woodrow Wilson's decision to involve himself personally in Europe's future through his Fourteen Points and negotiation of the Versailles Treaty. Wilson was too far ahead of public opinion. The depth of American action in that war had not been powerful enough to persuade citizens or their representatives that Europe now warranted full American involvement. The Senate refused to ratify his treaty and blocked membership of the League of Nations that Wilson himself had invented. In 1920 the nation overwhelmingly elected Warren Harding to the White House on a ticket of 'normalcy' and although the United States was involved in global politics in the 1920s, notably in the promotion of international disarmament, the general disinclination to get entangled in European affairs remained. Congressional reaction to the rising tension in Europe through the 1930s was a set of Neutrality Acts designed to frustrate Franklin Roosevelt's anti-Nazi instincts.

The Japanese attack on Pearl Harbor, coupled with Hitler's still curious decision to declare war on the United States in solidarity with his Asian ally, shattered hopes of remaining neutral through the Second World War and laid the ground for a wider internationalism. All-out American engagement in that conflict, the subsequent allied victory over fascism, the acquisition of superpower status, the possession of nuclear weapons and the rapid deterioration of relations with the Soviet Union with the consequent Cold War revolutionised American foreign policy. Through the Truman Doctrine of

1947 (assistance for free peoples struggling against communism), the Marshall Plan of the same year (massive economic aid to Europe) and the creation of NATO in 1949 (the first full commitment of American troops to Europe on a seemingly permanent basis), American selective engagement in international politics was transformed into a worldwide commitment to prevent the advance of communism, a commitment that had to coexist with the constraints and ambiguities laid down by the Constitution.

The Presidency, Congress, and foreign policy

As in so many areas, the Constitution of 1789 complicates the management of contemporary foreign policy through its deliberate failure to specify one office as uniquely responsible for it. Under the Constitution the President is named as Commander-in-Chief, is given the power to negotiate treaties with other nations, and has the right to appoint American Ambassadors. These functions can be blocked by the need for a majority of Congress to support a declaration of war and the power of one-third of the Senate to reject or attach killer amendments to treaties and one half to block nominations for ambassadorships. As congressional support is needed to pay for all foreign policy activities (notably the armed forces), then Congress can use this 'power of the purse' to emasculate presidential initiatives.

The Supreme Court has traditionally been reluctant to embroil itself in the dispute about where the balance of power lies. It has avoided pronouncing on which of the two branches controls foreign policy with the exception of a very controversial case in 1936, *US* v. *Curtiss-Wright*, where the majority opinion written by Justice Sutherland appeared to award the presidency a unique domain in international policy. However, whilst the Court has been reluctant to constrain the executive in its operation of overseas policies – especially where those activities appear to enjoy congressional support – it has not usually repeated Justice Sutherland's sweeping (and constitutionally debatable) views.

Most presidents from Washington onwards have encountered some difficulties with Congress. Treaties have been amended and even rejected (most notably the Treaty of Versailles). Congress was more reluctant than the White House to enter either world war. Indeed, it has been the issue of using American troops abroad – and the tendency of presidents to do so unilaterally – that has generated the fiercest conflict. Of the over two hundred occasions when US armed forces have been used in combat situations Congress has only formally declared war four times (the War of 1812, the Spanish–American War of 1898, and both world wars) and passed an approving joint resolution twice (the war to annex Texas in 1848 and the Gulf War of 1991). Conflicts as major and protracted as Korea (1950–53) and Vietnam could be described as 'presidential wars'.

For the twenty years after 1945 Congress was uncharacteristically generous to the presidency. New institutions such as the National Security Council and

---

The Constitution and foreign policy

As in many other areas the Constitution divides control over foreign policy. The President, as Commander-in-chief, with the right to appoint ambassadors, and the ability to negotiate treaties, has a very prominent role, but Congress alone can declare war and controls the funding of overseas operations. The Supreme Court has generally avoided deciding between competing claims over foreign policy, with the exception of *US* v. *Curtiss-Wright* (1936). In this case Justice Sutherland, writing for the majority, produced an extraordinary opinion which amounted to declaring a special presidential domain over foreign policy. Although all subsequent Presidents have referred to this case when convenient, few have though or acted as if it were the last word on the constitutional question.

---

the Central Intelligence Agency were created for it, and considerable deference was accorded to the President's judgement on how best to conduct the Cold War. The sole possession of nuclear weapons by the Commander-in-Chief also worked to the advantage of the White House. Presidents could conduct international relations through executive agreements (understandings between governments rather than countries) with other nations rather than proper treaties. This unusual degree of co-operation spawned the question of whether there were two presidencies, a relatively embattled one at home compared to a dominant one abroad.[2]

This era of mutual understanding was fatally undermined by the Vietnam War. President Johnson's personal decision to escalate the American presence to a peak of over 500,000 men started inter-branch disagreement. Richard Nixon continued it by his saturation bombing tactics (North Vietnam had more tonnage of bombs dropped on it than the rest of all the bombing in the history of mankind up until that point) and his secret (and probably illegal) extension of the war into neighbouring Cambodia and Laos, none of which seemed to increase American prospects of propping up South Vietnam.

An increasingly angry Congress used Nixon's political weakness during the Watergate crisis to undercut his policy in Vietnam and to return to an antagonistic relationship with the President. That Congress and the President were frequently from different political parties in this period did not help matters. From the late 1960s onwards Congress reasserted its constitutional prerogatives in three ways, a set of president-constraining legislation, opposition to policy options preferred by the White House, and an enormous increase in its use of scrutiny.

President-constraining legislation

The 1970s witnessed a torrent of legislation designed to curb what Congress now saw as presidential abuse of executive power. This started with the Case Act of 1972 which obliged the White House to notify Congress of executive agreements with other nations. That was followed by the highly controversial

---

Containment

For most of the two decades or so after the Second World War American policy towards the Soviet Union was characterised by Containment. This doctrine emerged from George Kennan's anonymous article in *Foreign Affairs* in 1947 and a key National Security Council document (NSC 68) agreed in1950. The doctrine stated that the United States should use a mixture of diplomatic and military means to keep the Soviet empire contained to its then boundaries in the belief that, after a period of time, a contained USSR would collapse because of its economic limitations and through popular discontent. A side-effect of the policy was the domino theory, which held that Communist gains in one country would quickly be followed by gains throughout that region. The consensus behind containment was badly mauled by the Vietnam War which seemed a direct consequence of it. However, the theory looks more respectable after events in Central Eastern Europe in 1989 at least coincided with its predictions.

War Powers Act of 1973 passed over Richard Nixon's veto. This obliged the President to notify Congress of the use of US troops and triggered a sixty-day period of unrestrained presidential action that could then be terminated if Congress did not approve of it. Alternatively, Congress could sanction a further limited period of presidential activity. The effectiveness of this has been a matter of great dispute. No president has ever recognised its constitutionality, although their actions have generally conformed with it. Some critics object to the idea of allowing presidents to fight wars for two months believing that Congress would not have the stomach to cancel military operations in progress. The importance of the Act lies in symbolising congressional opposition to presidential misuse of military might and thus represents a potent political warning.

The War Powers Act was swiftly followed by the Hughes–Ryan amendment to the Foreign Assistance Act of 1974 (requiring the CIA to notify Congress of covert operations). The overall act attempted to place human rights requirements on recipients of US aid. The International Development and Food Assistance Act of 1975 continued this theme. The Arms Export Control Act of 1976 gave Congress the chance to veto major arms sales. The Trade Act of 1974 and the Export Administration Act of 1979 gave Congress a greater say over international economic policy. The Foreign Intelligence Surveillance Act of 1978 and the Intelligence Oversight Act of 1980 placed greater controls still on the CIA. Together, this constituted an impressive set of weapons for restricting the institutional power of the presidency, even if the latter remained the premier actor abroad.

Opposition to presidential policy

Congress also went beyond this set of legislation to actively intervene against presidential policy initiatives. What remaining American assistance there was to South Vietnam was ended by Congress in 1975 and the regime there fell

---

Treaties and executive agreements

A treaty is a formal and legally binding pact between countries. In the United States a two-thirds majority of the Senate is required to endorse a treaty, an unusually high threshold. For this reason Presidents became increasingly keen on executive agreements, which are less legally powerful political understandings between governments, that future governments could reject. The distinction between the two entities is blurred, with Presidents using executive agreements to achieve treaty-like objectives. In response to this Congress passed the Case Acts in 1972 which obliged the White House to inform Congress of all executive agreements. Even so they are still used more regularly than treaties. For example, Ronald Reagan concluded 125 treaties during his tenure, compared with 1,371 executive agreements.

---

within weeks. Sensing that the Ford Administration might want to limit the spread of communism in Africa the Clark Amendment, banning US intervention of any kind in Angola, was passed in 1976. Opponents of Nixon and Ford's allegedly amoral policy of *détente* (closer relations) with the Soviet Union managed to harass the Administration so much that by 1976 the word had been banished from the presidential vocabulary.

Although the restoration of a Democrat to the presidency with Jimmy Carter's victory in 1976 eased tensions somewhat they were not eliminated. Carter's Panama Canal Treaty (proposing the return of the Canal to Panama in 1999) was eventually passed through the Senate on a 67–33 vote, the narrowest possible margin. Carter's decision to recognise the Communist Government of China and abandon the previous commitment to Taiwan was unsuccessfully challenged in the Supreme Court by a number of senators (*Goldwater* v. *Carter*, 1979). His arms control treaty with the Soviet Union – SALT II – was in deep political waters before it was withdrawn in 1980 in the light of the soviet takeover in Afghanistan.

With the return of Republican presidents in the 1980s inter-branch conflict resumed apace. In his first year Ronald Reagan narrowly persuaded the Senate to permit a proposed arms sale to Saudi Arabia (by a 52–48 split). He then suffered constant strife over his support for the right-wing government of El Salvador and his backing of the Contra rebel movement in Nicaragua (blocked by the Boland amendments). It was this failure that led to the Iran–Contra scandal.

Reagan was also pressurised into moving US troops out of the Lebanon for fear of seeing the War Powers restrictions used. His handling of the Cold War was tackled head-on by a nuclear weapons freeze resolution in the House of Representatives (although it fell in the Senate). Further arms sales to Saudi Arabia and Jordan in the mid-1980s had to be abandoned when it became clear that Congress would reject them. Reagan's planned Strategic Defense Initiative (or 'Star Wars') was greeted unenthusiastically. His policy

Major foreign policy inter-branch disputes		
President	*Dispute period*	*Subject*
Johnson	1965–68	Vietnam War
Nixon	1969–73	Vietnam War
	1970	Cambodian incursion
Ford	1975	South Vietnam aid
	1976	Angolan Civil War
Carter	1979	Panama Canal Treaty
	1979	SALT II ratification
Reagan	1981–89	Central America (Nicaragua)
	1981–87	Arms control
	1985–87	South Africa
Bush	1989–93	China relations
	1991	Gulf War support
Clinton	1993	Troops in Somalia
	1994	Troops in Haiti

of 'constructive engagement' or relatively benign relations with South Africa was struck down by the Anti-Apartheid Act of 1986 (passed over his veto). His interpretation of previous arms control treaties was challenged in the Senate who insisted on writing language of interpretation into his own Intermediate Nuclear Forces Treaty (the Byrd amendment).

Although Reagan's record of confrontation with Congress was somewhat exceptional George Bush also encountered trouble. His refusal to isolate China after the Tiananmen Square massacre of 1989 was constantly challenged (but not overturned) in the Senate. His authority during the Gulf crisis was threatened when the Senate only narrowly (52–47) backed the use of force to retake Kuwait after the resolution had passed by a much wider margin in the House of Representatives (250–183). Defeat in the Senate would have been a devastating blow. Bill Clinton's policies towards Bosnia, Haiti, and Somalia were all challenged in Congress even before the Republicans gained control of Congress after the 1994 elections.

Greater congressional scrutiny

Finally, Congress has flexed its constitutional muscles by much tougher scrutiny of presidential proposals. This has allowed the House of Representatives – otherwise dealt a relatively weak hand in foreign policy – to use its dominance in fiscal policy for foreign policy ends. This new scrutiny has taken several forms.

The Senate has paid much more attention to the details of proposed treaties. It has not always been especially consistent. The Senate Foreign Relations Committee voted to back President Carter's Panama Canal Treaty but the Armed Services Committee recommended rejection. The two committees proposed precisely the opposite combination in their judgement of Ronald Reagan's 1981 arms sale to Saudi Arabia.

Both wings of Congress have used their control over the budgetary process to impose their priorities in foreign aid and defence spending. From 1950 until 1969 Congress had rarely cut administration requests on defence by more than trivial amounts and always by less than for non-defence items. That trend was dramatically changed from 1969 until 1975 as Congress slashed defence spending while increasing the budget elsewhere. Congressional activism over the defence budget increased so spectacularly that strong complaints of micro-management were heard from the Reagan Administration. The number of hearings into presidential policy increased, the number of annual required reports (compulsory justification of an individual policy) rose from 79 in 1969 to an unbelievable 861 by 1990.[3] Congressional staff serving the House and Senate Armed Services committees expanded from 18 in 1969 to 72 by 1988.[4] Both chambers regularly vote through hundreds of amendments to the defence budget despite the Administration issuing an annual book justifying its decisions that now runs to over thirty thousand pages.

The creation of new Senate (1976) and House (1977) Intelligence Committees to monitor the CIA increased to ten (Appropriations, Armed Services, Budget, Foreign Relations and Intelligence in each chamber), the number of major committees who deal with foreign policy. The new Intelligence bodies quickly abandoned their initial inclination to automatically trust the CIA.

Congress has also attempted to write America's trade policy. In 1967 it refused to extend the President's negotiating powers over international trade agreements and only restored them in 1974 subject to a new set of conditions that made it easier for Congress to vote down or amend what had been agreed. The free-trade rhetoric of the Reagan Administration was frequently compromised in practice because of protectionist pressures in Congress.

This network of new laws, policy initiatives, powerful committees, and an enhanced scrutiny function have created unusual obstacles to the making of US foreign policy. This has not been helped by increasing disagreement within the executive branch itself.

Executive branch disputes

Not only have presidential–congressional relations become more fraught in the last twenty-five years but relations with the various international policy departments of the executive have frayed as well. This is the consequence of two main factors. The traditional dominance of the State Department over foreign policy has waned as other institutions – the National Security Council, the Defense Department, the Central Intelligence Agency and the presidency

---

Competing agencies in foreign policy

Diplomatic/strategic   *Economic*

State Department   Treasury Department
Defense Department   Commerce Department
National Security Council   US Trade Representatives
Central Intelligence Agency   Council of Economic Advisers

---

itself – have attempted to get the upper hand. Furthermore, the traditional superiority of security concerns within foreign policy have been challenged by other departments more concerned with economics such as the US Trade Representative, the US Treasury, and the Commerce Department, to name but a few.

Before the 1960s the State Department was clearly established as the premier overseas affairs actor. As a consequence US policy tended to be consistent and administrations spoke with one voice. As other institutions rivalled State that coherence became harder to retain and under Presidents Carter and Reagan open disagreement between different individuals and bodies became so pronounced that the basic credibility of its international position was undermined. This section outlines the main competitors for influence inside the foreign policy process and highlights the struggle for control it.

The State Department

Created in 1789, the State Department, which co-ordinates the activities of the vast number of American embassies throughout the world, holds the foreign aid budget, and manages day-to-day diplomacy, is theoretically the senior actor in foreign affairs. The department developed slowly, a full 'professional' diplomatic corps not being created until the Rogers Act of 1924 made necessary by the expanding number of US Embassies throughout the world. The Foreign Service Act of 1946 tried to give the department a greater strategic sense and a Policy Planning division was established to look at longer-run foreign policy goals.

The State Department has always suffered from two weaknesses. Its elite professional image and reputation for highly deliberative policy formulation aimed at the maximum possible consensus has not always endeared it to outsiders. Presidents from John F. Kennedy to Ronald Reagan have protested at its procrastination and lack of innovation. It was invariably accused of being too willing to seek diplomatic solutions to problems which others saw as needing a more aggressive approach. The department was the leading target of anti-Communist hysteria associated with Senator Joseph McCarthy in the 1950s and has remained a favourite enemy of conservatives. Furthermore, the Department lacks a sympathetic constituency in Congress. The major component of its budget – foreign aid – is frequently unpopular. The Department funds its various diplomatic endeavours around the world on a budget that is minuscule compared with the Defense Department. Other interests have capitalised on those weaknesses to try and marginalise its influence.

The presidency and the National Security Council

The most threatening challenge to the State Department comes from the frequent desire of presidents to be their own Secretary of State and their ability to use the National Security Council to that end. Several presidents have deliberately appointed low-key figures to head State so that the White House can dominate international relations. Franklin Roosevelt's appointment of Cordell Hull (1933–44), John Kennedy's selection and Lyndon Johnson's retention of Dean Rusk (1961–69) and Richard Nixon's choice of William Rogers (1969–73) have all been seen in this light.

The major vehicle for presidential takeovers of this kind is the National Security Council (NSC). This was established in 1947 to provide a formal structure and a supporting staff inside the White House for longer-term strategic planning. The actual Council must by law include the President, Vice-President, and Secretaries of State and Defense. In practice the composition is decided by the individual president and the NSC's power comes from its expert staff and their co-ordinator, the National Security Advisor. The attraction of the NSC to presidents is that it is entirely based in the White House, its budget is virtually beyond congressional scrutiny, and the position of National Security Advisor (NSA) does not require senatorial approval.

John Kennedy relied on his NSA, McGeorge Bundy, rather than the advice of the State Department, and Lyndon Johnson continued that process with Bundy's successor, Walter Rostow. Under Richard Nixon, Henry Kissinger was so powerful that he completely eclipsed the State Department until he finally took over as Secretary of State (while remaining NSA for two more years) in 1973. Jimmy Carter's NSA, Zbigniew Brzezinski, fought for control over the external agenda with Secretary of State Cyrus Vance until the latter resigned when his advice not to attempt the ill-fated mission to rescue the American hostages in Iran in April 1980 was ignored. Ronald Reagan's fourth NSA, John Poindexter, persuaded him to trade arms with Iran in return for US hostages in Beirut, despite the strong objections of Secretary of State George Schultz and Defence Secretary Caspar Weinberger.

The Defense Department

The Defense Department was created in 1947 from the former positions of Secretary for War and the Secretaries of the Army, Navy, and Air Force. Rivalry between these services had been legendary during the Second World War. The National Security Act of 1947 did little to rectify this, creating a Secretary of Defense and a Chairman of the Joint Chiefs of Staff answerable to the Chiefs of Staff of the Army, Navy, Air Force, and Marines. Without direct authority to fire or promote officers, the Defense Secretary was highly exposed to alliances between the service chiefs and Congressmen seeking more spending in their districts. In 1953 and 1958 the Act was amended to give more influences to the Defense Secretary and the Chairman of the Joint Chiefs. That process was to culminate with the Defense Reorganization Act of 1986 that finally established the Chairman of the Joint Chiefs as the senior military adviser to the President. From the 1960s onwards, starting with the influence of Defense Secretary Robert MacNamara on Kennedy and Johnson, the Pentagon has been willing to challenge the State Department, often lobbying against military action, as under President Clinton where the military had little taste for action in Bosnia or Somalia.

The Central Intelligence Agency

The Central Intelligence Agency (CIA) was also created by the National Security Act of 1947 and again reflected Cold War thinking. The official functions of the CIA are to gather intelligence information on global developments, make assessments of likely actions by foreign powers and to provide materials for longer-term analysis. Recent estimates suggest a staff of nearly twenty thousand. The CIA does not have a monopoly on intelligence gathering. Other bodies such as the Defense Intelligence Agency, the National Security Agency, the Federal Bureau of Investigation (FBI), the four military services, and various domestic departments all coexist (some would say compete) in these activities.

The agency's high-profile and controversial attempts at destabilising foreign regimes, notably in Iran (1953), Cuba (1961) and Chile (1973), led to calls for greater control over it. As noted earlier, this was met by the creation of House and Senate Intelligence Committees in the 1970s. Their arrival checked presidential supremacy over the Agency and led the White House to be more careful in their use of it. However, even after these Committees were established, Ronald Reagan's CIA Director, William Casey (1981–87), had considerable influence although the agency's power was checked after its involvement in the Iran–Contra scandal, and its whole purpose has been questioned given the collapse of the Cold War. It was also deeply embarrassed by the Aldrich Ames spy scandal in 1994.

The United Nations Ambassador

The post of American Ambassador to the United Nations (UN) was created in 1945 at the inauguration of that body. For most of its history it has not been of enormous importance in foreign relations. There have been some exceptions to this rule. Henry Cabot Lodge under President Eisenhower, Adlai Stevenson under President Kennedy, Andrew Young under President Carter, and Jeane Kirkpatrick under President Reagan were all influential characters whose personal advice, if not the institution of the UN Ambassador, made them significant.

The US Trade Representative

The post of US Trade Representative (USTR) was created in 1963 as the President's personal delegate to global trade negotiations. Its invention was something of a snub to the State Department which had previously handled the details of such deliberations but which was regarded by Congress as insufficiently tough in promoting US economic interests. Originally a non-Cabinet agency with a small staff, the USTR has achieved cabinet status, a much larger bureaucracy and considerable profile as questions of international economic policy – especially the GATT (General Agreement on Tariffs and Trade) process – increasingly enter the overseas agenda. Under President Carter Trade Representative Robert Strauss held considerable influence, as did Carla Hills under George Bush, and, especially, Mickey Kantor under Bill Clinton.

Other executive bodies

As if this plethora of institutions was not enough, other departments which might appear concerned with domestic policy also have an influence abroad. The United States Treasury, especially with James Baker serving under Ronald Reagan (1985–88), plays an increasingly vital role in the international economy in seeking economic co-operation through the Group of Seven major industrialised countries, promoting certain adjustments in global currency rates, and attempting to manage the issue of Third World debt. The Commerce Department has prime responsibility for the promotion of US exports (which often leads it to clash with the Trade Representative). The Department of Agriculture has significant international interests both in pushing grain sales abroad and in administering the Food for Peace programme, which involves billions of dollars worth of American produce. The Department of Energy, through its work on nuclear weapons, also has overseas responsibilities.

With this huge range of departments all seeking a prominent position in foreign policy the possibility of disputes is obviously high and the need for central bureaucratic management by the presidency much greater. Presidents who come to office with little prior experience in foreign affairs tend to react to their disadvantage by appointing advisers with a wide range of views. This arrangement is often troublesome as individual personality and philosophy differences are added to institutional rivalry. President Carter's administration gave the impression of frequently holding two foreign policies. A more accommodating line towards the Soviet Union represented by Secretary of State Cyrus Vance and UN Ambassador Andrew Young and a much harder line offered by NSA Zbigniew Brzezinski and Defence Secretary Harold Brown. Until its final two years in office the Reagan Presidency appeared to have several foreign policies as the State Department struggled with the National Security Council for control. Hardliners opposed moderates, and substantial differences of opinion also emerged between Secretary of State Schultz and Defence Secretary Weinberger.

This incoherence can be outlined in two sets of statistics. Between 1973 and 1983 there were six separate Secretaries of State (Rogers, Kissinger, Vance, Muskie, Haig, and Schultz). In the period 1980 to 1990 there were eight NSAs (Brzezinski, Allen, Clark, Macfarland, Poindexter, Carlucci, Powell, and Scowcroft), six of whom served President Reagan. This degree of fragmentation and such high levels of turnover hardly help the construction of policy and left US allies bewildered as to which of many apparent opinions actually represented American policy. Only when a president with substantial prior experience, George Bush, was elected did the constant public disagreements and selective leaking to newspapers stop. After four years though, Bush was out of office and another inexperienced president, Bill Clinton, assumed the White House.

The erosion of the State Department's supreme role in external matters and the increased importance of economics in foreign affairs may have created the space for such dissent and uncertainty. What strengthened it was the collapse of a policy consensus after the Vietnam War and the increasingly complex international system that American presidents had to work with, making it more probable that individual departments would disagree among themselves and that the president and Capitol Hill would clash.

The increasingly complex international system

In the twenty-year period from 1945 American foreign policy benefited from two distinct advantages. First, the United States was by far the largest economy in the world and dominated international economic discussions. It also possessed a clear nuclear superiority over the Soviet Union, witnessed by the Cuban missile crisis of 1962 when it was Nikita Khruschev rather than President Kennedy who ultimately backed down. Second, in this same period there was a broad consensus in American political thinking behind the policy of 'containment' (isolating and restricting the advance of the Soviet Union by a mixture of diplomatic and military means). The existence of such a consensus partly explains why Congress was so willing to defer to the presidency during this period and why conflict within the executive branch was muted. From the mid-1960s onwards both this American economic–military dominance and this basic containment consensus were severely stretched, complicating the operation of American overseas policy and fostering divisions amongst those making policy.

The United States came out of the Second World War in an astonishingly fortunate position. Unlike European powers, it had suffered no occupation or mass bombing of its territory and the process of becoming a wartime economy had not involved acquiring crippling debts. Its major trading rivals of the inter-war period (notably Britain) were exhausted and virtually bankrupt and it alone possessed the secret of nuclear weapons. The United States was by far the world's richest nation, its greatest creditor, and the dollar had become the undisputed global currency. The Bretton-Woods arrangements for post War international economic relations (1944) were concluded on terms largely dictated by the United States.

Unsurprisingly, given the torrid state of other trading nations, the United States had a massively disproportionate share of the world economy (estimated at 33 per cent of global GNP in 1950) throughout the 1950s. Also unsurprisingly, other nations did rebuild and recover so that the US proportion began to slide, reaching some 23 per cent by the mid-1980s where it has basically stabilised. Although this figure is no lower than the US position in 1940 it nevertheless did create a strong sense of relative decline and established new economic powers – notably Japan and Germany – who could not be ignored.

Although domestic economic performance (in terms of growth, inflation, and unemployment levels) was quite robust in the 1980s its external position was undermined by two developments. The spiralling budget deficit increased from an average of $63 billion between fiscal years 1978 and 1981 to an

Table 14.1. *Defence spending, 1965–94*

Year	Defence outlays as a percentage of GDP	Year	Defence outlays as a percentage of GDP
1965	7.5	1980	5.1
1966	7.9	1981	5.3
1967	9.0	1982	5.9
1968	9.7	1983	6.3
1969	8.9	1984	6.2
1970	8.3	1985	6.4
1971	7.5	1986	6.5
1972	6.9	1987	6.3
1973	6.0	1988	6.0
1974	5.7	1989	5.9
1975	5.7	1990	5.5
1976	5.3	1991	4.9
1977	5.1	1992	5.0
1978	4.8	1993	4.6
1979	4.8	1994	4.2

Note As the table shows, the Reagan-inspired defence build-up peaked in 1986, and there has been quite a dramatic reduction, accelerated by the end of the Cold War, since then, with defence spending projected at around 3 per cent of GDP by the year 2000.

average of $207 billion in fiscal years 1983–86.[5] The Reagan Administration ran a higher cumulative budget deficit than the entire cumulative budget deficits of presidents from Franklin Roosevelt to Jimmy Carter. This was worsened by the massively increased trade deficits with other countries. After 1983 trade deficits exceeding $100 billion annually became commonplace. The total cumulative trade deficits of the Reagan years matched the entire cumulative trade deficits of all presidents from George Washington to Jimmy Carter. The overall impact of this was to change a situation in 1981 where the United States had a net positive worth of $141 billion in international investments to one in 1988 where the US had a net negative worth of $532.5 billion.[6] The nation went from being the banker of the world to its chief debtor in the space of less than a decade.

The American monopoly of nuclear weapons ended in 1949 when the Soviet Union successfully produced atomic bombs as well. Through the 1950s the gap between the two nations' stockpiles of such weapons gradually narrowed

Table 14.2. *The US balance of trade, 1962–92*

Year	Balance on current account	Year	Balance on current account
1962	3,387	1978	15,143
1963	4,414	1979	−285
1964	6,823	1980	2,317
1965	5,431	1981	6,030
1966	3,031	1982	11,443
1967	2,583	1983	−43,623
1968	611	1984	−98,824
1969	399	1985	−121,721
1970	2,331	1986	−147,529
1971	−1,433	1987	−163,474
1972	−5,795	1988	−126,656
1973	7,140	1989	−101,143
1974	1,962	1990	−90,428
1975	18,116	1991	−3,682
1976	4,295	1992	−62,448
1977	−14,335		

Note This table shows that the United States, which had traditionally been in trade surplus, began to experience difficulties in the 1970s which then got much worse in the 1980s and into the 1990s.

and a major spurt by the USSR in the 1960s (after the humiliation of the Cuban crisis) led to rough balance or so-called strategic parity by 1970.

From 1947 onwards American policy towards the USSR was based on the idea of containment created by a State Department diplomat, and expert on the Russians, George Kennan. His original idea of containment – that the United States should prevent Communist advance in certain key regions such as Western Europe and Japan – was transformed by the Korean War into a worldwide commitment to guarantee nations under threat from Communist (or alleged Communist) subversives. This was backed by the domino theory, the belief that if one nation in a region fell to Communists the other nations in that area would also fall one by one. This expanded notion of containment was supported by Truman, Eisenhower, Kennedy and Johnson and by the overwhelming majority of the American political elite. The pursuit of it led the Americans straight into the quagmire of Vietnam.

The Vietnam experience smashed the containment consensus that had structured strategic thinking for a generation. No single grand theory ever replaced it. Politicians divided into various different schools. Some, notably conservative internationalists and neo-conservatives (hawkish Democrats), blamed the American defeat on the Johnson Administration's unwillingness to unleash the full might of American power. To others, isolationists and accommodationists (liberal internationalists), it showed the futility of combating the spread of radicalism by military means. Others clung to the notion of containment, insisting it had been misapplied in Vietnam but was still broadly the best option. Self-described realists, notably Richard Nixon and his foreign affairs guru Henry Kissinger, favoured recognising the reality of military equality with the Soviet Union and supported traditional ideas of balance-of-power theory, although in the past it had always proved too amoral for the United States.

For the last twenty years of the Cold-War period American presidents had to work against a background of relative economic decline, increasing overseas debt, no particular advantage in nuclear weapons, and substantial disunity within their own administrations, and between themselves and Congress about what the guiding principles of international relations should be. That US policy should frequently appear incoherent and uncertain as a consequence should surely be no shock. American foreign policy had become progressively harder to make. It remains difficult in the 1990s, despite the Soviet withdrawal from Eastern Europe in 1989 and the collapse of the USSR as a state in 1991 leaving the United States with the misleading luxury of sole superpower status.

American foreign policy beyond the Cold War

The collapse of the Soviet Union as the great world rival is only a mixed blessing for the United States. It creates new elements of complexity in its place in the international system, the two major dilemmas for the United States being: the

---

Post Cold War policy

The end of the Cold War international system has made it much harder to reach agreement on the United States' national interests and its role in the world. Public and congressional sentiment has favoured a disengagement from overseas commitments to concentrate on domestic problems, along with a new emphasis on American economic interests within foreign policy. The Clinton presidency started off with an emphasis on promoting democracy as the new watchword of US policy, but this ran into trouble in Bosnia, Haiti and Somalia. It shifted emphasis towards a lower international profile with much weight placed on trade issues. This was illustrated by the North American Free Trade Agreement (NAFTA), the invigoration of the Asia Pacific Economic Community (APEC), and the ratification of the Uruguay Round of the General Agreement on Tariffs and Trade (GATT). It is a shift in foreign policy that may well prove difficult for future administrations to reverse.

---

new relationship between economics and security factors that is likely to dominate the post Cold-War world; and the search for what the United States' national interests are and global role should be.

The demise of the Cold War is likely to make economics more important and traditional military muscle less important than has been the case in the last fifty years. In one sense, then, the United States has been unfortunate to find itself the premier, indeed undisputed, military nation on the planet (as was so visibly demonstrated in the Gulf War) when the value of possessing such vast military resources may be rapidly declining. Whilst the United States spent an increasing proportion of its income building high-technology armed forces in the 1980s its fundamental economic position was being undermined by the twin budget and trade deficits. It can now hardly escape the irony that its leading Cold-War rival, the Soviet Union, was no rival in economic terms: in fact it was one of the few major nations the US persistently ran trade surpluses with. Yet its leading Cold-War allies (especially Japan and Germany) were its leading economic adversaries. If economics is to prove pre-eminent in the new era then despite the overall size and strength of the American economy, a painful adjustment will be needed.

This process is more difficult still because while global rivalry between nations is increasing so is the degree of economic interdependence between them. The United States needs to adjust its foreign policy, which has been dominated for fifty years by military and diplomatic considerations, to take account of the new and complex role that international economics will play. The reaction of the Clinton Administration has been to create a National Economic Council to try and inject economic thinking into international strategy. However, this route was tried by President Eisenhower (via a Council on Foreign Economic Policy) and by President Nixon (through a Council on International Economic Policy) and was not notably successful. For the time being, international economics and international security remain starkly separated in American thinking.

One facet of this division between economics and security is the more assertive position the United States is taking in international trade discussions. Although disputes between the United States and other nations were common during the Cold-War era the fact that all the countries concerned were military partners always put a limit on how bad such disagreements could get. Despite the free-trade words of Ronald Reagan he presided over a steady advance of quasi-protectionist measures and his successors have come under great pressure to continue this unless trade concessions are made by other parties. To some extent the North American Free Trade Agreement between the United States, Canada, and Mexico is a thinly disguised insurance policy in case the world trading system collapses along with the Cold War. Such trade brinkmanship will not rest easily alongside efforts to retain traditional institutions such as NATO.

A wider, and more fundamental, uncertainty concerns what exactly America's national interests are now that it has no Communist bogeyman to resist, and what Americans want their global role to be. Different parts of the United States would appear to have varying interests. The north-eastern seaboard still instinctively looks towards involvement and collaboration with Europe. Although the major economic and political power-centres (New York and Washington, DC) are based there it has been depopulating compared with the rest of the nation for some decades now. California and the rest of the Pacific coast look towards the Far East for their major economic markets and for political co-operation. The rapidly growing southern states of Florida and Texas see ever-growing financial and strategic relations with Latin America as a natural extension of their concerns. To the heartland states of middle America many of these places seem remote and irrelevant. During the Cold-War era such divergent aspirations were subordinated to the overall goal of resisting the USSR and the spread of Communism. It is less certain that they can be so subordinated in the future.

Achieving a foreign-policy consensus about the US role in the world is equally problematic. Some favour a rapid and thorough withdrawal from commitments made during the superpower struggle. Others favour a more moderate version of the same thing. They would pursue a form of retrenched internationalism whereby America would remain politically engaged across the planet but that military expenditure overseas would be slashed to pay for social programmes at home. Others believe that the United States should remain fully engaged abroad. Some would like to see the United States vigorously asserting its status as the sole superpower, taking active measures to prevent others challenging American command. A stark alternative vision – New Internationalism – would have the United States working more fully with the United Nations to promote universal democracy, worldwide respect for human rights, and would take active measures to punish nations that refused to abide by these values. Another view is that the global system is breaking into three trade groups so that the United States should concentrate on Latin America and build itself up as a regional supremo.

The Bush Administration tried to avoid being forced into any of these options. Instead it strove to maintain the US role as the leading but not dominant nation that it had been in the late Cold-War period and to conduct business much as if the Cold War's collapse was unimportant. Uncharacteristically, and perhaps unwisely, George Bush used the occasion of his crusade against the Iraqi invasion of Kuwait to declare a 'New World Order'. Defining that order proved devilishly difficult.

President Clinton, as the first genuinely post-Cold War President, had a more difficult time still.[7] He had hoped for an assertive foreign policy based on promoting democracy and humanitarianism. This proved impractical and awkward in Bosnia (no military intervention), China (where human rights considerations were abandoned), Haiti (an enduring off–on invasion), North Korea (forced to bargain over that country's nuclear ambitions), Rwanda (a very modest response to a massive humanitarian crisis), and Somalia (an embarrassing withdrawal at the hands of Third World bandits). Although some of these problems may have been caused by Clinton's inexperience and relative disinterest in foreign affairs, much of it shows how even after the Cold War, American foreign policy will remain extremely difficult to make.

Notes

1 Dean Acheson quoted in Crabb and Holt, *Invitation to Struggle* (Washington, DC, Congressional Quarterly, 4th edn, 1992).
2 Aaron Wildavsky, 'The Two Presidencies' *Transaction*, December 1966.
3 Mackubin Owens, 'Micromanaging the Defence Budget' *The Public Interest*, Summer 1990.
4 Blechman, *The Politics of National Security*.
5 I. M. Destler in Charles O. Jones (ed.), *The Reagan Legacy*, (Chatham, New Jersey, Chatham House, 1988). American fiscal or budget years run from 1 October to 30 September.
6 Crabb and Holt, *Invitation to Struggle*.
7 Tim Hames, 'Foreign Policy and the American Elections of 1992', *International Relations*, April 1993 and 'Searching for the New World Order: The Clinton Administration and Foreign Policy in 1993', *International Relations*, April 1994.

Conclusion

At the outset of this book it was argued that there would be a number of consistent themes that would run throughout. Those major themes were:

o The importance of appreciating American political history and culture for an understanding of modern political outcomes.

o That the political system inherited from the Founding Fathers always made the United States a difficult nation to govern but that difficulty has multiplied.

o That one major cause of this has been growing conflict between the major political institutions in Washington, DC.

o That this has been further complicated by the expanding number of groups attempting to influence politics.

o That the consequence of all this has been rising public dissatisfaction in the American political system.

o Finally, that all of this has been made more challenging by the dramatically changed international context in which the United States now finds itself in the aftermath of the Cold War.

All of these factors have indeed loomed large in this examination of the contemporary United States. In concluding it would be appropriate to focus on the intense public dissatisfaction that has manifested itself over the last two decades and what the consequence of this crisis of faith might be.

The basic structure that the United States Constitution creates, and its fundamental principles – federalism, the separation of powers with checks and balances, and an emphasis on individual rights – remain broadly popular with American citizens and widely admired in the rest of the world. Public alarm seems less focused on this structure and much more related to how individual elements within it are working. It is quite easy to see why so many Americans are concerned about the federal government. The presidency, which for thirty years after the New Deal appeared such a dynamic force for good in American public life, lost its credibility in the carnage of the Vietnam War and the corruption of the Watergate scandal. Other institutions moved to check its authority and the Oval Office has never truly recovered. Most modern presidencies have been seen as flawed by voters who have ended them prematurely. Although Ronald Reagan demonstrated that it was still possible to make the presidency into a meaningful resource, even he had considerable problems. The institution seems unlikely to recapture its past glories.

The United States Congress has developed its own traumas. Its inability to produce internal organising systems that promote effective policy, or co-ordinate successfully with the White House, have seen its basic competence widely questioned. As outlined here, sets of scandals about behaviour of individual members and the collective body have tarnished its legitimacy in the eyes of the electorate.

The Supreme Court has also experienced a turbulent two decades. Whilst, unlike the other two branches, it has not seen either its efficiency or honesty challenged, its decisions in a wide range of issues, the essence of which has been to create an ever broader notion of rights, has engulfed it in explosive social policy controversies. Nor has the arrival of a more cautious majority under the stewardship of Chief Justice William Rehnquist soothed these concerns.

The extraordinary changes that have ensnared these bodies and eroded their authority can perhaps be best encapsulated through such recent events as: the wounding of the Reagan presidency over the Iran–Contra scandal in 1986/1987; the rejection of Judge Robert Bork from the Supreme Court in 1987; the enforced resignation of the Democratic Speaker of the House of Representatives, Jim Wright, on ethics charges in 1989; the astonishing confirmation hearings of Justice Clarence Thomas in 1991; the presidential election of 1992 with another incumbent defeated and the sudden arrival of Ross Perot; and the landmark 1994 congressional elections which saw a Democratic majority that had lasted forty years in the House of Representatives swept away. Surrounding all these individual dramas was the emergence in domestic policy of a large and destabilising federal budget deficit and a foreign policy turned upside down by the prosecution of, and the sudden end to, the Cold War. It illustrates why so many Americans feel alienated and confused.

However, it is, at least in part, the contention of the book that these spectacular developments in the formal political institutions of the United States have their roots in changes amongst those informal organisations – bureaucracy, political parties, interest groups and the media – that are so vital in trying to hold together what the constitutional settlement separates. American bureaucracy, as has been demonstrated, is divided and confused. Political parties have lost public esteem to a crippling degree. Interest groups have proliferated enormously but their activities have cast doubt on their legitimacy. The mass media has similarly seen a great profusion of activity and has been widely accused of fuelling public cynicism about the political process. When the glue that holds political institutions together begins to fail it becomes unsurprising that those institutions fall away from each other. This logically has an impact on policy where candidate-driven election campaigns produce fragmented results which have in turn spawned immobilism in economic policy and a crisis of purpose in foreign policy.

Modern American government is thus in a fraught condition. Some voters sought to recast it by electing Bill Clinton alongside a Democratic Congress in 1992. Others took the more dramatic decision to seek solace in Ross Perot. The public apparently wanted to end 'gridlock' in national politics. Either because they felt gridlock had not been eliminated or because they disliked the product of unified government they rejected their own handiwork, ushering in a Republican majority in Congress with a commitment, especially in the House of Representatives, to a fundamental set of reforms.

It is worth considering that agenda further because, unusually, it seems centred less on policy prescriptions then on wide-ranging institutional restructuring. Republicans promised far-reaching change in the committee system, staffing levels, and basic procedure of the House of Representatives that would be at least as important as the changes that liberal Democrats had forced through twenty-five years earlier. These changes included term limitations for the most significant members of Congress, partly meeting the public demand for such limits at every level of American politics. It includes a balanced budget amendment to the national Constitution that might well have a revolutionary effect on the role and nature of government in American life. This would be allied to the introduction of a line-item veto for the President which, while initially aimed at budgetary prudence, might have a much broader institutional significance. Within days of his electoral triumph Speaker-elect Newt Gingrich spoke of amending the Constitution to allow prayer in public schools, restoring an activity the Supreme Court struck down thirty years earlier. If all or most of this agenda were enacted it would constitute the biggest set of constitutional innovations since the Civil War, the most important institutional alteration since the First World War, and the most profound political change since the New Deal. It is too early to judge that success.

All of these changes – striking down congressional privileges, term limits, the balanced budget amendment, and the line-item veto – represent an attempt to deal with the basic complaints of an aggrieved public which believes government in Washington is too big, too remote, too ineffective, and too corrupt. Whether their adoption can be completed, or whether the voters will find them as attractive in practice as they do in theory, cannot yet be foreseen. Whether they can deliver change if the real source of present problems lies not in institutions but informal organisations is an unknown. Nor can the impact of term limits and a federal balanced budget on the one set of political institutions that have generally enjoyed greater esteem over the past two decades – the states – be predicted. Failure to adopt these changes, or others of equal consequence, could also lead to a collapse of the two-party system and a possible Independent/'Third Party' presidency, that would surely alter the American political structure quite dramatically.

None the less, the fact that changes of this scale are being contemplated due to the displeasure with the status quo on the part of ordinary Americans says something profound about the way politics has developed in this generation, even if it cannot foretell the concerns of the next one. The last two decades have been ones of uncertainty and turmoil in American politics. This seems set to continue.

Appendix

The Constitution

We the People of the United States, in order to form a more perfect union, establish Justice, insure domestic tranquillity, provide for the common defence, promote the general Welfare, and secure the Blessings of Liberty to ourselves and our Posterity, do ordain and establish this Constitution for the United States of America.

Article I

Section 1. All legislative Powers herein granted shall be vested in a Congress of the United States, which shall consist of a Senate and a House of Representatives.

Section 1. The House of Representatives shall be composed of Members chosen every second Year by the People of the several States, and the Electors in each State shall have the Qualifications requisite for the Electors of the most numerous Branch of the State Legislature.

No person shall be a Representative who shall not have attained to the Age of twenty-five years, and been seven Years a Citizen of the United States, and who shall not, when elected, be an Inhabitant of that State in which he shall be chosen.

Representatives and direct Taxes shall be apportioned among the several States which may be included within this Union, according to their respective Numbers, which shall be determined by adding to the whole Number of free Persons, including those bound to Service for a Term of Years, and excluding Indians not taxed, three fifths of all other Persons. The actual Enumeration shall be made within three Years after the first Meeting of the Congress of the United States, and within every subsequent Term of ten Years, in such Manner as they shall by Law direct. The Number of Representatives shall not exceed one for every thirty Thousand, but each State shall have at Least one Representative; and until such enumeration shall be made, the State of New Hampshire shall be entitled to chuse three, Massachusetts eight, Rhode-Island and Providence Plantations one, Connecticut five, New-York six, New Jersey four, Pennsylvania eight, Delaware one, Maryland six, Virginia ten, North Carolina five, South Carolina five, and Georgia three.

When vacancies happen in the Representation from any State, the Executive authority thereof shall issue Writs of Election to fill such Vacancies.

House of Representatives shall chuse their Speaker and other Officers; and shall have the sole Power of Impeachment.

Section 3. The Senate of the United States shall be composed of two Senators from each State, chosen by the Legislature thereof, for six Years; and each Senator shall have one Vote.

Immediately after they shall be assembled in consequence of the first Election, they shall be divided as equally as may be into three Classes. The Seats of the Senators of the first Class shall be vacated at the Expiration of the second Year, of the second Class at the Expiration of the fourth Year, and of the third Class at the Expiration of the sixth Year, so that one-third may be chosen every second Year; and if Vacancies happen by Resignation, or otherwise, during the Recess of the Legislature of any State, the Executive thereof may make temporary Appointments until the next Meeting of the Legislature, which shall then fill such Vacancies.

No Person shall be a Senator who shall not have attained to the Age of thirty Years, and been nine Years a Citizen of the United States, and who shall not, when elected, be an Inhabitant of that State for which he shall be chosen.

The Vice President of the United States shall be President of the Senate, but shall have no Vote, unless they be equally divided.

The Senate shall chuse their other Officers and also a President pro tempore, in the Absence of the Vice President, or when he shall exercise the Office of President of the United States.

The Senate shall have the sole Power to try all Impeachments. When sitting for that Purpose, they shall be on Oath or Affirmation. When the President of the United States is tried, the Chief Justice shall preside: And no Person shall be convicted without the Concurrence of two thirds of the Members present.

Judgment in Cases of Impeachment shall not extend further than to removal from Office, and disqualification to hold and enjoy any Office of honor, Trust or Profit under the United States: but the Party convicted shall nevertheless be liable and subject to Indictment, Trial, Judgment and Punishment according to Law.

Section 4. The Times, Places and Manner of holding Elections for Senators and Representatives, shall be prescribed in each State by the Legislature thereof; but the Congress may at any time by Law make or alter such Regulations, except as to the Places of chusing Senators.

The Congress shall assemble at least once in every Year, and such Meeting shall be on the first Monday in December, unless they shall by Law appoint a different Day.

Section 5. Each House shall be the Judge of the Elections, Returns and Qualifications of its own Members, and a Majority of each shall constitute a Quorum to do Business; but a small Number may adjourn from day to day, and may be authorized to compel the Attendance of absent Members, in such Manner, and under such Penalties, as each House may provide.

Each House may determine the Rules of its Proceedings, punish its Members for disorderly Behavior, and, with the Concurrence of two thirds, expel a Member.

Each House shall keep a Journal of its Proceedings, and from time to time publish the same, excepting such Parts as may in their Judgment require Secrecy; and the Yeas and Nays of the Members of either House on any question shall, at the Desire of either House of one fifth of those present, be entered on the Journal. Neither House, during the Session of Congress, shall, without the Consent of the other, adjourn for more than three days, nor to any other Place than that in which the two Houses shall be sitting.

Section 6. The Senators and Representatives shall receive a Compensation for their Services, to be ascertained by Law, and paid out of the Treasury of the United States. They shall in all Cases, except Treason, Felony and Breach of the Peace, be privileged from Arrest during their Attendance at the Session of their respective Houses, and in going to and returning from the same; and for any Speech or Debate in either House, they shall not be questioned in any other Place.

No Senator or Representative shall, during the Time for which he was elected, be appointed to any Civil Office under the Authority of the United States, which shall have been created, or the Emoluments whereof shall have been encreased during such time; and no Person holding any Office under the United States, shall be a Member of either House during his Continuance in Office.

Section 7. All Bills for raising Revenue shall originate in the House of Representatives; but the Senate may propose or concur with Amendments as on other Bills.

Every Bill which shall have passed the House of Representatives and the Senate, shall, before it become a Law, be presented to the President of the United States; If he approve he shall sign it, but if not he shall return it, with his Objections to that House in which it shall have originated, who shall enter the Objections at large on their Journal, and proceed to reconsider it. If after such Reconsideration two thirds of that House shall agree to pass the Bill, it shall be sent, together with the Objections, to the other House, by which it shall likewise be reconsidered, and if approved by two thirds of that House, it shall become a Law. But in all such Cases the Votes of both Houses shall be determined by Yeas and Nays, and the Names of The Persons voting for and against the Bill shall be entered on the Journal of each House respectively. If any Bill shall not be returned by the President within ten Days (Sundays excepted) after it shall have been presented to him, the Same shall be a Law, in like Manner as if he had signed it, unless the Congress by their Adjournment prevent its Return, in which Case it shall not be a Law.

Every Order, Resolution, or Vote to which the Concurrence of the Senate and House of Representatives may be necessary (except on a question of Adjournment) shall be presented to the President of the United States; and before the Same shall take Effect, shall be approved by him or being disapproved by him, shall be repassed by two thirds of the Senate and House of Representatives, according to the Rules and Limitations prescribed in the Case of a Bill.

Section 8. The Congress shall have Power To lay and collect Taxes, Duties, Imposts and Excises, to pay the debts and provide for the common Defence and general Welfare of the United States; but all Duties, Imposts and Excises shall be uniform throughout the United States;

To borrow Money on the credit of the United States;

To regulate Commerce with foreign Nations, and among the several States, and with the Indian Tribes;

To establish an uniform Rule of Naturalization, and uniform Laws on the subject of Bankruptcies throughout the United States;

To coin Money, regulate the Value thereof, and of foreign Coin, and fix the Standard of Weights and Measures;

To provide for the Punishment of counterfeiting the Securities and current Coin of the United States;

To establish Post Offices and post Roads;

To promote the Progress of Science and useful Arts, by securing for limited Times to Authors and Inventors the exclusive Right to their respective Writings and Discoveries;

To constitute Tribunals inferior to the supreme Court;

To define and punish Piracies and Felonies committed on the high Seas, and Offences against the Law of Nations;

To declare War, grant letters of Marque and Reprisal, and make Rules concerning Captures on Land and Water;

To raise and support Armies, but no Appropriation of Money to that Use shall be for a longer Term than two Years;

To provide and maintain a Navy;

To make Rules for the Government and Regulation of the land and naval Forces; to provide for calling forth the Militia to execute the Laws of the Union, suppress Insurrections and repel Invasions;

To provide for organizing, arming and disciplining the Militia, and for governing such Part of them as may be employed in the Service of the United States, reserving to the States respectively, the Appointment of the Officers, and the Authority of training the Militia according to the discipline prescribed by Congress;

To exercise exclusive Legislation in all Cases whatsoever, over such District (not exceeding ten Miles square) as may, by Cession of particular States, and the Acceptance of Congress, become the Seat of the Government of the United States, and to exercise like Authority over all Places purchased by the Consent of the Legislature of The State in which the Same shall be, for the Erection of Forts, Magazines, Arsenals, dock-Yards,and other needful Buildings; – And

To make all Laws which shall be necessary and proper for carrying into Execution the foregoing Powers, and all other Powers vested by this Constitution in the Government of the United States, or in any Department or Officer thereof.

Section 9. The Migration or Importation of such Persons as any of the States now existing shall think proper to admit, shall not be prohibited by the Congress prior to the Year one thousand eight hundred and eight, but a Tax or duty may be imposed on such Importation, not exceeding ten dollars for each Person.

The Privilege of the Writ of Habeas Corpus shall not be suspended, unless when in Cases of Rebellion or Invasion the public Safety may require it.

No Bill of Attainder or ex post facto Law shall be passed.

No Capitation, or other direct, tax shall be laid, unless in Proportion to the Census or Enumeration herein before directed to be taken.

No Tax or Duty shall be laid on Articles exported from any State.

No Preference shall be given by any Regulation of Commerce or Revenue to the Ports of one State over those of another; nor shall Vessels bound to, or from, on State, be obliged to enter, clear, or pay Duties in another.

No Money shall be drawn from the Treasury, but in Consequence of Appropriations made by Law; and a regular Statement and Account of the Receipts and Expenditures of all public Money shall be published from time to time.

No Title of Nobility shall be granted by the United States: And no Person holding any Office of Profit or Trust under them, shall, without the Consent of the Congress, accept of any present, Emolument, Office, or Title, of any kind whatever, from any King, Prince, or foreign State.

Section 10. No state shall enter into any Treaty, Alliance, or Confederation; grant Letters of Marque and Reprisal; coin Money; emit Bills of Credit; make any Thing but gold and silver Coin a Tender in Payment of Debts; pass any Bill of Attainder, ex post facto Law, or Law impairing the Obligation of Contracts, or grant any Title of Nobility.

No State shall, without the Consent of the Congress, lay any Imposts or Duties on Imports or Exports, except what may be absolutely necessary for executing its inspection Laws: and the net Produce of all Duties and Imposts, laid by any State on Imports or Exports, shall be for the Use of the Treasury of the United States; and all such Laws shall be subject to the Revision and Controul of the Congress.

No State shall, without the Consent of Congress, lay any Duty of Tonnage, keep Troops, or Ships of War in time of Peace, enter into any Agreement or Compact with another State, or with a foreign Power, or engage in War, unless actually invaded, or in such imminent Danger as will not admit of delay.

Article II

Section 1. The Executive Power shall be vested in a President of the United States of America. He shall hold his Office during the Term of four Years, and, together with the Vice President, chosen for the same Term, be elected, as follows.

Each State shall appoint, in such Manner as the legislature thereof may direct, a Number of Electors equal to the whole Number of Senators and Representatives to which the State may be entitled in the Congress: but no Senator or Representative, or Person holding and Office of Trust or Profit under the United States, shall be appointed an Elector.

The electors shall meet in their respective States, and vote by ballot for two Persons, of whom one at least shall not be an Inhabitant of the same State with themselves. And they shall make a List of all the Persons voted for, and of the Number of Votes for each; which List they shall sign and certify, and transmit sealed to the Seat of the Government of the United States, directed to the President of the Senate. The President of the Senate shall, in the Presence of the Senate and House of Representatives, open all the Certificates, and the Votes shall then be counted. The Person having the greatest Number of Votes shall be the President, if such Number be a Majority of the whole Number of Electors appointed; and if there be more than one who have such Majority, and have an equal number of votes, then the House of Representatives shall immediately chuse by Ballot one of them for President; and if no Person have a Majority, then from the five highest on the List the said House shall in like Manner chuse the President. But in chusing the President, the Votes shall be taken by States, the Representation from each State having one Vote; A quorum for this Purpose shall consist of a Member or Members from two thirds of the States, and a Majority of all the States shall be necessary to a Choice. In every Case, after the Choice of the President, the Person having the greatest Number of Votes of the Electors shall be the Vice President. But if there should remain two or more who have equal Votes, the Senate shall chuse from them by Ballot the Vice President.

The Congress may determine the Time of chusing the electors, and the Day on which they shall give their Votes; which Day shall be the same throughout the United States.

No Person except a natural born Citizen, or a Citizen of the United States, at the time of the Adoption of this Constitution, shall be eligible to the Office of President; neither shall any Person be eligible to that Office who shall not have attained to the Age of thirty five Years, and been fourteen Years a Resident within the United States.

In Case of the Removal of the President from Office, or of his Death, Resignation or Inability to discharge the Powers and duties of the said Office, the same shall devolve on the Vice President, and the Congress may by Law provide for the Case of Removal, Death, Resignation or Inability, both of the President and Vice President, declaring what Officer shall then act as President, and such Officer shall act accordingly, until the Disability be removed, or a President shall be elected. The President shall, at stated Times, receive for his Services, a Compensation, which shall neither be encreased nor diminished during the Period for which he shall have been elected, and he shall not receive within that Period any other Emolument from the United States, or any of them.

Before he enter on the Execution of his Office, he shall take the following Oath of Affirmation:– "I do solemnly swear (or affirm) that I will faithfully execute the Office of President of the United States, and will to the best of my Ability, preserve, protect and defend the Constitution of the United States."

Section 2. The President shall be Commander in Chief of the Army and Navy of the United States, and of the Militia of the several States, when called into the actual Service of the United States; he may require the Opinion, in writing, of the principal Officer in each of the executive Departments, upon any Subject relating to the Duties of their respective Offices, and he shall have Power to grant Reprieves and Pardons for Offences against the United States, except in Cases of Impeachment.

He shall have Power, by and with the Advice and Consent of the Senate, to make Treaties, provided two thirds of the Senators present concur and he shall nominate, and by and with the Advice and Consent of the Senate, shall appoint Ambassadors, other public Ministers and Consuls, Judges of the Supreme Court, and all other Officers of the United States, whose Appointments are not herein otherwise provided for, and which shall be established by Law; but the Congress may by Law vest the Appointment of such inferior Officers, as they think proper, in the President alone, in the Courts of Law, or in the Heads of Departments.

The President shall have Power to fill up all Vacancies that may happen during the Recess of the Senate, by granting Commissions which shall expire at the End of their next Session.

Section 3. He shall from time to time give to the Congress Information of the State of the Union, and recommend to their Consideration such Measures as he shall judge necessary and expedient; he may, on extraordinary Occasions, convene both Houses, or either of them, and, in case of Disagreement between them, with Respect to the Time of Adjournment, he may adjourn them to such Times as he shall think proper; he shall receive Ambassadors and other Public Ministers; he shall take Care that the Laws by faithfully executed, and shall Commission all the Officers of the United States.

Section 4. The President, Vice President and all civil Officers of the United States, shall be removed from Office on Impeachment for, and Conviction of, Treason, Bribery, or other high Crimes and Misdemeanors.

Article III

Section 1. The judicial Power of the United States, shall be vested in one Supreme Court, and in such inferior Courts as the Congress may from time to time ordain and establish. The Judges, both of the supreme and inferior Courts, shall hold their Offices during good Behaviour, and shall, at stated Times, receive for their services, a Compensation, which shall not be diminished during their Continuance in Office.

Section 2. The judicial Power shall extend to all Cases, in Law and Equity, arising under this Constitution, the Laws of the United States, and Treaties made, or which shall be made, under their Authority; – to all Cases affecting Ambassadors, other public Ministers and Consuls; – to all Cases of admiralty and maritime Jurisdiction; – to Controversies to which the United States shall be a Party; – to Controversies between two or more States; between a State and Citizens of another States; – between Citizens of different States, – between Citizens of the same State claiming Lands under Grants of different States, and between a state, or the citizens thereof, and foreign States, Citizens or Subjects.

In all Cases affecting Ambassadors, other public Ministers and Consuls, and those in which a State shall be party, the supreme Court shall have original Jurisdiction. In all other Cases before mentioned, the supreme Court shall have appellate Jurisdiction, both as to Law and Fact, with such Exceptions, and under such Regulations, as the Congress shall make.

The Trial of all Crimes, except in Cases of Impeachment, shall be by Jury; and such Trial shall be held in the State where the said Crimes shall have been committed; but when not committed within any State, the Trial shall be at such Place or Places as the Congress may by Law had directed.

Section 3. Treason against the United States, shall consist only in levying War against them, or in adhering to their Enemies, giving them Aid and comfort. No Person shall be convicted of Treason unless on the Testimony of two Witnesses to the same overt Act, or on Confession in open Court.

The Congress shall have Power to declare the Punishment of Treason, but no Attainder of Treason shall work Corruption of blood, or Forfeiture except during the Life of the Person attainted.

Article IV

Section 1. Full Faith and Credit shall be given in each State to the public Acts, Records, and judicial Proceedings of every other State. And the Congress may by general Laws prescribe the Manner in which such Acts, Records and Proceedings shall be proved, and the Effect thereof.

Section 2. The Citizens of each State shall be entitled to all Privileges and Immunities of Citizens in the several States.

A person charged in any State with Treason, Felony, or other Crime, who shall flee from Justice, and be found in another State, shall on Demand of the executive Authority of the State from which he fled, be delivered up, to be removed to the State having Jurisdiction of the Crime.

No Person held to Service or Labour in one State, under the Laws thereof, escaping into another, shall, in Consequence of any Law or regulation therein, be discharged from such Service or Labour but shall be delivered up on Claim of the Party to whom such Service or Labour may be due.

Section 3. New States may be admitted by the Congress into this Union; but no new State shall be formed or erected within the Jurisdiction of any other State; nor any State be formed by the Junction of two or more States, or Part of States, without the consent of the Legislatures of the States concerned as well as of the Congress.

The Congress shall have the Power to dispose of and make all needful Rules and Regulations respecting the Territory or other Property belonging to the United States; and nothing in this Constitution shall be so construed as to Prejudice any Claims of the United States, or of any particular State.

Section 4. The United States shall guarantee to every State in this Union a Republican Form of Government, and shall protect each of them against Invasion; and on Application of the Legislature, or of the Executive (when the Legislature cannot be convened) against domestic Violence.

Article V

The Congress, whenever two thirds of both houses shall deem it necessary, shall propose Amendment to this Constitution, or, on the Application of the Legislatures of two thirds of the several States, shall call a Convention for proposing Amendments, which, in either Case, shall be valid to all Intents and Purposes, as Part of this Constitution, when ratified by the Legislatures of three fourths of the several States, or by Conventions in three fourths thereof, as the one or the other Mode of Ratification may be proposed by the Congress; Provided that no Amendment which may be made prior to the Year One thousand eight hundred and eight shall in any Manner affect the first and fourth Clauses in the Ninth Section of the first Article and that no State, without its Consent, shall be deprived of its equal Suffrage in the Senate.

Article VI

All Debts contracted and Engagements entered into, before the Adoption of this Constitution, shall be as valid against the United States under this Constitution, as under the Confederation.

This Constitution, and the Laws of the United States which shall be made in Pursuance thereof; and all Treaties made, or which shall be made, under the Authority of the United States, shall be the supreme Law of the Land; and the Judges in every State shall be bound thereby, any Thing in the Constitution or Laws of any State to the Contrary notwithstanding.

The Senators and Representatives before mentioned, and the Members of the several State Legislatures, and all executive and judicial Officers, both of the United States and of the several States, shall be bound by Oath or Affirmation, to support this Constitution; but no religious Test shall ever be required as a Qualification to any office or public Trust under the United States.

Article VII

The Ratification of the Conventions of the nine States, shall be sufficient for the Establishment of this Constitution between the States so ratifying the Same.

Amendments to the Constitution

(The first ten amendments were proposed on 25th September 1789 and declared ratified on 15th December 1791.)

First

Congress shall make no law respecting an establishment of religion, or prohibiting the free exercise thereof; or abridging the freedom of speech, or of the press; or the right of the people peaceably to assemble, and to petition the government for a redress of grievances.

Second

A well regulated Militia, being necessary to the security of a free State, the right of the people to keep and bear Arms, shall not be infringed.

Third

No Soldier shall, in time of peace, be quartered in any house, without the consent of the Owner, or in time of war, but in a manner to be prescribed by law.

Fourth

The right of the people to be secure in their persons, houses, papers and effects, against unreasonable searches and seizure, shall not be violated, and no Warrants shall issue, but upon probable cause, supported by Oath or affirmation, and particularly describing the place to be searched, and the persons or things to be seized.

Fifth

No person shall be held to answer for a capital, or otherwise infamous crime, unless on a presentment or indictment of a Grand Jury, except in cases arising in the land or naval forces, or in the Militia, when in actual service in time of War or public danger; nor shall any person be subject for the same offence to be twice put in jeopardy of life or limb; nor shall be compelled in any Criminal Case to be a witness against himself, or be deprived of life, liberty, or property, without due process of law; nor shall private property be taken for public use, without just compensation.

Sixth

In all criminal prosecutions, the accused shall enjoy the right to a speedy and public trial, by an impartial jury of the State and district wherein the crime shall have been committed, which district shall have been previously ascertained by law, and to be informed of the nature and cause of the accusation; to be confronted with the witnesses against him; to have compulsory process for obtaining Witnesses in his favor, and to have the Assistance of Counsel for his defence.

Seventh

In suits at common law, where the value in controversy shall exceed twenty dollars, the right of trial by jury shall be preserved, and no fact tried by a jury shall be otherwise re-examined in any Court of the United States, than according to the rules of common law.

Eighth

Excessive bail shall not be required, nor excessive fines imposed, nor cruel and unusual punishments inflicted.

Ninth

The enumeration in the Constitution, of certain rights, shall not be construed to deny or disparage others retained by the people.

Tenth

The powers not delegated to the United States by the Constitution, nor prohibited by it to the States, are reserved to the States respectively, or to the people.

Eleventh

(Proposed 4th March 1794; declared ratified 8th January 1798)

The Judicial power of the United States shall not be construed to extend to any suit in law or equity, commenced or prosecuted against one of the United States by Citizens of another State, or by Citizens or Subjects of any Foreign State.

Twelfth

(Proposed 9th December 1803; declared ratified 25th September 1804)

The electors shall meet in their respective states, and vote by ballot for President and Vice-President, one of whom, at least, shall not be an inhabitant of the same state with themselves; they shall name in their ballots the person voted for as President, and in distinct ballots the person voted for as Vice-President, and they shall make distinct lists of all persons voted for as President, and of all persons voted for as Vice-President, and of the number of votes for each, which lists they shall sign and certify, and transmit sealed to the seat of the Government of the United States, directed to the President of the Senate; – The President of the Senate shall, in the presence of the Senate and the House of Representatives, open all the certificates and the voted shall then be counted; – The person having the greatest number of votes for President shall be the President, if such number be a majority of the whole number of Electors appointed; and if no person have such majority, then from the persons having the highest numbers not exceeding three on the list of those voted as President, the House of Representatives shall choose immediately, by ballot, the President. But in choosing the President, the votes shall be taken by states, the representation from each state having one vote; a quorum for this purpose shall consist of a member or members from two-thirds of the states, and a majority of all the states shall be necessary to a choice. And if the House of Representatives shall not choose a President whenever the right of choice shall devolve upon them, before the fourth day of March next following, then the Vice-President shall act as President, as in the case of the death or other constitutional disability of the President. The person having the great number of votes as Vice-President, shall be the Vice-President, if such number be a majority of the whole number of Electors appointed, and if no person have a majority, then from the two highest numbers on the list, the Senate shall choose the Vice-President; a quorum for the purpose shall consist of two-thirds of the whole number of Senators, and a majority of the whole number shall be necessary to a choice. But no person constitutionally ineligible to the office of President shall be eligible to that of Vice-President of the United States.

Thirteenth

(Proposed 31st January 1865; declared ratified 18th December 1865)

Section 1. Neither slavery nor involuntary servitude, except as a punishment for crime whereof the party shall have been duly convicted, shall exist within the United States, or any place subject to their jurisdiction.

Section 2. Congress shall have power to enforce this article by appropriate legislation.

Fourteenth

(Proposed 13th June 1866; declared ratified 28th July 1868)

Section 1. All persons born or naturalized in the United States, and subject to the jurisdiction thereof, are citizens of the United States and of the State wherein they reside. No State shall make or enforce any law which shall abridge the privileges or immunities of citizens of the United States; nor shall any State deprive any person of life, liberty, or property, without due process of law; not deny to any person within its jurisdiction the equal protection of the laws.

Section 2. Representatives shall be apportioned among the several States according to their respective numbers, counting the whole number of persons in each State, excluding Indians not taxed. But when the right to vote at any election for the choice of electors for President and Vice President of the United States, Representatives in Congress, the Executive and Judicial officers of a State, or the members of the Legislature thereof, is denied to any of the male inhabitants of such State, being twenty-one years of age, and citizens of the United States, or in any way abridged, except for participation in rebellion, or other crime, the basis of representation therein shall be reduced in the proportion which the number of such male citizens shall bear the whole number of twenty-one years of age in such State.

Section 3. No person shall be a Senator or Representative in Congress, or elector of President and Vice President, or hold any office, civil, or military, under the United States, or under any State, who, having previously taken an oath, as a member of Congress, or as an officer of the United States, or as a member of any State legislature, or as an executive or judicial officer of any State, to support the Constitution of the United States, shall have engaged in insurrection or rebellion against the same, or given aid or comfort to the enemies thereof. But Congress may by a vote of two-thirds of each House, remove such disability.

Section 4. The validity of the public debt of the United States, authorized by law, including debts incurred for payment of pensions and bounties for services in suppressing insurrection or rebellion, shall not be questioned. But neither the United States nor any State shall assume or pay any debt or obligation incurred in aid of insurrection or rebellion against the United States, or any claim for the loss or emancipation of any slave; but all such debts, obligations and claims shall be held illegal and void.

Section 5. The Congress shall have power to enforce, by appropriate legislation, the provisions of this article.

Fifteenth

(Proposed 26th February 1869; declared ratified 30th March 1870)

Section 1. The right of citizens of the United States to vote shall not be denied or abridged by the United States or by any State on account of race, color, or previous condition of servitude.

Section 2. The Congress shall have power to enforce this article by appropriate legislation.

Sixteenth

(Proposed 12th July 1909; declared ratified 25th February 1913)

The Congress shall have power to lay and collect taxes on incomes, from whatever source derived, without apportionment among the several States, and without regard to any census or enumeration.

Seventeenth

(Proposed 13th May 1912; declared ratified 31st May 1913)

The Senate of the United States shall be composed of two senators from each State, elected by the people thereof, for six years; and each Senator shall have one vote. The electors in each State shall have the qualifications requisite for electors of the most numerous branch of the State legislature.

When vacancies happen in the representation of any State in the Senate, the executive authority of such State shall issue writs of election to fill such vacancies: PROVIDED, That the legislature of any State may empower the executive thereof to make temporary appointments until the people fill the vacancies by election as the legislature may direct.

This amendment shall not be so construed as to affect the election term of any senator chosen before it becomes valid as part of the Constitution.

Eighteenth

(Proposed 18th December 1917; declared ratified 29th January 1919)

After one year from the ratification of this article, the manufacture, sale, or transportation of intoxicating liquors within, the importation thereof into, or the exportation thereof from the United States and all territory subject to the jurisdiction thereof for beverage purposes is hereby prohibited.

The Congress and several States shall have concurrent power to enforce this article by appropriate legislation.

This article shall be inoperative unless it shall have been ratified as an amendment to the Constitution by the legislatures of the several States, as provided in the Constitution, within seven years from the date of the submission hereof to the States by the Congress.

Nineteenth

(Proposed 4th June 1919; declared ratified 26th August 1920)

The right of citizens of the United States to vote shall not be denied or abridged by the United States or by any States on account of sex.

The Congress shall have power, by appropriate legislation, to enforce the provisions of this article.

Twentieth

(Proposed 2nd March 1932; declared ratified 6 February 1933)

Section 1. The terms of the President and Vice-President shall end at noon on the twentieth day of January, and the terms of Senators and Representatives at noon on the third day of January, of the years in which such terms would have ended if this article had not been ratified; and the terms of their successors shall then begin.

Section 2. The Congress shall assemble at least once in every year, and such meeting shall begin at noon of the third day of January, unless they shall by law appoint a different day.

Section 3. If, at any time fixed for the beginning of the term of the President, the President-elect shall have died, the Vice-President-elect shall act as President until a President shall have qualified; and the congress may by law provide for the case wherein neither a President-elect nor a Vice-President-elect shall have qualified, declaring who shall then act as President, or the manner in which one who is to act shall be selected, and such person shall act accordingly until a President or Vice-President shall have qualified.

Section 4. The Congress may by law provide for the case of the death of any of the persons from whom the House of Representatives may choose a President whenever the right of choice shall have devolved upon them, and for the case of the death of any of the persons from whom the Senate may choose a Vice-President whenever the right of choice shall have devolved upon them.

Section 5. Sections 1 and 2 shall take effect on the 15th day of October following the ratification of this article.

Section 6. This article shall be inoperative unless it shall have been ratified as an amendment to the Constitution by the legislatures of three-fourths of the several States within seven years from the date of its submission.

Twenty-First

(Proposed 20th February 1933; declared ratified 5th December 1933)

Section 1. The eighteenth article of amendment to the Constitution of the United States is hereby repealed.

Section 2. The transportation or importation into any State, Territory, or possession of the United States for delivery of use therein of intoxicating liquors, in violation of the laws thereof, is hereby prohibited.

Section 3. This article shall be inoperative unless it shall have been ratified as an amendment to the Constitution by convention in the several States, as provided in the Constitution, within seven years from the date of the submission hereof to the States by the Congress.

Twenty-Second

(Proposed 21st March 1947; declared ratified 3rd March 1951)

Section 1. No person shall be elected to the office of the President more than twice, and no person who has held the office of President, or acted as President, for more than two years of a term to which some other person was elected President shall be elected to the office of the President more than once. But this Article shall not apply to any person holding the office of President when this Article was proposed by the Congress, and shall not prevent any person who may be holding the office of President, or acting as President, during the term within which this Article become operative from holding the office of President or acting as President during the remainder of such term.

Twenty-Third

(Proposed 17th June 1960; declared ratified 3rd April 1961)

Section 1. The District constituting the seat of Government of the United States shall appoint in such manner as the Congress may direct:

A number of electors of President and Vice President equal to the whole number of Senators and Representatives in Congress to which the District would be entitled if it were a State, but in no event more than the least populous State; they shall be in addition to those appointed by the States, but they shall be considered, for the purposes of election of President and Vice President, to be electors appointed by a State; and they shall meet in the District and perform such duties as provided by the twelfth article of amendment.

Section 2. The Congress shall have power to enforce this article by appropriate legislation.

Twenty-Fourth

(Proposed 27th August 1962; declared ratified 4th February 1964)

Section 1. The right of citizens of the United States to vote in any primary or other election for President or Vice President, for electors for President or Vice President, or for Senator or Representative in Congress, shall not be denied or abridged by the United States or any state by reason of failure to pay any poll tax or other tax.

Section 2. The Congress shall have power to enforce this article by appropriate legislation.

Twenty-Fifth

(Proposed 6th July 1965; declared ratified 23rd February 1967)

Section 1. In the case of the removal of the President from office or of his death or resignation, the Vice President shall become President.

Section 2. Whenever there is a vacancy in the office of the Vice President, the President shall nominate a Vice President who shall take office upon confirmation by a majority vote of both Houses of Congress.

Section 3. Whenever the President transmits to the President pro tempore of the Senate and the Speaker of the House of Representatives his written declaration that he is unable to discharge the powers and duties of his office, and until he transmits to them a written declaration to the contrary, such powers and duties shall be discharged by the Vice President as Acting President.

Section 4. Whenever the Vice President and a majority of either the principal officers of the executive department of such other body as Congress may by law provide, transmit to the President pro tempore of the Senate and the Speaker of the House of Representatives their written declaration that the President is unable to discharge the powers and duties of his office; the Vice President shall immediately assume the powers and duties of the office as Acting President.

Thereafter, when the President transmits to the President pro tempore of the Senate and the Speaker of the House of Representatives his written declaration that no inability exists, he shall resume the powers and duties of his office unless the Vice President and majority of either the principal officers of the executive department or of such other body as Congress may by law provide, transmit within four days to the President pro tempore of the Senate and the Speaker of the House of Representatives their written declaration that the President is unable to discharge the powers and duties of his office. Thereupon Congress shall decide the issue, assembling within forty-eight hours for that purpose if not in session. If the Congress, within twenty-one days after Congress is required to assemble, determines by two-thirds vote of both Houses that the President is unable to discharge the powers and duties of his office, the Vice President shall continue to discharge the same as Acting President; otherwise, the President shall resume the powers and duties of his office.

Twenty-Sixth

(Proposed 23rd March 1971; declared ratified 30th June 1971)

Section 1. The right of citizens of the United States, who are 18 years of age or older, to vote shall not be denied or abridged by the United States or any state on account of age.

Section 2. The Congress shall have the power to enforce this article by appropriate legislation.

Twenty-Seventh

(Proposed 1789; declared ratified 7th May 1992)

No law varying the compensation for the services of the Senators and Representatives shall take effect, until an election of Representatives shall have intervened.

Bibliography

The following represents a short set of books covering each chapter in this text. The aim is to provide the student or general reader with a list of a reasonable but not overwhelming length for further reading and research. The accent here is on both 'classics' of the literature and recent publications.

General reading

M. Barone, *Our Country* (New York, Free Press, 1990).

M. Barone and G. Ujifusa, *The Alamanc of American Politics 1994* (Washington, DC, National Journal, 1994).

C. Campbell and B. Rockman (eds), *The Bush Presidency* (Chatham, NJ, Chatham House, 1991).

E. Drew, *On the Edge: The Clinton Presidency* (New York, Simon & Schuster, 1994).

P. Duncan (ed.), *Politics in America* (Washington, DC, Congressional Quarterly Press, 1994).

A. King (ed.), *The New American Political System* (2nd edn) (Washington, DC, AEI Books, 1990).

N. Ornstein *et al.*, *Vital Statistics on Congress 1993–1994* (Washington DC, Congressional Quarterly Press, 1994).

G. Peele *et al.* (eds), *Developments in American Politics 2* (London, Macmillan, 1994).

H. Smith, *The Power Game* (New York, Ballantine Books, 1988).

H. Stanley and R. Niemi, *Vital Statistics on American Politics* (Washington, DC, Congressional Quarterly Press, 1994).

Chapter 1: American history

S. Ambrose, *The Rise to Globalism: American Foreign Policy since 1938* (New York, Penguin, 1990).

D. Boorstein, *The Americans: The Colonial Experience* (New York, Vintage Books, 1958).

H. Brogan, *The Pelican History of the United States* (London, Penguin, 1986).

D. Hackett Fisher, *Albion's Seed: Four British Folkways in America* (New York, Oxford University Press, 1989

R. Hofstadter, *The American Political Tradition and the Men Who Made It* (New York, Vintage, 1974).

J. M. McPherson, *Battle Cry of Freedom: the Civil War Era* (New York, Ballantine Books, 1988).

W. Manchester, *The Glory and the Dream* (London, Michael Joseph, 1975).

C. Vann Woodward, *The Strange Career of Jim Crow* 3rd revised edn, (New York, Oxford University Press, 1974).

G. S. Wood, *The Radicalism of the American Revolution* (New York, Knopf, 1992).

H. Zinn, *A People's History of the US* (London, Longmans, 1980).

Chapter 2: Economy and society

J. Davidson Hunter, *Culture Wars: The Struggle to Define America* (New York, Basic Books, 1991).

T. Dye, *Who's Running America? The Bush Era* (Englewood Cliffs, NJ, Prentice-Hall, 1990).

T. Edsall with M. Edsall, *Chain Reaction: the Impact of Race, Rights, and Taxes on American Politics* (New York, Norton, 1992).

N. Glazer and D. Moynihan, *Beyond the Melting Pot: The Negroes, Puerto Ricans, Jews, Italians, and Irish of New York City* (Cambridge, MA, MIT Press, 1970).

R. Hughes, *Culture of Complaint: The Fraying of America* (New York, Oxford University Press, 1993).

K. Phillips, *The Politics of Rich and Poor* (New York, Random House, 1990).

R. Reich, *The Work of Nations: Preparing Ourselves for 21st Century Capitalism* (New York, Knopf, 1991).

A. J. Reichley, *Religion in American Public Life* (Washington, DC, Brookings Institution, 1985).

K. Sale, *Power Shift: The Rise of the Southern Rim and its Challenge to the Eastern Establishment* (New York, Random House, 1976).

C. Schultze, *Memos to the President* (Washington, DC, Brookings Institution, 1992).

Chapter 3: Political culture and the constitution

B. Bailyn, *The Ideological Origins of the American Revolution* (Cambridge, MA, Harvard University Press, 1967).

A. De Tocqueville, *Democracy in America* (New York, Knopf, 1951).

A. Hamilton, J. Madison and J. Jay, *The Federalist Papers* (New York, New American Library, 1961).

L. Hartz, *The Liberal Tradition in America* (New York, HBJ Books, 1955).

R. Hofstadter, *The Paranoid Style in American Politics* (Chicago, Phoenix Press, 1979).

S. Lipset, *The First New Nation: The United States in Historical and Comparative Perspective* (Garden City, NY, Anchor Books, 1967).

F. McDonald, *Novus Ordo Seclorum* (Lawrence, KS, University of Kansas Press, 1985).

B. Shafer (ed.), *Is America Different?* (Oxford, Oxford University Press, 1990).

G. Wills, *Explaining America: The Federalist* (London, Penguin, 1981).

G. Wood, *The Creation of the American Republic, 1776–1787* (New York, Norton, 1969).

Chapter 4: The presidency

J. Bond and R. Fleisher, *The President in the Legislative Arena* (Chicago, University of Chicago Press, 1990).

G. Edwards, *At the Margin* (Hartford, CT, Yale University Press, 1993).

C. Jones, *The Presidency in a Separated System* (Washington, DC, Brookings Institution, 1994).

C. Jones (ed.), *Separate but Equal* (Chatham, NJ, Chatham House, 1994).

S. Kernell, *Going Public* (Washington, DC, Congressional Quarterly Press, 1993).

P. Light, *The President's Agenda* (Baltimore, Johns Hopkins University Press, 1991).

D. Mervin, *The President of the United States* (New York, Harvester Books, 1993).

R. Neustadt, *Presidential Power and the Modern Presidents* (New York, Free Press, 1991).

R. Rose, *The Post-Modern President* (Chatham, NJ, Chatham House, 1991).

A. Wildavsky, *The Beleaguered Presidency* (New Brunswick, NJ, Transactions Press, 1991).

Chapter 5: Congress

R. Davidson and W. Oleszek, *Congress and its Members* 4th edn. (Washington, DC, Congressional Quarterly Press, 1994).

L. Dodd and B. Oppenheimer (eds), *Congress Reconsidered* (Washington, DC, Congressional Quarterly Press, 1993).

A. Ehrenhalt, *The United States of Ambition: Politicians, Power, and the Pursuit of Office* (New York, Random House, 1991).

M. Fiorina, *Congress: Keystone of the Washington Establishment* (New Haven, CT, Yale University Press, 1989).

G. Jacobson, *The Politics of Congressional Elections* 2nd edn, (Boston, Little Brown & Co., 1987).

D. Mayhew, *Congress: The Electoral Connection* (New Haven, CT, Yale University Press, 1974).

R. M. Peters Jr, *The American Speakership: The Office in Historical Perspective* (Baltimore, Johns Hopkins University Press, 1990).

B. Sinclair, *The Transformation of the U.S. Senate* (Baltimore, Johns Hopkins University Press, 1989).

S. Smith, *The American Congress* (Boston, Houghton Mifflin, 1995).

J. Sundquist, *The Decline and Resurgence of Congress* (Washington, DC, Brookings Institution, 1981).

Chapter 6: The Supreme Court

H. Abraham, *The Judicial Process* (New York, Oxford University Press, 1986).

R. Bork, *The Temptation of America* (New York, Free Press, 1990).

E. Bronner, *Battle for Justice: How the Bork Nomination Shook America* (New York, Norton, 1989).

S. Carter, *The Confirmation Mess: Cleaning Up the Federal Appointments Process* (New York, Basic Books, 1994).

R. Hodder-Williams, *The Politics of the US Supreme Court* (London, George Allen & Unwin, 1980).

A. Lewis, *Gideon's Trumpet* (New York, Random House, 1964).

D. M. O'Brien, *Storm Center: The Supreme Court in American Politics* (New York, Norton, 1986).

D. Savage, *Turning Right: The Making of the Rehnquist Supreme Court* (New York, John Wiley & Sons, 1992).

B. Woodward and S. Armstrong, *The Brethren: Inside the Supreme Court* (New York, Simon & Schuster, 1979).

Chapter 7: States and local government

T. Conlan, *New Federalism* (Washington, DC, Brookings Institution, 1988).

T. Dye, *American Federalism* (Lexington, MA, Lexington Books, 1990).

M. Kaplan, *The Governors and the New Federalism* (Boulder, CO, Westview Press, 1991).

J. Kincaid, *American Federalism: The Third Century* (Newbury Park, Sage, 1990).

R. Nathan, *Reagan and the States* (Princeton, NJ, Princeton University Press, 1987).

L. O'Toole, *American Intergovernmental Relations* (Washington, DC, Congressional Quarterly Press, 1993).

P. Peterson and B. Rabe, *When Federalism Works* (Washington, DC, Brookings Institution, 1986).

A. Rivlin, *Reviving the American Dream* (Washington, DC, Brookings Institution, 1992).

C. Van Horn, *The State of the States* (Washington, DC, Congressional Quarterly Press, 1993).

J. Zimmerman, *Contemporary American Federalism* (Leicester, Leicester University Press, 1992).

Chapter 8: Bureaucracy

J. Aberbach, *Keeping a Watchful Eye* (Washington, DC, Brookings Institution, 1990).

L. Galambos, *The New American State* (Baltimore, Johns Hopkins University Press, 1987).

W. Gormley, *Taming the Bureaucracy* (Princeton, Princeton University Press, 1989).

J. Gruber, *Controlling Bureaucracies* (Berkeley, University of California Press, 1987).

D. Osborne and T. Gaebler, *Reinventing Government* (Reading, MA, Addison-Wesley Press, 1992).

F. Rourke, *Bureaucracy, Politics and Public Policy* (Boston, Little, Brown & Co., 1984).

R. Stillman, *The American Bureaucracy* (Chicago, Nelson-Hall, 1989).

G. Wamsley, *Refounding Public Administration* (London, Sage, 1990).

R. Waterman, *Presidential Influence & the Administrative State* (Knoxville, TN, University of Tennessee Press, 1989).

J. Wilson, *Bureaucracy* (New York, Basic Books, 1989).

Chapter 9: Political parties

W. Burnham, *The Current Crisis in American Politics* (New York, Oxford University Press, 1982).

L. Epstein, *Political Parties in the American Mold* (Madison, University of Wisconsin Press, 1986).

N. Polsby, *Consequences of Party Reform* (New York, Oxford University Press, 1994).

N. Rae, *The Decline and Fall of the Liberal Republicans* (New York, Oxford University Press, 1989).

— *Southern Democrats* (New York, Oxford University Press, 1994).

A. J. Reichley, *The Life of the Parties: A History of American Political Parties* (New York, Free Press, 1992).

B. Shafer, *Quiet Revolution* (New York, Russell Sage Foundation, 1983).

D. Shea and J. Green (eds), *The State of the Parties* (Lanham, MY, Rowman & Littlefield, 1994).

J. Sundquist, *Dynamics of the Party System* (Washington, DC, Brookings Institution, 1983).

M. Wattenberg, *The Decline of American Political Parties: 1952–1980* (Cambridge, MA, Harvard University Press, 1984).

Chapter 10: Interest groups

A. Cigler, *Interest Group Politics* (Washington, DC, Congressional Quarterly Press, 1991).

J. Heinz *et al.*, *The Hollow Core* (Cambridge, MA, Harvard University Press, 1993).

L. Makinson, *Open Secrets* (Washington, DC, Congressional Quarterly Press, 1994).

M. Petracca, *The Politics of Interest Groups* (Boulder, CO, Westview Press, 1992).

A. Rosenthal, *The Third House* (Washington, DC, Congressional Quarterly Press, 1993).

L. Sabato, *PAC Power* (New York, Norton, 1985).

M. Smith, *Pressure, Power and Policy* (New York, Harvester Wheatsheaf, 1993).

W. Stone, *Republic at Risk* (Pacific Grove, CA, Brooks/Cole Press, 1990).

J. Walker, *Mobilizing Interest Groups in America* (Ann Arbor, MI, University of Michigan Press, 1991).

B. Wolpe, *Lobbying Congress* (Washington, DC, Congressional Quarterly Press, 1990).

Chapter 11: The media

T. Crouse, *The Boys on the Bus* (New York, Random House, 1973).

E. Diamond and S. Bates, *The Spot* (Cambridge, MA, MIT Press, 1993).

R. Entman, *Democracy Without Citizens: Media and the Decay of American Politics* (New York, Oxford University Press, 1989).

D. Graber, *Mass Media and American Politics* (Washington, DC, Congressional Quarterly Press, 1989).

K. Jamieson, *Packaging the Presidency* (New York, Oxford University Press, 1984).

T. Mann and G. Orren (eds), *Media Polls in American Politics* (Washington, DC, Brookings Institution, 1992).

G. R. Orren and N. W. Polsby (eds), *Media and Momentum: The New Hampshire Primary and Nomination Politics* (Chatham, NJ, Chatham House, 1987).

T. Patterson, *The Mass Media Election: How Americans Choose Their President* (New York, Praeger, 1980).

A. Ranney, *Channels of Power: The Impact of Television on American Politics* (New York, Basic Books, 1983).

Chapter 12: Elections

P. Davies, *Elections USA* (Manchester, Manchester University Press, 1992).

G. Jacobson, *The Politics of Congressional Elections* (Boston, Little, Brown & Co., 1987).

—— *The Electoral Origins of Divided Government* (Boulder, CO, Westview Press, 1990).

R. Neimi and H. Weisberg, *Controversies in Voting Behaviour* (Washington, DC, Congressional Quarterly Press, 1993).

M. Nelson (ed.), *The Elections of 1992* (Washington, DC, Congressional Quarterly Press, 1993).

G. Pomper (ed.), *The Elections of 1992* (Chatham, NJ, Chatham House, 1993).

A. J. Reichley (ed.), *Elections – American Style* (Washington, DC, Brookings Institution, 1987).

B. Shafer (ed.), *The End of Realignment?* (Madison, WI, University of Wisconsin Press, 1991).

B. Shafer and W. Clagget, *The Two Majorities* (Baltimore, Johns Hopkins University Press, 1995).

M. Wattenberg, *The Rise of Candidate Centered Politics* (Cambridge, MA, Harvard University Press, 1992).

Chapter 13: Economic policy

J. Cogan, *The Budget Puzzle* (Stamford, CA, Stamford University Press, 1994).
D. Franklin, *Making Ends Meet* (Washington, DC, Congressional Quarterly Press, 1993).
A. Hyde, *Government Budgeting* (Pacific Grove, CA, Brooks/Cole Press, 1992).
M. Kostess, *Fiscal Politics & the Budget Enforcement Act* (Washington, DC, American Enterprise Institute, 1992).
A. Mayer, *The Evolution of US Budgeting* (New York, Greenwood Books, 1989).
T. Mayer, *The Political Economy of US Monetary Policy* (Cambridge, Cambridge University Press, 1990).
P. Peretz (ed.), *The Politics of American Economic Policy Making* (Armonk, NJ, Sharpe, 1994).
J. Pfiffner, *Economic Policy and the President* (Philadelphia, ISHI, 1986).
A. Shick, *The Capacity to Budget* (Washington, DC, Urban Institute, 1990).
J. White and A. Wildavsky, *The Deficit and the Public Interest* (Berkeley, University of California Press, 1991).

Chapter 14: Foreign policy

B. Blechman, *The Politics of National Security* (New York, Oxford University Press, 1990).
R. Dallek, *The American Style of Foreign Policy* (New York, Oxford University Press, 1983).
J. Dumbrell, *The Making of U.S. Foreign Policy* (Manchester, Manchester University Press, 1990).
J. Gaddis, *Strategies of Containment* (Oxford, Oxford University Press, 1992).
T. Mann (ed.), *A Question of Balance* (Washington, DC, Brookings Institution, 1990).
R. Melanson, *Reconstructing Consensus* (New York, St. Martin's Press, 1991).
B. Roberts (ed.), *US Foreign Policy after the Cold War* (Cambridge, MA, MIT Press, 1992).
J. Rosati, *The Politics of US Foreign Policy* (Orlando, FL, HBJ Books, 1993).
J. Spanier, *American Foreign Policy since World War II* (Washington, DC, Congressional Quarterly Press, 1992).
D. Yankelovich and I. Destler (eds), *Beyond the Beltway* (New York, Norton, 1994).

Index